# IRELAND AND MEDICINE IN THE
SEVENTEENTH AND EIGHTEENTH CENTURIES

The History of Medicine in Context

Series Editors: Andrew Cunningham and Ole Peter Grell

Department of History and Philosophy of Science
University of Cambridge

Department of History
Open University

Titles in this series include

*Contraception, Colonialism and Commerce*
*Birth Control in South India, 1920–1940*
Sarah Hodges

*Crafting Immunity*
*Working Histories of Clinical Immunology*
Edited by Kenton Kroker, Jennifer Keelan and Pauline M.H. Mazumdar

*Before My Helpless Sight*
*Suffering, Dying and Military Medicine on the Western Front, 1914-1918*
Leo van Bergen

*Negotiating the French Pox in Early Modern Germany*
Claudia Stein

*Hospital Politics in Seventeenth-Century France*
*The Crown, Urban Elites and the Poor*
Tim McHugh

# Ireland and Medicine in the Seventeenth and Eighteenth Centuries

*Edited by*

JAMES KELLY
*St Patrick's College, Dublin City University, Republic of Ireland*

*and*

FIONA CLARK
*The Queen's University of Belfast, UK*

LONDON AND NEW YORK

First published 2010 by Ashgate Publishing

2 Park Square, Milton Park, Abingdon, Oxon OX14 4RN
711 Third Avenue, New York, NY 10017, USA

*Routledge is an imprint of the Taylor & Francis Group, an informa business*

First issued in paperback 2016

Copyright © James Kelly and Fiona Clark and the contributors 2010

James Kelly and Fiona Clark have asserted their right under the Copyright, Designs and Patents Act, 1988, to be identified as the editors of this work.

All rights reserved. No part of this book may be reprinted or reproduced or utilised in any form or by any electronic, mechanical, or other means, now known or hereafter invented, including photocopying and recording, or in any information storage or retrieval system, without permission in writing from the publishers.

Notice:
Product or corporate names may be trademarks or registered trademarks, and are used only for identification and explanation without intent to infringe.

**British Library Cataloguing in Publication Data**
Ireland and Medicine in the Seventeenth and Eighteenth Centuries. –
 (The History of Medicine in Context)
 1. Medicine – Ireland – History – 17th century. 2. Medicine – Ireland – History – 18th century. I. Series II. Clark, Fiona. III. Kelly, James.
 610.9'415'09032-dc22

**Library of Congress Cataloging-in-Publication Data**
Ireland and Medicine in the Seventeenth and Eighteenth Centuries /
 [edited by] Fiona Clark and James Kelly.
   p. ;   cm. – (The History of Medicine in Context)
 Includes index.
 1. Medicine – Ireland – History – 17th century. 2. Medicine – Ireland – History – 18th century. I. Clark, Fiona, 1972– . II. Kelly, James, 1959– . III. Series: History of Medicine in Context.
 [DNLM: 1. History of Medicine – Ireland. 2. History of Medicine – Northern Ireland. 3. History, 17th Century – Ireland. 4. History, 17th Century – Northern Ireland. 5. History, 18th Century – Ireland. 6. History, 18th Century – Northern Ireland. 7. Physicians – Ireland. 8. Physicians – Northern Ireland. WZ 70 GI6 I65 2009]
 R498.6.I74 2009
 610.9415'.09032–dc22                                                          2009019700

ISBN 978-0-7546-6556-4 (hbk)
ISBN 978-1-138-26197-6 (pbk)

# Contents

| | |
|---|---|
| *List of Tables* | *vii* |
| *List of Contributors* | *ix* |
| *Acknowledgements* | *xi* |
| *List of Abbreviations* | *xiii* |

Introduction     1

1    The Role of Graduate Physicians in Professionalising
Medical Practice in Ireland, c. 1619–54     17
*Mary Ann Lyons*

2    Medical Practice and Gaelic Ireland     39
*Charlie Dillon*

3    Medicine and Miracles in the Late Seventeenth Century: Bernard
Connor's *Evangelium Medici* (1697)     53
*Liam Chambers*

4    Medicine, Religion and Social Mobility in Eighteenth- and
Early Nineteenth-Century Ireland     73
*Laurence Brockliss*

5    Domestic Medication and Medical Care in Late Early
Modern Ireland     109
*James Kelly*

6    Institutional Medicine and State Intervention in Eighteenth-Century
Ireland     137
*Andrew Sneddon*

7    Gendered Medical Advice within Anglo-Irish Correspondence:
A Case Study of the Cary-Jurin Letters     163
*Wendy D. Churchill*

8    The Wider Cultures of Eighteenth-Century Irish Doctors     183
*Toby Barnard*

| 9 | Advancing the Medical Career Abroad: The Case of Daniel O'Sullivan (1760–c.1797)<br>*Fiona Clark* | 197 |

*Index*                                               *217*

# List of Tables

| | | |
|---|---|---|
| 4.1 | Number of graduates in medicine from Ireland per decade 1640–9 to 1790–9 | 77 |
| 4.2 | Diocesan origin of Irish medical graduates at Reims in the seventeenth and eighteenth centuries | 80 |
| 4.3 | Place of previous education of Reims graduates in medicine from Ireland, 1749–93 | 84 |
| 4.4 a–c | Dublin physicians, 1768, 1778, 1798 | 89 |
| 4.5 | Reims doctorates in medicine awarded to students from the British Isles and the British colonies: decennial totals (number studying at Leiden in brackets) | 94 |
| 4.6 | Army surgeons in the French wars: country of origin | 98 |
| 4.7 | Army surgeons: county of birth | 100 |
| 6.1 | Heads of bills and bills initiated in the Irish parliament and relating to institutional medicine, 1695–1800 | 157 |

# List of Contributors

**Toby Barnard**, F.R.Hist.S., F.B.A., M.R.I.A. (Hon), is a Fellow of Hertford College, Oxford. His main research interests are in the fields of the political, social and cultural histories of Ireland and England, c.1600–1800. Among his recent publications are *A New Anatomy of Ireland* (2003), *Irish Protestant Ascents and Descents, 1641–1779* (2003), *The Kingdom of Ireland, 1641–1760* (2004), *Making the Grand Figure: Lives and Possessions in Ireland, 1641–1770* (2004) and *Improving Ireland?: Projectors, Prophets and Profiteers, 1641–1786* (2008).

**Laurence Brockliss** is Professor of Early Modern French History at Oxford and Fellow of Magdalen College. He has written extensively on the history of education, science and medicine in early modern France and Britain. His major publications include *The Medical World of Early Modern France* (with Colin Jones) (1997), *Calvet's Web: Enlightenment and the Republic of Letters in Eighteenth-century France* (2002), *Nelson's Surgeon: William Beatty, Naval Medicine, and the Battle of Trafalgar* (with John Cardwell and Michael Moss) (2005), and *Advancing with the Army: Medicine, the Professions and Social Mobility in the British Isles 1790–1850* (with Marcus Ackroyd, Michael Moss and Kathryn Retford) (2006).

**Liam Chambers** is lecturer in History at Mary Immaculate College, University of Limerick. His research interests lie in the areas of seventeenth and eighteenth-century Ireland and the intellectual history of early modern Europe, with a particular focus on the Irish in Europe 1600–1800 and the Irish colleges in Europe. His publications include *Rebellion in Kildare, 1790–1803* (1998) and *Michael Moore c.1639–1726: Provost of Trinity, Rector of Paris* (2005).

**Wendy D. Churchill** was a Hannah Postdoctoral Fellow at the Wellcome Trust Centre for the History of Medicine at University College London during 2005–6. She is currently an Assistant Professor of History at the University of New Brunswick. She has published on the subject of medicine, gender and class, including 'Bodily Differences?: Gender, Race, and Class in Hans Sloane's Jamaican Medical Practice, 1687–1688', in *Journal of the History of Medicine and Allied Sciences* (2005).

**Fiona Clark** is Lecturer in Spanish and Portuguese Studies at the Queen's University of Belfast. In 2004–6, she was an Irish Council for the Humanities and Social Sciences postdoctoral fellow at St Patrick's College, Dublin City University. Her research interests include the development of the scientific literary periodical press in colonial Spanish America and transatlantic scientific/medical networks. Her recent publications include 'Read All About It: Science, Translation, Adaptation and Confrontation in the *Gazeta de Literatura de México* (1788–1795)' in Daniela Bleichmar et al. (eds) *Science and Medicine in the Spanish and Portuguese Empires* (2008).

**Charlie Dillon** is Lecturer in Irish and Celtic Studies at the Queen's University of Belfast. His research interests are Irish language and literature of the seventeenth and eighteenth centuries, native Irish historiography, the Irish in continental Europe in the early modern period, and the history and practice of Irish translation. He is editor (with Ríona Ní Fhrighil) of *Aistriú Éireann* (2008).

**James Kelly**, M.R.I.A., is the Cregan Professor of History and Head of the History Department at St Patrick's College, Dublin City University and Honorary Research Professor in History at the Queen's University of Belfast. He has published widely on the social, political and religious history of late early modern Ireland. His recent publications include *The Liberty and Ormond Boys: Faction Fighting in Eighteenth-Century Dublin* (2005), *Poynings' Law and the Making of Law in Ireland, 1660–1800* (2007), and *The Proceedings of the House of Lords, 1771–1800* (3 vols, 2008).

**Mary Ann Lyons** is a Senior Lecturer in History at St Patrick's College, Dublin City University and Co-Director of the Irish in Europe Project. She is currently joint editor of *Irish Historical Studies*. She has embarked on a biographical study of the influential seventeenth-century Irish physician Thomas Arthur. Her publications include *Church and Society in County Kildare c.1470–1547* (2000) and *Franco-Irish Relations, 1500–1610: Politics, Migration and Trade* (2003). She has edited several volumes in the *Irish in Europe* series and is general editor of the *Maynooth Guides for Local History*.

**Andrew Sneddon** is lecturer in international History at the University of Ulster. He was a postdoctoral research fellow (2004–6) on the Leverhulme Foundation funded 'Irish Legislation 1692–1800' project in the School of History and Anthropology at the Queen's University of Belfast and a research fellow (2007–8) in the Institute of Irish Studies in the same institution. His monograph, *Witchcraft and Whigs: the Life of Bishop Francis Hutchinson* was published by Manchester University Press in 2008.

# Acknowledgements

Research into the history of medicine in Ireland is still in its infancy, though there have been a number of important recent initiatives to suggest that this is about to change. One of the most notable has been the establishment of a number of cross-institutional research programmes and, in 2006, of a Centre for the History of Medicine in Ireland based at the University of Ulster and the School of History and Archives at University College Dublin. This welcome trend notwithstanding, the priority long accorded to the institutional and biographical approach, and to the nineteenth and twentieth centuries, serves to underline the importance of exploring the earlier history of medicine in Ireland, and the need to open up new avenues in the way and manner in which both the history of medicine is conceived, and medical subjects are explored. This is the purpose of this collection, which comprises papers presented to a symposium on Ireland and medicine in the seventeenth and eighteenth centuries hosted by the Centre for Eighteenth-Century Studies at Queen's University Belfast on 25 and 26 April 2008. Both the symposium upon which this book is based, and the preparation of the text, have been assisted by financial and other supports forthcoming from the Wellcome Trust, the Royal Historical Society, the Centre for Eighteenth-Century Studies, the School of Spanish and Portuguese Studies, the School of History and Anthropology at Queen's University, and the History Department at St Patrick's College. Dr Clark, in particular, would like to thank Professor James Kelly and Dr Marian Lyons for making possible the initial process that led to the symposium, and for their continued support and encouragement, and express her gratefulness to the administrative staff in the School of Languages, Literatures and Performing Arts, and to Dr Simon Davies and colleagues in the Centre for Eighteenth-Century Studies at Queen's. Professor Kelly wishes to thank his colleagues in the History Department, St Patrick's College, and, particularly, Dr Marian Lyons for her continuing support and commitment to the project. Both editors wish to thank the contributors for their participation in the symposium, and for the efficient way in which they have assisted in making this volume possible.

*November 2008*

# List of Abbreviations

| | |
|---|---|
| Add. MS | Additional Manuscript |
| ADM | Admiralty Series |
| AGI | Archivo General de Indias, Seville |
| AGN | Archivo General de la Nación, México |
| AGS, SGU | Archivo General de Simancas, Secretaría del Despacho de Guerra |
| AHFM–UNAM | Archivo Histórico de la Facultad de Medicina – Universidad Nacional Autónoma de México |
| ARS | Archive of the Royal Society, London |
| BL | British Library, London |
| BMR | Bibliothèque Municipale, Reims |
| BNF | Bibliothèque Nationale de France |
| CUP | Cambridge University Press |
| *EHR* | *English Historical Review* |
| FCP | Four Courts Press |
| GA | Guild of Apothecaries, Apothecaries Hall, Dublin |
| HMC | Historical Manuscripts Commission |
| JRUL | John Rylands University Library, Manchester |
| LS | Linnean Society, London |
| MS(S) | Manuscript(s) |
| NAI | National Archives of Ireland |
| NLI | National Library of Ireland |
| NLW | National Library of Wales |
| NLS | National Library of Scotland |
| NUI | National University of Ireland |
| NUL | Nottingham University Library |
| *ODNB* | *Oxford Dictionary of National Biography* (60 vols, Oxford, 2004) |
| OUP | Oxford University Press |
| PRONI | Public Record Office of Northern Ireland |
| QUB | Queen's University Belfast |
| RANM | Real Academia Nacional de Medicina, Madrid |
| RCBL | Representative Church Body Library, Dublin |
| RCPI | Royal College of Physicians of Ireland, Dublin |
| RDS | Royal Dublin Society |
| RIA | Royal Irish Academy, Dublin |
| *RIA proc.* | *Royal Irish Academy, proceedings* |
| RSA | Royal Society of Arts |

| | |
|---|---|
| TCD | Trinity College Dublin |
| TNA | The National Archives, Public Record Office |
| UCD | University College Dublin |
| WL | Wellcome Library, London |
| WO | War Office |

# Introduction

Consistent with the ascendancy of the institution and the medical professional in modern medicine, most medical history published in Ireland to date has been written from an institutional and biographical perspective. Indeed, it has largely been written by medical practitioners with an interest in history rather than by historians. This explains the particular focus on institutions (the rise of the hospital and the development of the medical school), organisations (specifically professional bodies), the emergence of the professional medical elite, and the lives and achievements of doctors.[1] Much fine work has been accomplished in each of these areas, and, as a result, it is possible not only to consult solid narrative histories of most of the main medical institutions, colleges, as well as hospitals,[2] but also to pursue the life histories of many of the major medical figures of the seventeenth, eighteenth, nineteenth and twentieth centuries.[3]

---

[1] For a traditional overview, see John Fleetwood, *History of Irish medicine* (2nd edn, Dublin: Skellig Press, 1983). This has been superseded by Tony Farmar, *Patients, potions, physicians: a social history of medicine in Ireland 1654–2004* (Dublin: A&A Farmar, 2004), which employs a less traditional approach and is less preoccupied with organisations and institutions. However, in keeping with the fact that it was written to honour the anniversary of the Royal College of Physicians of Ireland, the history of that venerable institution features prominently on its pages.

[2] See, for examples of this approach, O'Donel T.D. Browne, *The Rotunda Hospital, 1745–1945* (Edinburgh: E. and S. Livingstone, 1947); Peter Gatenby, *Dublin's Meath Hospital* (Dublin: Town House, 1996); F.O.C. Meenan, *St Vincent's Hospital, 1834–1994: an historical and social portrait* (Dublin: Gill and Macmillan, 1995); Helen Burke, *The Royal Hospital Donnybrook: a heritage of caring, 1743–1993* (Dublin: Royal Hospital Donnybrook and the Social Science Research Centre, UCD, 1993); C.A. Cameron, *History of the Royal College of Surgeons in Ireland, and of the Irish schools of medicine, including numerous biographical sketches* (Dublin: Fannin and Company, 1886); J.D.H. Widdess, *The Royal College of Surgeons in Ireland and its medical school, 1784–1966* (2nd edn, Edinburgh: E. and S. Livingstone, 1967); J.D.H. Widdess, *A history of the Royal College of Physicians of Ireland 1654–1963* (Edinburgh: E. and S. Livingstone, 1963); T.P.C. Kirkpatrick, *History of the medical teaching in Trinity College, Dublin, and of the School of Physic in Ireland* (Dublin: Hanna and Neale, 1912). A fuller listing of institutional histories can be located in Fleetwood, *History of Irish medicine* (2nd edn), pp. 333–54, and in notes 4, 7, 8 and 14 in Greta Jones and Elizabeth Malcolm, 'Introduction: an anatomy of Irish medical history' in Jones and Malcolm (eds), *Medicine, disease and the state in Ireland 1650–1940* (Cork: Cork University Press, 1999), pp. 10–11, 12.

[3] See, for example, T.W. Belcher, *Memoir of Sir Patrick Dun* (Dublin: Hodges, Smith and Co., 1866); Sir William Stokes, *William Stokes, his life and work (1804–1878)* (London: T. Fisher Unwin, 1898); J.B. Lyons, *Brief lives of Irish doctors* (Dublin: Blackwater, 1978);

The value of such inquiry is undeniable. It has provided the student of the history of medicine in Ireland with a series of standard narratives and, in many instances, the foundation documents of the main medical institutions, and perspectives on the personnel and personalities that contributed, individually and severally, to the evolution of medical practice in Ireland since the seventeenth century. Moreover, given the different approaches employed in the histories that have been prepared of emblematical institutions, such as the Dublin Lying-in Hospital (The Rotunda), which has had its story chronicled on at least seven occasions, it is apparent that certain institutions can profitably be revisited to provide answers to new questions and to demonstrate the potential of new approaches to and new perspectives on the history of medicine.[4]

The value of the institutional and the biographical approach has not been exhausted, therefore, not only because both can assist with the application of new methodologies, but also because the history of many institutions and the lives of many practitioners (particularly at local level) has hardly been considered. Moreover, whole categories of eighteenth and early nineteenth-century foundations – infirmaries, dispensaries, houses of industry, workhouses, lunatic asylums, nursing homes and private sanatoria – remain seriously under-explored when they have been considered at all. Furthermore, because the approach in much institutional history to date has prioritised the physical growth, organisational development and, more recently, the cultural impact of the hospital, too little is known of the range, nature and impact of the course of therapies offered. This is even more so the case with a host of crucial issues appertaining to the care of patients, recovery rates, the evolution of the practitioner–patient relationship, the significance of gender, the impact and import of the moral, religious and political attitude of hospital staff, the adoption and impact of medication, the aetiology and impact of disease, and so on. In the case of medical practitioners, the attention accorded the physician, and specifically officeholders, innovators and leaders has overshadowed the no less important contribution of the ordinary practitioner, and still more so the impact and import of the surgeon and the apothecary, who were the other branches of the trinity of medical professionals responsible for dispensing medical assistance.

Their perceived limitations, notwithstanding, it is to works that employ an institutional and biographical focus that one must look for information to describe

---

Davis Coakley, *Irish masters of medicine* (Dublin: Town House, 1992); Eoin O'Brien, *Conscience and conflict: a biography of Sir Dominic Corrigan, 1802–80* (Dublin: The Glendale Press, 1983).

[4] For a review of the histories of the Rotunda see Jones and Malcolm, 'Introduction: an anatomy of Irish medical history' in Jones and Malcolm (eds), *Medicine, disease and the state*, pp. 1–17 (2–3). In addition to those discussed by Jones and Malcolm, see Ian Campbell Ross (ed.), *Public virtue, public love: the early years of the Dublin Lying-in hospital: the Rotunda* (Dublin: the O'Brien Press, 1986); G.A. Boyd, *Dublin 1745–1922: hospitals, spectacle and vice* (Dublin: FCP, 2006).

the early phases of the emergence of modern diagnostic medicine in Ireland.[5] They also constitute our main source of information on the evolution of the medical professions, which explains why this continues to be presented in primarily institutional terms; thus the emergence of the surgeon has been explored against the backdrop of the campaign to establish the College of Surgeons, and the expanding role of the physician in the context of the history of the College of Physicians.[6] As a result, those branches of medicine that do not possess equivalently venerable institutions – the apothecary, general practitioner and the dentist[7] – want for comparable histories, while the role and contribution of other carers – such as the nurse – have attracted still less notice.[8]

The strengths and weaknesses of Irish medical historiography, referred to in the preceding paragraphs, is well known. It was described in comparable terms nearly a decade ago by Jones and Malcolm, in the introduction to a collection of essays that stands out as the most ambitious attempt to date to apply a more modern approach to the history of medicine in Ireland.[9] A number of other collections currently in preparation aspire to build on this achievement,[10] and the recent surveys, though different in nature, purpose and focus, prepared by Tony Farmar and Laurence Geary suggest that the observations of Jones and Malcolm have not passed unnoticed.[11] However, in all of these works the nineteenth and twentieth centuries preponderate. As a result, the modern period overwhelms the early modern, leading to an insufficient acknowledgement of the complexity of medical practice in the seventeenth and eighteenth centuries.

---

[5] For an attempt, which draws heavily on such scholarship, see James Kelly, 'The emergence of scientific and institutional medical practice in Ireland, 1650–1800' in Jones and Malcolm (eds), *Medicine, disease and the state*, pp. 21–39.

[6] Widdess, *The Royal College of Surgeons in Ireland*; Widdess, *A history of the Royal College of Physicians of Ireland 1654–1963*; Cameron, *History of the Royal College of Surgeons in Ireland*.

[7] For an initial attempt to explore the emergence of the dentist see James Kelly, '"I was glad to be rid of it": dental medical practice in eighteenth-century Ireland' in Margaret Preston and Margaret Ó hÓgartaigh (eds), *Gender, medicine and the state in Ireland, the United States and Australia* (Syracuse: Syracuse University Press, forthcoming).

[8] There is a history of nursing – Pauline Scanlon, *The Irish nurse: a study of nursing in Ireland in history and education, 1718–1981* (Manorhamilton; Drumlin Press, 1991) – but the prominence afforded development in the twentieth century underlines the potential for further enquiry into the history and evolution of nursing care.

[9] Jones and Malcolm, 'Introduction: an anatomy of Irish medical history', in Jones and Malcolm (eds), *Medicine, disease and the state*, pp. 1–17.

[10] Preston and Ó hÓgartaigh (eds), *Gender, medicine and the state in Ireland, the United States and Australia*; Maria Luddy and Catherine Cox (eds), *Cultures of care in Irish medical history, 1750–1950* (Basingstoke: Palgrave, forthcoming).

[11] Farmar, *Patients, potions, physicians*; Laurence M. Geary, *Medicine and charity in Ireland, 1718–1851* (Dublin: UCD Press, 2004).

There is much, certainly, that requires detailed exploration before a balanced new synthesis can be generated. We do not, for example, possess even a hazy picture of the number of medical practitioners working in the country at any given point prior to the availability of censal figures in the mid-nineteenth century, though this is a prerequisite to any attempt to establish the availability of trained medical assistance, the level of public access and, not least, the permeation of new techniques and methods of diagnosis and care. Apart from the select number of students that were admitted to Trinity College, Irish physicians generally trained abroad. As the findings of Innes Smith, Underwood and Froggatt on Leiden, and Laurence Brockliss's pioneering work on Reims in this volume demonstrate, it should be possible to establish with some confidence the number that studied abroad by combing the registers of the relevant universities in Britain and Europe and thereby to construct a general time series.[12] It will be less easy, as Brockliss observes below (Chapter 4), to identify the number that returned to practice in Ireland, and still less to establish with any reliability how they interacted with the larger number of almost wholly domestically trained surgeons and apothecaries with whom they rubbed shoulders, or their relationship with the serried ranks of charlatans, quacks, and healers that were also a feature of the medical landscape. Moreover, we know little of the medicine that they practiced. While major claims have been advanced in respect of the influence of a number of the great practitioners of the age, most notably Herman Boerhaave, the 'paucity of Irish Catholics at the premier [medical] schools in the eighteenth century', combined with the predilection of Irish medical students to gravitate to those institutions where a degree could be secured cheaply, suggests that excellence was not always a priority, or always guaranteed.[13] What is apparent is that further, closer inquiry is required into the education of Irish physicians to establish the extent to which the Galenist humoral approach retreated (if at all) during the seventeenth and eighteenth centuries in the face of new knowledge, new medical theories and new styles of practice.

This will be of limited use, of course, in illuminating the more tenebrous world of popular medicine, particularly as practiced by the large Gaelic-speaking component of the public following the destruction of the traditional medical schools that flowed from the extension of English power in the sixteenth and seventeenth centuries. Based on the conclusion that medieval and early modern Irish medical texts 'contain some of the best medical literature available in contemporary Europe' and that they were not 'simply an academic exercise divorced from the

---

[12] R.W. Innes Smith, *English-speaking students of medicine at the University of Leiden* (Edinburgh: Oliver and Boyd, 1932); E.A. Underwood, 'The first and final phase of the Irish medical students at the University of Leiden' in Eoin O'Brien (ed.), *Essays in honour of J.D.H. Widdess* (Dublin: Cityview Press, 1978), pp. 5–42; Peter Froggatt, 'Irish students at Leiden and the renaissance of medicine in Dublin', in *Journal of the Irish College of Physicians and Surgeons*, 22 (1993): 124–32.

[13] Froggatt, 'Irish students at Leiden', 126.

reality of the doctor's practice',[14] it can reasonably be assumed that their echo reverberated long after the medical schools had disappeared. Yet this can only be conjectured in the absence of more focussed research, and a clearer appreciation of the relationship of the essentially Galenist medicine promoted in the medical schools with the herbal, religious and magical remedies that circulated among the *menu peuple*.

What is apparent, based on the testimony of contemporaries dating from the early seventeenth to the early nineteenth century, is that the number and distribution of medical practitioners with appropriate qualifications was wholly inadequate to the needs of the population. As a consequence, people of all traditions, cultures and classes were obliged to assume direct and personal responsibility for their own health and well-being. This resulted in the palpably more fluid doctor–patient relationship wherein the paying patient had more agency than became the case in the nineteenth century. This was symbolised by the fact that in Gaelic Ireland, medical manuscripts were frequently transcribed, not in the medical schools, but in the houses of the gentry on whom practitioners were dependent, as Charlie Dillon's account of the life of Risteard Ó Conchubhair (1561–1625) illustrates (Chapter 2).[15] Old English physicians likewise visited and stayed with their patients when summoned to do so, and the situation was only slightly different in anglophone Ireland at the end of the eighteenth century, as William Drennan's experience at Newry amply illustrates.[16] This arrangement persisted because of the gulf in social and economic status that separated members of the landed elite from those in medicine – a small cadre of well-connected physicians apart. Yet the fact that wealth was no security against ill-health facilitated the upwards mobility that was a feature of all branches of medicine – female midwives and unorthodox practitioners excepted. As a result, those with access to professional medicine by virtue of their social position and geographical location, could, and did in many instances, develop a close and trusting relationship with one or more of the slowly expanding number of graduate physicians, skilled surgeons and knowledgeable apothecaries that plied their skills. However, because recovery, even from minor complaints and conditions, could not be guaranteed, and because the curatives that were administered were perturbingly fallible, patients inevitably regarded the medical professions with understandable scepticism, and had no hesitation, in the eighteenth century, either in seeking other opinions or appealing to unorthodox practitioners, to family knowledge and to the expanding array of proprietary medication that were available for purchase. Moreover, though the origins of hospitalisation, and of the hospital as an institution, can be securely located in the eighteenth century, only a small proportion of those that were ill ever saw the

---

[14] Aoibheann Nic Dhonnchadha, 'Early modern Irish medical writings', in *Newsletter of the School of Celtic Studies*, 4 (1990): 39.

[15] Nic Dhonnchadha, 'Early modern Irish medical writings', 35–9.

[16] See Lyons, chapter 1 in this collection; Jean Agnew, *The Drennan–McTier letters* (3 vols, Dublin: Irish Manuscripts Commission, 1998–9), vol. 1 *passim*.

inside of such an institution. It is not possible at present to estimate the number or social station of those who did receive hospital attention, but the absence of any reference to their engagement with such institutions other than in a charitable capacity indicates that members of the social elite never attended a hospital as a patient. Illness was treated primarily in the home, and given the deficiencies of many medical practitioners, the therapies they proffered and the available medications, it is not surprising that those blighted by ill-health did not hesitate to try all the options available to them. As a result, the seventeenth and eighteenth centuries sustained a more varied medical culture than that which existed in the nineteenth century, when, during the golden age of Irish medicine, the medical professional and the hospital achieved the ascendancy it retains to the present.

As the preceding overview suggests, the diversity that was emblematical of Irish medicine in the seventeenth and eighteenth centuries pertaining to such a variety of medical approaches provides the main rationale for this current volume. To this end, the collection aspires both to open up new areas of enquiry, and to re-engage with others in order to broaden the interpretative context within which the medical history of late early modern Ireland is situated. It is thus appropriate that the collection includes a preliminary exploration by Charlie Dillon of the character and impact of the native medical tradition (Chapter 2), and, in particular, of the medical schools that Gaelic Irish society sustained. As Dillon points out, medical practice was one of the hereditary arts in Gaelic Ireland into the early modern period. Like the better-known poetic tradition, it was unsustainable in the absence of the clan structure, which was the main casualty of the collapse of the Gaelic political order in the face of Tudor expansion, and the imperious extension of English settlement and political influence in the seventeenth century. Though it is possible from the surviving record to establish who the main Gaelic medical families were, and, from the extant corpus of medical manuscripts the tradition of medical learning they promoted and developed, we are less well informed as to how medicine was practised. Gaelic medical practitioners seem to have been located securely within the Galenist framework then dominant in Europe, and to have tended primarily (and perhaps exclusively) to members of the landed elite, both of the Gaelic and Anglo-Norman/Old English traditions. One of the best documented medical schools was at Aghmacart in county Laois, but the fact that it disappears from the record in 1611 is in keeping with the fact that the native medical tradition was so inextricably bound up with the Gaelic order it could not survive its collapse.[17]

Based both on the content of the medical knowledge contained in the hundred plus 'manuscripts dating from the fifteenth to the seventeenth centuries which are almost entirely medical in content', and the assessments of reliable contemporary observers, the Gaelic medical tradition was laudably practical in its approach and

---

[17] Aoibheann Nic Dhonnchadha, 'The medical school of Aghmacart, Queen's County', in *Ossory, Laois and Leinster*, 2 (2006): 11–43.

orientation.[18] Significantly, its admirers included Johannes Baptista van Helmont, the influential critic of contemporary medical practice, who was induced by his antipathy to what was transmitted within university medical schools on the continent to applaud the reliance of Irish medical practitioners on observation and 'vernacular' remedies.[19] The long-term legacy of Aghmacart, and of comparable institutions is elusive, but Dillon's contentions that the practice of Irish people going to Europe for medical training is evidence of continuity with a ruptured past, and that the Gaelic tradition of medical learning may also have influenced the vibrant folk tradition of healing and cures that persisted into the nineteenth century is suggestive. As matters stand, there is a glaring chasm in our knowledge as to what the ordinary public did for medical assistance, assuming they had at least some access to the learning promoted by the professional medical schools, between the early seventeenth and the early nineteenth centuries when their reliance on folk medicine can be tracked.

It is clear that the collapse of the Gaelic order did not halt the practice of Galenist medicine in Ireland. The Old English descendants of the Anglo-Norman settlers, who dominated much of the urban environment and who were a powerful political as well as economic force in various parts of the provinces of Leinster and Munster, also sustained a medical infrastructure. It remains to be fully excavated, but it would appear that medical practitioners from this background traditionally went abroad for their medical education, largely but not exclusively to England. This pattern was disrupted by the confessional and political upheavals of the sixteenth century, though the presence of Dermot O'Meara at Oxford University in the early seventeenth century indicates that the indulgence shown to medical practitioners by the New English authorities meant the Catholics continued to have access to English medical learning past the completion of the Tudor conquest. However, in common with those who sought theological training, members of this community made their way increasingly to Catholic Europe from the early seventeenth century. Whatever their precise destination, the impact of their training and the best practice they encountered abroad convinced them that the approach adopted by the multitude of what Dermot O'Meara famously caricatured as 'cursed mountebanks, ignorant barbers and shameless quacks' then practicing in Ireland 'profane[d] the holy temple of Asculapius'.[20] Conceiving that this should not be allowed to continue, a number of the most ambitious and talented practitioners sought to promote a programme of reform and professionalisation, whose most ambitious manifestation was a scheme to establish a college of physicians at Dublin, in order to police practitioners and to regulate standards. Their plans proved still born, but Lyons' account (Chapter 1) of their efforts in the late 1620s,

---

[18] Nic Dhonnchadha, 'Early modern Irish medical writings', 35.

[19] Quoted from van Helmont's *Opera Omnia* (1682) in Kirkpatrick, *History of the medical teaching in Trinity College*, p. 31.

[20] Cited in Kelly, 'The emergence of scientific and institutional medical practice in Ireland, 1650–1800', p. 22.

and her exploration of the practice of Ireland's premier physician, Thomas Arthur, demonstrates that the kingdom was not the medical wasteland in the first half of the seventeenth century that an unquestioning acceptance of O'Meara's oft-cited description might imply. The absence of proper regulation did permit a permissive environment that unqualified practitioners successfully availed of, but the fact that these were not always without skill demonstrates that the history of medicine in seventeenth-century Ireland is about more than the foundation of a graduate college of physicians, which finally took place in 1654.

Thomas Arthur was one of the earliest Irish graduates of the University of Reims, and one of the first of many Irish Catholics who were obliged, because of the absence of a vibrant school of medical training and the intensifying confessional cleavage that gripped Irish society in the seventeenth century, to have recourse to continental Europe for medical training. The country did have a university, Trinity College established in 1592, with the authorisation to prepare medical graduates. However, theology took precedence, and this, in combination with the institution's confessional character, ensured that the bulk of the country's medical graduates during the seventeenth, eighteenth and early nineteenth centuries were trained abroad.[21] Reims was the destination long favoured by Catholics, as Laurence Brockliss points out (Chapter 4), in large part because it was cheaper and easier to secure a medical degree there than elsewhere. However, because of the substantial number of Irish Catholic students who aspired to a medical qualification, they were also to be found in medical faculties across the continent. The numbers graduating from Paris, Montpellier and Prague was palpably smaller than from Reims, but it may be that they were more highly motivated, better educated and, perhaps, more influential in shaping medical practice in the eighteenth century when, with the Protestant ascendancy firmly rooted, their number appreciated sharply.[22]

It is clear, moreover, that the number of medical students grew in the course of the eighteenth century because medicine was one of the few professions from which Catholics were not disbarred or inhibited by law.[23] This is not to suggest that medicine held no interest for members of the Church of Ireland. Beginning in the 1660s, a slowly appreciating trickle of students, overwhelmingly members of the Church of Ireland, opted to travel to Leiden in the Dutch Republic, where, during the 38 years that Herman Boerhaave taught there (1700–38), they received a medical training of exceptional quality. A total of 236 Irish students registered at Leiden over a period of three centuries, 122 during 'the Boerhaavian period' alone. Their number declined appreciably following Boerhaave's death (only 87 Irishmen matriculated between 1739 and 1817), but by then Trinity College had a functioning medical school, while Oxford and Cambridge also attracted some

---

[21] Kirkpatrick, *History of the medical teaching in Trinity College Dublin*, pp. 25–6.

[22] For an assessment of the influence of Leiden see Peter Froggatt, 'Irish students at Leiden', 124–32.

[23] See Patrick Fagan, *Catholics in a Protestant country: the papist constituency in eighteenth-century Dublin* (Dublin: FCP, 1999), chapter three.

Irish students.[24] Presbyterians, meanwhile, were strongly drawn to Scotland, and the development at Glasgow and Edinburgh of vigorous medical schools proved an attractive option, to which many had recourse. Much work needs to be done on the registers and records of these institutions, but based on the fact that 'no less than 354' Irish men graduated MD from Edinburgh University between 1794 and 1816, it is apparent that the medical school there must be placed alongside Reims, Leiden, and Trinity College as the most formative influences on the manner in which medicine was practised in Ireland during the period covered by this book.[25] There were other institutional influences, of course, not least the British military, as Laurence Brockliss also highlights. The British army and navy proved an attractive source of employment for many Irish medical practitioners during the late eighteenth and early nineteenth centuries, and though many of these never returned to practise in Ireland, others contributed in a direct and impressive manner to the rise in numbers and in medical expertise available to the population of Ireland in the early nineteenth century.[26]

One of the most striking implications of the work of Innes Smith, Underwood, Froggatt and Brockliss on the education of Irish physicians, besides their impressive number and confessional diversity, is its international character. This means that any account of Irish medicine during the seventeenth, eighteenth and early nineteenth centuries must also note the fact that not only did the careers of most Irish doctors possess an international dimension, but also that many chose to live their lives entirely abroad and to use their medical knowledge in a manner that would serve to advance humanity rather than their own careers. This is manifest from two essays in the collection – those by Liam Chambers on Bernard Connor (Chapter 3), and by Fiona Clark on Daniel O'Sullivan (Chapter 9). Both Connor and O'Sullivan were exceptional men, and their interests extended beyond the formal practice of medicine to engage with the broader implications for society of developments in the realm of medicine, as well as with the increasingly scientific approach to knowledge and understanding that was intrinsic to the so-called scientific revolution. This is most apparent in the case of Bernard Connor, who not only practised medicine in Poland and London, but also engaged actively with the major intellectual challenges posed by medical discovery and intellectual enquiry in the early Enlightenment to the traditional, intrinsically religious conception of mankind and its place in the world. Focusing in particular on one of Connor's works, *Evangelium Medici* (1697), which he locates within the contemporary discourse on miracles, Chambers' account of Connor is revealing of how medical training shaped attitudes on a wider intellectual plain as the ancients and moderns battled for intellectual pre-eminence. Connor's career also exemplifies the personal,

---

[24] Froggatt, 'Irish students at Leiden', 127–9.
[25] Froggatt, 'Irish students at Leiden', 125.
[26] As well as his chapter in this volume, see Brockliss, et al., *Advancing with the army: medicine, the professions and social mobility in the British Isles, 1790–1850* (Oxford: OUP, 2007).

intellectual and, one can conjecture, professional difficulties some Irish medical practitioners experienced in an era in which traditional medical knowledge and understanding encountered new ideas, new discoveries and new thinking that challenged long-cherished assumptions, and that encouraged new approaches to illness. Significantly, though Connor was both familiar with and largely convinced by the arguments of the moderns in a variety of fields, he was unwilling simply to discard the knowledge and learning of the ancients. Just as his medical theory combined aspects of the Galenic approach, Paracelsian and iatrochemical thinking, and the mechanical approach favoured in the late seventeenth century, so his treatise on miracles, *Evangelium Medici*, contrived to reconcile miracles with human reason. Though this was a matter about which he had long pondered prior to his entry into print in 1697, possibly in response to the publication of John Toland's notorious deistical manifesto, *Christianity not Mysterious* (1695), Connor's career is at once an illustration of the practical challenges of negotiating a way through the shoals and eddies of contemporary intellectual discourse, and of the particular difficulties confronting an individual from an Irish Catholic background with a medical qualification from a French university, who sought to establish a successful medical practice in Protestant London.

By contrast, within the context of the Iberian-Atlantic world, Daniel O'Sullivan's Catholic background did not constitute an insuperable barrier to his advancement, but he was to encounter still more forbidding obstacles in the shape of vested interests, which reflexively joined forces to resist the criticisms and ideas of the outsider. An Irish physician, trained in France, O'Sullivan entered the Spanish colonial service and was posted to Mexico. It was a difficult location, which for an aspiring physician demanded considerable diplomatic skills as well as medical knowledge, as Clark makes clear (Chapter 9). O'Sullivan possessed the latter but not the former, with the result that his efforts to assist in the identification of a cure for venereal disease succumbed to the infighting and petty jealousies at play within the medical ranks of late colonial Mexico. His experience illustrates how individuals in positions of authority could use and manipulate the authority that came from their position to frustrate both the ideas and ambitions of those around them and, as in this instance, is revealing of how medical ideas were received, rejected and reconfigured. Late colonial Mexico was particularly complex, but the problems O'Sullivan encountered were illustrative of the intricate and varied nature of the web of tightly woven social, scientific and political relationships that many Irish-born but foreign-trained physicians must have experienced. It thus highlights the need for more in-depth examination of the various means of advancement adopted by these individuals, such as rhetorical or discursive practices and practical networking, as they negotiated varied structures and demands of empire, whether in late seventeenth-century London, eighteenth-century Mexico or in the nineteenth-century British military.

Of course, they could simply have returned to Ireland, where their services were much needed. Indeed, the shortage of medical practitioners was a crucial factor, Kelly argues (Chapter 5), in sustaining a vibrant practice of domestic and auto-medication during the seventeenth and eighteenth centuries. This was probably most developed (it is certainly most visible) among the anglophone element of the population, and it is no surprise therefore that the pattern of 'domestic medicine' that flourished bears direct comparison with that identifiable in England. It would appear also that responsibility for dispensing care in the home was assumed primarily by women, and that they embraced roles and performed functions that, in an institutional environment, would have been the preserve of medical professionals. Many of the skills required to perform these functions were learned as part of the routine business of household management that women were expected to master, but households also equipped themselves with knowledge in the form of 'receipt books', in which they recorded remedies to enable them to deal with illness when it arose. Receipt books were passed between generations, and they were thus a repository of hereditary knowledge, but one of the most striking features of the increased availability of medical information in print in the eighteenth century is the embrace of remedies and nostrums from a great variety of sources. Moreover, as Kelly points out, the increased availability of compendious medical guides provided households with ever more comprehensive instructions to assist with medicating in a domestic setting, while the appreciating range of proprietary medicines that was widely advertised and available for purchase at a multiplicity of outlets meant that the public had access to an unprecedented volume of medication.[27] Much of what was offered for sale was of doubtful value – some nostrums were positively dangerous – but in a world where auto-diagnosis was commonplace, where professional medical assistance was not always readily available, and where no single approach to curing had attained a decisive moral ascendancy, it was deemed still better than doing nothing.

A wide variety of factors encouraged patients to engage in auto-diagnosis, to delegate that task to someone without formal qualification, and to pursue cures in a domestic setting; several essays in this collection explore these issues. A particular concern was the failure of the Irish parliament, though it met in regular session from 1692 until its abolition in 1800, either to establish an appropriate regulatory environment or to provide the funds that would have sustained an institutional infrastructure capable of providing care to the population at large. It may be observed in defence of the legislature that it was reluctant to intervene in the regulation of interests that were overseen by corporations or chartered bodies, particularly when, as demonstrated by the charter granted to the College of Physicians in 1692, it provided that body with extensive powers. It is the case, of course, that the College wished to have these powers put on statutory foundation, as Andrew Sneddon relates (Chapter 6). But the realisation that this might serve, as the surgeons and apothecaries reiterated, to confine their ability to diagnose and to proscribe, and increase the burden on the poor, was sufficient to dissuade

---

[27] For a perspective on the growth in the availability of patent and proprietary medicine see James Kelly, 'Health for sale: mountebanks, doctors, printers and the supply of medication in eighteenth-century Ireland', in *RIA proc.*, 108C (2008): 1–38.

parliament from strengthening the regulatory powers of the cadre of physicians that maintained a tight grip of the College of Physicians. This elitist impulse may well have served to ensure that standards were maintained within this, the most eminent, branch of the medical profession and kept within bounds in other ranks, but the regulatory weaknesses of the Barber-Surgeons' Guild, and, following its establishment in 1747, of the Apothecaries' Guild ensured that examples of malpractice were commonplace. This was virtually inevitable, given the sheer number of irregulars, the respect accorded healers, and the receptivity of the people at large to quacks and charlatans. Parliament did not completely ignore the problems this caused, but it did little enough, and was, for example, only persuaded to intervene to regulate the apothecary trade in 1735 by the exposure by Charles Lucas, himself an apothecary, of egregious abuses. Moreover, this can hardly be described as a turning point. It is notable that several further initiatives pressed by Lucas in the 1760s failed to make it into law, and that a majority of the medical legislation approved in the later eighteenth century may reasonably be described as institutional rather than strictly medical. It is indicative of the enduring disinclination of MPs and peers to engage in any detailed or systematic way in the regulation of medicine, and of their determination to confine themselves to larger structural issues, that they tended to follow rather than to anticipate developments taking place within the medical arena, as exemplified by the legislation establishing the College of Surgeons in 1784 and the Apothecaries Hall in 1791. In both instances, the statutory intervention constituted acknowledgement of the fact that the surgeon and the apothecary were as crucial to the existing medical system as the physicians, who had been accorded institutional recognition more than a century previously.

Of course the influence and impact of the medical practitioners was not solely confined to the medical arena. Medicine was the career of choice for some of the brightest and ablest people of every generation. The involvement of a number of prominent physicians to the Dublin Philosophical Society in the late seventeenth century has been explored by K. Theodore Hoppen.[28] More recently, Eamon O'Flaherty has described the intellectual activities of a variety of eighteenth-century eminences,[29] but it is a measure of the range of activity of medical men that this is but to scratch the surface of this phenomenon. Toby Barnard's assessment of the social impact of physicians across Ireland as agents of knowledge and enlightenment in the seventeenth and eighteenth centuries (Chapter 8) highlights the disproportionate influence medical practitioners had as avatars of improvement. They were able to do this, he suggests, because unlike many other areas of life, the absence of confessional prohibitions meant a wider pool of ability and experience

---

[28] K. Theodore Hoppen, *The common scientist of the seventeenth century: a study of the Dublin Philosophical Society, 1683–1708* (London: Routledge Kegan Paul, 1970)

[29] Eamon O'Flaherty, 'Medical men and learned societies in Ireland, 1680–1785', in Howard Clarke and Judith Devlin (eds), *European Encounters* (Dublin: UCD Press, 2003), pp. 253–69.

was available to the medical profession. In support of this thesis, Barnard not only engages with individual doctors who made a substantive intellectual and cultural contribution, he explores the specific contribution of a quite distinctive improving society, the Medico-Philosophical Society, which sought through its efforts to combat poverty, to improve the reliability of medicines, and to discourage the consumption of spirits to better Irish society. It was only partly successful, but it arguably best exemplifies the importance of the link between the medical profession and learning, and the impact of medical practitioners on the wider culture of Ireland. Significantly, this body has, to date, attracted little of the attention that has been lavished on the sequence of improving and antiquarian societies that also populated the Irish intellectual landscape. But in Charles Smith, a talented apothecary and until now a remarkably shadowy presence on the Irish medical and intellectual horizon, it had a figure of particular interest. Significantly, it emerges from Barnard's account that though Smith made as important a contribution to the Medico-Philosophical Society, as he had previously to the Physico-Historical Society, and that he promoted the inculcation of an increasingly scientific approach to knowledge and understanding, he was also possessed of less than enlightened opinions on the confessional order that obtained in eighteenth-century Ireland. This point needs making, moreover, because it highlights that though Catholics were admitted to all ranks of the medical profession, medicine was not immune to the sectarian passions that characterised Irish society in the mid-eighteenth century.

Smith was not, of course, the only remarkable medical personality of the era whose life and labours remain to be disinterred. There were, as Barnard also illustrates, other medical practitioners whose contribution to the cultural life of eighteenth-century Ireland was expressed in ways other than through their medical endeavours. What this underlines is that the exploration of the life and activities of an individual, or even an aspect of the life of an individual medical practitioner or patient, can serve to illuminate a particular trend. Medical correspondence is a case in point. During the eighteenth century epistolary consultation was a crucial feature of the prevailing culture of self-diagnosis and domestic medication and a vital medium of communication in a world of refined homo-sociability. Yet, it is frequently difficult to overcome the limitations of the scattered shards of correspondence from which so much of the patient–practitioner discourse has to be constructed in order to penetrate beneath the surface to establish how the various parties in a medical correspondence regarded the exchange, and precisely what it says both about being a doctor and being ill. The letters exchanged between Mordecai Cary, the Church of Ireland bishop of Clonfert, and James Jurin, a physician resident in London in the mid-1730s permit one to peel away some of the obscurity that characterises most such exchanges because of the nature of the exchange and the familiarity of the participants. Intriguingly, as Wendy D. Churchill observes (Chapter 7), the subject of their correspondence was Cary's wife, which allows many questions to be addressed on the importance of gender in contemporary medical practice. On first consideration, the fact that Mordecai

Cary was the author of the correspondence, and not his wife, suggests that Mrs Cary's voice was silent and she a passive recipient of the results of the ongoing medical discourse. But Churchill's nuanced argument and reasonable conclusion that the primary concern was Mrs Cary's health allows her to offer a reading of the exchange wherein Mrs Cary is the invisible yet guiding agent in both description and implementation, thereby rejecting any sense of the passive in support of an active, if apparently silent, role of women in medical correspondence. Seen from another perspective, the Cary–Jurin correspondence attests further to the international context in which the history of Irish medicine in the seventeenth and eighteenth centuries belongs; as far as those members of the English elite who resided in Ireland were concerned they were part of a British cultural world, and they had no hesitation in travelling or writing to Britain for medical direction and guidance, because in medicine, as in so many other walks of life, they perceived Ireland as provincial and less developed.

This may not seem a positive note on which to conclude this attempt to locate the papers in this collection within the historiography of Irish medicine. Be that as it may, the essays presented here aspire, together and individually, not only to examine the role of institutions and individuals anew, but also to open up new areas for consideration in order to extend the parameters of Irish medical history. This is necessary because for all the achievements of its founding fathers, Irish medical history will be enriched if it embraces new approaches. This is not to suggest either that the work of previous generations is consigned to the library shelf or that the role of the individual practitioner and of the major medical institutions should not continue to attract their share of notice. It is obvious from several essays in this volume that these dimensions are important if we are to deepen our understanding of the culture of medicine, the status of the medical practitioner, the nature, character and priorities of the main medical interests, and the bodies that represented them. However, it is important also to embrace other themes: medical training, medical practice, the availability of medicine and medical information, the attitude of the patient and the experience of illness, the number and distribution of medical practitioners and their place in society, and so on.

It is crucial also to locate the history of medicine in Ireland in its wider geographical and cultural sphere. Medical practitioners may not, as several contributors to this volume note, have suffered as severely as other elements of the Catholic intellectual and professional elite from repression and exclusion, but the dislocation and disruption that shaped Irish history in the sixteenth and seventeenth centuries, and the starkly confessional order that was sustained from the 1660s was not without negative impact. It was not that Ireland was deprived of skilled medical practitioners; those that could pay for the services of Thomas Arthur in the seventeenth century or Sir Edward Barry in the eighteenth had access to the best medical advice, as many of their patients testified.[30] However, there were insufficient numbers of skilled practitioners in all branches of medicine. This can be attributed partly to the unwillingness of the Irish parliament to intervene. It may be anachronistic to suggest that it should have taken steps to ensure that the country possessed a network of medical practitioners to whom all had access, but it could have taken steps to ensure there were more trained practitioners, and, by following the example of France, have instituted a regulatory regime that placed a premium on good practice and on standardised qualifications, which would have had major implications in terms both of the standard and availability of care. Instead, it permitted the emergence of a medical free for all in which the quack and the qualified practitioner competed equally for custom, and in which large amounts of damaging and dangerous proprietary medications were proffered for sale.

The fact that in Ireland, as in England, 'there was no single privileged medicine' contributed in no small manner to the diverse character of Irish medicine and to the vigour of domestic medicine, which is one of the main themes addressed in this collection, and which must be one of the priorities of the historians of medicine to reveal.[31] Another is its international character. The medical history of seventeenth- and eighteenth-century Ireland cannot properly be understood in an island setting. It is integral to the history of the Irish diaspora to continental Europe, as well as to the island's embrace within the consumer culture that flourished in England in the eighteenth century. It is for this reason that developments in the university sector on continental Europe are as pertinent to the history of medicine in Ireland as the importation and sale of large volumes of proprietary medicine of English origin.[32] There are, of course, other points of comparison with England, such as the pattern of institutional development. Yet the crucial point about the history of medicine in Ireland is that its story is particular, not because Ireland was colonised or because of the intimacy and extent of the connections with continental Europe, but because of the interplay of these and a diversity of other factors, ordinary and extraordinary, that shaped its development. This book will have served a useful purpose if, as well as demonstrating this point and stimulating others to engage in exploring that diversity, it throws light on these and other aspects of medicine in seventeenth and eighteenth-century Ireland.

---

[30] For Arthur, see Lyons, chapter 1; for a brief biography of Barry, who was a prominent member of the College of Physicians, physician-general, 1745–76, and MP for Charleville from 1744 to 1760, until he moved to London in the late 1750s: see E.M. Johnston-Liik, *History of the Irish parliament, 1682–1800* (6 vols, Belfast: Ulster Historical Foundation, 2002), vol. 3, pp. 138–9.

[31] Roy Porter, 'The people's health in Georgian England', in Tim Harris (ed.), *Popular culture in England* (New York: St Martin's Press, 1995), p. 126.

[32] See Kelly, 'Health for sale', 1–38.

Chapter 1

# The Role of Graduate Physicians in Professionalising Medical Practice in Ireland, c. 1619–54

Mary Ann Lyons

**Introduction**

The 1610s witnessed the beginnings of what was to be a significant departure in the professionalisation of medical practice in Ireland, as four precocious young Catholic men, graduates of the Faculty of Medicine at the University of Reims in north-eastern France, returned home to embark on their medical careers. These were Gerald Fennell, who graduated in 1614, Dermot O'Meara in 1616, Christopher Talbot in 1618 and Thomas Arthur in 1619.[1] Given their shared university experience and the fact that all became eminent members of Ireland's tiny coterie of successful and influential physicians during the first half of the seventeenth century, it was only to be expected that they should come to know each other, and, in some instances, to form life-long personal friendships. We know that Arthur and Talbot were acquainted as they were both students at Reims at the same time. Arthur and Fennell were lifelong friends and colleagues; Arthur took Fennell's advice on business matters in the late 1630s and counted Fennell as a 'brother' among the medical fraternity in Dublin in the early 1650s.[2] O'Meara and Talbot were sufficiently close to collaborate in the unsuccessful attempt to found an Irish College of Physicians in the mid-1620s. While little can be acertained about the backgrounds of Fennell and Talbot, both O'Meara and Arthur were members of well-established, prominent and influential families, albeit from contrasting cultural backgrounds. Dermot O'Meara belonged to a family that had long-standing associations with the earls of Ormond. He is thought to have been the son of the last O'Meara chief, Domhnail of Lisaniskey, and brother to William O'Meara who was sheriff of the county palatine of Ormond in 1616.[3] The

---

[1] See the graduate register of the Reims faculty, BMR, MS 1085, fols 46, 89, 123.

[2] Miscellaneous entry-book of Thomas Arthur, M.D., of Limerick (BL, Add. MS 31885, fol. 116) (hereafter Arthur entry-book); J.D.H. Widdess, 'A notable Irish physician', in *Irish Journal of Medical Science*, 373 (1957): 21–31 (27).

[3] P. Logan, 'Dermot and Edmund O'Meara, father and son', in *Journal of the Irish Medical Association*, 43 (1958): 312–15; Dermot F. Gleeson, *The last lords of Ormond* (rev.

Arthurs were a wealthy, urbane Old English merchant family who were deeply involved in Limerick civic life and who ranked among the city's four leading patrician families.[4] The paths these men took to Reims also differed. O'Meara initially studied at Oxford and, after a sojourn in Ormond during which time his son, Edmund, was born (1614), he resumed his studies in Reims.[5] By contrast, Thomas Arthur recounts in his autobiographical verse how, as an immature boy, he commenced his university career studying arts at the University of Bordeaux, and then proceeded to Paris where he matriculated in 1616. It was there that he embarked upon his medical training and having graduated in 1617 with a Master's degree, he moved to Reims to complete his studies.[6]

At this time, Reims was a new university, founded in 1548. Prior to Gerald Fennell's graduation in 1614, only one Irishman, Jacobus Fildens, had graduated from the institution.[7] Yet, the university's faculty of medicine had a formative impact on the professionalisation of medicine in early seventeenth-century Ireland because it afforded Irish Catholics of modest means the opportunity to pursue a course of studies, which was academically less challenging than that at Leiden, at a fraction of the cost.[8] The fact that the number of Irish medical graduates from Reims increased appreciably in the 1610s and that all returned to Ireland and set up practices, apparently without impediment from government authorities, is evidence of the growing in confidence of middle-ranking Catholics in Jacobean Ireland. Thomas Arthur was so confident he could pursue a lucrative career as a physician in Ireland that, just a year after his return to Limerick, he commenced building a substantial stone house on Mungret Street on the southern suburbs of Limerick as his future family residence. Such was its size that as late as 1649 it was

---

edn, Nenagh: Relay Books, 2001), p. 194, n. 43; *ODNB, sub* Dermot O'Meara.

[4] See Widdess, 'A notable Irish physician', 21–31; *ODNB, sub* William Arthur; Maurice Lenihan, *Limerick: its history and antiquities* (reprint, Cork: Mercier Press, 1967); John Canon Begley, *The diocese of Limerick in the sixteenth and seventeenth centuries* (Dublin: Browne and Nolan, 1927); Colm Lennon, *An Irish prisoner of conscience of the Tudor era: Archbishop Richard Creagh of Armagh, 1523–1586* (Dublin: FCP, 2000); Colm Lennon, *Urban patriates of early modern Ireland: a case-study of Limerick* (Dublin: National University of Ireland, 2000).

[5] Logan, 'Dermot and Edmund O'Meara', 312–13; Gleeson, *Last lords*, p. 194, n. 43; *ODNB, sub* Dermot O'Meara.

[6] Arthur entry-book, fol. 190r; Acta rectoria Universitatus Parisiensis, 1616–1633, fol. 9v (BNF, MS Latin 9958).

[7] Graduate register of the Reims faculty, fol. 46 (BMR); for the foundation and early history of the faculty of medicine at Reims see Robert Benoit, *Vivre et mourir à Reims au Grand Siècle 1580–1720* (2nd edn, Arras: Artois Presses Université, 1999), p. 589; Laurence Brockliss and Colin Jones, *The medical world of early modern France* (Oxford: OUP, 1997).

[8] See Tony Farmar, *Patients, potions and physicians: a social history of medicine in Ireland, 1654–2004* (Dublin: A&A Farmar, 2004), p. 35.

still under construction.⁹ Dermot O'Meara entertained equally high expectations of success. Emboldened by the fact that he was physician to Walter Butler, eleventh earl of Ormond, and that he had a university qualification, he published a treatise on hereditary disease, *Pathologia hereditaria Generalis*, in Dublin in 1619, which he dedicated to the Lord Deputy, Sir Oliver St John. St John had published a number of regulations against Catholics two years previously.¹⁰ Since his patron, the eleventh earl of Ormond, was imprisoned around the time he published his book, O'Meara may have hoped to impress St John with his university credentials in order to secure his patronage. Further evidence of the relatively tolerant climate in which these recently qualified and ambitious Catholic physicians operated is the direct involvement of both Dermot O'Meara and Christopher Talbot, along with Lord Deputy Falkland's physician, Paul Delaune, in the attempt to establish an Irish college of physicians in the mid-1620s. In the longer term, the careers of Thomas Arthur and Gerald Fennell reveal that their Roman Catholicism did not serve as a serious impediment to the professional advancement of skilled medical practitioners, though both were high profile advocates in the 1640s of the Confederate Catholic cause.

## Medical practice in Ireland in the early seventeenth century, and the response of graduate physicians

It is instructive to consider the milieu in which these graduate physicians embarked on their professional careers and how they defined their status and their role. In 1619 there was only one medical corporation in Ireland, the Barber-Surgeons' Guild in Dublin. It was originally founded for barbers in 1446 by royal charter of Henry IV. However, Elizabeth I concluded that the fraternity of barbers needed to become more skilled in the art of surgery in order to improve standards of health care in the city. Consequently, in 1577 she issued a charter uniting the fraternity of barbers and the society of surgeons in one corporation to be called the Master, Wardens, and Fraternity of Barbers and Surgeons of the Guild of the Blessed Mary Magdalene. To strengthen the newly constituted guild's monopoly over medical practice in Dublin and to improve the standard of care, Elizabeth's charter explicitly prohibited any person from practicing as either barber or surgeon in the city or suburbs who had not been admitted under the common seal of the guild corporation: anyone who did so was liable to a heavy penalty of 100*s.* per month for as long as he continued to offend. In a context in which neither physicians nor apothecaries operating in Ireland were incorporated, the 1577 charter was the sole regulatory instrument appertaining to medical standards in Ireland until 1667

⁹ Arthur entry-book, fols 238v–241r.
¹⁰ J.B. Lyons, *Aspects of the history of medicine in Ireland* (Dublin: no publisher details given, 1997), p. 2; Logan, 'Dermot and Edward O'Meara', 312; Tony Sweeney, *Ireland and the printed word* (Dublin: de Burca, 1997), p. 494; *ODNB, sub* Dermot O'Meara.

when Charles II granted the long promised letters patent for the foundation of a College of Physicians in Dublin.[11]

In policing medical practice in Dublin, the guild was supported by the City's Corporation, which restricted admission to the franchise to fully qualified physicians, surgeons, barber-surgeons and apothecaries, and the small number admitted to this privilege provides the most reliable guide to the diminutive size of the cohort of medical professionals in the city at the time. During the years 1579 to 1600, the franchise was granted to two physicians, five surgeons, four barber-surgeons and seven apothecaries (a total of eighteen), while between 1601 and 1620, though no physician and only one surgeon was enfranchised, the admission of 14 barber-surgeons and three apothecaries ensured that the total mirrored the figure for the final decades of the sixteenth century.[12] Apart from the physicians, who were university graduates, a majority of these practitioners were admitted upon completion of an apprenticeship, often under the supervision of a family member with an established practice in the city.

In a further initiative aimed at improving the standard of medical care in Dublin, the Corporation appointed a physician, Nicholas Hickey, in 1590, to attend to the needs of the citizenry. Hickey had been admitted to the franchise ten years previously and presumably had a well-established practice at the time of his appointment. His salary was set at £10, and specific terms and conditions were set down in defining his role. He was, for instance, permitted to maintain a private practice within the city and could travel to tend to private patients who were resident within a radius of 60 miles of the city. However, he was not authorised to minister to patients who were more than three hours distance from Dublin, and he was obliged to be on call whenever the mayor might choose to summon him. Failure to do so would result in the forfeiture of half of his annual stipend.[13] Cork

---

[11] See Charter of Elizabeth I, with translation, 1577, grant of arms, 1645 (TCD, MS 1447); Henry F. Berry, 'The ancient corporation of barber-surgeons, or guild of St Mary Magdalene, Dublin', *Royal Society of Antiquaries of Ireland Journal*, 33 (1903): 217–38; Charles A. Cameron, *History of the Royal College of Surgeons in Ireland and of the Irish schools of medicine* (Dublin: Fannin and Company, 1916), pp. 69–78; J.D.H. Widdess, *A history of the Royal College of Physicians of Ireland, 1656–1963* (Edinburgh and London: E. and S. Livingstone, 1963), p. 12; John F. Fleetwood, *The history of medicine in Ireland* (2nd edn, Dublin: Skellig Press, 1983), pp. 65, 81; J.B. Lyons (ed.), *Dublin's surgeon-anatomists and other essays by William Doolin: a centenary tribute* (Dublin: Royal College of Surgeons of Ireland, 1987), pp. 136–8; Mary Clark and Raymond Refaussé, *Directory of historical Dublin guilds* (Dublin: Dublin Public Libraries, 1993), p. 15; J.B. Lyons, *A pride of professors: the professors of medicine at the Royal College of Surgeons in Ireland, 1813–1985* (Dublin: A. & A. Farmar, 1999), p. 1.

[12] John T. Gilbert (ed.), *Calendar of ancient records of Dublin* (19 vols, Dublin: Dollard, 1889–1944), vol. 2, pp. 138, 141, 151, 160, 163, 175, 179, 235, 237, 251, 273, 287, 295, 309, 324, 329–30, 365, 369, 392, 415, 419, 422, 430, 476, 536, vol. 3, pp. 35, 40, 43, 46, 87, 93, 94, 97, 101, 102.

[13] Gilbert (ed.), *Calendar of ancient records*, vol. 2, pp. 146–7, 151.

Corporation had a comparable system. In 1616, it invited a Mr Meade, doctor of physick, to practice in the city, also for the sum of £10 per year, but since it was hoped (rather than ordered or agreed) that he would 'minister the poor physick, out of charitable disposition *gratis*', it is apparent that access to medical assistance was something of a lottery in the city.[14]

Prior to Elizabeth I's charter of 1577, the guild of barbers had actively policed medical practice in Dublin city, arresting unqualified practitioners and instituting legal proceedings for their punishment. Empowered by the charter, the newly constituted Barber-Surgeons' Guild contrived, with some degree of success, to increase surveillance: in the late 1570s and early 1580s, one offender was arrested and another had his shop forcibly closed.[15] However, they were unable to prevent unqualified practitioners, who were not members of the guild, from trying their luck, and the Guild's frustration at the persistence of quackery was justified given the damage wrought by unqualified practitioners. The case of William O'Moltolly is indicative. By the time of his second arrest, in 1578, O'Moltolly had left a disturbing trail of destruction. One of his patients, Patrick Crosbie, who paid 30*s*. for a course of treatment, was found to have been left 'in worse case than he found him'. O'Moltolly was also discovered to have let blood from the nose of a glower from Bridge-foot in the city, causing the man's entire face and head to swell and impostume. It was only thanks to the intervention of a brother of a guild member that the patient's life was saved. In another case of malpractice, O'Moltolly set the broken leg of a woman in such a crooked fashion that, according to members of the guild, 'she was never able to do herself no good till she died'.[16]

More generally, the response to the outbreak of plague that occurred in the city in 1604–5 reinforces the impression provided by other sources that the medical provision available in Dublin was primitive and essentially *ad hoc*. Like many other cities, Dublin was prone to outbreaks of epidemic plague (as a result of the major outbreak in 1575 the city was so depopulated that grass grew on some of its busiest thoroughfares[17]), but it was so ill-prepared infrastructurally that in 1604–5 the Corporation was obliged to rent a house and adjoining small yard on St George's Lane to act as a temporary pest house. It was also necessary for the mayor and Corporation to issue instructions for the purchase of provisions for those that were infected. In addition, all those named in a cess book were to make a weekly contribution, which would go towards relief of sick and infected persons, and help to defray the costs of guarding the pest house and burying the dead. Fees for burying men, women and children from the pest house were itemised. The duties of four strong men charged with guarding the pest house, preventing inmates from escaping and burying the dead were specified. It was expressly ordered that when these men approached the city centre bearing a corpse, they

---

[14] Quoted in Fleetwood, *History of medicine*, pp. 52–3.
[15] Berry, 'Ancient corporation', 225.
[16] Berry, 'Ancient corporation', 225–6.
[17] Berry, 'Ancient corporation', 227.

were to carry long white staves and they were not to pass the home of the city's mayor. Furthermore, each inhabitant of the city was ordered by the mayor to burn a fagot at his door each Monday, Wednesday and Saturday night and on other mights as he should think fit in order to purify the air.[18] However, it is telling as the Corporation instructions make no reference to the role of the city's physicians, barber-surgeons, or apothecaries in combating this outbreak of plague. Neither does it appear to have made any extraordinary financial provision or to have recruited dedicated medical personnel to assist them in their response. There was, however, a general awareness of the importance of medical help in overcoming the threat to life, as was indicated in 1575 when a Doctor Collier was admitted a freeman of the city in gratitude for his having risked his life to attend the mayor and others during an outbreak of plague.[19]

Given the weak and inadequately unregulated character of medical practice in early seventeenth-century Dublin, it is a matter of little surprise that, in the dedication to his *Pathologia hereditaria Generalis*, Dermot O'Meara was forthright in highlighting the inadequacies of current practice, and in drawing attention to the superior qualities of university-trained physicians. The publication of this work, the first medical text published in Ireland, signalled the arrival of a new breed of graduate physician in the country and the professionalisation of Irish medicine, and it is significant that others were to follow his example. A succession of Irish-born graduate physicians, that included O'Meara's son, Edmund, Conly Cassin, and of course John Stearne, published medical texts in Dublin and London in subsequent decades.[20] In this way, O'Meara set in motion a process whereby continentally trained Irish graduate physicians increasingly came to resemble members of the London College of Physicians, many of whom also wrote medical tracts and treatises.[21]

O'Meara was clearly shocked by the amateur nature and appallingly low standards of what was passing for medical practice in the capital. He was scandalised that:

> Here not only cursed mountebanks, ignorant barbers, and shameless quack compounders, but also persons of every other craft whatsoever, loose women, and those of the dregs of humanity who are either tired of their own proper art

---

[18] Gilbert (ed.), *Calendar of ancient records*, vol. 3, pp. 536–9.

[19] Berry, 'Ancient corporation', 227.

[20] J.B. Lyons, *Brief lives of Irish doctors* (Dublin: Blackwater, 1978), pp. 29–30; Sweeney, *Ireland and the printed word*, pp. 146, 494, 538–9, 757–8. There were, in addition, publications by Irish graduate physicians such as Neil Ó Glacán on the Continent.

[21] See William Munk, *The roll of the Royal College of Physicians of London* (3 vols, 2nd edn, London, 1878), vol. 1 (1518–1700).

and craft or inflamed with an unbridled passion for making money, all have free leave to profane the holy temple of Esculapius.[22]

Thomas Arthur, who owned a copy of the *Pathologia*, shared O'Meara's outrage at the incompetence, ignorance, lack of training and professionalism that characterised medical practice in Ireland.[23] His frustration and indeed, at times, anger, stemmed largely from the pointless suffering and harm inflicted on patients by shoddy amateur practitioners. Like his fellow physicians, Arthur had personal experience of attending patients who were the victims of botched treatments administered by incompetent doctors and quack practitioners. Indeed, within a week of formally commencing in practice in Limerick in May 1619, Arthur conducted an autopsy on a 50-year-old local woman, named Anna Gould, who had died as a result of one such course of mistreatment. Gould had been married for 19 years to her second husband when she first visited Arthur, prior to the formal opening of his practice, claiming that she was ill. Arthur diagnosed that she was pregnant, but, he recorded in his feebook, 'some senior medics, in whom she placed a greater trust, destroyed her with medicines to draw off dropsy after eight months [of] pregnancy, in spite of my protestations'. The woman and her unborn child died as a consequence, and Arthur recounted how, having been granted permission to conduct an autopsy, he 'cut open the womb of this dead woman [and] according to the declaration of my opinion ... took [out] of her a dead girl, complete with all her limbs'.[24] Eight years later, in 1627, Arthur was called upon to attend the wife of George Devenish, a councillor in Dublin, who had recently given birth. He found her seized by dropsy brought on by an inappropriate suppression of white loach she had taken on the advice of 'a certain ignorant mid-wife'.[25] Mrs Devenish recovered but, in other instances, Arthur was powerless to offer any assistance. For example, when he visited Sir Basil Brooke who suffered from a blockage at the neck of his bladder in 1633, Arthur found him in the throes of intolerable suffering and fever brought on by 'a certain wreckless physician [who] had prescribed beetles to be eaten'. Knowing that the patient did not have long to live, Arthur simply advised him to 'look out for the safety of his soul and have regard as quickly as possible for the disposal of his affairs'.[26]

In his critique of medical practice in Dublin, Dermot O'Meara counselled that because 'the misuse of no other art can be more harmful', the art of medicine needed

---

[22] Dermot O'Meara, *Pathologia hereditaria generalis* (Dublin, 1619) (dedication); Logan, 'Dermot and Edmund O'Meara', 312; James Kelly, 'The emergence of scientific and institutional practice in Ireland, 1650–1800' in Greta Jones and Elizabeth Malcolm (eds), *Medicine, disease and the state in Ireland, 1650–1940* (Cork: Cork University Press, 1999), p. 22.

[23] Arthur entry-book, fol. 9v.
[24] Arthur entry-book, fol. 15r.
[25] Arthur entry-book, fol. 27r.
[26] Arthur entry-book, fol. 45r.

to be learned 'clearly and properly from learned teachers ... in a university'. It should, he pronounced, be 'learned with hard work and with thought'. 'Instruction from his youth, diligence and time' were, he claimed, essential 'for not without long labour, time and practice is a doctor made perfect'.[27] O'Meara complained that although there was no shortage of practitioners in Dublin city, very few of them possessed the six qualifications that Hippocrates identified in his *De Lege Naturae* as necessary in a medical doctor, namely 'keenness of mind, power of judging, kindness, moderation, discretion, knowledge'.[28]

Like O'Meara, Arthur attributed his superior medical skills to his university training, which he described in idealised terms in rude verse in his entry book:

> ... in his diligence he hastened to Paris
> and there he listened to the physicians with avid ears.
> Busily he ... introduced the venerable lectures and performances
> of the learned men to parchment pages with reed-quill pens.
> There with his mind he drank deep of the authoritative announcements of the Apollinean cauldron on healing and became acquainted with the stern teachings of Hippocrates.
> There he also unfolded several volumes of your teaching, great Galen,
> on the healing powers of clover.
> There he examines the inner secrets of the art of Paracelsus,
> to see if from that he may be able to bring forth any assistance to the sick.
> Soon decorated with the honour of a doctorate at Reims,
> he returns in grateful celebration to the household gods of his fatherland.
> There he vigorously perfected under favourable omens
> the healing skills of Paeonius which he practiced in his youth.[29]

Arthur set, as this suggests, great store by his university qualifications, styling himself 'doctor of philosophy and of medicine', but he was also acutely conscious of the implications of his university qualifications his reputation as a practising physician, remarking that it was 'the numerous recognised documentary proofs of his outstanding learning [that] made him well known'.[30]

Dermot O'Meara's recourse to the printing press in 1619 to draw attention to the poor standard of medical practice in the capital and to emphasise the superior skills of graduate physicians was opportune. Two years previously, in a move to hasten the regularisation of medical training and practice in England, James I had reincorporated the College of Physicians in London.[31] Moreover, O'Meara and

---

[27] O'Meara, *Pathologia* (dedication).
[28] O'Meara, *Pathologia* (dedication).
[29] Arthur entry-book, fol. 190r.
[30] Arthur entry-book, fols 183v and 190r.
[31] See *Register of the king and queen's college of physicians in Ireland* (Dublin, 1866), p. 7; Widdess, *History*, p. 3.

Arthur's concern at the lack of appropriate regulation in Ireland was shared by other recently qualified Irish physicians, and even more importantly, by a handful of physicians intimately connected with the Dublin administration. In 1626 a combination of factors created a fleeting circumstance in which these joined forces in an attempt to professionalise medical practice in the capital through the foundation of a college of physicians based on the London college model.

O'Meara was deeply involved in initiating these proceedings with his fellow Reims graduate, Christopher Talbot and another Irish physician, John Verdon (about whom little is known). Although all three were Catholic, they were pragmatic enough to recognise the need to cultivate a close, positive relationship with the Dublin Castle administration if they were to progress their plan and more generally to advance their own careers as practitioners. This was true also of Thomas Arthur who left Limerick in the mid-1620s to develop a lucrative practice in the metropolis, where much of his client base centred round the Lord Deputy and the Castle administration.

O'Meara, Talbot and Verdon were supported by James Metcalfe and Paul Delaune, two physicians attached to Dublin Castle. Metcalfe (d. 1635) had served as State Physician between 1610 and 1615 and was, as a result, well aware of the standards of medical practice in Ireland.[32] Paul Delaune, a graduate of Cambridge and of Padua universities, and a fellow of the London College of Physicians, had come to Ireland as physician to Lord Falkland, when the latter was appointed lord deputy in 1622.[33] This alliance of five of Ireland's most able and well-placed physicians, at least two of whom were Roman Catholic, constituted a powerful lobby in favour of medical reform, but it is unlikely that they would have come together at this moment but for a shift in official policy towards Catholics that provided Catholic physicians with the encouragement to join with Delaune in composing a petition seeking royal approval for the foundation of a college of physicians in Ireland.

In 1626, with a war against Spain looming, Charles I, in return for the promise of substantial financial subventions, signalled his readiness to concede property rights and religious freedom to the Old English gentry, the so-called Graces, and held out the prospect of official toleration for Catholicism. In this context, Charles's readiness to entertain petitions from Catholic physicians for founding an Irish college of physicians, and Falkland's decision in the summer of 1622 to overlook Thomas Arthur's Catholicism in order to appoint him physician to the viceregal household can be seen as part of a larger more significant shift in official attitude towards Catholics.[34]

Having considered the five physicians' petition, Charles I was disposed to respond positively. In August 1626, he informed Falkland and Adam Loftus, the

---

[32] *Calendar of the state papers relating to Ireland, James I, 1608–1610* (London, 1874), p. 507.
[33] Widdess, *History*, p. 46; *ODNB*, sub Paul Delaune.
[34] Arthur entry-book, fol. 24v.

Lord Chancellor, that he had 'taken it into our consideration, that the establishing [of] a practice of learning and humane sciences ... amongst others, that laudable and most necessary art of physic is not a little available' in Ireland and that:

> amongst others, that laudable and most necessary art of physic ... is daily abused, in that our kingdom, by wandering ignorant mountebanks and empirics, who for want of restraint do much abound to the daily impairing of the healths and hazarding of the lives in general of our good subjects there.[35]

Perceiving that it was necessary therefore to bring about 'the reformation of ... this abuse' of the art of physic, Charles instructed Falkland, the Lord Chancellor and the Irish Privy Council, 'with the advice of some of our learned counsel of that realm, by letters patent', to establish in Dublin 'a college, society, and corporation of physicians, according to the rule and form of the charter ... granted to the physicians in our city of London, for the incorporating of them'.[36] He went on to state that the fellows of the Irish college should enjoy the same articles and privileges as their London counterparts. The college was also to be granted a license to purchase manors, lands, tenements and hereditaments in Ireland, though their annual value was not to exceed £40 Irish, and they were to hold such property from Dublin Castle. Charles indicated in addition that he would, in due course, grant the society and corporation of physicians the authority to formulate laws and ordinances for governing the college, supervising its members, regulating the practice of physic in the city and within a twenty mile radius, and managing the college's revenues and possessions.[37]

Having elicited this encouraging response from the king, the five physicians sought to press ahead with their plans to bring into being a college, of which all would be members. They wrote to the London College of Physicians, announcing that in response to their petition the king had been pleased to establish a college in Dublin in order to regulate medical practice and to repress unqualified practitioners. To enable them to progress their preparations, they requested the London College

---

[35] James Morrin (ed.), *Calendar of the patent and close rolls of chancery in Ireland of the reign of Charles the first* (Dublin, 1863), p. 227. Given the similarities in terminology and comparable observations made by Charles I and Dermot O'Meara in their assessment of medical practice in Ireland, and the fact that O'Meara was a signatory of the 1626 petition, it may be that O'Meara was Charles's source of information, though whether he was guided by O'Meara's 1619 publication or O'Meara rewrote his published commentary for the petition is unknown.

[36] Morrin (ed.), *Calendar of patent and close rolls ... of the reign of Charles the first*, p. 277.

[37] Morrin (ed.), *Calendar of patent and close rolls ... of the reign of Charles the first*, pp. 277–8; *Calendar of the state papers relating to Ireland of the reign of Charles I, 1625–1632* (London, 1900), p. 148; T.W. Belcher, *Memoir of John Sterne* (Dublin, 1865), pp. 18–20.

to send copies of its statutes, charters and other documentation pertaining to its foundation and governance. However, the officers of the London College were unwilling to incur the expense of copying the relevant documentation. Instead, they advised the petitioners that it would be better for them to dispatch a carefully selected representative to London so that he might see first-hand how the College functioned and receive pertinent advice and information. As a result, he would be able on his return to explain to them precisely what the king had granted and also the extent of the grant. It has been suggested that this unenthusiastic response by the London College reflected its officers' belief that Charles was not genuinely committed to the foundation of an Irish equivalent, and it may be that this was the conclusion arrived at by the five Irish physicians. In any event, the proposal to establish an Irish college was dealt a decisive and devastating blow by its very architects when, in their response soon afterwards to the London College's communiqué, the hitherto enthusiastic physicians rather lamely indicated that none among them was in a position to accept the invitation to travel to London because they could not afford to take leave from their private and business affairs for the length of time required.[38]

However, Paul Delaune did not let the matter rest there. Eager to identify another way forward, he approached the provost of Trinity, William Bedell, in 1628 and outlined the physicians' efforts to obtain a patent for an Irish college. Delaune evidently suggested to Bedell that Trinity College ought to consider availing of this opportunity to redress the imbalance that existed between its overwhelmingly dominant theology faculty on the one hand and its comparatively neglected faculties of law and physic on the other.[39] (The first statues of the university and the college set out regulations both for degrees in medicine and for establishing a medical fellowship. The fact that in 1618 and 1620, the fellowship was awarded to Sir John Temple and Thomas Beere respectively, neither of whom had a medical qualification or had taken medical degrees in the University, is indicative of the underdeveloped character of medical studies in Trinity College at that time.[40]) Delaune's proposal clearly resonated with Bedell. He was not averse, in principle, to the idea of constituent colleges functioning under the auspices of the university, particularly as it stood to benefit Trinity by accelerating the pace of development of the university's physic and law faculties. In a letter to James Ussher, Archbishop of Armagh, he acknowledged: 'I suppose it hath been an error all this while to neglect the faculties of law and physic, and attend only to the ordering of one poor College of Divines'. Looking back over the time that had elapsed since the university's foundation in 1592, Bedell remarked wistfully that 'with a little more labour and

---

[38] See George Clark, *A history of the Royal College of Physicians of London* (2 vols, Oxford: Clarendon Press, 1964), vol. 2, p. 250; Farmar, *Patients, potions and physicians*, p. 14.

[39] Belcher, *Memoir*, pp. 17–18.

[40] T. Percy C. Kirkpatrick, *History of the medical teaching in Trinity College Dublin and of the school of physic in Ireland* (Dublin: Hanna and Neale, 1912), p. 245.

a few privileges attained, a great many more good wits might have been allured to study', in areas other than theology, at the University.[41] Anxious to acquire more information, Bedell wrote in January 1628 to the master of Sidney College, Cambridge, inquiring about the amount of money the professors of law and physic paid to the university for their chairs and whether physicians and lawyers made any profession when taking their doctoral degrees.

Events, however, overtook Bedell's tentative explorings. In 1629, he was appointed bishop of Kilmore and immediately resigned his position as provost.[42] The recall of Viscount Falkland to London in April of the same year, which put an end to Delaune's sojourn in Ireland, was still more significant as it effectively deprived the scheme of its most committed champion. As a result, the plan for founding an incorporated Irish college of physicians was shelved and not reanimated for several decades. The failure of his plan, notwithstanding, Delaune had made a lasting contribution to the professionalisation of physicians' practice in Ireland. According to T.W. Belcher, Delaune was the originator of the idea that the University of Dublin should replicate the English university model by establishing dedicated constituent colleges, which specialised in theology, law and physic. Just two years after his discussion with Bedell, Trinity College opened its first university hall or college, with its own master and scholars, and it was one of these halls that became the cradle of John Stearne's fraternity of physicians in the mid-1650s.[43] In the interim, however, Ireland was left without an incorporated college or even a fraternity or society of physicians empowered to regulate and protect the professional standards of this key cohort of medical practitioners.

## The medical practices of Thomas Arthur and John Clavell, 1630–54

The failure of this attempt to establish a college of physicians in Dublin in the 1620s left the Irish medical marketplace in a highly unregulated condition, and open to all-comers for several decades thereafter. The varied nature and character of physicians' practices that this permitted is exemplified by reference to the careers of two contrasting practitioners: the university trained professional, Thomas Arthur, and the charismatic quack, John Clavell.[44]

Acknowledged by contemporaries as the leading physician in Ireland until at least the late 1640s, Arthur epitomised the new breed of modern, graduate physician practising in Ireland from the late 1610s. An examination of his thriving Dublin practice in the late 1620s and 1630s throws into sharp relief the contrast between the professionalism with which university trained physicians conducted themselves

---

[41] Kirkpatrick, *History*, p. 279; Belcher, *Memoir*, p. 17.
[42] Kirkpatrick, *History*, p. 29.
[43] Belcher, *Memoir*, p. 18.
[44] J.H.P. Pafford, *John Clavell, 1601–43: highwayman, author, lawyer, doctor* (Oxford: Leopard's Head Press, 1993); *ODNB, sub* John Clavell.

and their practices, and the intrinsically opportunistic, even unprincipled activities of rival unlicensed and unqualified practitioners such as Clavell.

Thomas Arthur was, first and foremost, a shrewd businessman and this is clearly reflected in his utterly methodical approach to his practice as physician. Dissatisfied with the relatively modest income that he earned when he commenced in practice in Limerick in 1619, Arthur moved to Dublin in the mid-1620s, and quickly established a lucrative and high profile practice in the capital. Yet, ever the pragmatic businessman, even with a flourishing practice in Dublin, he made a point of spending a few months every year in Limerick where he maintained a profitable client base. This arrangement stood him in particularly good stead in the 1640s when, fearing for his safety in Dublin, he returned to Limerick where he had enough clients to sustain his livelihood. Arthur's business-like approach to his work as a physician is typified by his systematic recording of every consultation in his feebook throughout his professional practice, which extended for 47 years from 1619 until 1666. He used abbreviated Latin to record payment received for every patient he saw and (tellingly) there is not a single entry for a patient in which money did not change hands. Even in the case of beggars and fishermen, a fee was paid. Furthermore, regardless of the number of repeat visits for treatment of the one ailment, the patient was obliged to pay a fee.[45]

It is significant also that Arthur, who was the country's leading physician, only devoted part of his time to his medical practice. While in the early 1630s Arthur saw in the region of 175 to 180 patients a year, as a result of which his income rose from £145 13s. 6d. sterling (June 1630–March 1631) to £278 4s. 4d. (March 1633–March 1634). His returns from investments in rents, mortgages and loans exceeded his income from his medical practice, sometimes by a factor of three.[46] Moreover, he was not unusual in thus dividing his time. It appears that the income from a physician's practice, regardless of how successful it may have been, was not considered adequate or sufficiently stable to permit physicians, whether they were university-trained or not, to concentrate wholly on their medical work. John Clavell, for instance, practised as a lawyer as well as a physician while in Ireland during the 1630s.[47] When Dermot O'Meara found himself without a patron around 1620, he worked for a short spell as a tutor teaching logic and humanities in Roscrea, county Tipperary before resuming his medical practice.[48] In Arthur's case, however, it was the desire to accumulate capital that prompted him to augment the already substantial income from his medical practice from other sources.

Arthur's practice contrasted in many important respects with that of the unlicensed practitioners, who operated in Dublin in the 1620s and 1630s. For instance, John Clavell solicited business, and although he did not pose a significant

---

[45] See, for example, entries for Robert Bonny's visits during 1631–2: Arthur entry-book, fols 38v, 39r, 39v, 40r, 41r, 41v, 42r; Widdess, 'A notable Irish physician', 25.
[46] Arthur entry-book, fols 36r, 48r.
[47] Pafford, *John Clavell*, chapter 6.
[48] Logan, 'Dermot and Edmund O'Meara': 313; *ODNB, sub* Dermot O'Meara.

threat to Arthur's client base, he did poach at least one of Thomas Arthur's prominent patients, namely Adam Loftus, the Lord Chancellor.[49] By contrast, as a rule Arthur was sought out by patients, and then from as far away as Carrickfergus and Dunluce, county Antrim. This was how he came to attend his most important client, James Ussher, the Church of Ireland Archbishop of Armagh, at his palace in Drogheda in March 1626.

Arthur's university training was very evident in the studied, scientific and pastoral approach he brought to bear to diagnosis and treatment – an approach exemplified by his treatment of Ussher. Arthur recorded, when he first visited Ussher, who was afflicted with a mysterious illness which the royal physicians in England were unable to diagnose or cure, that he listened to the prelate's own account of his sickness and examined the royal physicians' records. He studied closely the symptoms that presented throughout the history of the entire disease and then carried out 'a slight experiment' to test his 'conjecture'. He recounts how, having 'perfectly diagnosed the disease, I confidently undertook his cure [and] nor did my hopes deceive me'.[50] Arthur took Ussher to Lambay Island off the coast of Dublin where the Ussher family had a house and, after a period of almost two months, the patient was deemed cured.[51]

This was not a unique episode. Arthur employed the same methodical approach in his treatment of Robert Bonny, a bailiff who presented with symptoms of melancholy on 7 November 1631.[52] Bonny was Arthur's only patient on that day. He questioned the patient at length about his symptoms and duly recorded these as sadness, panic, nocturnal apparitions, vague gaseous moistures rising and vanishing of their own accord, nocturnal suffocation, a poor appetite, an overly full belly and a constant pain in the stomach, following which he devised a course of treatment (see below).

Arthur's exceptional understanding of medical science, combined with his appreciation that medical diagnosis could not be rushed, set him and graduate physicians like him apart in the minds of those contemporaries, who took an interest in medical matters, and who were guided in their choice of their own physician by those whom they cured. Significantly, following his successful treatment of Archbishop Ussher, Arthur was questioned by the then lord deputy, Viscount Falkland about the prelate's disease, the points on which the royal physicians had erred, and his reasons for spending time on Lambay Island. According to Arthur, he explained his diagnosis and treatment 'so scientifically' that Falkland was entirely satisfied; indeed, he was so impressed he appointed Arthur as his personal physician.[53]

---

[49] Pafford, *John Clavell*, pp. 256–8.
[50] Arthur entry-book, fol. 24r.
[51] Arthur entry-book, fol. 24v; R. Buick Knox, *James Ussher, Archbishop of Armagh* (Cardiff: University of Wales Press, 1967), p. 34; *ODNB, sub* James Ussher.
[52] Arthur entry-book, fol. 38v.
[53] Widdess, 'A notable Irish physician', 25.

What were Arthur's scientific views? Like the majority of physicians at the time, he was a quintessential Galenist who pursued the humoralist approach. He believed that blockages (which he often termed 'stubborn obstructions') resulted in the accumulation of black and yellow bile, choler, mucus, catarrh and blood. This, in turn, caused patients to experience seizures and heart tremors, and their livers, spleens, stomachs, intestines and kidneys to become inflamed and painful. For instance, in diagnosing a patient named John Dumbill in March 1633, Arthur concluded that, as a result of a hot impurity in the patient's liver, there had been a build-up of excessive bile, which caused him to experience daily bouts of diarrhoea.[54] For Arthur, as for other physicians, restoring the balance between the four bodily humours was the key to curing most illnesses, and to that end he systematically planned his frequently protracted treatments. For example, in treating the aforementioned Robert Bonny for melancholy he prescribed a medication which Bonny was to take for one month in late 1631 and for another month the following spring (Bonny made a return visit in April 1632). This had the effect of causing the patient to pass an enormous amount of mucus and phlegmatic fluid but did not lessen his symptoms, and Bonny required a further consultation at the end of May. Confident in his diagnosis and in the benefits to be derived from his plan of treatment, Arthur persevered and ordered Bonny to take the same medication at the end of the following autumn (Bonny attended him again on 13 October, presumably to receive the medication). The treatment was successful. Arthur triumphantly recorded Bonny's recovery, recounting in graphic detail how, as a result of the proscribed concoction, 'he copiously excreted the hidden and deep-seated black bile fluid and then the gnaw worms, threadworms, intestinal worms and worms of various forms, of various colours, languid, lively and dead. From there he emerged free from all the reviewed diseases'.[55] Another patient, Thady O'Derleo, having taken 'an emetic by the ingestion of a glass of [toxic sulphide], expelled through his excrement a worm thirty feet long and was relieved of the terrible cholics with which he had been tortured for a long time'.[56] Arthur appears to have cured Thomas Luttrell of 'gripes of the intestines' in a similar fashion.[57]

Despite the fact that Galen's views were under serious attack from the 1650s, Arthur remained steadfast in his adherence to the Galenist approach that he learned as a disciple of the *Ecole française*. This is evident from his reading; his purchase of Neil Ó Glacán's opus, *Cursus Medicus*, published in Bologna in 1655, which has been described by J.B. Lyons as 'orthodox, based firmly on Galen, making no attempt to foster new ideas', is indicative.[58] Arthur's enduring reliance on Galen is also borne out by the conspicuous absence from his impressive library

---

[54] Arthur entry-book, fol. 43v.
[55] Arthur entry-book, fol. 38v.
[56] Arthur entry-book, fol. 19r.
[57] Arthur entry-book, fol. 38r.
[58] Lyons, *Brief lives*, p. 29.

of a number of ground-breaking seventeenth-century medical texts, most notably William Harvey's classic *De Motu Cordis et Sanguinis*, published in 1628, which challenged Galen's entire interpretative paradigm, and Thomas Willis's work on cerebral anatomy and the nervous system, published in London in 1644.

Compared with unlicensed practitioners such as Clavell, who engaged in prompt diagnosis and who promised complete cure, Arthur invested a lot of time and energy in treating individual patients. This can be attributed in part to the fact that his casebook bustled with patients with exceptionally problematic conditions, such was his reputation. Nevertheless, it is still noteworthy that most courses of treatment were prolonged, and it was not unusual for individuals, including Archbishop Ussher, who had serious illnesses to remain on his books for years. Unlike most unqualified practitioners, who were unwilling to admit to failure, Arthur was prepared to acknowledge the instances in which his services were 'to no purpose'.[59] This honesty contributed to Arthur's reputation, and ensured that surgeons from as far away as Ulster referred patients and, in at least one instance, even paid the patient's fee. Occasionally other practitioners challenged his diagnosis. When, in May 1632, Arthur showed that Sir William Talbot was suffering from a stone in the bladder, his diagnosis ran contrary to the opinion of other doctors whom Talbot had attended, and elicited protests from the lithotomists who were involved with this case.[60]

Arthur's surviving papers have little to say about the compounds he prescribed for patients. There is some evidence to indicate that he had an apothecary in Dublin city, who made up and, on occasion, administered medications (in one case, two glisters [clysters] and some juleps).[61] It is possible also that he used the brass kettles and distilling pots that he had in his home in Limerick to prepare medicinal compounds but one cannot be certain of this.[62]

Graduate physicians such as Arthur were set apart from their less qualified practitioners by the breadth of their training and their extensive skills set. The range of his competencies is suggested by the works contained in his library: works on midwifery, surgery, botany, chemistry, and epidemics such as the plague.[63] Like most physicians, Arthur largely left the business of surgery to barber-surgeons, but he was sufficiently familiar with the surgeon's scalpel to carry out autopsies, and when Limerick city was besieged by the Parliamentary forces in 1651 to attend to war casualties, one of whom, a Dr Credanus, had to have his hand amputated.[64]

In the absence of a monitoring agency other than the Barber-Surgeons' Guild in Dublin, unqualified, unlicensed and incompetent practitioners circulated in seventeenth-century Ireland with little impediment or fear of interruption,

---

[59] Arthur entry-book, fol. 16v.
[60] Arthur entry-book, fol. 41r.
[61] Arthur entry-book, fol. 122r.
[62] Arthur entry-book, fol. 195r.
[63] Arthur entry-book, fols 8r–10r.
[64] Widdess, 'A notable Irish physician', 26.

competing with qualified physicians for clients and with apothecaries for sale of potions and cures. The experience of John Clavell, an English-born highwayman turned author, lawyer and self-styled physician, indicates how open the medical market was at this time. Though unlicensed, Clavell practised extensively as a physician in both Cork and Dublin during a sojourn spanning the period December 1634 to June 1637.[65] Significantly, he only ever practised as a physician in Ireland. Although he may, for this reason, typify the rogue unlicensed practitioners criticised by Dermot O'Meara, his career demonstrates that some amateur practitioners had sufficient command of the science of medicine to convince senior officials in the Dublin administration of their competence.

Clavell effectively established himself as *persona grata* in the highest strata of Dublin society during his first visit to Ireland, which lasted for just over two years, from August 1631 to September 1633. Within five months of his arrival in the capital for the second time, he consolidated his position by marrying the nine-year-old heiress of a rich Dublin vintner (he was 33 at the time and she was his second wife). Through that union, Clavell was able to forge a close and immensely advantageous friendship with Lord Chancellor Loftus, who strongly approved of the marriage and, taking Clavell into his confidence, actively recommended him as a physician within his circle of colleagues, friends and family in the greater Dublin area. As a result, Clavell soon built up a considerable, and by his own account, very successful practice, first in Cork and later in Dublin and surrounding districts. According to his biographer, J.H.P. Pafford, it is highly improbable that Clavell possessed either training or a qualification in medicine; rather, his 'extravagant claims are typical of the quack' practitioner.[66] Clavell recounted that he was frequently summoned to attend a patient when other doctors had failed, and claimed that he invariably cured even incurable patients with great speed. As a result, by comparison with Arthur and other university-trained physicians, he saw great numbers of patients: he recorded 19 cures, 'a few of many', which he claimed he had achieved in Dublin in the space of one month.[67]

Regardless of what his detractors thought of him, and irrespective of the fact that his supposed fame was ephemeral and unrecorded except by himself, it is significant that Clavell managed to convince two leading officials in Dublin Castle of his curative skills. He claimed, for example, to have cured Adam Loftus, the Lord Chancellor, of a serious kidney disease ('passion of the reins'), in the space of just one day, and to have relieved one of Loftus' kinswomen from kidney stones. He maintained also that he cured the Lord Chief Baron's daughter of epilepsy in

---

[65] Their ability to convince lay in the fact that they were well informed of the therapeutic qualities of even mundane and exotic herbs, spices, and skilled in concocting potions and remedies. See Pafford, *John Clavell*, pp. 220–58.

[66] Clavell boasted: 'I fail in none I undertake' and '... such as are great and learned and have made ... [the art of physic] the study of their life, cannot come near me' (Pafford, *John Clavell*, pp. 232–6).

[67] Pafford, *John Clavell*, pp. 232–6.

a week and that he had cured a neighbour of the Lord Chief Baron's son who had a worm, in the course of four days; in the latter case, he claimed to have brought from the boy's bowel a worm with two heads, with the result that the pain faded and the patient was restored to good health. What is undeniable is that Clavell came to possess such a formidable reputation as a therapist of ability that he was invited to treat a gentleman named Marwood when he was in the service of Lord Deputy Thomas Wentworth, and that he boasted this was one of his most impressive cures. Marwood had been ailing for several years to the point that 'all his D[octo]rs had left him'. Yet within a fortnight of Clavell treating him for diarrhoea and fits, Marwood had made such a complete recovery he was able to travel to England and back.[68]

His suspiciously successful record apart, Clavell's impact as a practitioner can be attributable to the manner in which he pursued clients with promises of a cure. Writing to the Lord Chancellor, Adam Loftus, when he was so debilitated by kidney disease he could not attend the law courts for an entire term, Clavell grabbed his attention by conveying a detailed account of a course of treatment that would bring him relief:

> I will undertake within 8 or 10 days to bring from all parts of your body insensible by siege at least 3 gallons of jelly, like soap half melted. What I administer I will daily take in full quantity my self before you. I shall not make you sick; it shall not hinder you a day from dispatch of business; you may do in your whole course as usually you do at all other times. I will, by the help of God, free you from all obstructions and gross vapours which force drowsiness, from all shortness of breath and unwieldiness. It will rid you from all gross humors and troublesome sweats. I will corroborate your stomach and palliate thirst. I shall debar all hydropsic humors and colics. I shall in general make you as lightsome, lively and able of body as you have ever been …. And if I fail in the least little of any of these, or come short a spoonful of the quantity of jelly, besides the loss of your Lordship[']s favour for ever, I will never again practice physic whilst I live.[69]

In addition, Clavell's claim never to take payment from a patient before the cure was 'perfected' enhanced his credibility with the public, who did not set it aside his equally doubtful boast that he never failed.

Clavell's standard method of diagnosis was to examine a patient's urine and symptoms. When treating serious illnesses, he compounded and personally tested his own physic, on the ostensible grounds that since his receipts were uncommon, and there was no 'trusty apothecary' in Ireland, it was the only way open to him to guarantee a patient's safety.[70] While the remedies he used were unrefined, it must

---

[68] Pafford, *John Clavell*, pp. 232–6.
[69] Pafford, *John Clavell*, pp. 256–8.
[70] Pafford, *John Clavell*, pp. 236–7.

be acknowledged in his defence that there are no instances of prescriptions based merely on charms and superstition. Clavell aspired to be both scientific and serious in his practice. He used what he termed only 'lawful means of physic', and did not have recourse to witchcraft or to astrology.[71] His potions combined mundane and exotic ingredients: everything from rhubarb, honey, wine and nutmeg to goose turds, arsenic and frankincense. Among his cures for epilepsy, for instance, was a broth or curdle containing powdered sea crab, which was to be taken every full moon, every noon, and when a patient fell into a fit. An alternative was to take a live raven and to cook it in a hot oven until it was burnt. The powdered ashes, mixed in a little ale, were to be drunk by the patient every morning and evening.[72]

As the different methods to which Thomas Arthur and John Clavell had recourse vividly attest, there was considerable diversity in terms of qualifications, experience and approach among the small cohort of practitioners that styled themselves physicians in 1630s Dublin. It is equally evident, moreover, though graduate physicians such as O'Meara and Arthur echoed their counterparts abroad and complained insistently about the anti-medicine administered by medical charlatans, the sick in Dublin, which included members of the Castle administration, saw no radical incommensurability between trained and untrained medical practitioners, and that this was a crucial factor in sustaining the buoyancy of the varied and largely unregulated medical market that existed in the capital.

## Conclusion

The extent to which the new generation of graduate physicians who set up practice in the late 1610s enhanced the status of the university-trained physician in Ireland was manifest in the 1640s when three Reims graduates – Arthur, Fennell and O'Meara – possessed sufficient public stature to feature in despatches and to exercise significant influence in the negotiations that took place at Kilkenny and Limerick. Arthur[73] and O'Meara were vocal supporters of the Catholic Confederates (indeed, O'Meara[74] was indicted for high treason by James Butler, twelfth earl of Ormond in 1642), while Gerald Fennell, 'a doctor of physick for Ormond's house',[75] served

---

[71] Pafford, *John Clavell*, p. 237.

[72] Pafford, *John Clavell*, pp. 237–56.

[73] See John T. Gilbert, *A contemporary history of affairs in Ireland from 1641 to 1652* (3 vols, Dublin, 1879), vol. 1, part 2, p. 698; John T. Gilbert, *History of the Irish Confederation and the war in Ireland, 1641–9* (7 vols, Dublin, 1882–91), vol. 3, p. 214, vol. 6, pp. 130, 131.

[74] O. Ogle and W.H. Bliss, *Calendar of the Clarendon state papers preserved in the Bodleian Library* (5 vols, Oxford, 1872–1970), vol. 1, p. 234; Logan, 'Dermot and Edmund O'Meara', 313; *ODNB*, sub Dermot O'Meara.

[75] Gilbert, *Contemporary history of affairs in Ireland*, vol. 1, part 1, p. 22; Charles McNeill (ed.), *The Tanner letters* (Dublin: Irish Manuscripts Commission, 1943), *passim*;

as a member of the Supreme Council at Kilkenny. Yet they emerged at the end of the conflict with their reputations little injured, and the esteem in which Arthur and Fennell were held by physicians within the Cromwellian administration and army is remarkable testimony to their high professional standing. In the 1650s, both physicians, by then in their sixties, were resident in Dublin, where Arthur tended to government officials, who included Charles Fleetwood and Henry Cromwell, and other military and civilian Cromwellian settlers.[76]

Dublin in the 1650s was a very different from the city Arthur had left in 1641. The Confederate Wars had brought an influx of English and continentally-trained physicians, apothecaries and surgeons, such as, Arnold Boate, physician general to the English army, William Currer, physician to the English army in Munster, Benjamin Worsley, surgeon general to the army, Jonathan Goddard, physician-in-chief to the army, Marmaduke Lyne and Sankey Sulliard, two apothecaries, and Owen O'Shiel, physician to the Irish army.[77] Most importantly, the wars brought Abraham Yarner and Sir William Petty to Dublin. Yarner, a physician, was an officer in the Lord Lieutenant's horse troop and Petty, a fellow of the Royal College of Physicians in London, was appointed physician to the army in Ireland in September 1652.[78] As a result, for the first time in the early 1650s, Dublin possessed a critical mass of accomplished physicians, some with ties to the Royal College of Physicians in London as well as to Oxford and Cambridge universities. Abraham Yarner, who was later president of the College of Physicians in Dublin, was a pivotal figure in fostering an *esprit de corps*, and it is notable that he made a point of including both Thomas Arthur and Gerald Fennell in social and philosophical gatherings, as his invitation to both men to attend a 'pleasant banquet and philosophical gathering' in Dublin in the early 1650s indicates. Yarner's invitation demonstrates that bonds of professional affinity among physicians continued to transcend religious, political, and even cultural interests and identities. Moreover, the feeling was reciprocated. When he was unable to accept the invitation to dine owing to business commitments outside of Dublin, Arthur wrote to 'the most loving and able Dr A. Yarner and to the other medical worthies dining with him' to record his apologies and to thank Yarner for 'his usual generosity' in inviting

---

Pádraig Lenihan, *Confederate Catholics at war, 1641–49* (Cork: Cork University Press, 2001), p. 79.

[76] Arthur entry-book, fols 85r, 86r, 146r; Gilbert, *Calendar of ancient records*, vol. 4, p. 567.

[77] Patrick Logan, 'Medical services in the armies of the Confederate Wars, 1641–52', in *The Irish Sword*, 4 (1959–60): 217–26 (218); Patrick Logan, 'Owen O'Shiel, ?1584–1650', in *The Irish Sword*, 6 (1963–4): 192–5; Lyons, *Brief lives*, p. 28; T.C. Barnard, *Cromwellian Ireland: English government and reform in Ireland, 1649–1660* (Oxford: OUP, 2000), pp. 240–42, 247–8; *ODNB, sub* Gerard Boate, Jonathan Goddard, William Currer and Benjamin Worsley.

[78] Widdess, *History*, p. 613; Fleetwood, *History of medicine*, p. 545, Barnard, *Cromwellian Ireland*, p. 248; *ODNB, sub* William Petty.

him and his 'brother Dr Fennell'. Arthur's reply encapsulated the strong fraternal affinity shared by physicians in Dublin, which had assisted him to negotiate the Confederate wars. In genuinely warm terms, he offered his heartfelt thanks to the physicians 'for the unparalleled kindness with which you, sirs, have aided me when tossed about with the storms of war and with cares, and ... steadied me with your advice and succoured me with your patronage'.[79] Within just a few years, John Stearne advanced the process of giving that professional fraternalism formal, institutional expression in the foundation of the Royal College of Physicians in Dublin in 1654, and in the process set the process of professionalisation of Irish medicine onto a new plain.

---

[79] Widdess, 'A notable Irish physician', 279.

Chapter 2
# Medical Practice and Gaelic Ireland

Charlie Dillon

Despite its location on the periphery of Europe, Gaelic Irish society in the medieval and early modern era sustained a learned medical profession. Pursuing an approach grounded on Galenist principles as they were interpreted and mediated by some of the major medical writers of the age, Gaelic Irish medicine flourished until the political and social upheavals of the sixteenth and, particularly, the seventeenth centuries undermined that social order and, with it, the economic and social foundations that supported the medical profession. Prior to this, skilled physicians enjoyed the patronage of the ruling Gaelic elite, and belong therefore with the other hereditary professionals – judges, poets, artists, historians, annalists, lawyers and negotiators – each of which performed a specific function in the service of ruling clans and great dynastic families. These professions were generally the preserve of particular families, which explains the presence of individuals bearing the same surnames in the service of successive generations of identifiable dynasties until the Gaelic order was undermined. Until this happened, the hereditary practitioners of medicine, like members of the other professions, enjoyed benefits appropriate to their elevated status and their access to the ruling families of Gaelic Ireland. These included grants of land and exemption from the tributes and taxes exacted by magnates from those who gave them allegiance.[1]

Medical families, whose professional *raison d'être* was the health and well-being of the social elite, existed in Gaelic Scotland as well as Ireland. Approximately, 20 are known to have operated in Ireland in the later Tudor/early Stuart period, but a full dated listing of these individuals extending over the duration of this phenomenon, including the clans and families to which they were attached, has yet to be attempted. This is not to suggest that the picture is entirely opaque. In Ulster, the Ó Duinnshléibhe (Donlevy) family were hereditary physicians to the Ó Dónaill (O'Donnell) kindred of Tir Chonaill, while other prominent northern medical families included the Ó Casaide (Cassidy), who were physicians to Mag Uidhir (Maguire), rulers of Fermanagh, and the Ó Siadhail family, who were attached to the Mac Mathghamhna (McMahon) family of Oriel. The pattern was similar in the provinces of Connacht, Munster and Leinster; the Ó Liaigh (Lee) gave medical service to the ruling Ó Flatharta (Flaherty) family in county Galway, the Ó Callanáin (Callanan) to Mac Carthaigh (McCarthy) of Carbery, county Kerry, Ó hIceadha (Hickey) to Ó Briain (O'Brien) of Thomond (county Clare),

---

[1] K.W. Nicholls, *Gaelic and Gaelicised Ireland* (Dublin: Gill and Macmillan, 1972).

and Ó Meara (O'Mara) to the Anglo-Norman Butlers of Ormond.[2] These eminent medical families owed their high standing to their attachment to these major ruling houses as well as to their medical expertise; there were other, smaller, medical kindred whose attachment to lesser rulers, to gentry families of Anglo-Norman descent or lack thereof, brought them less fame and fortune.

An examination of the meaning and etymology of the surnames of some medical kindred sustains the notion of healing as the hereditary preserve of particular families, and by extension that this was a practice of long standing. Ó Liaigh, for example, translates to English as 'descendant of the doctor', and Ó hIceadha as 'descendant of the healer'. The name of the principal medical kindred of Gaelic Scotland, the Mac Bethad family (Anglicised Beaton), has a comparable etymology; Mac Bethad translates as 'descendant of life'.[3] In a society that valued continuity and heritage, medical knowledge distinguished and defined these families and secured them a place among the Gaelic intellectual elite, and direct access to the ranks of the Gaelic aristocracy.

The practice of vesting medical expertise in a hereditary family attached to a ruling family had practical advantages. It enabled physicians to acquire an intimate knowledge of the ailments and conditions to which a ruling family was prone, and access to medical records maintained over generations may have encouraged the administration of courses of treatment of proven efficacy. The hereditary Gaelic physician was, in effect, immersed in the health of his patron, and educated specifically to deal with his complaints, sometimes with the aid of a generational casebook, as the renowned medical chemist, Johann Baptista Van Helmont (1579–1644), visiting from Brussels in the early part of the seventeenth century, noted approvingly:

> The Irish nobility have in every family a domestic physician, who has a tract of land free for his remuneration, and who is appointed, not on account of learning he brings away in his head from colleges, but because he can cure disorders. These doctors obtain their medical knowledge chiefly from books belonging to particular families left them by their ancestors, in which are laid down the symptoms of the several diseases, with the remedies annexed: which remedies are vernacula – the productions of their own country.[4]

---

[2] See Brian Ó Cuív, 'The Irish language in the early modern period', in T.W. Moody, F.X. Martin and F.J. Byrne (eds), *A new history of Ireland* vol. 3 (Oxford: OUP, 1976), pp. 518–9; John Fleetwood, *History of medicine in Ireland* (Dublin: Browne and Nolan, 1951), chapter 4.

[3] For the Scottish medical tradition, see John Bannerman, *The Beatons: a medical kindred in the classical Gaelic tradition* (Edinburgh: John Donald, 1986).

[4] Cited in Francis Shaw, 'Irish medical men and philosophers' in Brian Ó Cuív (ed.), *Seven centuries of Irish learning 1000–1700* (Cork and Dublin: Mercier Press, 1961), pp. 87–101.

Though Van Helmont may have overestimated the strictly vernacular character of the medical diagnoses and remedies administered by the hereditary Irish physicians, pre-Norman sources indicate that medicine was already defined as a profession in Ireland in the first millennium. Much information is to be found in the early Irish law texts on the roles, responsibilities and social status of the physician. The profession was classed legally on a par with that of other skill – or knowledge-based professions – the cleric, poet, judge, advocate, druid, craftsman and smith. The term 'ollam' was used to distinguish those who achieved mastery of the profession. Early Irish law dictated that, 'a physician required public recognition before he was free to practise medicine'; it also laid out conventions on how payment was made, and made the practitioner liable should he cause undue harm – to cause bleeding was acceptable, but when a joint or sinew was cut inadvertently, the physician was subject to a fine, and made liable for the cost of the patient's ensuing convalescence (or 'sick maintenance').[5]

Members of the Gaelic knowledge-based professions were responsible for maintaining and augmenting the corpus of knowledge upon which they and their successors drew. Thus the lawyers were keepers of law-texts, the poets maintained *duanairí*, or dynastic poem books, while historians kept chronicles and annals of events pertaining to a dynasty or region. The medical equivalent was the medical manuscript: translations and copies of medical texts of continental European provenance that embraced native and established therapies. Access to continental texts was crucial in shaping the Irish medical mind throughout the early modern period, as evidenced by the volume of translation and transcription of such texts that took place between the mid-fourteenth and the mid-seventeenth century.[6] Indicatively, over thirty medical manuscripts survive from the sixteenth century alone, and these show clearly that Irish physicians drew on the canonical medical texts of the period: texts that represented the best of European medical thinking, such as the *Lilium Medicinae* (1305) of Bernard de Gordon (fl.1283–1308), professor of medicine in the university of Montpellier, and the *Rosa Anglica* (1314) of the Oxford physician John of Gaddesden (c.1280–1361). It was on the information and instruction contained in these and other texts that Gaelic physicians developed the bodies of knowledge that guided and informed their practice.

Irish medical scholars did not engage in the copying and translation of continental medical texts after a passive fashion, however. Very often physician scribes translated freely, interpolating their new text with commentary on, and variations from, the original Latin version to which they had access. In some instances, shorter passages by other authors on specific ailments were added as appropriate to amplify the options available to the Irish practitioner. For example, despite the fact that Gaddesden's *Rosa Anglica* drew heavily on Bernard de

---

[5] Fergus Kelly, *A guide to early Irish law* (Dublin: Dublin Institute for Advanced Studies, 1988), pp. 57–9.

[6] Aoibheann Nic Dhonnchadha, 'The medical school of Aghmacart, Queen's County', in *Ossory, Laois and Leinster*, 2 (2006): 11–43.

Gordon's *Lilium Medicinae* in its original version, its translator into Irish, who was possibly a member of the Ó hIceadha (Hickey) family, introduced new or extended extracts from the *Lilium*, thereby creating an Irish version that is an elaborate amalgam of the two original Latin works (see Appendix One for a translated extract).[7] Moreover, following their initial translation into Irish, texts were repeatedly transcribed, copied, synopsised and combined with other treatises to form new compositions, which served to ensure that the information contained in the original was widely disseminated among Gaelic physicians, albeit in a modified form.

This scribal activity took place largely in what can loosely be described as medical schools: dedicated centres, under the patronage of a ruling family, where individuals could pursue scholarly activity, be it composition, transcription, scribal work or instruction. The survival of a number of manuscripts belonging to the medical school run by members of the Ó Conchubhair medical kindred at Aghmacart, county Laois, provides a useful perspective on one such institution in the late sixteenth and early seventeenth centuries.[8] At that time, the school was under the stewardship of Donnchadh Ó Conchubhair, *ollamh re leges* (master-practitioner of medicine) to the Mac Giollapádraig family. His kinsman Risteard Ó Conchubhair prepared a copy of *Lilium Medicinae* in 1590 at Aghmacart, and, as is the case with a number of medical manuscripts, the scribal colophons, marginalia and other additions he incorporated into his version of the *Lilium* are revealing, not only of the milieu of this medical school at the end of the sixteenth century but also of the movements and contacts of Ó Conchubhair as he carried on the work. It also attests to the high esteem in which he held his tutor, Donnchadh; he describes him in glowing terms as 'ullamh Osraighi re leghes agus rogha legha Erenn ina aimsir fen gan dul a hÉrinn do dhenam foghluma.' ['Ossory's master-practitioner of medicine and the best physician of Ireland in his own time having never left Ireland to study.'][9]

The reference in Risteard Ó Conchubhair's encomium to the fact that Donnchadh achieved his medical proficiency without having gone abroad to study medicine is noteworthy. The motive for the statement is unclear; perhaps Risteard is extolling the pre-eminence of Aghmacart and the Ó Conchubhair kindred as a centre of study, or indeed he may be marvelling at the status gained by Donnchadh given the widely shared opinion that the standard of medical education was higher abroad, and that the most knowledgeable physicians had trained in Britain or on the continent. Regrettably, only two works by Donnchadh Ó Conchubhair survive: Irish translations of a chapter on stretching and yawning from the *Collectorium* of

---

[7] Winifred Wulff (ed.), *Rosa Anglica* (London: Irish Texts Society, 1929), p. xv. Wulff qualifies her identification of the Ó hIceadha family with the observation that dialectal evidence within the translation suggests a northern translator (p. xxxiv).

[8] Nic Dhonnchadha, 'The medical school of Aghmacart, Queen's County', 18.

[9] Author's translation. See Paul Walsh (ed.) *Gleanings from Irish manuscripts* (2nd edn, Dublin: At the Sign of the Three Candles, 1933), p. 135.

Nicolaus Bertrucius (d. 1347) and of a short passage on sahaphati, a type of skin disease, by Valescus de Taranta (fl. 1382–1418). There must have been others, for as Nic Dhonnchadha notes, his role as head of the medical school would have required texts on a wider range of conditions.[10]

Risteard Ó Conchubhair's marginalia also provide a valuable perspective into the social milieu in which Gaelic physicians operated at the end of the sixteenth century. They are particularly informative on his movements and lodgings, and on the gentry families, both Gaelic and Old English of county Kildare and county Kilkenny, with whom he stayed during the period when he was engaged in transcribing the *Lilium*. Commencing with a visit to John Lye of Clonaugh of county Kildare (an Englishman, who was an interpreter in the service of Dublin Castle), he subsequently stayed with Calbhach, son of O'More of Ballina, the Birminghams of Carbery, James Fitzgerald of Donore, all in county Kildare and with Edmund, Viscount Mountgarret in county Kilkenny prior to taking up residence in the house of Mac Giollapádraig where he completed transcribing the manuscript.[11] The high social standing of those who received Risteard during this period bear witness to the fact that he was a physician of some repute, as well as to the fact that Aghmacart (and by association, Donnchadh Ó Conchubhair) were both acknowledged as sources of sound medical knowledge and treatment.

Risteard Ó Conchubhair's visits to gentry and aristocratic families in Leinster were in keeping with the peripatetic character of medical practice in medieval and modern Ireland. Such visitations were probably conducted on a regular basis. Ó Cuív has observed that Irish medical men travelled a great deal to minister to the needs of the Anglo-Norman gentry and aristocratic families and Gaelic clans who sought and who could afford their services, as well as in pursuit of knowledge.[12] Since Ó Conchubhair was evidently at ease among Gaelic Irish and Old English alike, it is tempting to suggest that the lack of harsh criticism and abusive treatment of Gaelic practitioners of medicine was indicative of the respect with which they were regarded across this profoundly divided society. This was not the case for New English treatment of other hereditary professional classes, such as the poets, with whom it was forbidden to interact. Ó Cuív has speculated that this may be attributed to the continental provenance of the practitioners' expertise, and to the fact that their skills were not esoteric or threatening. Whatever the precise reason, the fact remains that Gaelic medical men were able to continue to practice their medical skills for some time following the eclipse of the Gaelic order as a consequence of the military defeat and flight into exile of the leadership of the major Ulster clans at the beginning of the seventeenth century. The changed environment cannot have been easy, but the medical tradition that the hereditary clans represented survived until the mid-seventeenth century when it succumbed

---

[10] Nic Dhonnchadha, 'The medical school of Aghmacart', 17–20.
[11] Walsh, *Gleanings*, pp. 125–33.
[12] Ó Cuív, 'The Irish language in the early modern period', p. 519.

in the face of the Cromwellian conquest and still more draconian land confiscation that followed.

The texts identified by Gaelic physicians for translation and induction into the Gaelic medical canon attest to the high respect in which mainstream European medical thinking was held in Gaelic Ireland and Scotland, though Bannerman has correctly pointed out that 'Gaelic medicine remained at the conservative wing of the European medical spectrum.'[13] It is noteworthy, for instance, that cutting-edge renaissance innovation in the study of anatomy failed to find its way into the Gaelic tradition. The translated texts do, however, display a felicity in language not to be found in the works of professional historians and poets, which are encumbered with archaisms borne of an over-zealous devotion to the preservation and practise of traditional forms. Medical texts, by contrast, are written in the spoken language of the scribes, and this innovative disposition is mirrored by the willingness to interpolate, comment and adapt the source text to the requirement of the Irish environment. In so doing, Irish medical scholars like the Ó Conchubhair were exceptional in Europe, as Gaelic, in the words of John Bannerman, 'joined Greek, Arabic and Latin as one of only four languages in which this body of medical knowledge was formally and systematically studied and taught over the centuries from Hippocrates to Riverius.'[14]

Despite the fact that Gaelic physicians were afforded greater tolerance by the New English than the bardic poets and others among the Irish learned classes, the destruction of the society, both Old English and Irish, which gave them patronage, inevitably deprived them of the opportunity to practise their skills in the traditional way. As the power of the Gaelic Irish aristocracy diminished, so too did their capacity to support a learned elite, and, as the ruling classes of Ireland became Anglicised, Gaelic men of letters were obliged to attempt to get by in an increasingly difficult environment. Many chose exile, and the presence of hundreds of Irish names on the rolls of the medical faculty of continental Catholic universities indicates not only that medicine did not lose its appeal as a profession, but also that aspiring medical practitioners of Catholic ancestry were prepared to travel to the continent for medical training.[15] Charles University, Prague was never as popular as the Sorbonne, Reims or Leiden as a destination of Irish students, but the presence there during the seventeenth and eighteenth centuries of a steady stream of Irish students provides an opportunity to explore how the existence on the continent of a network of Irish Colleges, and sponsors in the shape of Irish nobles and soldiers, helped to sustain a native medical tradition that remains opaque in the extreme.

---

[13] Bannerman, *The Beatons*, p. 91.
[14] Bannerman, *The Beatons*, p. 97.
[15] For a fuller engagement with the pattern of Irish medical students abroad see Brockliss, chapter 4 in this collection.

## Irish presence in Prague

Irish Catholics were attracted to Prague in the seventeenth century because the Austrian Hapsburgs, who had recently assumed a commanding influence in Bohemia, were eager to inoculate the city against Protestant efforts to regain control, and the university was a key element in their strategy to strengthen the city's Catholic character. Outsiders were welcomed, especially those who brought skills and a willingness to work for the civic, and Catholic, good. Robinson-Hammerstein has described this strategy as 'a vigorous and deliberate policy of settling the country with "all comers" who were willing to contribute to the Hapsburg idea of a Catholic common good and turn it into reality.'[16] The Irish were ready to participate, and a key step was taken when Patrick Fleming, an Irish Franciscan from county Louth, visited Vienna in search of permission from the Hapsburg Emperor to build an Irish Franciscan foundation within the Habsburg empire. Fleming was instructed to build in Prague and an Irish Franciscan College opened its doors in that city in 1632. The college was built with the financial help of local Catholic noble families, but the Franciscans could also count on the assistance of other Irish in exile, notably soldiers in the Irish regiments of Colonels Patrick Taafe and Walter Butler.[17] As a consequence, Irish Franciscans soon came to exert a significant influence on Catholic spiritual life in the city; for example, as well as fulfilling their duties teaching Irish seminarians in the Irish college many of their number contributed to the education of priests for the local diocese in the local seminary. They assumed these extra duties at the behest of Cardinal Arnošt Harrach of Prague, whose object was to improve the education of the local priesthood (in line with Council of Trent guidelines). He greatly welcomed the assistance of the Irish Franciscans, as he was enabled thereby to exclude the local Jesuits, who he found altogether less agreeable.[18]

Irish religious and military presence in the city was a crucial consideration in persuading Irishmen of university age to travel to Prague to study in the seventeenth and eighteenth centuries. Like the Irish colleges elsewhere on continental Europe, the college in Prague became a focal point for scholarly activity. Moreover, service in the regiments of Taafe and Butler allowed many to fund medical study,

---

[16] Helga Robinson-Hammerstein, 'The university, the common good and Irish medical students as refugees in early eighteenth-century Prague', in Helga Robinson-Hammerstein (ed.) *Migrating scholars: lines of contact between Ireland and Bohemia* (Dublin: Navicula Publications, 1988), p. 55.

[17] For recent account see Jan Pařez, 'The Irish Franciscans in seventeenth- and eighteenth-century Prague' (pp. 104–17), and Micheal MacCraith and David Worthington, 'Aspects of the literary activity of the Irish Franciscans in Prague, 1620–1786' (pp. 118–34) in Thomas O'Connor and Mary Ann Lyons (eds), *Irish migrants in Europe after Kinsale, 1602–1820* (Dublin: FCP, 2003).

[18] Parez, 'The Irish Franciscans in seventeenth- and eighteenth-century Prague', p. 106.

and military service may have been an avenue of practice and employment for medical graduates. The practice of coupling medical study with military service is well attested in the university's book of matriculation, and can be illustrated by the example of Johannes Ludovicus Matthias O'Devlin, Hibernus, who only graduated in 1718, eight years after he matriculated because he combined study with soldiering.[19] The surname O'Devlin suggests that he was from Ulster; the Ó Doibhlin were a family who traditionally gave allegiance and service to the Ó Néill dynasty. Others took more direct and orthodox pathways. Edmund O'Neill, who is listed as nobleman of Dungannon in the faculty rolls, graduated in 1737 having written a dissertation on the nature and medicinal properties of camphor.[20] A dissertation on the use and abuse of purgative medicines was prepared by a Michael de Boyne, nobleman of Cashel who matriculated in 1701 and graduated three years later. Significantly, in the introductory pages of his dissertation, he gave thanks to his patron, Colonel Taafe, which attests to the continuing importance of the Irish community in supporting Irish students into the eighteenth century.[21] This is reinforced by the presence on the medical roll for the period between 1651 and 1783 of such other Irish names as Lynch, Brady, McNamara, Mulledy, Flanagan, O'Quinn, Trench, O'Gormly, Kelly, Maguire, and O'Hehir.

The presence of such a visible stream of Irish medical students at Charles University permits some tentative conclusions as to the fate of the traditional medical families of Gaelic Ireland following the disintegration of the medical schools and the Gaelic social order that had long nurtured the medical profession in Ireland. Saliently, some of the Gaelic medical kindred are represented on the Prague student roll though their precise biographies are generally too fragmentary to permit definitive conclusions. William O'Cassidy of Fermanagh, who entered the medical faculty in 1728, is a case in point; the university roll tells us nothing else of him, which probably means he did not graduate, at least not from Prague.[22] Yet, it is tempting to speculate that he may have been a descendant of the O'Cassidy, who long provided medical assistance to the Maguire dynasty of Fermanagh. It is reasonable to assume, moreover, that he had an awareness of the *importe* of his name and of his family's traditional role in the service of Maguire; the oral tradition in which he was raised would have ensured this. However, since it is not known if he, or what proportion of the other Irishmen who studied medicine at Prague, returned to Ireland to practice their chosen profession, it is impossible at present to assess what impact continentally trained medics had on the medical provision available in rural Ireland. One might surmise from this that medical students resembled the clergy, who returned in large numbers throughout the seventeenth

---

[19] Robinson-Hammerstein, 'The University', p. 67.
[20] Robinson-Hammerstein, 'The University', p. 75.
[21] Robinson-Hammerstein, 'The University', p. 66.
[22] Robinson-Hammerstein, 'The University', p. 73.

and eighteenth centuries, but though it is evident that a considerable proportion may have done so, their distribution and impact remains to be revealed.[23]

## Mac Domhnaill's *Fealsúnacht*

If the subsequent careers of those Irish students who studied medicine at Prague remain elusive, the medicine practiced in Gaelic society in Ireland from the mid-seventeenth century is still more so. One of the inevitable consequences of the destruction of Gaelic society was the loss of the medical knowledge that percolated out of the medical schools. As a result, there was widespread recourse to potions, charms, holy wells, healers and general quackery among the uneducated and poorer elements of the community. A sub-current of medical thinking, probably always latently present among the rural poor, became more mainstream in the absence of Aghmacart and comparable institutions. As a result, lay healers, who were wont to attribute strange ailments and ill-health to the supernatural, may have proliferated.[24] Yet, there is some tantalising evidence to suggest that remnants of the more learned medicine practised by hereditary medical families survived; folklore sources maintain that the skills required to heal specific complaints were handed down from generation to generation, in keeping with the pattern previously identified with hereditary medical families.

To investigate the practice of medicine among the Gaelic Irish in this period is to pull back a veil on that which has been famously characterised as a 'hidden Ireland': an Ireland that existed off the official record, its population immersed in a subculture that is only visible to the historian's gaze when it clashed with authority or when travellers such as Thackeray encountered it on their travels. It is reasonable to conclude, based on the existence of fewer manuscripts, that the practice of medicine amongst the Irish did not enjoy the renaissance that was the experience of other native arts, such as poetry and creative literature, when they were liberated from the conservative strictures that the Gaelic professional classes encouraged. A vivid, imaginative literature in Irish exists from this period, which owes its vitality and originality to the fact that it mirrored the voice of the common people, who were its composers and its audience. Due to the fact that learned medicine required its practitioners to operate to a high level of exactitude, which was not possible in the unfavourable social and political environment of the late seventeenth and eighteenth centuries, the practice of learned medicine among the Irish-speaking population weakened and declined, but it did not entirely disappear.

---

[23] See Lyons, chapter 1 in this collection.

[24] Tales of demonic possession, fairy kidnap and evil eyes as causes of illness abound in the folklore gathered in the early twentieth century, which suggests that such phenomena had a still tighter grip on some two centuries earlier.

There is one Irish textual source from the early nineteenth century, which gives the lie to the suggestion that no science was applied by the Gaelic Irish in the manner in which they practiced medicine. Its author, Aodh Mac Domhnaill, had no medical training, nor did he claim to possess it; he was a teacher and Gaelic scribe born in 1802 in county Meath but resident in county Antrim. He first comes to light between 1839 and 1842 as a teacher of the Bible to native Irish speakers while in the employ of the Home Mission, a group set up by the Ulster Presbyterian Synod to proselytise the Irish speaking population in the north of the country.[25] It should not, however, be concluded that Mac Domhnaill was, by his actions, committed to the proselytes' cause; he was one of a large number of Irish speakers employed in this activity, and his motivation was most likely the wage he received.

It was between the years 1842 to 1856, however, that Mac Domhnaill engaged in the endeavour for which he is best remembered. This period saw him in the almost constant employ of Robert McAdam, the Belfast industrialist who spearheaded the Irish revivalist movement in the city. McAdam learned to read Irish and to speak it fluently, and was secretary, aged 22, of the Ulster Gaelic society, founded in 1832. He perceived that a rich literary culture was in danger of being lost, and set about collecting, transcribing, cataloguing and preserving manuscripts containing songs, proverbs and native lore of all descriptions.[26] The remit of Mac Domhnaill, as a native scholar, was to source and transcribe material from the populace, and he prepared many manuscripts with this in view, which are to be found in the collections of Belfast libraries today. His work took him all over the northern part of the country, and it can be safely presumed that this frequent contact with the ways and customs of the Gaelic Irish, not to mention his own upbringing in Meath, informed his only prose work, the *Fealsúnacht* or *Philosophy*.[27]

It is a substantial text, written entirely in Irish, the central thesis of which is that, in order better to understand the mysteries of God, the logic and order of his creation must be observed and understood (see Appendix Two for an extract). He maintained that the five bodily senses must engage with what they encountered before the three spiritual senses – will, memory and understanding – could be fully employed. Mac Domhnaill maintained that these three spiritual senses were the true gifts of God, and were what gave humankind dominance over the animal kingdom. Original sin, however, had left humankind prone to disease, but the remedy for all disease in creation is to be found within creation itself – in the flora and fauna which inhabit it. It was thus incumbent on humans to know and study nature, and to acquire knowledge of its healing properties. The main section of the *Fealsúnacht*, which follows on logically from this, provides a comprehensive

---

[25] Colm Beckett (ed.), *Fealsúnacht Aodha Mhic Dhomhnaill* (Dublin: An Clóchomhar, 1967), pp. 2–3.

[26] See A.J. Hughes, 'The Ulster Gaelic Society and the work of McAdam's Irish scribes', in Fionntán de Brún (ed.), *Belfast and the Irish language* (Dublin: FCP, 2006), pp. 65–100.

[27] As note 26.

list of names of herbs and plants with healing properties, in Irish with a parallel English translation. Mac Domhnaill also assembled a description of how this pharmacopoeia should be administered to ease those who were ill and indisposed, in the manner of the following examples:

> Ground ivy, boiled in water, cures coughs, kidney and liver complaints, and bleeding in the urine.
> Cranesbill is a tonic which stops bleeding and which cures bruising, and is a cure for all bleeding, both internal and external; its sap should be drunk, or a poultice made of it.
> The dock is a common herb, and it contains many benefits, but the root is best. Boiled in water and new milk, it cleans the blood and cures breaking out of the skin.[28]

What is striking about the cures listed in Mac Domhnaill's *Fealsúnacht* is the minimal recourse to magic and superstition. The author's priority was to identify the tangible medical properties of the indigenous flora of the Irish countryside, with the result that there are only two examples where supernatural powers were at issue. Thus the rowan tree, or mountain ash, is recommended as a shield against magic on the grounds that this was a traditional Irish belief stretching back into prehistory and the legendary Tuatha De Danann.[29] He also claimed that the field mouse, the smallest of mammals, possessed special powers. It could be boiled, and the water given to children to prevent bed-wetting. Alternatively, if one slept with a field mouse through which one had driven pins under one's pillow, then a vision of the person's future spouse would appear. Saliently, he noted that this behaviour was on the wane, albeit not because of declining belief in its efficacy or in the general merits of superstition, but due to a dearth of field mice.[30]

Like the canonical medical texts from the early modern period, Mac Domhnaill's text is of great linguistic value. However the *Fealsúnacht* is still more interesting as a witness to an approach to medical thinking in Gaelic Ireland for which there are few reliable sources. It bears witness to the existence of a community that relied on herbal remedies for a wide variety of ailments. It is unlikely that Mac Domhnaill was personally familiar with each of the remedies he incorporated into his text, and more likely that he picked many of them up in the course of his travels through Ulster on behalf of Robert McAdam. Their number and character gave him the idea to set them in the context of his own views on creation and natural law. His vision of the earth is of a mother of all worldly things who cares for all of her offspring in the same manner as a mother cares for her children. She has provided, therefore, natural cures for all diseases to which humans and animals

---

[28] Beckett (ed.), *Fealsúnacht*, pp. 126–7.
[29] Beckett (ed.), *Fealsúnacht*, p. 155.
[30] Beckett (ed.), *Fealsúnacht*, p. 203.

are prone, and which, as his listing and description makes clear, it is incumbent on human beings to learn.

The *Fealsúnacht* never saw the printing press during Mac Domhnaill's lifetime.[31] It is, in any event, unlikely that there would have been many readers for such a work in the Irish language in the middle of the nineteenth century, though it can reasonably be assumed that Mac Domhnaill intended it for publication. That it was not published, or indeed extensively copied by hand, stands in sharp contrast to the vigorous scribal transcription, interrogation, modification and commentary of the medical works that came into the hands of Gaelic physicians in the late medieval and early modern era. Such circumstances attest to the extent of the decline of native medical practice in the intervening centuries.

## Conclusion

The energetic culture in learned medicine that operated in Gaelic Ireland in the medieval and early modern eras drew on continental as well as indigenous learning in the compilation of the medical texts that provide the most vivid illustration of its character. This culture was supported by, and, as a result, largely sustained by the Gaelic elite, and their eclipse hastened its marginalisation. Medical practitioners fared better than poets, but by the early seventeenth century traditional medicine was already under pressure, and it was effectively eclipsed by the dramatic shift in power and influence that saw the New English emerge as the most commanding force in the country. Obliged to look to Europe for medical training, a steady stream of Irish students travelled throughout the seventeenth and eighteenth centuries to continental university medical faculties in Catholic Europe. Some returned to Ireland (more probably did not return), but their number and impact has yet to be established. Whatever the outcome, it is clear that medicine did not emulate literature or, probably, religion in its capacity to adapt to the changed environment, and that one consequence of this was an increased reliance on herbal medicine by the Irish speaking population. Yet the tradition of hereditary medical care did not entirely disappear, as the compendium of popular remedies gathered by Aodh MacDomhnaill from across Ulster in the nineteenth century bears witness. Such remedies were probably commonly resorted to. However, the fact that MacDomhnaill's *Philosophy* was not published is indicative of the lack of appeal of traditional medicine to the growing Anglophone population, for whom proprietary (quack) medicine and the expanding network of medical professionals and medical institutions offered greater hope of a medical cure. The era of traditional Gaelic medicine may not have been completely over, but there was no prospect of its ever reanimating the halcyon days of an earlier era.

---

[31] Belfast Public Library, MS XIX A. The manuscript is in Mac Domhnaill's own hand, in a bound copy book of 122 pages.

## Appendix 1

Extract with English translation from Irish version of *Rosa Anglica* by John of Gaddesden from Winifred Wulff, (ed.), *Rosa Anglica* (London: Irish Texts Society, 1929), pp. 14–15, wherein is described the diagnosis of tertian fever:

> Comartha na heslainti so do leth in fuail .i. fual seim doinderg tanaide 7 is i a cuiss a beith a ndeirge .i. tes an cuirp, 7 cuis a tanachta tirmacht leanna ruaid. Item fual doinderg ina dath 7 tanaidhe ina folud 7 solas ina ichtar 7 dorcha ina uachtar ag duine og coilirda maille risna neithib randquidhigiss riu signidi sin terciana fire. Item fual dub iba dath 7 tanaidi ina folud 7 dorcha na uachtar signidi sin a nduine flegmatacha 7 a mnai terciana dubullta. Item fual doinderg ina dath 7 tana ina folud 7 dorcha na uachtar a macamaib signidi sin in fiabras re nabar terciana continua. Item fual derg ard ina dath 7 buartha ina folud 7 dath an luaigi na uachtar signidi sin terciana continua o linn ruad nadurdha.

> Signs of this disease as regards the urine .i. subtle thin red-brown urine; and the cause of its being red is the heat of the body, and the cause of its thinness is the dryness of choler. *Item* urine red-brown in colour and thin in substance, bright below and dark above, in a young choleric person along with the particular matters, signifies true tertian fever. *Item* urine black in colour and thin in substance, and dark above in a phlegmatic person and in a woman, signifies double *tertiana*. *Item* urine red-brown in colour and thin in substance and dark above in youths, signifies the fever called *tertiana continua*. *Item* urine red and high in colour, and troubled in substance, and leaden-coloured above, signifies *tertiana continua* from natural choler.

## Appendix 2

Extract (with translation) from the introduction to the *Fealsúnacht/Philosophy* of Aodh Mac Domhnaill (Colm Beckett (ed.), *Fealsúnacht Aodha Mhic Dhomhnaill* (Dublin: An Clóchomhar, 1967), p. 95).

### AN CHEAD CEABHADOIL DON BHFEILSONACHT, AIR CCRUTHADH

> An té ar mian leis fis udar agus chailaighacht corpa talmuidh agus corpa neamha a chuartadh no a scrudamh amach is eigin do an dá chinal duar a chur a ccumpair anus go mbarde bo leir do na cheadfuidh na nithe dorcha so do bhreaneadh agus go murmar gach cleantach sa leanan dobh a ré a mbeatha no a marthana. Deir udair gur be dia a rinne na huile nithe agas go rabh sé leatha aige criochnadh na hoibre amhuil agus bheithadh neach air bith eile aige criochnadh gnoithe saoilta agus mur an cceadna nach rabh ni air bith aige le andeanamh dhe acht a mhor

chumhachta fein amhain ionus gur be so a creadas furmhor an domhain agus na mor nach huabhar leobh amharc taobhasteach do cracan ni ar bith acht a bheith sasta le gac ni a cclunid ú gach fafaire agus gan uirid le úsat a dhanamh de na cceadfuidh fein marsin is coir damhsa agus do mo leid eile amharc a steach go grinn gringealeach an gach cluid de na rundhiamhuir so.

## THE FIRST CHAPTER OF THE PHILOSOPHY: ON CREATION

He who wishes to search for or examine the reasoning and qualities of earthly bodies and heavenly bodies, must first compare both elements, so that the observation of these unclear things, and especially all their traits and tendencies during their existence, would make them clear to his senses.

Writers say that God made all things, and that he did so in six days, in much the same way as any other person would finish worldly business, and also that he had no instrument for creation other than is own great power. This is what is believed by most people, yet they fail to look under the skin of anything, but are content with what they are told by every sort of fool, never using their own senses. It is thus proper for me and my likes to peer closely into every corner of these mysteries.

Chapter 3
# Medicine and Miracles in the Late Seventeenth Century: Bernard Connor's *Evangelium Medici* (1697)

Liam Chambers

The people of seventeenth-century Ireland lived in what Raymond Gillespie has called 'a world of wonders', where everyday and unusual occurrences were understood in the context of God's providential role in people's lives.[1] While the official doctrine of the Church of Ireland held that miracles had long ceased, ill-health and recovery were ascribed by followers of all Christian denominations to divine intervention and studied for the religious messages that they could reveal. However, Gillespie also notes that 'by the end of the century there was increasing scepticism about wonder stories as the educated looked for alternative explanations, a development which helped to destroy the comfortable world of hearsay, tradition and private judgement.'[2] Improving standards of medical knowledge and training in the seventeenth century had a significant part to play in effecting this change. The Irish physician, Bernard Connor (c.1666–98), provided an illustration in 1698, when he recalled an episode he had witnessed in Rome a few years earlier:

> ... passing by chance through the Strada del Popolo I saw a multitude of people hurrying a man to St Mark's Chappel, which belongs to the Venetian Embassadors; they told me he was possess'd by the devil, and that they were carrying him to be exorcis'd; I crowded through the throng into the church, and felt the man's pulse; I found him in a Fever, making hideous grimaces and motions with his face, eyes, tongue, and all his limbs, which were nothing else but a fit of convulsive motions all over his body, occasion'd by a disorder of his blood and spirits, being a hypochondriacal person. The clergy and people began very devoutly to fright the pretended devil out of him, and in a little time his disorderly motions ceased, which as they thought to be the miraculous effect

---

[1] Raymond Gillespie, *Devoted people: belief and religion in early modern Ireland* (Manchester: Manchester University Press, 1997), p. 108.

[2] Gillespie, *Devoted people*, p. 108.

of their prayers, I attributed to the natural abatement and the usual cessation of such fits.[3]

Connor believed that 'wilful mistakes' and 'ignorance' elevated natural events, like this, into supernatural ones. However, he also maintained that miraculous events could happen and argued that the physician was ideally placed to distinguish between them and natural occurrences.[4] In 1697 he published a controversial work on miracles, *Evangelium Medici: seu Medicina Mystica; De Suspensis Naturæ Legibus, sive De Miraculis*, which illustrates the implications of the mechanical philosophy for both medicine and the miraculous.[5] The book attempted to reconcile the possibility of miracles with novel medical ideas, especially those associated with the mechanical philosophy. Connor's work is particularly interesting on account of his Irish Catholic background, his extensive continental connections and his apparent religious ambiguity.

Connor's brief but remarkable career has not passed unnoticed. The Irish medical historians John Knott (1907), W.R. Le Fanu (1964) and, more recently, Davis Coakley (1992) have summarised his achievements.[6] Baruch S. and Jean L. Blumberg (1958) have highlighted his authorship of one of the first known descriptions of ankylosing spondylitis.[7] S. Szpilczynski (1974) has contributed an important article on Connor's 'contribution to the development of medical

---

[3] Bernard Connor, *The history of Poland, in several letters to persons of quality ... with several letters relating to physick ... publish'd by the care and assistance of Mr. Savage* (2 vols, London: 1698), vol. 1, pp. 317–18[II]. The pagination in both volumes of this work is irregular. In volume one pp. 1–352 are followed by a new pagination bearing the numbers 289–322. In volume two, pp. 1–236 are followed by new pagination numbered pp. 1–120 and an unpaginated table of contents. References to the second series of page numbers in volumes one and two are indicted by '[II]'.

[4] Connor, *The history of Poland*, vol. 1, pp. 317–18[II].

[5] The title may be translated as: 'The gospel of a doctor, or, mystic medicine; concerning the suspension of the laws of nature, or concerning miracles'. References in this article are to the first edition published in London in 1697. The pagination in the work is irregular. Pages 1–208 are followed by a new pagination numbered pp. 1–38 and an unpaginated table of contents. References to the second series of page numbers are indicted by '[II]'.

[6] John Knott, 'Bernard Connor: a forgotten Irish medical exile and scientific pioneer of the seventeenth century (1666–1698)', *Dublin Journal of Medical Science*, 133 (January–February 1907): 131–44; W.R. Le Fanu, 'Two Irish doctors in England in the seventeenth century', *Irish Journal of Medical Science* (July 1964): 303–9; Davis Coakley, *Irish masters of medicine* (Dublin: Town House, 1992), pp. 15–25.

[7] Baruch S. Blumberg and Jean L. Blumberg, 'Bernard Connor (1666–1698) and his contribution to the pathology of ankylosing spondylitis', *Journal of the History of Medicine and Applied Sciences,* 13 (1958): 349–66.

thinking' in which he traces the sources of Connor's medical ideas.[8] Research on Connor was synthesised and augmented in 1981 by R.H. Dalitz and G.C. Stone in an article that focused primarily on Connor's *History of Poland*, an important two-volume work published in 1698.[9] Yet, Connor's most controversial book, *Evangelium Medici*, has received little attention. Knott provided an idiosyncratic assessment, concluding that 'every sentence scintillates with originality of thought and brilliancy of genius'.[10] Le Fanu was less convinced, noting that 'it is full of unusual observation and strange speculations, but its general effect is the opposite of what he intended'.[11] This paper locates *Evangelium Medici* in the debates about religion, medicine and the mechanical philosophy that took place in the late seventeenth century. It briefly assesses conceptions of the miraculous during this period and considers Bernard Connor's medical ideas, before assessing the genesis and content of *Evangelium Medici*.

## Conceptions of the miraculous in the seventeenth century

Connor's work on miracles may be situated within three overlapping contexts: Irish (especially Catholic) attitudes to miracles, attempts to work out the implications of the mechanical philosophy for the miraculous, and the 'great debate' about miracles generated by the deist challenge of the later seventeenth century.

Irish Catholics, with the encouragement of their clergy, understood ill-health, disease, recovery and death within a theology of the miraculous. In his work on miracles the Irish Jesuit, Richard Archdekin, argued that miracles were 'an assured token and proofe of true religion'.[12] He recognised an important role for

---

[8] S. Szpilczynski, 'Bernard O'Connor from Ireland: aulic physician to the Polish King Jan III Sobieski. A contribution to the development of medical thinking at the turn of the seventeenth century', *Proceedings of the XXIII international congress of the history of medicine* (London: Wellcome Institute of the History of Medicine, 1974), pp. 762–71.

[9] R.H. Dalitz and G.C.Stone, 'Doctor Bernard Connor: physician to King Jan III Sobieski and author of the History of Poland (1698)', *Oxford Slavonic Papers*, 14 (1981): 14–35; Gerald Stone has also authored the entry on Connor in the *ODNB*, *sub* Bernard Connor. The present author contributed a short entry on Connor to Thomas Duddy (ed.), *Dictionary of Irish philosophers* (Bristol: Thoemmes, 2004), pp. 83–6. Róisín Healy has recently assessed Connor's *History* in 'The view from the margins: Ireland and Poland–Lithuania, 1698–1798' in Richard Unger, with the assistance of Jakub Basista (eds), *Britain and Poland–Lithuania: contact and comparison from the Middle Ages to 1795* (Leiden: Brill, 2008), pp. 355–74. I wish to thank Dr Healy for her comments on an earlier draft of this article.

[10] Knott, 'Bernard Connor', 143.

[11] Le Fanu, 'Two Irish doctors', 308.

[12] Richard Archdekin, *A treatise of miracles together with new miracles and benefits obtained by the sacred reliques of S. Francis Xaverius exposed in the Church of the Soc. of Jesus at Mechlin* (Louvain, 1667), p. 3.

medical practitioners in the authentication of miracles. To accusations of trickery, Archdekin responded that:

> Catholicks never use to give out for miracles any effect that can be performed by human arte, but onely such things as are found to surpasse the ordinarie reach and power of nature, as the raising of the dead, the curing of some incurable sickness; or where the cure was soe suddain that by acknowledgment of doctors it could not be naturally performed in so short a time.[13]

Archdekin stressed three levels of authority: ecclesiastical approval, legally certified evidence and the testimony of 'skillful doctors, surgeons and other witnesses who could have knowledge of the matter'.[14] The miracles recounted in his work, which took place in Mechelen and various parts of Ireland and involved the relics of the Jesuit saint, Francis Xavier, frequently occurred in cases where physicians were unable to assist their patients. Indeed, physicians encouraged patients to seek divinely inspired remedies.[15] The testimony of physicians was very important. In one case, involving the cure of a young woman, the official account recorded that 'the two prime doctors and professors of medicine' in Louvain agreed that 'this recovering of strength in so short a tyme, was above the ordinary force of nature and could not otherwise be obtained than by divine favour.'[16]

While the miraculous remained important in seventeenth-century Ireland and England, the growing influence of an experimental and mechanical natural philosophy ensured that alleged miraculous events were subject to more intense scrutiny.[17] Jane Shaw has identified the healing activities of Valentine Greatrakes, 'the Irish stroker', in England during 1666 as a turning point. Robert Boyle and others took a keen interest in Greatrakes' activities and sought to identify mechanical explanations. However, they also wished to leave open the possibility that miracles *could* happen. Shaw comments that 'many suggested or implied that natural or mechanical explanations would be offered in the majority of cases that people claimed as miracles, but that divine intervention remained a plausible explanation, at least upon very great evidence.'[18] In Ireland, the Dublin Philosophical Society is

---

[13] Archdekin, *A treatise*, p. 22.

[14] Archdekin, *A treatise*, p. 36.

[15] Archdekin, *A treatise*, pp. 45–7, 51, 57, 59–60, 64–6, 69–70, 74–5, 77, 79, 82–3, 84–8, 90, 95–6, 105.

[16] Archdekin, *A treatise*, p. 60.

[17] For Ireland see Gillespie, *Devoted people*, pp.107–26. For England see Jane Shaw, *Miracles in Enlightenment England* (New Haven and London: Yale University Press, 2006); William E. Burns, *An age of wonders: prodigies, politics and providence in England, 1657–1727* (Manchester: Manchester University Press, 2002); Peter Dear, 'Miracles, experiments and the ordinary course of nature', *Iris*, 81/4 (1990): 663–83

[18] Shaw, *Miracles*, pp. 96–7; Caoimhghin S. Breathnach, 'Robert Boyle's approach to the ministrations of Valentine Greatrakes', *History of Psychiatry*, 10 (1999): 87–109.

not recorded as discussing miracles specifically, but Hoppen has pointed out that members saw no contradiction between their natural philosophy and their religious sympathies.[19] In December 1683, Robert Huntington explained that 'several of the number meet at five upon Sunday nights (as the whole Company does on Mondays) to discourse theologically, of God suppose, and his attributes, and how to establish religion, and confute atheism, by reason, evidence, and demonstration'.[20] One Dublin Philosophical Society member, Richard Bulkeley, who gained a reputation as an inventor and experimentalist, even threw his lot in with the French Prophets, a miracle-working Huguenot group, when they arrived in England in the early eighteenth century.[21] However, most natural philosophers of the period preferred to chart a course between what they thought of as two extremes: the fanaticism of a Bulkeley or Archdekin and an opposing and increasingly influential tendency, the denial of miracles by the deists.

The 'great debate on miracles' was underway in England and Scotland by the end of the seventeenth century and culminated in Hume's famous essay of 1748.[22] Baruch Spinoza's outright denial of miracles in the *Tractatus Politico-Theologicus* (1670) was one important influence on a generation of English deists. As Jonathan Israel has pointed out: 'since miracles were seen as the "first pillar" of faith, authority and tradition by theologians at the time, Spinoza's rejection of the possibility of miracles seemed to bring all accepted beliefs, the very basis of contemporary culture, into question.'[23] Spinoza's chapter on miracles was translated (rather freely) into English by Charles Blount and published anonymously in *Miracles, no violations of the laws of nature* (1683). The response was muted, and it was not until the publication of John Toland's *Christianity not mysterious* (1696) that the deist attack on Christian revelation and the miraculous can be said to have taken shape. 'When all other shifts prove ineffectual', wrote Toland, 'the partizans of mystery fly to miracles as their last refuge'.[24] Toland's work was published towards the end of 1695 (though it was dated 1696 to avoid complications arising

---

[19] K. Theodore Hoppen, *The common scientist in the seventeenth century: a study of the Dublin Philosophical Society, 1683–1708* (London: Routledge and Kegan Paul, 1970), pp. 80–84.

[20] K. Theodore Hoppen, 'The Royal Society and Ireland II', *Notes and Records of the Royal Society of London*, 20/1 (1965), 78–99 (79).

[21] On Bulkeley, see Shaw, *Miracles*, pp. 151–7; Hoppen, *Common scientist*, pp. 40, 186; Toby Barnard, 'Reforming Irish manners: the religious societies in Dublin during the 1690s', *Historical Journal*, 35/4 (1992): 805–38 (818).

[22] R.M. Burns, *The great debate on miracles from Joseph Glanvill to David Hume* (London: Bucknell University Press, 1981).

[23] Jonathan Israel, *Radical Enlightenment: philosophy and the making of modernity, 1650–1750* (Oxford: OUP, 2001), p. 219, and pp. 599–627 for Spinoza's influence on English deism.

[24] John Toland, *Christianity not mysterious* (London, 1696), p. 144.

from the Licensing Act) and his comments on miracles are relevant to Connor's *Evangelium Medici*, published less than two years later. For Toland:

> A miracle then is some action exceeding all human power, and which the laws of nature cannot perform by their ordinary operations ... Now whatever is contrary to reason can be no miracle, for it has been sufficiently prov'd already, that contradiction is only another word for impossible or nothing. The miraculous action must therefore be some thing in itself intelligible and possible tho the manner of doing it be extraordinary.[25]

Since Toland rejected John Locke's case for accepting propositions 'above reason', it is difficult to assess the 'divine miracles' that Toland appeared to retain.[26] In any event, just as Bernard Connor arrived in England, probably for the first time, the debate about miracles was well underway, and a cause of considerable dissension among the intellectual elite.

### The life and medical ideas of Bernard Connor

Bernard Connor was born in Ireland, possibly in county Kerry, around 1666.[27] In the sermon he preached at Connor's funeral, William Hayley stated that Connor was born a Catholic and that he 'remained in his own country, as I am informed by his friends, till about the twentieth year of his age; when in order to cultivate his studies, and to apply his mind to physick, and work out his fortune, he betook himself to travel.'[28] Connor graduated as a doctor of medicine from the University of Reims on 18 September 1693, but he also had associations with medical circles in Montpellier and Paris.[29] Connor mentioned that he lived for a time in Montpellier, and eighteenth-century authorities state that he studied there.[30] Connor also claimed that he lectured at Paris, possibly in connection with his

---

[25] Toland, *Christianity*, pp. 144–5.

[26] Toland, *Christianity*, pp. 146–51. For Locke on miracles see Burns, *The great debate*, pp. 57–69; J.J. Macintosh, 'Locke and Boyle on miracles and God's existence' in Michael Hunter (ed.), *Robert Boyle reconsidered* (Cambridge: CUP, 1994), pp. 193–214.

[27] For discussion of this point see Dalitz and Stone, 'Doctor Bernard Connor', 15–16.

[28] William Hayley, *A sermon preached in the parish Church of St. Giles in the Fields at the funeral of Bernard Connor, M.D. who departed this life, Oct. 30. 1698, with a short account of his life and death* (London, 1699), p. 27.

[29] For discussion of Irish attendance at these universities see Lyons chapter 1 and Brockliss chapter 5 in this collection.

[30] For discussion on this point see Dalitz and Stone, 'Doctor Bernard Connor', 16–18.

membership of the Chambre Royale de Medicine.[31] Assuming that Connor arrived in France in the mid to late 1680s, he would have encountered a medical curriculum based on an elastic Galenism, which had integrated aspects of the iatrochemical approach. However, evidence from the University of Paris indicates that the more fundamental shift, involving the challenge of iatromechanism, occurred only in the mid-1690s.[32] This may explain Connor's attraction to the Chambre Royale which, as Brockliss and Jones have noted, was 'an institutional front for iatromechanism in a period when the new medical ideology had no support within the faculties.'[33]

The Chambre Royale was dissolved as a result of pressure from the Paris Faculty of Medicine in the early summer of 1694. Later that year Connor accompanied the sons of Jan Wielopolski, the crown chancellor of Poland, on a journey from Paris to Warsaw. The trip amounted to a grand tour through the Italian states and central Europe, as well as Poland, and it provided Connor with an opportunity to expand his medical knowledge. Along the way, he met with leading medical thinkers, including Marcello Malpighi, Lorenzo Bellini and Francisco Redi, as well as Irish and English travellers.[34] Connor's medical education and networking meant he was well schooled in the university curriculum and the novel ideas of the iatromechanists. His published work in the 1690s reflects these influences and his commitment to integrate them into a 'new' system.

Connor's sceptical attitude to Aristotelian and Galenic authority in natural philosophy and medicine emerge clearly from his account of his Polish sojourn. As a result of connections he made in Venice, Connor was engaged as a physician to the ailing Polish king, John Sobieski.[35] Shortly after his arrival Connor was consulted on the illness of the king's sister. He diagnosed 'an ague fomented by an abcess of the liver' and delivered a much bleaker prognosis than his Polish colleagues. When the princess died, Connor's diagnosis was confirmed and his medical reputation was correspondingly enhanced.[36] In general, Connor was critical of the state of medical knowledge in Poland.[37] Logic and metaphysics were, he believed, rooted in Aristotle's philosophy, though there was little agreement among his followers.[38] There were few native physicians because the expense of studying medicine was

---

[31] Bernard Connor, *Dissertationes medico-physicae* (Oxford, 1695), title page; Connor, *History*, vol. 1, p. 289[II].

[32] Laurence Brockliss and Colin Jones, *The medical world of early modern France* (Oxford: OUP, 1997), pp. 90–169, 411–33; L.W.B. Brockliss, *French higher education in the seventeenth and eighteenth centuries: a cultural history* (Oxford: OUP, 1987), pp. 391–443; L.W.B. Brockliss, 'Medical teaching at the University of Paris, 1600–1720', *Annals of Science*, 35 (1978): 221–251.

[33] Brockliss and Jones, *The medical world*, p. 419, n. 38.

[34] Connor, *History*, vol. 1, p. 289[II].

[35] Connor, *History*, vol. 1, p. 2. On his Venetian connections see p. 153.

[36] Connor, *History*, vol. 1, pp. 198–201.

[37] Connor, *History*, vol. 2, pp. 74–97[II].

[38] Connor, *History*, vol. 2, pp. 78–9[II]; also notes a penchant for Albertus Magnus.

too great for any but the wealthiest, who were generally unprepared to invest the time and effort necessary to qualify.[39] As a result, Polish medical practice was 'very imperfect' and 'the medicines which they use are altogether Galenical, and those always of the worser sort'.[40]

These criticisms notwithstanding, Connor noted approvingly that the monarch was interested in the 'modern philosophy', and on one occasion encouraged a debate involving Connor and a number of Polish bishops and clergy concerning the location of the soul in the body.[41] By his own account, Connor reluctantly proffered his view that the soul 'must be only in the brain which is the seat of sensation, and the origin of all the nerves, which are the organs of perception and motion.'[42] Father Vota, a Jesuit, responded that if the soul resided only in the brain, the rest of the body would be dead, because the soul was 'the life of the whole body'.[43] Connor rejected this Aristotelian conception of the soul and instead proposed one consistent with a mechanical philosophy:

> That the rational soul was not the life of the body, but the blood only and the animal spirits, and that this blood and spirits circulated equally all over the body, and gave it its natural heat and motion, which is properly its life: and that this circulation of the blood and spirits could not possibly depend on the rational soul, because it was an involuntary motion formed by the mechanical structure of the body and by the natural impulse of the heart, which is the *primum mobile* of the whole machine; and that tho they all held, not only in Poland, but in other countries, that the rational soul perform'd every minute action in the body, yet this opinion was irreconcilable with the free will of the mind, which they all admitted, for since they allow that whatever the soul does, not only it is conscious of it, but likewise does it freely without being necessitated thereto; when as it is evidently obvious to everyone, that the vital motions in our bodies, I mean the motion of the heart, and that of respiration, with the peristaltic motion of the stomach and guts, are performed naturally with such mechanism that the soul can't stop them, no nor as much as hasten or retard them, and that the soul is not at all conscious of them; for if we think of any object, or not think at all, as when we are asleep, or in an apoplex, those vital motions go on equally the same.[44]

To the objection that human beings were therefore no different to animals, Connor responded that the soul 'performed all voluntary motions' and therefore acted like

---

[39] Connor, *History*, vol. 2, p. 82[II]; he makes an interesting aside on the same page noting that persons of the meanest birth make the best scientists.
[40] Connor, *History*, vol. 2, p. 89[II].
[41] Connor, *History*, vol. 1, pp. 179–80.
[42] Connor, *History*, vol. 1, p. 181.
[43] Connor, *History*, vol. 1, p. 181.
[44] Connor, *History*, vol. 1, pp. 181–2.

a pilot in the body.[45] A consequence of Connor's theory was that death was not caused by the departure of the soul from the body, rather it was the 'cessation of the motions of the heart, of the blood and of the spirits', which did not depend on the soul. The soul departed the body only after this cessation.[46] The Jesuit priest condemned Connor's 'heretical opinions (as they called them)'. For Connor, the debate illustrated the strength of clerical attachment to Aristotelianism 'not only in Poland, but in Spain, Italy and in most other countries where their power is very great' and the fear that 'if experience and reason shake the foundation, the superstructure would fall to the ground, as doubtless it would for the most part.'[47]

John Sobieski's deteriorating health and Connor's insecure position at the Polish court prompted him to leave. In January 1695, he accompanied Princess Teresa Cunegunda on a journey to Brussels before travelling on, via Holland, to England, where he arrived in February 1695.[48] He quickly established himself in English medical and scientific circles. During 1695 and 1696 Connor gave anatomical demonstrations in Oxford, London and Cambridge. He was also elected a fellow of the Royal Society and admitted as a licentiate of the Royal College of Physicians.[49] By October 1695, he had established a medical practice in London.[50]

Connor's rapid assimilation into the English medical establishment was assisted by the patronage network that he cultivated. He had, as already noted, made the acquaintance of a number of English and Irish aristocrats while on the continent, most significantly William Legge, first earl of Dartmouth, whom he treated.[51] He was fully aware of the value of eminent patrons, as his published works each contain a series of dedications to members of the English peerage and to eminent medical practitioners.[52] It is difficult to know how many of these were known personally to Connor, but such evidence as there is suggests that

---

[45] Connor, *History*, vol. 1, pp. 181–2.

[46] Connor, *History*, vol. 1, p. 183.

[47] Connor, *History*, vol. 1, p. 184.

[48] Connor, *History*, vol. 1, pp. 193–8. He passed through Mechelen, the location of the miracles recounted by Richard Archdekin, *en route* (p. 198). Connor was consulted on the king's health after his departure (pp. 201–4).

[49] For an account see, Dalitz and Stone, 'Doctor Bernard Connor', 22–27. Connor was ineligible for a fellowship of the Royal College of Physicians on account of his foreign MD. On the distinction between fellows and licentiates see Harold J. Cook, *The decline of the old medical regime in Stuart London* (Ithaca and London: Cornell University Press, 1986), pp. 72–4.

[50] Connor, *History*, vol. 1, p. 290[II].

[51] Connor, *History*, vol. 1, p. 2.

[52] For dedications in the *History* see Dalitz and Stone, 'Doctor Bernard Connor', 28–9. The *Dissertationes* were dedicated to Thomas Herbert, eighth earl of Pembroke and fifth earl of Montgomery, John Radcliffe, Edward Browne and Hans Sloane. *Evangelium Medici* was dedicated to Charles Montagu, Earl of Halifax (1661–1715); this work also

he possessed strong links to the medical and intellectual elites, including Hans Sloane, who assisted him in early 1695.[53] Another prominent fellow of the Royal Society, Richard Waller let it be known that he was translating a treatise by Connor in 1697.[54] Connor was also in contact with John Radcliffe and James Tyrrell.[55] The latter, who was described by Connor as 'a true friend', was in turn a close friend of Locke and a brother-in-law of Charles Blount (who died before Connor arrived in England in 1693). A grandson of James Ussher, he visited Ireland in the early 1670s and wrote an uncomplimentary essay 'On the Irish' in 1673.[56] Connor noted in *Evangelium Medici* that he had discussed miracles with 'D.B.M.', who he described as a 'kinsman' of 'the author of Religio medici'. Presumably this was Dr Edward Browne (a physician who had travelled and written extensively on Eastern Europe) or, possibly, his son Thomas Browne, respectively the son and grandson of Sir Thomas Browne. The connection would explain the controversial title of Connor's work.[57] In early 1696, he was working on 'chymical and anatomical experiments' in the library of Thomas Tenison, Archbishop of Canterbury.[58]

Connor had published on a range of medical subjects in 1693 and 1694, while he was still resident on the continent.[59] Indeed, a paper written by him on a 'large

---

contained a letter to his 'friend', 'D.B.M', and an essay entitled 'De Secretione Animali' dedicated to Edward and Robert Southwell.

[53] Bernard Connor to Hans Sloane, 28 May 1695 (BL, Sloane MS 4036, fols 213–14v). Sloane studied in Paris and Montpellier in the early 1680s, *ODNB, sub* Hans Sloane.

[54] Margaret J.M. Ezell, 'Richard Waller, F.R.S.: "In the pursuit of nature"', *Notes and Records of the Royal Society*, 38 (1984): 215–33 (220–21). Ezell identifies this as Connor's contribution to the *Philosophical Transactions*, but it was more likely to have been *Evangelium Medici*. Presumably the adverse publicity surrounding the publication put Waller off.

[55] Connor to Sloane, 28 May 1695 (BL, Sloane MS 4036, fols 213–14v).

[56] Connor, *History*, vol. 1, p. 301[II]; J.W. Gough, 'James Tyrrell, Whig historian, and friend of John Locke', *Historical Journal*, 19 (1976): 581–610.

[57] *Evangelium Medici*, epistola, pp. i, vii. Connor dedicated one of the sections of his *Dissertationes* to Edward Browne and mentions to Hans Sloane that he was forwarding a copy to 'Dr Browne' (Connor to Sloane, 28 May 1695, see note 55). A 'T. Brown' gave a positive account of *Evangelium Medici* to Joseph Raphson, a fellow of the Royal Society, on behalf of the author in 1697 (John Wilmot, *Familiar letters* (2nd edn, London, 1697), pp. 114–17). See also footnote 52.

[58] Connor, *History*, vol. 1, p. 307[II].

[59] 'Description physique d'une masse de chair pesant quarante deux livres et un quart, trouvée dans le ventre d'une femme qui l'avoit portée pendant vingt cinq ans', *Journal des Sçavans* (Amsterdam, 1693); 'Lettre écrite a M. le Chevalier G. de Waldegrave, premier médecin de sa majesté Britannique, par M. Bernard O'Connor ... contenant une description physique de la fabrique surprenante d'un tronc de squelette humain, où les vertèbres, les côtes, l'os sacrum, et les os des iles, qui naturellement sont distincts et séparés, ne sont qu'un seul os continu et inséperable', *Journal des Sçavans* (Amsterdam, 1693), pp. 590–617. The latter was published separately as: *Lettre écrite a Monsieur le Chevalier*

tumour' may have been read to the Royal Society before his arrival in London.[60] While in Oxford he published a new version of these papers: *Dissertationes medico-physicæ* (1695).[61] He also published an English language version of his paper on ankylosing spondylitis in the *Philosophical Transactions* in the same year.[62] Connor's fascination with natural curiosities and wonders was shared by the fellows of the Royal Society and he presented specimens collected in Poland to them a few weeks after he arrived in London, in March 1695.[63] This interest in wonders emerges elsewhere in his published work. *The History of Poland* contains discussions of 'rarities', feral children raised by bears in Lithuania, and 'two diseases that are peculiar to the Poles'.[64]

Connor's medical ideas were presented as 'A new plan of an animal oeconomy' to those who attended his anatomical demonstrations at Oxford, London and Cambridge in 1695 and 1696. They also appeared in print (in outline form) in *Evangelium Medici* and as an appendix to the first volume of his *History of Poland* titled: 'A compendious plan of the body of physick'.[65] Connor's 'new plan' drew together medicine, anatomy, chemistry and natural philosophy. His ideas were novel, he claimed, at least in the sense of amalgamating ideas and practices from different disciplines and 'tho several may be more capable of it, yet none can be more willing to communicate it to the publick than I am.'[66] Moreover, Connor strongly asserted a freethinking impulse: 'Since therefore reason and experience

---

*Guillaume de Waldegrave ... contenant une dissertation physique sur la continuité de plusieurs os, a l'occasion d'une fabrique surprenante d'un tronc de squelltte humain, etc* (Paris, 1693?) Connor also published: *Ζωοθανασιον θαυμαστον seu mirabilis viuentium interitus in charonea Neapolitana crypta. Dissertatio physica, etc.* (Cologne or Venice? 1694). The latter contains a paper titled: 'Nouissimum vesuuii montis incendium'.

[60] *Details of a large tumour by M B Connor*, n.d., (ARS, MS Cl.P/12i/37). This is described as an offprint from a 'journal' printed in Paris, presumably the *Journal des Sçavans*, and was apparently read to the Royal Society on 13 May 1691[recte 1693?].

[61] This contained four separately paginated papers: 'De antris lethiferis'; 'De montis vesuuii incendio'; 'De stupendo ossium coalitu'; 'De immani hypogastrii sarcomate'.

[62] 'An extract of a letter to Sir Charles Walgrave, published in French at Paris, giving an account of an extraordinary human skeleton, whose vertebrae of the back, the ribs and several bones down to the *os sacrum*, were all firmly united into one solid bone, without jointing or cartilage', *Philosophical Transactions*, 19 (1695): 21–7.

[63] Dalitz and Stone, 'Doctor Bernard Connor', 23.

[64] Connor, *History*, vol. 1, pp. 342–50, vol. 2, pp. 82–9, 91–7[II]; Connor, *Evangelium Medici*, pp. 181–3.

[65] Connor, *History*, vol. 1, pp. 289–310[II]; Connor, *Evangelium Medici*, pp. 1–34, 23–38[II].

[66] Connor, *History*, vol. 1, p. 310[II]. His application of a mechanical philosophy to animal oeconomy (that is, physiology) was certainly not new *per se*. The College of Physicians had adopted iatromechanism from the 1660s. On this issue see Theodore Brown, *The mechanical philosophy and the 'animal oeconomy'* (New York: Ayer Publishing, 1981), pp. 121–91.

are our only guides, no body is to take it amiss if I censure such as wrote before me, with as much justice as they did their predecessors; for I'm sworn to no master.'[67]

Szpilczynski has maintained that Connor's medical theory amalgamated aspects of Galenic ideas, Paracelsian and iatrochemical influences, and late seventeenth-century mechanical approaches.[68] Drawing on a range of sources, Connor adopted a materialist and atomist theory of the human body and emphasised the importance of anatomy and chemistry for understanding how the body was structured and, ultimately, the effects of remedies for diseases.[69] His medical theory stressed the importance of the circulation of the blood and the role of 'animal spirits': 'The life of man is the correspondence between the soul and the body; but the life of the body is the natural motion of the blood and spirits'.[70] Health depended on the 'due disposition' of the 'organs, springs and humours of the body'. Diseases arose from a 'ferment or matter' caused by some external source, and had their origin in the blood, which transferred them around the body. These destroyed the body's disposition, leading to death. Medicines therefore operated on the 'whole mass of the blood' and could be divided into two classes: 'evacuating' and 'alterating'.[71] Above all Connor rejected Galenic pessimism, for if the 'operations of the body are performed by natural causes without miracles' and diseases and their cures can be made 'intelligible', then 'that vulgar maxim, that there's no certainty in physick, will be found most erroneous'.[72]

While Connor considered 'the theory and practice of physick ... one and the same thing', there is little evidence on the nature of Connor's medical practice in London.[73] However, one pamphlet suggests that he was one of those to take advantage of the new opportunities that opened up in the aftermath of the Glorious Revolution for the treatment of scrofula, or the king's evil.[74] In 1697, Maurice Tobin, an apothecary, published a pamphlet announcing to the public that he had a secret cure for the disease.[75] Tobin had acquired the cure from Timothy Beaghan,

---

[67] Connor, *History*, vol. 1, p. 310[II]. This is a reference to the motto of the Royal Society.

[68] Szpilczynski, 'Bernard O'Connor from Ireland', 766–71.

[69] Connor, *History*, vol. 1, p. 302–10[II].

[70] Connor, *History*, vol. 1, p. 298[II]. Generated from blood in the brain, animal spirits 'furnish the soul with ideas in the brain, and convey'd through the nerves to all parts of the body, they are the causes of motion in the muscles and of sense in the five organs, which convey the impression of exterior bodies to the soul.' (p. 297[II]).

[71] Connor, *History*, vol. 1, pp. 298–9[II].

[72] Connor, *History*, vol. 1, pp. 292[II].

[73] Connor, *History*, vol. 1, pp. 292[II].

[74] This was despite Connor's argument that a detailed knowledge base was essential to good medical practice and his rejection of 'quacks and other ignorant pretenders': see Connor, *History*, vol. 1, p. 302[II].

[75] Maurice Tobin, *A true account of the celebrated secret of Mr Timothy Beaghan, lately killed at the Five Bells Tavern in the Strand, famous for curing the King's Evil*

an illiterate, one-legged ex-soldier, who had in turn acquired it from his wife. After Beaghan was murdered at the Five Bells Tavern in London, Tobin, who had acted as a front for him, sought to publicise the cure.[76] To avoid conflict with the Royal College of Physicians, Tobin imparted the secret to Bernard Connor: 'being an expert anatomist, and well versed in medicines, and in the practice of physick, and having experience myself of his skill in curing often intricate diseases, I have communicated this secret to him, and desired him to appear in it'.[77] Connor sought confirmation that the ingredients were the same as those used by Beaghan and to assure themselves that the result was not harmful, both Tobin and he drank a bottle, which they 'found very agreeable'.[78] Arising out of this, Tobin requested that 'all persons infested with the king's evil, may repair to Doctor Connor in Bowstreet for his advice', while Tobin confined himself to the preparation of the medicine.[79] It seems reasonable to assume that both Tobin and Beaghan, like Connor, were of Irish extraction.[80]

## The genesis and content of *Evangelium Medici*

As he established himself in London, Connor was also working on a treatise on miracles. The origin of this work, according to the author, lay in his participation in a number of 'disputes' in London at which miracles were denied.[81] This was a subject on which Connor was well versed: he had, he observed, 'formerly discoursed with others, both in this and other countries, upon the same subject, and had some years ago drawn up a rude scheme of an essay towards the clearing of this point'.[82] The novelty of Connor's contribution to the debates about miracles was his argument that it was possible to illustrate the manner in which miracles occurred in terms acceptable to human reason.[83] Connor's colleagues urged him to publish his work and he reluctantly prepared a draft essay. However, this was made

---

(London, 1697).

[76] Beaghan was murdered on 10 August 1697. William Bird was later acquitted of the murder (The Proceedings of the Old Bailey, ref. F16970901–1 [www.oldbaileyonline.org] accessed on 30 July 2008).

[77] Tobin, *A true account*, pp. 6–7.

[78] Tobin, *A true account*, p. 7.

[79] Tobin, *A true account*, p. 7.

[80] On the conflict between the apothecaries and the Royal College of Physicians in the 1690s see Cook, *The decline of the old medical regime*, pp. 227–240. An apothecary called William Lilley was one of the executors named in Connor's will (Dalitz and Stone, 'Doctor Bernard Connor', 32).

[81] Connor, *History*, vol. 1, p. 311[II]; Connor, *Evangelium Medici*, epistola, pp. i–ii.

[82] Connor, *History*, vol. 1, p. 312[II].

[83] Connor, *History*, vol. 1, p. 312[II]; Connor, *Evangelium Medici*, epistola, pp. ii–iii.

public against his wishes, and was not well received. Therefore, Connor explained, 'I at last resolv'd to publish it as soon as I could, seeing persons industriously reported things I never thought of'.[84] In the meantime, Connor published two defences of his work in 1696, one addressed to the Archbishop of Canterbury, the other addressed to 'D.B.M.'[85] The controversy contributed to further publication difficulties. The Royal Society refused to grant a license to the book on the grounds that the subject matter was 'theological and the council therefore thought it not within the cognizance of the society, so it was judged proper not to meddle with it'.[86] The Royal College of Physicians was less reticent and granted imprimatur on 9 April 1697.[87] *Evangelium Medici* was published in London later in the year. The work generated considerable interest, for a second edition appeared in 1697 and, following Connor's premature death two further editions were published abroad in Amsterdam in 1699 and in Jena in 1724.

*Evangelium Medici* posited three states of the human body: natural or healthy, diseased, and supernatural.[88] Flowing from his mechanical conception of the human body, Connor argued that it was possible to, 'reconcile' miracles with the:

> structure of the human body and with reason ... For since the human body is entirely composed of matter, and since all this matter arises from countless particles which are separate one from another and possess diverse bulk, position and shape, its condition cannot be changed or preserved in a supernatural manner without the bulk, position and shape of its particles being either varied or preserved.[89]

Connor argued that natural phenomena are produced as a result of three laws of motion:

---

[84] Connor, *History*, vol. 1, p. 313[II]; Connor, *Evangelium Medici*, epistola, p. iv.

[85] *A Copy of a Letter sent his grace \*\*\* from Dr. Connor ... concerning his medicina arcana de mystico corporis humani statu: or, a Latin treatise, in which he designs to explain the miracles relating to human bodies, by the principles of physick* (London, 1696); *A letter to his worthy friend, D. B. M. from Dr. Connor ... concerning his medicina arcana de mystico corporis humani statu: or, a Latin treatise, in which he designs to explain the miracles relating to human bodies, by the principles of physick* (London, 1696).

[86] See Dalitz and Stone, 'Doctor Bernard Connor', 30.

[87] Connor, *Evangelium Medici*, unpaginated.

[88] Connor, *Evangelium Medici*, pp. 1–41.

[89] Connor, *Evangelium Medici*, pp. 36–7. All subsequent translations are by Mr J.R.T. Holland.

1. A body which is moved is moved by another body.
2. A body placed in motion communicates the motion to bodies it encounters, provided that they are not of a huge bulk.
3. A body placed in motion always continues in motion until it communicates the motion to a second body.[90]

Connor then considered the 'true nature of a miracle'.[91] He rejected the proposition that a miracle is 'an amazing effect which strikes the senses with consternation and surpasses the grasp of the intellect'.[92] Many natural phenomena were astonishing, but they were not miracles. Connor also rejected what he termed the 'common' definition of a miracle, that is, 'a supernatural phenomenon produced at the particular command of God'.[93] Connor argued that both natural and supernatural phenomena flowed from God.[94] Since the motion of bodies flowed not from the bodies themselves, but from God, this 'common' definition did not sufficiently distinguish natural and supernatural effects. Therefore Connor proposed a third definition:

> A miracle can therefore be correctly defined as an effect produced by the suspension of a law of nature, or of motion. Yet laws can only be suspended by Him who established the laws. Since then the laws of motion have been sanctioned by God alone, they can only be suspended or abolished by God alone. And consequently God alone will be able to perform miracles, or at the least be able to grant to others the power to perform them.[95]

Moreover, Connor argued that miracles occur 'for some particular purpose ... so as to reveal God's own decrees'.[96]

The real novelty in Connor's argument is in the next step. He argued that one can conceive of the effects produced by the suspension of the laws of motion, that is, miracles.[97] Just as there were three laws of motion, Connor argued that there were three ways in which they could be suspended:

1. The body will be able to move without the occasion of the motions of a

---

[90] Connor, *Evangelium Medici*, p. 57.
[91] Connor, *Evangelium Medici*, p. 58.
[92] Connor, *Evangelium Medici*, pp. 58–9.
[93] Connor, *Evangelium Medici*, p. 60.
[94] Connor, *Evangelium Medici*, pp. 41, 56.
[95] Connor, *Evangelium Medici*, p. 62.
[96] Connor, *Evangelium Medici*, pp. 62–3.
[97] Connor, *Evangelium Medici*, p. 63.

second body that collides with it.
2. On the given occasion of the colliding body, the body will be incapable of motion.
3. The body placed in motion will be able suddenly to lose its motion, without communicating the same motion to a second ambient body.[98]

Connor claimed that this accounted for a series of biblical miracles, to which he confined his discussion.[99]

However, his mechanical philosophy of the human body also ensured that some alleged miracles could not happen. Specifically, he rejected the possibility of bilocation.[100] Clearly different parts of bodies could exist in different places and human bodies could be multiplied, for example, through reproduction.[101] However, because the human body 'is in truth nothing except matter', bilocation is impossible.[102] Yet, Connor still conceived the possibility that God could, in 'a sort of hitherto and unheard of, and yet unique manner' act on a human body so that it was in two places at once, though not with the same size. Even in this case, Connor was unable to accept that a person's soul could be in two places at once.[103] In the end, therefore, Connor concluded that bilocation could not happen. He claimed that he had previously revealed his argument to 'a large number of candid, honest and learned men' who advised him not to make it public, for fear of 'new quarrels among academics ... civil disagreements, and possibly to certain disturbing errors', to which Connor had agreed.[104]

For the most part, *Evangelium Medici* concentrated on the human body. However, Connor also explored the possibility of miracles involving the soul. Human beings, argued Connor, were composed of both matter and rational soul, which performed operations of mental reflection.[105] The human soul reflected on something when an external body impacted on the five senses. In other words, knowledge was derived from sense experience and 'it is not surprising if recently born children have no, or only very few, concepts of things'.[106] As a parallel to the suspension of the laws of motion relating to the body, Connor argued that there were two ways in which God could suspend the laws of motion governing the relationship between the senses and the soul: first, the soul could think without the impact of a sense experience; and, second, the soul would be unable to think even

---

[98] Connor, *Evangelium Medici*, p. 64. Connor pointed out that the suspension of motion is not the same as the suspension of the law of motion (p. 66).
[99] Connor, *Evangelium Medici*, pp. 58–159.
[100] Connor, *Evangelium Medici*, pp. 160–171; Connor, *History*, vol. 1, p. 315–16[II].
[101] Connor, *Evangelium Medici*, pp. 163, 167–8.
[102] Connor, *Evangelium Medici*, p. 169.
[103] Connor, *Evangelium Medici*, p. 170.
[104] Connor, *Evangelium Medici*, p. 170–71.
[105] Connor, *Evangelium Medici*, p. 194.
[106] Connor, *Evangelium Medici*, p. 196.

when a sense experience was impressed on one of the five senses.[107] This opened up the possibility of miracles not accounted for in terms of the human body alone: knowledge of the 'nature and existence of things'; abilities of prediction; dream interpretation; perception of 'spectres, ghosts and other phantasms of shadow, though they do not truly affect the organs of the senses'; and inability to perceive a sensation despite interaction with an object, for example, a hand placed in boiling water.[108]

Connor's *Evangelium Medici* was evidently controversial. The Newtonian John Keill attacked the work in 1698, adducing it as evidence that 'our moderns are as wild, extravagant, and presumptuous as any of the ancients'.[109] In response, Connor offered a defensive English language account in an appendix to the first volume of his *History of Poland*.[110] It was published as a letter to 'his Reverend Friend Dean J.R.', tentatively identified by Davis Coakley as Dean John Richards of Ardfert in county Kerry.[111] The letter provided a convenient summary of his argument, but he also took the opportunity to reject accusations that he had encroached on theology. Connor insisted that he had not sought to prove that particular miracles had or had not happened; this was the responsibility of clergymen. Rather he had explained 'the mode and mechanism with which we may conceive how they might have been performed'.[112] He had undertaken his work with the advice of senior clergymen and had limited himself to aspects of the miraculous in which physicians were competent to judge, citing as an example the alleged miracle he had witnessed in Rome. Physicians versed in anatomy and chemistry, he maintained, were especially well placed to judge between natural and supernatural occurrences and to unmask trickery posing as the miraculous. As a further example, Connor cited Pope Innocent XII's imprisonment of the alchemist Giuseppe Francesco Borri at the Castel Sant'Angelo in August 1695, implicitly raising suspicions. Connor and his colleagues therefore offered protection against the Catholic trickery which, as Raymond Gillespie has pointed out, so worried seventeenth-century Protestants.[113] In the end, Connor, accepting that his theory may not have been well understood, 'resolv'd not to meddle any more with matters of this kind, but to apply myself entirely to the practice of physick'.[114]

---

[107] Connor, *Evangelium Medici*, p. 197.
[108] Connor, *Evangelium Medici*, pp. 200–201.
[109] John Keill, *An examination of Dr Burnet's theory of the earth* (2nd edn, Oxford and London: H. Clements and S. Harding, 1734), pp. 9–10.
[110] Connor, *History*, vol. 1, pp. 311–22[II].
[111] Coakley, *Masters*, p. 22.
[112] Connor, *History*, vol. 1, p. 317[II].
[113] Connor, *History*, vol. 1, pp. 317–322. Connor mistakenly wrote Clement X.
[114] Connor, *History*, vol. 1, p. 322.

## Conclusion

Dalitz and Stone concluded that 'it would seem that questions of real religious or national loyalty were of less importance to Connor than the need to gain the approval of the medical and social establishment, without which he could not have practised his profession so successfully'.[115] The establishment of a professional patronage network was clearly an important consideration for a recently arrived migrant. This may have induced Connor to publish his work on miracles in what must ultimately be deemed a misjudged attempt to overcome suspicions concerning his political and religious allegiances. Shortly after his arrival in England, Connor appears to have changed his name from O'Connor to Connor and conformed to the established church.[116] However, as a French-educated Irish Catholic, Connor was clearly vulnerable to allegations of disloyalty. In 1695, Sir William Trumbull, a government official who maintained a network of informers and who was instrumental in uncovering the Jacobite Fenwick plot, received information from Oxford that Connor had left the city when it was discovered that 'his work was to get Ireland out of the English hands'.[117] The same source later informed Trumbull that Connor was a French spy.[118] These allegations were not taken seriously, but suspicions relating to Connor's religious beliefs may have had more foundation. Connor fell ill in 1698. He requested in his will that a local Church of England minister, William Hayley, would preach a sermon at his funeral, so Hayley attended him two days before his death. Hayley assumed that part of his motivation was to overcome accusations of heterodoxy. Therefore he questioned Connor closely on his religious beliefs, and especially on miracles, to which he provided satisfactory answers. Hayley's sermon later recounted that 'when I discoursed him on the subject of that book of his, which occasion'd suspicion of his principles, he declared that he had no intention to prejudice religion thereby'.[119] Following a second discussion, Hayley concluded that Connor had 'sufficiently purged himself from the imputation of deism, socinianism or popery, I lookt on him as a true penitent member of the Church of England, and I gave him the

---

[115] Dalitz and Stone, 'Doctor Bernard Connor', 32.

[116] For discussion of his name change see Dalitz and Stone, 'Doctor Bernard Connor', 18; Blumberg and Blumberg, 'Bernard Connor', 350. Hayley's *Sermon* noted that he converted to the Church of England shortly after arrival in England (p. 28).

[117] Dr Robert George to Sir William Trumbull, 16 July 1695 in HMC, *Report on the manuscripts of the Marquess of Downshire*, 1, part 2 (London: Her Majesty's Stationary Office, 1924), pp. 508–9.

[118] George to Trumbull, 24 July 1695 in HMC, *Downshire*, p. 516. The same collection contains an anonymous letter addressed to William III reporting Connor's movements on the continent in 1694, though the letter is undated (ibid., p. 603). Trumbull was well aware of an Irish dimension to Jacobite plotting (Éamonn Ó Ciardha, *Ireland and the Jacobite cause, 1685–1766: a fatal attachment* (Dublin: FCP, 2002), pp. 91, 98).

[119] Hayley, *Sermon*, p. 30

sacrament'.[120] Hayley later discovered that Connor was also visited by an Irish Catholic priest, who administered the last rites with Connor's permission, though Hayley concluded that Connor's 'judgment was now quite decayed, and that he did not know what he did'.[121] Connor died on 30 October 1698.[122]

Was Hayley's conclusion correct? The evidence of *Evangelium Medici* is that Connor was operating within an orthodox Church of England theology of the miraculous. Connor accepted that the age of miracles had ended and his references were to biblical miracles.[123] He was pointedly critical of perceived 'Catholic' miracles.[124] *Evangelium Medici* was not a veiled deist tract and it seems more reasonable to conclude that it was one aspect of Connor's attempts to establish a medical reputation and practice in London by raising his social, professional and intellectual status in the face of suspicions aroused by his Irish Catholic background, his continental connections and his novel medical ideas. The choice of subject matter may have been dangerous, but it was also topical. In late 1695 John Toland's *Christianity not Mysterious* had shocked readers. Toland and Connor were of a similar age and had been raised as Catholics in remote parts of Ireland (if Connor's origins lay in county Kerry). Connor must have been well aware of the sensational impact of Toland's work. Toland was a vocal character in the coffee houses of Oxford not long before Connor gave popular anatomy demonstrations in the city and both men knew James Tyrrell. In *Christianity not Mysterious* Toland rejected, as unintelligible, beliefs that were against or above reason. Connor's *Evangelium Medici* argued that miracles were intelligible within a mechanical philosophy of nature and the human body. As Connor noted: 'By this I hope to convince our scepticks, the Deists, who must give their assent, when they have the same evident reason to conceive the possibility, and consequently to believe the truth of such miraculous effects, that are authentically related, as they

---

[120] Hayley, *Sermon*, pp. 31–2.

[121] Hayley, *Sermon*, p. 33.

[122] His essay on the anatomy of muscles was published posthumously in John Browne's *Myographia Nova: or, a graphical description of all the muscles in the humane body, as they arise in dissection* (London, 1698). The work was first published in 1681. It was later demonstrated that Browne's text was plagiarised. Connor's essay first appeared in the 1698 edition. On Browne see K.F. Russell, 'John Browne, 1642–1702, a seventeenth-century surgeon, anatomist and plagiarist', *Bulletin of the History of Medicine*, 33 (1959): 393–414, 503–75.

[123] Connor provided a list of biblical references for miracles discussed in his text (*Evangelium Medici*, pp. 205–8).

[124] Alexandra Walsham has argued recently that miracles played an important role in the counter-reformation missionary effort in sixteenth and seventeenth-century England; see 'Miracles and the Counter-Reformation mission to England', *Historical Journal*, 46/4 (2003): 779–815.

have to conceive that straw can burn in a flaming fire'.[125] It is possible therefore to read *Evangelium Medici,* in part at least, as an early response to *Christianity not Mysterious.*

Bernard Connor was not a deist, but his work reflects an increasing scepticism concerning miracle claims at the end of the seventeenth century and illustrates how medicine played an important role in that process. Connor wished to chart a middle way between outright denial and simple credulousness. While he was a self-conscious free-thinker, keen to disseminate novel ideas, Connor believed that the most recent theories concerning the workings of the human body could be developed to explain and reinforce biblical miracles. In doing so, he presented a radical accommodation of the mechanical philosophy and the supernatural that reflected a significant tendency among mechanical philosophers in later seventeenth-century England.[126] However, Connor stands out on account of his Irish Catholic background. His explicit rejection of Aristotelianism in favour of an amalgam of medical and natural philosophical ideas illustrates how Irish Catholics educated in French universities could develop novel, even radical, ways of thinking.[127] While very different to John Toland, Bernard Connor also represents something of the early Irish Enlightenment in his appeal to 'experience and reason as our only guides'.[128] Moreover, his life and career suggest that scholars should pay closer attention to role of Irish Catholic doctors in the development of early modern intellectual as well as medical history.

---

[125] Connor, *History,* vol. 1, p. 314[II]. Connor made a very similar point at the start of *Evangelium Medici*: 'I have promised myself that those Pyrrhos and deists in our religion will be convinced and will at once give their assent at least to those miracles which the most reliable authors record, since they will realize that these same events occur no less clearly than the stubble burns when fire is applied' (Epistola, p. v). He also noted that unusual events which were mistakenly taken for miracles had 'given so great an occasion to scepticism and increase of Deism' (Connor, *History,* vol. 1, p. 314[II]).

[126] See Shaw, *Miracles,* pp. 74–97, 144–73. Peter Harrison has argued that a late seventeenth- and early eighteenth-century group of Newtonians shifted the debate in a new direction: see 'Newtonian Science, miracles and the laws of nature', *Journal of the History of Ideas,* 56 (1996): 531–53.

[127] Cf. Liam Chambers, *Michael Moore, c.1639–1726: Provost of Trinity, Rector of Paris* (Dublin: FCP, 2005); Liam Chambers, 'Irish Catholics and Aristotelian scholastic philosophy in early modern France, c.1600–c.1750' in James McEvoy and Michael Dunne (eds), *The Irish contribution to European scholastic thought* (forthcoming 2009). While Connor was influenced by Cartesianism, he rejected some aspects of Descartes' thought. See Connor, *History,* vol. 1, p. 304[II].

[128] Connor, *History,* vol. 1, p. 310[II].

Chapter 4
# Medicine, Religion and Social Mobility in Eighteenth- and Early Nineteenth-Century Ireland

Laurence Brockliss

According to the 1851 census, there were 3,649 male medical practitioners in Ireland, 1,223 physicians, 1,864 surgeons and apothecaries, and 562 druggists, chemists and other unspecified healers. If the Irish women who declared themselves to be midwives or nurses are added to this number, then there were some 7,000 people across the island in the mid-nineteenth century offering some sort of medical care, or one medical practitioner per 933 inhabitants. Compared with England and Wales where the ratio was one to 302, Ireland was (to use the jargon of the *Annales*) under-medicalised.[1] There again, the 1851 census only reveals those who described their occupation as medicine or medicine-related. It provides information about full-time, trained practitioners but is silent about the medical penumbra, the countless part-time healers – clergymen, faith healers, ladies-bountiful, bone-setters, wart-charmers, potion-sellers, and so on – who were frequently and chiefly found in the countryside. It is more than likely that in a rural country such as Ireland, fringe healers and alternative practitioners outnumbered the educated and were the first port of call for the sick poor.[2]

What the medical provision for Ireland was like in the seventeenth and eighteenth centuries on the other hand is still more difficult to establish. Before 1858 and the establishment of medical registration throughout the United Kingdom, medicine on both sides of the Irish Sea was an unregulated occupation. In most parts of Central and Western Europe, medicine in the late middle ages and the sixteenth and seventeenth centuries had become a corporate profession

---

[1] Penelope J. Corfield, *Power and the professions in Britain 1700–1850* (London and New York: Routledge, 1995), p. 158 (table). On the *Annales* and the concept of 'medicalization', see the critical essays in Roy Porter and Andrew Wear (eds), *Problems and methods in the history of medicine* (London: Croom Helm, 1987), pt. i.

[2] For the range of 'popular' medical practice in two parts of Europe, see David Gentilcore, *Healers and healing in early-modern Italy* (Manchester: Manchester University Press, 1998), especially chapter 4, and Matthew Ramsey, *Professional and popular medicine in France 1770–1830: the social world of medical practice* (Cambridge: CUP, 1988), pt. ii.

divided into three distinct branches: physic, surgery and pharmacy. Physic – the science of medical diagnosis and prescription – was a learned skill; surgery and pharmacy were its subordinate arts. Physicians therefore had to have a university degree in medicine, while surgeons and apothecaries learnt on the job: they were initially apprenticed, then served for a time as travelling journeymen before being examined and admitted as masters by a local guild. Such guilds, which had a legal monopoly of practice, were to be found in most continental towns by 1700, and in the larger cities even graduate physicians had to become members of a specialist corporation before they could set up their plate. In the course of the eighteenth century, moreover, the regulations became even tighter as the state began to take a hand in licensing medical practitioners and demand that surgeons as well as physicians should be formally trained. In Spain, for instance, no one in theory could practise any branch of medicine in town or country unless he had first been examined by officials appointed by the king's *protomedicato* or chief physician. From the turn of the nineteenth century no one could become a surgeon who had not attended one of the new specialist colleges of surgery.[3] This is not to say that there was not a legion of uncertified healers in every continental state, nor that certificated practitioners kept to their last. It does mean, though, that the unlicensed and the boundary-breaker operated outside the law and could be challenged in the courts.[4] It also means that the number of licensed practitioners in the different regions of mainland Western Europe can be recovered with some precision as the work of Jean-Pierre Goubert and François Lebrun on Brittany and Anjou has demonstrated.[5]

In the British Isles in contrast medicine never developed into a corporate profession. Under the common law of England and Ireland, anyone (male or female) could practise medicine, subject only to the penalties of the criminal law if the patient suffered harm. The continental distinction between trained and untrained practitioners was understood, as was the distinction between the learned art of physic and the manual crafts of surgery and pharmacy, but neither

---

[3] For an introduction to medical corporatism, see Laurence Brockliss, 'Organization, training and the medical marketplace in the eighteenth century', in Peter Elmer (ed.), *The healing arts: health, disease and society in Europe, 1500–1800* (Manchester: Manchester University Press, 2004), chapter 13. For the specific cases of France and Spain, see Laurence Brockliss and Colin Jones, *The medical world of early modern France* (Oxford: OUP, 2007), chapters 3 and 8, and M.C. Burke, *The Royal College of San Carlos: surgery and Spanish medical reform in the late eighteenth century* (Durham, NC: Duke University Press, 1977), chapters 3–5.

[4] For boundary-breaking by certificated practitioners, see Brockliss and Jones, *Medical world*, pp. 605–17.

[5] François Lebrun, *Les hommes et la mort en Anjou aux XVIIe et XVIIIe siècles* (Paris: Editions de l'Ecole des Hautes Etudes en Sciences Sociales, 1975), chapter 6; Jean-Pierre Goubert, *Malades et médecins en Bretagne 1770–1790* (Rennes: Université de Bretagne, 1974), chapter 2.

had general legal warranty.⁶ In the eighteenth century, medical corporations of the continental kind did exist in the three capital cities and Glasgow, but only London had long-established charted communities of physicians, barber-surgeons (from whom the surgeons seceded in the 1740s to form a separate corporation) and apothecaries. In Dublin a college of physicians was initially set up in the 1660s (which from 1692 operated a *numerus clausus* of 14 with regard to its fellowship), but there was no formal society of apothecaries until 1745 and no chartered corporation of surgeons, distinct from the Barber-Surgeons' Guild, until 1784.⁷ In the eighteenth century, moreover, the rights and privileges of these corporations, though important, were limited. Though they had a theoretical monopoly over the practice of their particular branch of the art within the city and its suburbs, they had little chance of legally enforcing this right after a landmark case of 1704. In that year the London College of Physicians took an apothecary called Rose to court for practising physic. The case was appealed to the House of Lords, and the judges found for the boundary-breaker.⁸ Thereafter the authority of the medical corporations in all three kingdoms was greatly diminished. To all intents and purposes anyone could practise within their jurisdictions without being licensed by the relevant medical guild.

It would be going too far to represent the medical world of eighteenth-century Britain and Ireland as a free-for-all, or a market place where the consumer was king, as the late Roy Porter continually did when writing about England.⁹ The age-old distinctions, if not enshrined or protected in law, did have social meaning. Graduate physicians, specialist surgeons and apothecaries were visible and honoured parts of the medical community in the capital cities and larger towns, and, where possible, the rich and socially prominent liked to use their services. It was the poor who flocked to empirics; the rich, again *pace* Porter, tended to seek their services only *in extremis*. But the educated medical practitioner had to

---

⁶ In theory in England and Ireland would-be healers were supposed to receive a licence from their local bishop but in the eighteenth century no one bothered.

⁷ J.D.H. Widdess, *A history of the Royal College of Physicians of Ireland* (London: E. and S. Livingstone, 1963), chapters 1–7; and J.D.H. Widdess, *The Royal College of Surgeons in Ireland and its Medical Schools, 1784–1984* (3rd edn, Dublin: Royal College of Surgeons, 1984), pp. 5–49. Glasgow had only one distinctive medical guild: a combined 'faculty' of physicians and surgeons (founded 1599); the city also had an 'incorporation' of surgeons and barbers (1656). See also Lyons chapter 1 and Sneddon, chapter 6, in this collection.

⁸ Sir George Clark, *A history of the Royal College of Physicians of London* (2 vols, Oxford: OUP, 1964–66), vol. 2, pp. 476–79. See also Sneddon chapter 6 in this collection for reference to this case.

⁹ Among his many books, see in particular, *Health for sale: quackery in England 1660–1850* (Manchester: Manchester University Press, 1989); and with Dorothy Porter, *Patient's progress: doctors and doctoring in eighteenth-century England* (Cambridge: CUP, 1989). The term 'medical marketplace' was made popular by Hal Cook in *The decline of the old medical regime in Stuart London* (Ithaca, NY: Cornell University Press, 1986).

practise cheek by jowl with quacks and charlatans, and the theoretical divisions between the three branches of the profession easily became blurred. Outside the chief towns, apprenticed-trained medical practitioners, even occasionally graduate physicians, practised all three branches of the art and called themselves surgeon-apothecaries.[10] As a result, the structure of medical practice in the three kingdoms in the long eighteenth century is too inchoate to allow the number and distribution of medical practitioners to be easily recovered.

Admittedly, it is possible to make a stab at mapping England. A medical directory was published in the late 1770s and the early 1780s, which, if incomplete, is still informative about the geographical spread of medical practitioners across the country. Further information can be gleaned about some individual towns from trade directories.[11] In Ireland's case, however, there is no obvious route to pursue. There was no Irish medical directory before the early 1840s, and there is a dearth of trade directories before 1800, except for Dublin.[12] That said, it would be wrong to conclude that the history of Irish medical practitioners in the long eighteenth century remains statistically a closed book. I propose to examine two distinctive groups of medical practitioners: graduate physicians in the period 1640–1800 and army and navy surgeons during the French revolutionary wars at the turn of the nineteenth century.

**Irish graduate physicians, 1640–1800**

Information on the Irish graduate physicians is based on the study of the extant matriculation and graduation registers of a number of Europe's universities. The figures are imperfect (many registers are lost and many others have not been perused), but it is safe to say that some 1,300 Irishmen gained a medical degree across the period 1640 to 1800. The number who did so expanded dramatically from the end of the seventeenth century. Before 1670 only a handful are known to have graduated in medicine, but thereafter the number steadily swelled in stages to reach a peak in the 1730s, when some 150 Irishmen received a degree. Although the decennial total fell dramatically in the following decade, it slowly expanded again to reach a second peak at an even higher level in the 1780s.

---

[10] The best study of provincial general practice is Irvine Loudon, *Medical care and the general practitioner, 1750–1850* (Oxford: OUP, 1986).

[11] [Samuel Foart Simmons], *The medical register for the year 1779 [1780, 1783]*. For the number of practitioners outside London recorded in the 1783 edn, broken down by county, see Jane Lane, 'The role of apprenticeship in eighteenth-century medical education in England', in W. F. Bynum and Roy Porter (eds), *William Hunter and the eighteenth-century medical world* (Cambridge: CUP, 1985), pp. 80–81 (table).

[12] [Henry Croly], *Irish medical directory* (1843 and 1846). The 1846 edn lists 1,989 physicians and surgeons and 513 apothecaries, 500 fewer than in the 1851 census.

Table 4.1 Number of graduates in medicine from Ireland per decade 1640–9 to 1790–9[a]

| | Angers | Leiden plus other Dutch universities | Leuven | Montpellier | Prague | Reims | Dublin | Edinburgh | Glasgow | Total |
|---|---|---|---|---|---|---|---|---|---|---|
| 1640–49 | 10 | | | | | | 1 | | | 11 |
| 1650–59 | 2 | 1 | 2 | | | 2 | 2 | | | 9 |
| 1660–69 | 5 | 1 | 2 | | | 3 | 3 | | | 14 |
| 1670–79 | 13 | | 3 | | 1 | 1 | 1 | | | 19 |
| 1680–89 | 2 | 2 | 1 | | | 21 | 7 | | | 33 |
| 1690–99 | 6 | 5 | 3 | | 1 | 18 | 6 | | | 39 |
| 1700–1709 | | 8 | 3 | 3 | 1 | 21 | 3 | | | 39 |
| 1710–19 | 2 | 4 | 7 | 6 | 2 | 62 | 9 | | | 92 |
| 1720–29 | 1 | 6 | 2 | 9 | 3 | 59 | 8 | | 2 | 90 |
| 1730–39 | 5 | 5 | 3 | 22 | 5 | 117 | 9 | | 2 | 168 |
| 1740–49 | | 7 | | 8 | 7 | 57 | 9 | 8 | 1 | 97 |

|  | Angers | Leiden plus other Dutch universities | Leuven | Montpellier | Prague | Reims | Dublin | Edinburgh | Glasgow | Total |
|---|---|---|---|---|---|---|---|---|---|---|
| 1750–59 | 7 | 7 | 3 | 8 | 3 | 54 | 12 | 29 | 4 | 120 |
| 1760–69 | 11 | 11 | 2 | 2 | 1 | 66 | 12 | 14 | 2 | 110 |
| 1770–79 | 11 | 11 | 7 | 12 | 1 | 71 | 5 | 34 | 7 | 148 |
| 1780–89 | 10 | 10 | 1 | 2 |  | 39 | 2 | 83 | 37 | 174 |
| 1790–99 | 2 | 2 |  |  |  | 8 | 17 | 103 | 22 | 152 |
| Total | 46 | 80 | 39 | 72 | 25 | 600 | 105 | 271 | 77 | 1,315 |

*Sources*

Angers: 'Students from the British Isles at the ancient faculty of medicine at Angers', *Notes and Queries*, 1 April, 1933, 218–21; Leiden: R. W. Innes Smith, *English-speaking students at the University of Leyden* (London: Oliver & Boyd, 1932); Leuven: Jeroen Nilis, 'Irish students at Leuven University, 1548–1797', *Archivium Hibernicum*, 60 (2006–7): 1–304. Medical graduates at Leuven contented themselves with either the baccalaureate or the licence; they did not become doctors; Montpellier: Louis Dulieu, *La médecine à Montpellier*, vol. 4. *L'époque classique*, pt. iii, (4 vols, Avignon: Les presses universelles, 1975–1990), vol. 2 (biographical register); Prague: *A Bohemian refugee: Irish students in Prague in the eighteenth century* (Dublin 1997): pamphlet prepared for an exhibition in Trinity College Dublin, December 1997 to May 1998; Reims: BM Reims MS 1085. Dublin: G. D. Burtchaell (ed.), *Alumni Dublinenses: a register of the students, graduates, professors and provosts of Trinity College in the University of Dublin (1593–1860)* (Dublin: A. Thom & Co., 1935); Edinburgh: *Nomina ... graduum medicinae doctoris ex academia Jacobi Sexti* (Edinburgh, 1886). Glasgow: W. Addison, *A roll of the graduates of the University of Glasgow from 31 December 1727 to 31 December 1897 with short biographical notes* (Glasgow: Maclehose, 1898); Medical students from Ireland did graduate from other French and continental European universities, but only in very small numbers, for example Hans Sloane took a degree at Orange in 1683. A few also took degrees from St Andrews and the two Aberdeen universities, where doctorates could be had on demand, but again hardly any: only eight Irishmen graduated from Aberdeen in the period.

Note: A few had doctorates from more than one university. Thus two had degrees from Leiden and Dublin, two from Reims and Dublin, and one from Reims and Leiden. The handful of doctorates given by Dublin that were awarded to medics not born in Ireland are not included in the totals.

Significantly, most medical graduates in the years 1670 to 1770 took their degree on the continent. It was only in the 1780s and 1790s that the number of Irishmen graduating in a university in the British Isles exceeded the number taking their degree on mainland Europe. Even then the Irish continued to leave Ireland to gain their doctorate, for the new favoured port of call was Edinburgh and to a lesser extent Glasgow. During the seventeenth and eighteenth centuries there appear to have been only six continental faculties that frequently bestowed medical degrees on Irishmen: three in France (Angers, Montpellier and Reims), two in the Low Countries (Leiden and Leuven) and one in the Holy Roman Empire (Prague). Of these, Reims was by far the most important, graduating 554 Irish doctors of medicine in the course of the eighteenth century alone (see Table 4.1).

The number of Irish graduates in medicine in the eighteenth century is impressive. Admittedly, it is not staggering – a maximum of 15 to 16 per year. But it is significant when it is remembered that a degree was not required in Ireland to practise physic (even in Dublin) and that, pre-1670, there existed a virtual absence of graduates. In France, where the profession was closely regulated and the population six to eight times as large, native Frenchmen only gained 160 medical degrees each year on the eve of the Revolution, proportionally not that different.[13] Moreover, the Irish total stands up well in comparison with the number of English medical graduates across the period 1640–1800. Although England was a much more prosperous and populous kingdom, it probably only produced about 400 more graduate physicians.[14]

Unfortunately, most of the extant graduation registers seldom provide information about Irish doctors beyond their name and nationality '*hibernus*'. The Reims' register, however, allows us to identify the regional origins of medical graduates with some precision.[15] If the Reims cohort was typical (and there is no reason to suggest it was not), then Irish medical graduates in the seventeenth and eighteenth centuries were drawn from all over the island of Ireland. Given that study outside Ireland would have been expensive, it might have been expected that a significant proportion would have come from Dublin and its hinterland, the richest and most urbanised part of the country. In fact, among the Reims graduates,

---

[13] Dominique Julia and Jacques Revel, 'Les étudiants et leurs études dans la France moderne', in Dominique Julia and Jacques Revel, *Les universités européennes du XVIe au XVIIe siècle. Histoire sociale des populations étudiantes* (2 vols, Paris: EHESS, 1989), vol. 2, pp. 290–92.

[14] 1,460 English medical graduates have been identified across the period, but the figure does not include the medical doctorates awarded at Cambridge, which, given the figure for Oxford, must have been in the order of 300. Per head of the population, Scotland produced more medical graduates than either England or Ireland: just under 1,000. These totals are the result of unpublished ongoing research and may well be subject to readjustment. They can be safely taken as relative orders of magnitude, however.

[15] The Edinburgh and Leiden lists only give nationality. The Glasgow and Leuven lists sometimes give the diocese, county or parish of origin but never consistently.

less than 10 per cent came from the city and diocese of the Irish capital. In contrast the south-west and west were surprisingly well-represented. More Irishmen passed through Reims from the dioceses of Cork and Limerick than from Dublin, and impressive contingents came from relatively isolated Ardfert and Aghadoe, and Tuam. Ulster on the other hand was poorly represented, only the diocese of Armagh providing a significant cohort of graduates (see Table 4.2).

Table 4.2  Diocesan origin of Irish medical graduates at Reims in the seventeenth and eighteenth centuries[a]

| **Ecclesiastical Province of Armagh** | |
|---|---|
| Raphoe | 1 |
| Derry | 5 |
| Connor | 2 |
| Clogher | 8 |
| Armagh | 22 |
| Down | 8 |
| Dromore | 0 |
| Kilmore | 24 |
| Ardagh | 5 |
| Meath | 27 |
| Clonmacnoise | 0 |
| Total | 102 |
| **Ecclesiastical Province of Dublin** | |
| Kildare | 8 |
| Dublin | 41 |
| Leighlin | 1 |
| Ossory | 18 |
| Ferns | 4 |
| Total | 72 |
| **Ecclesiastical Province of Cashel** | |
| Waterford | 7 |
| Lismore | 6 |
| Cloyne | 13 |
| Cork | 49 |
| Ross | 0 |
| Ardfert and Aghadoe | 36 |
| Limerick | 46 |
| Emly | 3 |
| Cashel | 37 |
| Killaloe | 28 |
| Kilfenora | 4 |
| Total | 229 |

| Ecclesiastical Province of Tuam | |
|---|---|
| Kilmacduagh | 0 |
| Clonfert | 10 |
| Tuam | 35 |
| Killala | 4 |
| Achonry | 8 |
| Elphin | 18 |
| Total | 75 |

*Source*: BM Reims MS 1054.

*Note*

[a] The total number of students whose diocesan origin is known is 478 out of 600. Students at French universities were expected to cite their home diocese. Protestant Irishmen, however, may have simply given their county or town of birth, which in many cases bears the same name as the diocese. It is thus impossible to know how many of the Reims graduates who claimed they came from Dublin, Cork or Limerick were natives of the city, the county or the diocese. As Irish dioceses were often combined, there must be also several cases where graduates gave the name of the neighbouring diocese to the one they hailed from. It is likely, for instance, that some of the 49 from Cork were born in Ross.

The predominance of the continent as a place of graduation until the 1780s is scarcely surprising. Before the second half of the eighteenth century, there was no university or any other centre of medical teaching in the British Isles that provided a proper medical education. The existing eight universities, including Dublin, which had had a medical faculty of sorts from the 1740s, did offer medical degrees, but high-quality tuition especially in practical anatomy and surgery, and bedside care had to be sought elsewhere. The situation was broadly no different for English, Welsh and Scottish medical students, who can be found travelling abroad from the early sixteenth century.[16] The lure of the continent remained unchallenged until the mid-eighteenth century. It then began to be undermined by the emergence of the Edinburgh faculty of medicine as one of the leading European centres of medical instruction (although it had only been properly established in 1726), and the concomitant development of the teaching role of the London hospitals. Following the outbreak of war with France in 1793, the pull of the European

---

[16] The chief difference in the English case was that in most decades before 1750 the majority of English graduate physicians, wherever they had trained, nearly always gained their degree in England (on the assumption that Cambridge gave as many medical degrees as Oxford each year). In the 1720s more than half appear to have graduated on the continent. Otherwise it was no more than a third, and the proportion fell rapidly from 1750 once Englishmen began to take degrees in Scotland as well. Scots graduate physicians, on the other hand, almost exclusively took their degree abroad until the 1740s; thereafter the percentage nose-dived. The Irish ceased seeking a degree on the continent some thirty or forty years after their English and Scottish counterparts.

mainland dwindled further, particularly encouraged by the emergence of Dublin and Glasgow as significant centres of medical teaching.[17]

The peculiar attraction of Reims from the 1680s requires further attention. There were a number of highly prized centres of medical instruction on the continent in the second half of the seventeenth and eighteenth centuries – Padua (though no longer as highly thought of as before 1650), Montpellier, Paris, Leiden, and, after 1750, Göttingen and Vienna, were the most famous.[18] Reims was definitely not one of them. Established in 1548, its faculty provided public lectures on medical theory throughout the seventeenth and eighteenth centuries, and from 1680 a course in anatomy and botany, but it never acquired a reputation as a centre of learning. Nor was Reims an important site of extra-faculty instruction: the only series of private lectures known to have been given there was a course in midwifery established in the town shortly before the Revolution. It was just one of some 15 or so French cities that supported minor medical faculties and whose professors offered run-of-the-mill instruction for those too lazy or too poor to seek enlightenment in a prestigious institution.[19] How then can we explain the number of Irishmen – 600 *in toto* – who gained a medical degree there? The answer lies in the corporative structure of the continental medical profession, alluded to above. No Irishman

---

[17] For Edinburgh and London, see Lisa Rosner, *Medical education in the age of improvement: Edinburgh students and apprentices 1760–1826* (Edinburgh: Edinburgh University Press, 1991), and Susan S. Lawrence, *Charitable knowledge: hospital pupils and practitioners in eighteenth-century London* (Cambridge: CUP, 1996). There is no good study of the growth of Dublin as a medical centre, but for Glasgow, see Derek Dow and Michael Moss, 'The medical curriculum at Glasgow in the early nineteenth century', *History of Universities*, 7 (1988): 227–57. Edinburgh had some 400 students at the end of the eighteenth century and was probably the most populous faculty in Europe: Friedrich Colland, *Kurzer Inbegriff von dem Ursprunge der Wissenschaften, Schulen, Academien und Universitäten in ganz Europa, besonders aber der Academien und hohen Schule zu Wien* (Vienna: Taubstummeninstitutsdruckerey; Trattner, 1796), p. 105.

[18] See Ole Grell and Andrew Cunningham (eds), *Centres of excellence: in search of the best medical education in early-modern Europe* (forthcoming). Throughout the early modern period, Padua was one of the leading centres of medical instruction in Europe but hardly any Protestant medical student from the British Isles graduated there in the eighteenth century: see E. Morpurgo, 'English physicians – "Doctorati" – at the University of Padua in the "Collegio Veneto Artista" (1617–1771)', *Proceedings of the Royal Society of Medicine*, 20 (1926–1927): 1369–80. The 'Collegio Veneto Artista' was created in 1616 as an institution where Protestants could gain a medical degree without swearing allegiance to the pope. Morpurgo also lists the Scottish and Irish graduates. The most famous English physician to study at Padua was William Harvey, who took his MD there in 1602.

[19] Basic details in A. Finot, *Les facultés de médecine de province avant la Révolution* (Paris: Le Grand, 1958). See also Laurence Brockliss, 'Medicine and the small university in eighteenth-century France', in Gian Paolo Brizzi and Jacques Verger (eds), *Le università minori in Europa (secoli XV–XIX)* (Soveria Mannelli: Rubbettino Editore, 1998), pp. 239–72.

actually studied at Reims. A separate register provides information on the prior education of those who graduated in the faculty between 1749 and 1793.[20] It is clear that the vast majority of Irish graduates – 194 out of 241 – had previously studied in Paris (see Table 4.3). They had either attended the Paris faculty, the city's surgical college (founded in the 1720s), or one or more of the many private medical schools that existed in the French capital.[21] The rest attended medical schools all over Europe – including 23 who had studied at nearby Leuven and nine at distant Prague. A handful, a sign of the changing climate, even claimed to have gained some medical training in the British Isles: three in London, five in Dublin and nine in Edinburgh. Had information existed about the prior training of the Irish graduates before 1749, it seems likely that Paris would have occupied the dominant position in the earlier period, too. On the other hand, before the mid-eighteenth century, it is clear that an important number of the graduates had passed through another leading medical centre, Leiden, a faculty unrepresented at a later date. We know that some 240 Irish medical students matriculated in the Dutch faculty between 1650 and 1799 of whom 80 graduated somewhere in the United Provinces. A further 43 took their degree at Reims, all but two before 1750.[22]

Some of the Irish graduates from Reims only spent a short time on the continent, probably less than a year. But most who had passed through Leiden or Leuven had spent a couple of years abroad, and some even longer. Ephraim Thwaites (simply described as Irish), for example, matriculated at Leiden in September 1714 after taking an MA at Glasgow in 1711. He did not graduate at Reims until May 1718. Thomas Simcockes from the Cork region was away even longer. He arrived in Leiden in December 1725 and did not take a degree at Reims until March 1731.[23] It is impossible to know the precise length of time Paris-educated graduates had been on the continent as the 1749 to 1793 register seldom records how many years of study a candidate completed. The few occasions where these details appear does suggest, however, that a number of the cohort had been away from Ireland

---

[20] BM Reims MS 2654.

[21] Paris was particularly famous for the quality of its instruction in anatomy and surgery: see Toby Gelfand, *Professionalising modern medicine: Paris surgeons and medical science and institutions in the 18th Century* (Westport: Greenwood Press, 1980). For an idea of some of the private courses available, see *Johannes Gessners Pariser Tagebuch, 1727*, ed. Urs Boschung (Bern: Hans Huber, 1985), and A. Rouxeau, *Un étudiant en médecine quimpérois (Guillaume-François Laennec) aux derniers jours de l'ancien régime* (Nantes: L'Imprimerie du 'Nouvelliste', 1926), chapters 2–6 (letters home, 1769–1772).

[22] Information from R. W. Innes Smith, *English-speaking students at the University of Leyden* (London: Oliver and Boyd, 1932). Innes Smith went through the Reims graduation register in preparing his biographical dictionary. The two Irishmen who attended Leiden post 1750 did so after graduating at Reims and therefore the fact is not recorded in BM Reims MS 2654. A handful of the Irishmen recorded in Innes Smith only turn up in the registers of other Dutch medical faculties, but it is assumed they had spent time at Leiden.

[23] Innes Smith, *English-speaking students*, pp. 212 and 233; BM Reims MS 1085, fols 120, 125.

for three or four years studying in the French capital. Some, too, were absent for a long while for they had taken their MA in France and presumably studied philosophy there, like John Hally, MD 1754 (possibly from Ballygalley, county Antrim) who spent three years in the Paris faculty and had a master's degree from Caen.[24] One graduate who had studied at Prague was abroad for at least a decade. This was John Keogh of county Dublin, who received his Reims degree in 1752; he claimed to have gained his MA at Ingolstadt in 1743, then to have spent four years studying medicine at Prague.[25]

Table 4.3   Place of previous education of Reims graduates in medicine from Ireland, 1749–93

| Academy/school | |
| --- | --- |
| Caen | 1 |
| Douai | 2 |
| Dublin | 5 |
| Edinburgh | 9 |
| London | 3 |
| Louvain | 23 |
| Montpellier | 3 |
| Paris (not faculty.) | 66 |
| Paris Faculty | 128 |
| Prague | 9 |
| Vienna | 2 |
| Unknown | 7 |
| Total | 258 |
| Two centres attended | 16 |
| (Paris and one other) | 14 |
| Three centres | 1 |
| (Paris and two others) | 1 |

[24] BM Reims MS 2654, fol. 19 (from 'Ballyalensis').
[25] BM Reims MS 2654, fol. 13.

| Academy/school | |
|---|---|
| Number of students attending more than one centre | 17 |
| Total number of students | 241 |

*Source*: BM Reims MS 2654.

The Irish then only came to Reims to graduate, and they did so because it was cheap and easy. A degree from most continental faculties brought with it the right to practise physic in the faculty town itself: it gave membership of the local corporation of physicians. It was therefore not handed over lightly. Paris was a wealthy city of 600,000 people in the eighteenth century: a medical Mecca. A doctor who practised there was promised a large income. In consequence, the faculty's doctorate was costly in time and money. It demanded that the candidate study for six years in the French capital (two in philosophy, four in medicine), required him to sustain numerous vivas and practical examinations for a further two years, and cost between 5 and 7,000 *livres* (some £200 to £300).[26] Reims, on the other hand, offered three types of doctorate: an expensive one (2,000–3,500 *livres*) for those who wanted to set up in the city (which was home to 32,000 inhabitants in 1789); a cheaper variety for native Frenchmen who were intent on practising in their home town (300 *livres*); and a third for foreigners, 'a quicky' (probably the same price) that was not valid in France. The attraction of a Reims degree for the Irish medical student who simply sought a doctoral diploma is obvious. Although the university's venal practices were a national joke – the faculty of law was just as accommodating – taking a degree *à la hâte,* as the practice was called, made good economic sense.[27] All the candidate had to do was take the morning coach

---

[26] Consequently, only a handful of doctors graduated each year: see Brockliss and Jones, *The medical world*, pp. 195–96, 482, 213, 517 (table), 603.

[27] On venality at Reims and in other French medical faculties, see Julia and Revel, 'Les étudiants et leurs études dans la France moderne', pp. 279–88. The relatively low cost of a medical degree also helps to explain the attraction of some of the other faculties in which Irish students are known to have graduated. Angers was another minor French medical faculty. An Angers doctorate for those who wished to practise in the town at the beginning of the eighteenth century cost 1,360 *livres*; in contrast a so-called *doctorat forain* cost 200 *livres* (probably about £15): see Julia and Revel, 'Les étudiants', p. 280 (table). A Leiden doctorate admittedly was expensive and prestigious (see Colland, *Kurz Inbegriff*, p. 113), so the fact that 66 of the 80 Irish students who gained a degree in the Netherlands graduated there rather than in one of the minor Dutch universities, such as Harderwijk, which gave 'easy' degrees, suggests they came from well-to-do backgrounds. The exact requirements to gain a degree at Leuven and Prague are unknown to the author, but it should be noted that some Irish students were allowed to graduate for free at the Czech university, in one case and doubtless in the others too, on condition that the new doctor did not practise

from Paris, undergo a brief oral examination, pay a token sum, and then catch the evening coach back to the French capital. This arrangement lent itself to abuse. From the comments in the Reims graduate register, some of the candidates who presented themselves for examination were clearly incompetent. James De Laney from county Tipperary, who was examined on 26 April 1777, was described as feeble. But he was awarded his degree anyway. He merely had to promise that he would continue his studies and not practise for two years.[28]

We know little about these Irish Reims graduates beyond their date of graduation, diocese of origin, and, for 40 per cent of the contingent, their earlier educational experience. They certainly did not all return home. Some became medical officers to the Irish regiments abroad or even served in foreign armies. Francis Dease from county Westmeath, who graduated at Reims in 1735, joined the Russian military after studying philosophy at Leuven and medicine at Leiden, only to die six years later at the young age of 32.[29] Some, such as Barthelomey Murrhy (Murray) of county Clare, may have set up in practice in France, even if they had no legal right to do so as. A Reims graduate in 1728, he seems to have moved to the capital, where he had presumably studied, for nine years later he regularised his position by becoming a doctor of the Paris faculty. When he died in the French capital in 1767, he was a rich man with a fine house and had already committed funds to support the education of 25 students at the city's Irish college, established in 1676 to train Catholic priests for the Irish mission. It is likely he had powerful patrons among the French Irish community.[30]

---

in the city: see *A Bohemian refugee; Irish students in Prague in the eighteenth century* (Dublin, 1997: pamphlet prepared for an exhibition in Trinity College Dublin, December 1997 to May 1998), pp. 34–35 (case of Edmund John O'Neill, MD 1737, from Dungannon, county Tyrone). Even Montpellier, though a prestigious faculty and one that demanded the candidate sustain several theses and pass a serious set of vivas and practicals in the course of six months, peculiarly gave cheap degrees: 300 *livres* in the early eighteenth century; 580 *livres* in the 1770s; moreover, if the candidate could prove he had already studied medicine for three years, he could begin his examinations on arrival: Julia and Revel, 'Les étudiants', p. 280; Rouxeau, *Un étudiant*, pp. 80–89.

[28] BM Reims MS 2564, p. 77. The Reims professors made a lot of money from 'selling' cheap degrees. One Louis-Jérome Raussin averaged 782 *livres* per annum as an examiner between 1750 and 1784: BM Reims MS 2564, pp. 403–04.

[29] BM Reims MS 1085, fol. 32; Innes Smith, *English-speaking students*, p. 65; Jeroen Nilis, 'Irish students at Leuven University, 1548-1797', *Archivium Hibernicum*, 60 (2006–2007): 1–304 (188, no. 732). Another Irish physician in a foreign army was Raymond Magrath (d. 1780), who served the Austrians: he probably trained at Leuven: see Nilis, 'Irish students', 6.

[30] BM Reims MS 1085, fol. 94; J. Brady, *Catholics and Catholicism in the eighteenth-century press* (Maynooth: Catholic Record Society of Ireland, 1965), p. 167; P. O'Connor, 'Irish clerics in the University of Paris, 1570–1770' (unpublished Ph.D. thesis, NUI Maynooth 2006), 209, 220. Once equipped with a medical doctorate, it was possible to gain a Paris degree simply by sitting the various prescribed exams over a two-year period

A few graduates appear to have settled in England. These include John Baillie (1700–1745), who took a degree at Reims in 1728, having earlier graduated with a BA from Trinity College Dublin (TCD). Once a doctor, he moved to Leiden to complete his training before settling in England, incorporating his medical degree at Cambridge and becoming physician to St George's Hospital, London. He worked at St George's from 1735 to 1744, and died the following year at Ghent whilst serving as a physician in the British army during the War of Austrian Succession.[31] Other graduates, such as the botanist Patrick Browne (1720–90), moved to the colonies. Originally from a gentry family in county Mayo, Browne spent a short time in Leiden after his graduation in 1742, later emigrating for a number of years to the West Indies, where he had already spent some time before his medical training.[32]

Most Reims graduates, though, found their way back to Ireland and became physicians in the county and port towns that comprised an affluent Protestant elite and the stirrings of a Catholic middle class. However, the dearth of Irish urban directories before the early nineteenth century, and the fact that most graduates seem to have kept a low profile, leaving no trace, means that the whereabouts of a large majority of graduates cannot be quickly uncovered. They were certainly to be found in Limerick. According to the one directory for the city – for 1769 – seven out of the 10 physicians practising in the town appear to have been Reims graduates. The most interesting amongst them was James Clanchy, who took his degree in 1765 after studying at Leuven and was a leading Limerick freemason.[33] Reims graduates also settled in Cork according to a database produced from book subscription lists.[34] Twenty-five of the 121 Reims graduates with surnames A to C turn up in this database, and at least three were based in the southern port, notably John Callanan (MD 1737) who subscribed to six different titles.[35]

---

for the same high fee. Murray was not the only Irishman practising in the French capital in the eighteenth century. Another was Andrew Cantwell FRS of Tipperary (d. 1764) who took a doctorate at Montpellier in 1729, then another at Paris in 1742: *ODNB*, *sub* Andrew Cantwell.

[31] BM Reims MS 1085, fol. 5; Innes Smith, *English-speaking students*, p. 11; Lawrence, *Charitable knowledge*, p. 343.

[32] BM Reims MS 1085, fol. 15; *ODNB*, *sub* Patrick Browne. Cf. the case of the Toulouse graduate, Daniel O'Sullivan, in Clark chapter 9 in this collection.

[33] *The Limerick Directories*, (2nd edn, Limerick, 1769), pp. 38–39; BM Reims MS 2654, fol. 45; Nilis, 'Irish Students', 223–4, no. 876. The directory lists two of the ten as simply MD, five as MDR, one as MDEd, one as MDT [Toulouse?] and one as MDLB [Leiden?]. The last in fact had studied at Leiden but graduated from Reims.

[34] Peter J. Wallis and Ruth Wallis, *Eighteenth-century medics: subscriptions, licences, apprenticeships* (Newcastle: Project for Historical Bibliography, 1985).

[35] Wallis and Wallis, *Eighteenth-century medics*, p. 98. Two different John Callanans from Cork took a degree at Reims, so this may be J.C. who graduated in 1769 (BM Reims MS1085, fol. 19). Twenty-five is a maximum; only six specifically identified themselves as MDs of Reims. Five lived outside Ireland and ten gave no place of residence.

Unsurprisingly, a not insignificant minority also set up their plate, if not immediately, in Dublin, the second largest town in the empire. Thanks to the existence of Wilson's annual *Dublin Directory* from the mid-eighteenth century, this is easily the most visible group (see Table 4.4 a–c). Fourteen of the 46 physicians in the capital in 1768 had graduated in the Champagne faculty; 14 out of the 45 ten years later. On both occasions they formed the largest contingent. Moreover, these physicians were not the only Reims graduates to be found in the capital. A number of others were practising Dublin surgeons who decided to take a medical degree, often in mid career. The most notable was George Daunt, the lithotomist and founding member of the Royal College of Surgeons, who was described as mediocre when he graduated in 1778 after studying in Paris.[36] There again hardly any Reims graduate was at the heart of the Dublin establishment. In the mid-eighteenth century one or two at most in any given year were members of the Royal College of Physicians (either fellows or licentiates).[37] By the turn of the nineteenth century, furthermore, it is clear that Reims graduates were a fast disappearing breed in the city; in 1798 they were only five out of 66 listed physicians and the largest contingent was now formed by Edinburgh students.[38]

---

[36] BM Reims MS 2654, p. 88. Daunt was already a surgeon in 1750: Sir Charles A. Cameron, *History of the Royal College of Surgeons in Ireland and of the Irish schools of medicine* (Dublin, 1886), pp. 41–42, 113.

[37] Although the size of the fellowship was fixed (see above p.75), the College was free to licence as many physicians as it wished. When the fellowship was full, would-be fellows could be elected candidate-members and gain a reversionary right to the next vacancy.

[38] Reims graduates may have been better represented among the Dublin medical establishment earlier in the eighteenth century. According to *The Gentleman and Citizen's Almanach* for 1737 the Royal College of Physicians had 14 fellows and seven licentiates in that year: four of the latter were Reims doctors, including Ephraim Thwaites mentioned above pp. 83–4. All four had studied at Glasgow and Leiden. The *Almanach* does not list the Dublin physicians who were not part of the College.

Table 4.4    Dublin physicians, 1768, 1778, 1798

4a: Dublin physicians in 1768

| Faculty from which doctorate obtained | All physicians | Licentiates of Royal College | Fellows of Royal College |
|---|---|---|---|
| Dublin | 14 | 3 | 7 |
| Edinburgh | 4 | 1 | |
| Glasgow | 3 | | |
| Leiden | 5 | 1 | |
| Reims | 14 | 2 | 2 |
| Unknown | 8 | 1 | 2 |
| Total | 46* | 8 | 9 |

* The two Reims graduates who were fellows of the Royal College were also Dublin graduates

4b: Dublin physicians in 1778

| Faculty from which doctorate obtained | All physicians | Licentiates of Royal College | Fellows of Royal College |
|---|---|---|---|
| Dublin | 13 | 2 | 6 |
| Edinburgh | 4 | 1 | 1 |
| Glasgow | 3 | | 1 |
| Leiden | 3 | 2 | |
| Reims | 14 | 1 | 2 |
| Unknown | 10 | 2 | 1 |
| Total | 45* | 8 | 9 |

* The two Reims graduates who were fellows of the Royal College were also Dublin graduates

4c: Dublin physicians in 1798

| Faculty from which doctorate obtained | All physicians | Licentiates of Royal College | Fellows of Royal College |
|---|---|---|---|
| Dublin | 11 | 2 | 8 |
| Edinburgh | 23 | 9 | 6 |
| Glasgow | 1 | 1 | |
| Leiden | 4 | 3 | |
| Reims | 5 | 2 | |
| Vienna | 1 | | |
| Unknown | 21 | 6 | |
| Total | 66 | 23 | 14 |

*Source*: Wilson's *Dublin Directory*

Since the Reims graduates in Dublin were not usually part of the medical establishment, hardly any had an appointment at one of the eight Dublin hospitals that were founded during the course of the eighteenth century.[39] One who did was Frederick Jebb (d. 1781), the son of an apothecary from county Roscommon, who was master at the Rotunda, the Dublin Lying-in Hospital founded in 1745. Like Gaunt, Jebb appears to have taken his degree in mid-career. He first settled in Dublin in 1764, perhaps as a surgeon-apothecary, and was made assistant master at the Rotunda in 1769. Shortly after this he must have received leave of absence, as he turns up in the Reims record in 1771 after apparently studying in the Paris faculty for an unspecified period. The degree was enough to get him the mastership two years later; a post he held for seven years and that left him enough time to write a number of pamphlets attacking any idea of a union with Britain. In the 1778 *Dublin Directory*, he describes himself as a physician. Presumably his early career had given him the wherewithal to go abroad and improve his status.[40]

Only a handful of the Irish graduates from Reims can be said to have had an illustrious medical career. Those who were highly successful were usually to the manor born, such as Nathaniel Barry (c. 1724–85). Barry, a Reims graduate in 1749, was the son of a leading Dublin practitioner, professor of physic, fellow of the Royal Society and medical author, Edward Barry (1696–1776), who had taken his degree at Leiden. Understandably, Nathaniel enjoyed a privileged education, matriculating as a pensioner at Trinity in 1739, taking his BA five years later and his BM in 1748. The following year, he was appointed to the new Dun

---

[39] Judgement based on the study of T.P.C. Kirkpatrick, *History of Dr Steevens' Hospital Dublin* (Dublin: University Press, 1924); O'Donel T.D. Browne, *The Rotunda Hospital (1745–1945)* (Edinburgh: E. and S. Livingstone, 1947); J.D.H. Widdess, *The Richmond, Whitworth and Hardwicke Hospitals: St Laurence's Dublin, 1772–1972* (no publisher, n. d. [1972]); Eoin O'Brien, *The Charitable Infirmary 1718–1987: a farewell tribute* (Monkstown, Dublin: Anniversary Press, 1987); Elizabeth Malcolm, *Swift's Hospital: a history of St Patrick's Hospital Dublin, 1746–1989* (Dublin: Gill and Macmillan, 1989); J.P. Lyons, *Story of Mercer's Hospital* (Dublin: Glendale, 1991); Helen Burke, *The Royal Hospital Donnybrook: a heritage of caring, 1743–1993* (Dublin: Royal Hospital Donnybrook, 1992); and Peter Gatenby, *Dublin's Meath Hospital 1753–1996* (Dublin: Townhouse, 1996). For the establishment of a hospital system in eighteenth-century Ireland, see Laurence M. Geary, *Medicine and Charity in Ireland, 1781–1851* (Dublin: DCU Press, 2005), chapters 1 and 2. Some Reims graduates must have held appointments in the numerous provincial hospitals created after 1765, though they usually only employed surgeons. John Barrett (MD Reims 1741) was one of the two physicians attached to the Limerick county infirmary in 1769: *Limerick Directories*, p. 36.

[40] BM Reims MS 2654, fol. 63; Browne, *Rotunda*, pp. 261–62 (does not mention his Reims degree). Jebb does not appear in either the 1766, 1767 or 1768 *Dublin Directory*, so may have gone abroad *before* his appointment. The one hospital with a respectable Reims presence was the Charitable Infirmary where three Reims doctors were physicians and another, Sheffield Grace (DM 1743), the surgeon: O'Brien, *Infirmary*, p. 261. Daunt also held a hospital appointment – at the Mercer's – where he was surgeon from 1738–86.

professorship in surgery and midwifery, though it is doubtful if he ever taught. At this juncture he must have crossed over to Paris to complete his medical training, for on graduating at Reims he claimed to have been studying in the French capital. On returning from the continent, he gained a second doctorate at Trinity in 1751, and then joined the Royal College when a vacancy occurred in 1758. For the rest of his life he practised in Dublin as a society doctor, sharing with his father the office of Physician General to the Irish army and ultimately inheriting his father's baronetcy.[41]

The only Reims graduate to cut a dash on the national medical stage who came from a relatively humble background was the social reformer, Sir Jeremiah Fitzpatrick (1740–1810). Nothing is known about Fitzpatrick's upbringing beyond that he was born in Kilbeggan, county Westmeath, to parents of modest substance. He successfully reached Leuven by unknown means, where he matriculated in 1765. He graduated from Reims two years later and returned to Ireland to set up his plate in Dublin in 1783. Fitzpatrick was knighted in 1782 but historians have no idea why; he had done nothing to merit the honour. Thereafter his career blossomed. From 1783 to 1794 he was employed by the Irish government as an inspector of hospitals, schools and prisons, then from 1794 to 1802 by the British government as a roving inspector of army hospitals. In the years before his death, he enjoyed the substantial income of £1,400 per annum.[42]

A few Reims graduates achieved fame for non-medical reasons. Bernard O'Connor (c.1666–98) supposedly studied medicine at Paris and Montpellier before graduating at Reims in 1693. The following year he became physician to the king of Poland before moving to London, where he cultivated the Irish-born Hans Sloane and became a fellow of the Royal Society. His contemporary fame was largely due to his publication of a history of Poland, a much acclaimed eye-witness account of a country about which the English knew little.[43] Another Reims graduate to make a name for himself as a historian was the Dublin merchant's son, John Curry (1702/3–80) who took his degree in 1730. For fifty years he belonged to the group of Dublin practitioners who were never members of the Royal College of Physicians. He is remembered today, however, for his various pro-Catholic accounts of the mid-seventeenth century Irish civil wars, and the development

---

[41] Burchaell, *Alumni*, pp. 44, 45; *ODNB*, sub Edward Barry; Widdess, *Royal College of Physicians*, pp. 77, 79, 91.

[42] BM Reims MS 2624, fol. 5; Nilis, 'Irish Students', 231, no. 911. For his general career, see Oliver MacDonagh, *The Inspector General: Sir Jeremiah Fitzpatrick and social reform, 1783–1802* (London: Croom Helm, 1981), especially pp. 19–26. Both the Leuven and Reims records give him of Philipstown, King's County. MacDonagh does not mention Fitzpatrick's Reims degree but there is no reason to doubt that the Reims graduate is the social reformer.

[43] BM Reims MS 1085, fol. 16; *ODNB*, sub Bernard Connor. See also Chambers chapter 3 in this collection.

of Catholic relief.[44] Curry was not the only Reims graduate to become involved in politics. His virtual contemporary, Charles Lucas (1713–71), renowned as 'the Irish Wilkes' for the long war he waged in defence of Irish 'liberties', also had a degree from the Champagne faculty. In his case, though, it was obtained in mid-career, in 1751, after studying in Paris when he was on the run on the continent to escape being imprisoned for his radical opinions.[45]

The fact that the large majority of Irish Reims graduates played a relatively minor role in the medical world suggests that, given the realities of confessional patronage, most were Catholics. This is supported too by the fact that Irish Protestant medical students seem to have had a different educational cursus. According to Peter Froggatt, Protestants chiefly went to Calvinist Leiden before the emergence of Edinburgh and Glasgow as medical centres. Catholics on the other hand preferred to attend Catholic continental faculties.[46] If this was the case, and the surname evidence seems to support his conclusion,[47] then the Irish Protestants who graduated at Reims must have been in a distinct minority. As we saw above, Irish students at Leiden did graduate in the Champagne faculty in the first half of the eighteenth century, yet they only formed a mere eight per cent of the 600-odd Irishmen who took a degree there across the period 1670–1800. Most of the cohort, it was earlier argued, passed through Paris. Admittedly, there were some Protestants among the Reims graduates who studied in the French capital. Barry is an obvious example: fellows of the Royal College of Physicians could not be Catholics until the last third of the eighteenth century;[48] the Dublin MP Lucas, who was unfairly labelled a Protestant bigot by nineteenth-century Irish historians, was clearly another. But the number must have been small. A significant proportion of the Irish Leiden students turn up in the matriculation registers of TCD and Glasgow as students in arts, confirming their Protestant credentials. This is equally true of those who eventually graduated at Reims (13 of the 45 were at Trinity, five at Glasgow). On the other hand, hardly any other Irish graduate at Reims appears in these registers; apart from Barry, mentioned earlier, only a further three,

---

[44] BM Reims MS 1085, fol. 29; *ODNB*, *sub* John Curry. He was one of the Reims doctors to hold a position at the Charitable Infirmary.

[45] BM Reims MS 2654, fol. 9. After Reims, Lucas went on to Leiden and took a degree there in 1752: Innes Smith, *English-Speaking Students*, p. 145. For his life, see *ODNB*, *sub* Charles Lucas. For Lucas and medical politics, see Sneddon, chapter 6 in this collection.

[46] Peter Froggatt, 'Irish students at Leiden and the renaissance of medicine in Dublin', *Journal of the Irish Colleges of Physicians and Surgeons*, 22/ 2 (1993): 124–32 (126).

[47] As does the fact that over a quarter of the Irish medics at Leiden could afford to graduate there: see above n. 27.

[48] Widdess, *Royal College of Physicians*, p. 104.

for instance, passed through Trinity, which is surely indicative.[49] It is extremely unlikely that Protestants formed more than 10 per cent of the Reims cohort.[50]

It is also the case that the Reims graduates who were successful were nearly all Protestants or had 'elastic' consciences. O'Connor was raised a Catholic but was happy to conform in London. Fitzpatrick seems to have been a prudent convert, if he rejoined the Catholic Church towards the end of his life. Curry was the one exception to the rule – a Catholic who never changed his allegiance – but his notoriety, as we saw, owed little to his medical skills. There again, a word of caution is necessary. If the Irishmen who passed through Reims were principally Catholics, then this must have been true of the large majority of Irish graduates up to 1780. Probably at most a third of Irish doctors of medicine were Protestants before this date; less than a quarter in the thirty years from 1710 to 1739.[51] This makes sense given the fact that medicine was the one respectable lay career open to Catholics, and an attractive one in that elites across Europe were expanding in size and seem to have been much more ready to invest heavily in health care in the Age of Enlightenment than they had in previous centuries. It also makes sense in that aspirant Catholic medical practitioners would arguably want a degree more than their Church of Ireland cousins in order to trade on its social cachet in finding clients among Protestant elites. Yet it seems odd that a Reims degree was not equally attractive to non-conformist Irish physicians who must equally have craved respectability. There is nothing to suggest Protestants were discouraged from graduating in the Champagne faculty, since, until 1750, Englishmen and Scots graduated at Reims in quite large numbers as well: the Irish were not the only nation from these islands looking for a cheap and easy degree. But most of the Britons who passed through Reims must have been Protestants, given the small size of Great Britain's Catholic population and the fact that a large proportion of

---

[49] Conclusion based on a study of Innes Smith, *English-speaking students* (this gives details of Leiden matriculands earlier education); G. D. Burtchaell (ed.), *Alumni Dublinenses: a register of the students, graduates, professors and provosts of Trinity College in the University of Dublin (1593–1860)* (Dublin: A. Thom & Co., 1935); and W. Innes Addison, *The matriculation albums of the University of Glasgow from 1728 to 1858* (Glasgow: Maclehose, 1913). There is no Edinburgh matriculation register and no evidence that any Irish Reims medical graduate attended Oxford or Cambridge. It must be stressed that there was no requirement that a foreign graduand should have attended a university arts course. Most medical graduates in the British Isles in the eighteenth century would only have attended a grammar school or learnt Latin from a private tutor, often the local clergyman.

[50] It seems likely too that the Protestants who claimed to have studied in Paris (if they could be identified) would be medical students, like Barry, who can only have spent a few months in the city, or, like Jebb and Daunt (whose religious affiliation admittedly is not known for certain), who travelled to the continent in mid-career.

[51] Based on the information in Table 4.1, and assuming that all Dublin, Leiden, Edinburgh and Glasgow graduates were Protestants before 1780, plus 60 graduates from Reims.

the Scottish contingent (some 50 per cent) had also attended Calvinist Leiden (see Table 4.5).

Table 4.5  Reims doctorates in medicine awarded to students from the British Isles and the British colonies: decennial totals (number studying at Leiden in brackets)

|  | England/ Wales | Scotland | Ireland | Empire | Britain (simply 'Britannicus') | Total |
|---|---|---|---|---|---|---|
| 1580–89 | 2 |  |  |  |  | 2 |
| 1590–99 | 1 |  |  |  |  | 1 |
| 1600–1609 |  |  | 1 |  |  | 1 |
| 1610–19 | 1 |  | 3 |  |  | 4 |
| 1620–29 | 2 |  | 1 |  | 1 | 4 |
| 1630–39 | 3 |  | 3 |  |  | 6 |
| 1640–49 |  |  | 1 |  |  | 1 |
| 1650–59 | 2 | 2 | 2 |  |  | 6 |
| 1660–69 |  |  | 3 |  |  | 3 |
| 1670–79 |  |  | 1 |  |  | 1 |
| 1680–89 | 6 (2) | 32 (11) | 21 |  |  | 59 |
| 1690–99 | 6 (3) | 11 (6) | 18 (2) |  |  | 35 |
| 1700–1709 | 1 | 20 (11) | 21 (2) |  |  | 42 |
| 1710–19 | 17 (8) | 42 (27) | 62 (13) |  | 1 | 122 |
| 1720–29 | 25 (8) | 47 (30) | 59 (10) |  | 1 | 132 |
| 1730–39 | 21 (9) | 44 (24) | 117 (9) |  | 1 | 183 |
| 1740–49 | 17 | 16 (3) | 57 (5) | 3 (3) |  | 93 |
| 1750–59 | 7 | 12 (2) | 54 (2) | 2 | 1 | 76 |
| 1760–69 | 2 | 1 | 66 | 1 |  | 70 |
| 1770–79 | 5 (1) | 1 | 71 | 1 |  | 78 |
| 1780–89 | 4 | 2 | 39 | 1 |  | 46 |
| 1790–99 |  |  | 8 |  |  | 8 |
| Total | 122 (31) | 230 (114) | 608 (43) | 8 (3) | 5 | 973 |

*Source*: BM Reims MS 1085; Innes Smith, 'English-speaking students'.

Obviously, before any solid judgement can be reached, we need to know much more about the confessional contours of Irish medical practice across the eighteenth century. Were Protestant practitioners largely grouped in Dublin and

Cork? Was the profession generally viewed by the ascendancy as unsuitable for its sons, simply by dint of the fact that it was open to Catholics? Were non-conformist Protestants in the first half of the eighteenth century failing to glimpse the same market opportunities as their English *confrères*, Quakers especially?[52] Or were the non-conformists largely confining their field of practice to their own religious communities and did not feel the need to burnish their credentials with a diploma? What is required above all is a prosopographical study of the 240 Irish students at Leiden, most of whom we can assume were Protestants but less than two-thirds of whom appear to have graduated.[53] This will be difficult to complete, given that the Leiden register seldom reveals the town or county of Ireland in which a matriculand was born. But it should be possible using the newspapers from the second half of the century to take the analysis of the Irish medical graduate community considerably further than has been achieved in the present study, where such evidence has not been deployed.

It is also the case that much more needs to be uncovered about how Irish medics, graduates and non-graduates funded their studies abroad. Studying for one or two years on the continent was not cheap. A medical student in Paris could expect to spend a minimum of 600–700 *livres* a year in the early 1770s (about £30), but the amount rose quickly if he chose to take private courses, which could cost as much as 72 *livres* each. Add to this the money spent in travelling to and fro and the inevitable purchase of books and mementoes, and it is hard to imagine a stay abroad costing parents less than £50 a year.[54] As most Irish medical students probably came from a mercantile or farming background, this would have been a heavy charge on a family's income.[55] Doubtless this was another reason why

---

[52] In eighteenth-century England the Quaker physician was a common phenomenon and included leading practitioners such as John Fothergill (1712–80) and John Coakley Lettsom (1744–1815). One English-born Quaker trained at Leiden, John Rutty, actually ended up practising in Dublin: see Widdess, *Royal College of Physicians*, p. 73.

[53] Besides the 80 who graduated in the Netherlands and the 45 who took a Reims degree (one of whom was also a Leiden doctor), 20 graduated at Dublin (four with degrees from either Leiden or Reims), six at Edinburgh and eight at other universities. A further 13 claimed to have doctorates when they registered at Leiden but there is no proof that they did: information from Innes Smith, *English-speaking students*.

[54] For a good idea of the cost of studying in the French capital, see Rouxeau, *Un étudiant*, chapters 2–6; information regarding course fees, books, board and lodging, and so on paid by Guillaume-François Laennec.

[55] Judgement based on only a small number of examples chiefly found in the *ODNB*. By and large nothing is known about the background of the Irish graduates from any faculty. The only register that provides information about social origin is the matriculation album for TCD but this is scarcely likely to be typical. Of the 19 Dublin alumni who graduated at Reims one was a merchant's son, two had a clerical background (one the son of a bishop of Limerick), three came from a medical family, nine described their father as *generosus* suggesting a landowner, one a *vestarius* (a vestreyman?) and one a citizen of Dublin. Two gave no information.

Catholics gravitated towards Paris rather than Leiden. Not only was there a large exile community in the French capital to which they could turn for help, but the city's Irish college, whose purpose was to prepare priests for the Irish mission, seems to have been willing to shelter a number of medical students. Presumably some if not all would have been initially destined for the Church in their youth, then discovered that they had no vocation.[56] However, our knowledge of the life of the Irish physician on the continent remains rudimentary. No equivalent to the letters home written by William Drennan during his stay at Edinburgh in the 1770s has surfaced.[57]

**Army and Navy Surgeons**

Given the shortage of data it is likely that we will never know for certain the relative ratio of Catholics and Protestants among the legions of non-graduate surgeon-apothecaries and general practitioners who lived and worked in small-town and rural Ireland in the first three-quarters of the eighteenth century. By the turn of the nineteenth century, however, if not before, there was one fast-expanding area of general practice that Irish Protestants were embracing with gusto: service in the army and navy medical corps. The armed services had employed surgeons and a small number of graduate physicians from the mid-seventeenth century. But before the outbreak of war with France in 1793, the army in particular was small and almost completely run down in peace time. The twenty-year conflict with Revolutionary and Napoleonic France created an unprecedented demand for medical personnel and offered young medical practitioners from modest backgrounds a novel opportunity to earn a good salary, mix with their social betters, and see the world at the state's expense. By the last years of the war, the navy had 1,400 medical practitioners on its books and the army 1,270.[58] Who these

---

[56] In the second half of the eighteenth century the scholars in the Irish college were divided into a community of priests and a community of clerics. Six out of the 60 inhabitants of the community of clerics in 1772, three already tonsured, would become Reims graduates; by the time that they did so the three who had not been tonsured would have spent from seven to eight years in Paris at least: P. Boyle, *The Irish College at Paris, 1598–1901* (London, 1901), pp. 200–201. Between 1762 and 1793 several holders of the Moloney scholarship attached to the college went on to study medicine after they had studied arts but none graduated at Reims: see Liam Chambers, 'Irish *fondations* and *boursiers* in early modern Paris, 1682–1793' in *Irish Economic and Social History*, 35 (2008): 1–22, n. 77. (My thanks to the author for a copy of his paper.) It is always possible that some priests gained an acquaintance with medicine while abroad to allow them to augment their income or improve their usefulness to their parishioners when they returned.

[57] See Jean Agnew, *The Drennan – McTier letters, 1776–1793* (3 vols, Dublin: Irish Manuscripts Commission, 1998), vol. 1.

[58] Laurence Brockliss, M. John Cardwell, and Michael Moss, *Nelson's surgeon: William Beatty, naval medicine, and the Battle of Trafalgar* (Oxford: OUP, 2005), p. 11;

men were, their background, career record and so on can be established from the personnel records in the War Office and Admiralty papers in the National Archive at Kew. Information about the members of the army medical service is especially rich. In 1815/16, the then Director General, Sir James McGrigor (1771–1858) – an Aberdonian who had been Wellington's chief medical officer in the Peninsula – sent out a *pro forma* to all army physicians asking them to provide details about their place of birth, education and service record. Nothing comparable exists for the navy but service records were compiled for all the surgeons employed during the French wars who were still alive in the mid-1830s in order to ascertain their pension rights. These say nothing of their background but give invaluable information about where they were living on half-pay or in retirement.[59]

Irishmen had served in the army and navy medical corps from the early eighteenth century. Besides members of the Royal College of Physicians who held semi-honorific positions at the head of the Irish army's medical establishment, such as Nathaniel Barry, a number of less privileged Irish physicians, humble surgeons, joined the armed forces on finishing their training. An example was the Ulsterman, David MacBride (1726–78), who served in the Royal Navy before setting up in his birthplace, Ballymoney, and then moving to Dublin to practise physick after taking a degree at Glasgow in 1764.[60] However, the surnames of army surgeons across the century collected by Drew suggest that Irishmen were under-represented in this branch of the services.[61] This changed after 1793. In the course of the war, approximately one-third of recruits to the army medical service and probably a similar proportion to the navy were from Ireland. In all a total of

---

Marcus Ackroyd, Laurence Brockliss, Michael Moss, Kate Retford, and John Stevenson, *Advancing with the army: medicine, the professions and social mobility in the British Isles 1790–1850* (Oxford: OUP, 2006), p. 45 (table).

[59] TNA, WO 25/3904–11; ADM 104/12–14. These two sources formed the starting-point for the two studies cited in n. 58 above. They provided the basic details for two prosopographical databases containing information on 454 army and 430 navy surgeons (respectively one-third and one-half of the names recorded in the two documentary collections). The databases are held on the Oxford University mainframe and continue to be updated. References to individuals in the databases given below cite the distinctive identity number given to each doctor (DID) and allow a researcher to locate relevant data in the numerous specific tables (on wealth, wives, relations and so on). Some of the names in the army database are of surgeons who joined the army in the years after 1815 for 16 per cent of the pro formas (scattered at random in the collection) refer to later entrants: see Ackroyd, et al., *Advancing with the army*, pp. 16–19.

[60] Addison, *Roll of graduates*, p. 350.

[61] Sir R. Drew, *Commissioned officers in the medical services of the British Army, 1660–1960* (2 vols, London: Naval and Military Press, 1968). This is a biographical dictionary, arranged by year of entry to the service, which draws on documents in the WO collection, including WO 25/3904–11. But it only contains information about the surgeons' army careers, not their background and education.

about 1,700 to 2,000 Irish medical practitioners entered the two services.[62] This is not to imply that the Irish were over-represented but they were definitely the largest national contingent. The Scottish presence was totally out of proportion to the size of Scotland's population but it was still under 30 per cent of the total, while the English were grossly under-represented (see Table 4.6).

Table 4.6    Army surgeons in the French wars: country of origin[a]

|  | Definite | Putative | Total | Percent |
|---|---|---|---|---|
| **Abroad** | 10 | 1 | 11 | 2.42% |
| Canada | [1] |  |  |  |
| France | [1] |  |  |  |
| Jersey | [1] |  |  |  |
| W. Indies | [7] |  |  |  |
| **England** | 85 | 45 | 130 | 28.63% |
| **Ireland** | 95 | 47 | 142 | 31.27% |
| **Scotland** | 117 | 18 | 135 | 29.74% |
| **Wales** | 5 | 3 | 8 | 1.76% |
| Unknown | 142 |  | 28 | 6.16% |
| Total | 454 | 114 | 454 |  |

*Source*: Ackroyd et al., *Advancing with the army*, p. 61.

*Note*

[a]    *Definite*: country of birth as given in the *pro forma* returns. *Putative*: country of apprenticeship. In some cases surgeons did not give their country of birth but did reveal where they were apprenticed. In virtually every case where place of birth and place of apprenticeship are given, they are in the same country, so it seems reasonable to use information about the second to deduce the first when it is not recorded. In the few cases where a surgeon was apprenticed in more than one country, the country of his first apprenticeship has been used.

The background of naval surgeons is not known with such certainty. But working from several sources, John Cardwell has calculated that 33.6 per cent of the cohort in the navy doctors' database came from Ireland: see Cardwell, unpublished paper (2008), p. 5.

These recruits were drawn from the non-graduate section of the Irish medical community at the turn of the nineteenth century. Although many of them took a degree later in life – often after the end of the French war – they were usually not

---

[62]    On the assumption that between 5,500 and 6,000 practitioners entered the two services altogether. Figures based on the information in Drew, *Commissioned Officers*, for the years 1793–1815, *Steel's Navy List* (1793–1813), and *Navy List* (1814–15). Navy numbers cannot be known accurately; the published lists rank in order of seniority, but Steel only records the names of full surgeons, not their mates or their assistants, about half the total.

doctors of medicine when they entered the service.[63] On the other hand, they were not poorly educated. Contemporaries attempting to persuade the government to set up a school of military medicine, as existed in several other countries, claimed that the medical practitioners who joined the army and navy were ignorant sawbones who gained what little knowledge they had by practising on the bodies of the nation's heroic soldiers and sailors.[64] This was a completely unfair assessment. Irish recruits, like their English and Scottish counterparts, had attended a local grammar school, then served a medical apprenticeship for three to five years – in their case somewhere in Ireland, sometimes with a relative, often locally, but frequently in Dublin.[65] Next they had usually studied at Edinburgh or London, attending public or private courses and walking the wards often for two or more years.[66] Typical was John Hennen from Castlebar, county Mayo, born in 1779, who joined the service in 1800. He served his time in his home town under a surgeon also called John Hennen, presumably his father. He then spent a period attached to the county hospital before crossing to Edinburgh for three years of study in the university and the infirmary. He did not graduate, however, and only took his Edinburgh degree in 1819.[67] A number of Irish recruits, born after the conflict began, had also attended lectures and walked the wards in Dublin before joining up. Thus Robert Shekleton, a merchant's son, born purportedly in 1793 in Dundalk, had been apprenticed in Dublin to one Ralph Smith, before attending the lectures of Abraham Colles and Richard Dease at the Royal College of Surgeons in 1805–7 and assisting at Dr Steevens' hospital.[68]

---

[63] Fifty-nine of the 95 surgeons in the army database definitely born in Ireland gained doctorates; only 12 had taken the degree before the year in which they entered the army and six in the same year (of whom three were post-1815 entrants).

[64] For example, John Bell, *Memorial concerning the present state of military and naval surgery* (Edinburgh, 1800), especially p.16.

[65] Of the 74 Irish-born surgeons in the army database for whom there are apprenticeship details, 31 spent all or part of their apprenticeship in the Irish capital. The army *pro forma* does not reveal if army surgeons had attended a grammar school. This, though, is suggested by the number of the army cohort who eventually had an Edinburgh degree (102); this required the candidate to write a lengthy thesis in Latin. A smaller proportion of the navy cohort (42) went on to take an Edinburgh degree. See army doctors' database/table: degrees; navy doctors' database/table: degrees.

[66] Ackroyd *et al.*, *Advancing with the Army*, chapter 3; navy doctors' database/table: lectures/courses (based on identifying members of the cohorts in the Edinburgh faculty and London hospitals' class lists).

[67] Army doctors' database, DID 28. The information supplied by Hennen's pro forma is confirmed in 'Life of the Author by his son, Doctor John Hennen' [another army surgeon], preface to the posthumous *Principles of military surgery, comprising of observations on the arrangement, police, and practice of hospitals, and on the history, treatment, and anatomies of variola and syphilis* (Edinburgh, 1829), pp. vii–viii.

[68] Army doctors' database, DID 57.

Parents and patrons had invested heavily in their education, just as heavily as those eighteenth-century Irish families whose sons studied abroad for three or more years before gaining a degree at Reims.[69] They differed, however, from the Reims cohort in their geographical provenance. Again they came from all over the island – 27 counties – but the balance is different. Dublin (city and county) provided nearly 20 per cent of the recruits (a much more respectable total), while the counties of Cork, Kerry and Galway only mustered 12 per cent between them. The big swing was towards Ulster. Only 10 per cent of Reims graduates came from the present-day six counties; among entrants to the army this figure was nearly three times as high. County Londonderry was a particularly important centre of recruitment (see Table 4.7). Naval recruits, too, were drawn heavily from Ulster if the place to which they retired is any indication. Curiously, of those still alive in the 1830s, at least twenty were living in Newtownstewart.[70]

Table 4.7    Army surgeons: county of birth

| County | Total | Town (A) | Town (B) | Town (C) | Rural |
|---|---|---|---|---|---|
| Antrim | 4 | 1 | 1 | 1 | 1 |
| Armagh | 3 (1) | 2 | | | |
| Carlow | 1 | 1 | | | |
| Cavan | 2 | 1 | | 1 | |
| Cork | 6 (1) | 3 | | 2 | |
| Donegal | 4 (2) | 1 | | 1 | |
| Down | 5 (3) | 1 | | 1 | |
| Dublin | 17 | 17 | | | |
| Fermanagh | 4 (3) | | | | 1 |
| Galway | 3 (1) | 1 | | 1 | |
| Kerry | 3 (1) | 1 | | 2 | |
| Kildare | 1 | 1 | | | |
| Kilkenny | 1 (1) | | | | |
| Limerick | 2 | 2 | | | |

---

[69]   Overall, they possibly had to commit more resources. Neither London nor Edinburgh were cheap cities at the turn of the nineteenth century: £50 per annum could easily have been spent on board and lodging and a further £50 on clothing, books and courses. There again prices doubled in the late eighteenth and early nineteenth centuries, so it is impossible to make an easy comparison with the cost of studying in Paris in the early 1770s: see Ackroyd et al., *Advancing with the Army*, pp. 124–25, 146–47.

[70]   Navy doctors' database / table: half pay. This list 12 living in Newtonstewart but the database contains information concerning only half of the surgeons extant in the 1830s: above, n.39.

| County | Total | Town (A) | Town (B) | Town (C) | Rural |
|---|---|---|---|---|---|
| Londonderry | 7 (3) | 1 | | 3 | |
| Longford | 2 | 1 | | 1 | |
| Louth | 1 | | | 1 | |
| Mayo | 3 (1) | | | 2 | |
| Meath | 4 (1) | | | 3 | |
| Monaghan | 5 (4) | | | 2 | |
| Queen's | 1 | | | 1 | |
| Roscommon | 1 | 1 | | | |
| Sligo | 2 (2) | | | | |
| Tyrone | 3 (1) | 1 | | 1 | |
| Waterford | 1 (1) | | | | |
| Wexford | 2 (1) | | | | 1 |
| Wicklow | 1 (1) | | | | |
| County not Given | 6 (6) | | | | |
| Total | 95 (34) | 36 | 1 | 23 | 3 |
| Percentage | (33.68%) | 37.89% | 1.05% | 24.21% | 3.15% |

*Key:*

Town (A): county or cathedral town (including Dublin)

Town (B): industrial town (Belfast)

Town (C): small market town or port (e.g Bandon, county Cork)

Rural: village, farm or estate (e.g. Killygowan, county Wexford)

(3): no specified location within county.

*Source*: Ackroyd et al., *Advancing with the army*, p. 63.

*Note*: It is possible that a number of Irish surgeons born in the countryside gave the local town as their birth place. Gibney of Dormiston castle (see below) claimed to come from Navan.

If the importance of Ulster suggests a distinctly Protestant flavour to the army and navy intake, this is confirmed by clearer analysis of the army contingent. Catholics were not forbidden from entering the two medical services. Army surgeons had officer's rank and enjoyed the privileges of the mess, but there seems to have been no requirement for them to be members of the established church. A significant proportion of English recruits were Protestant nonconformists. It is possible, then, to find Irish Catholics in the army medical corps. One such example is Oliver Dease of Dublin who belonged to a prominent Catholic medical family in the capital, headed by Richard Dease, one of the professors at the College of Surgeons. Oliver joined up in 1809 and was stood down in 1816. At this juncture, a promising career beckoned because Oliver, thanks to his Dease relatives, was elected a surgeon of a Dublin hospital. Unfortunately he died almost immediately, leaving his wife, Anne, and their five children in dire straits. Yet, despite their confessional creed, they suffered no discrimination from the army medical service. Anne received a widow's pension, then for 10 years from 1826, she was paid between £15 and £25 out of the orphans' fund to support her children.[71]

Catholics, though, were definitely in a minority. Moreover, some went out of their way to hide their origins. Gabriel Rice Redmond from a Wexford gentry family, the Redmonds of Killygowan house, seems to have come from a confessionally mixed family. He was distantly related on his mother's side to the Duke of Wellington, but his father, a younger son, had the ominous name of Thomas Ignatius. When Gabriel joined up he gave his uncle's name, John, as his father.[72] Other recruits, too, converted to Protestantism before they entered the army. The most interesting example is James William Macauley, whose father was James McGauley (c. 1723–83), a successful builder, timber merchant, grazier and real estate developer, who at the end of his life bought Stormanstown House at Drumcondra outside Dublin. James William was born in 1789 and baptised at St Michael's Roman Catholic Church, Rosemary Lane, Dublin. However, both his father and mother were dead by the time he was 15 and he and his two sisters were put in the care of a Protestant maternal relative, the Dublin apothecary, William Armstrong. Having been apprenticed to a surgeon at Kilmainham, he entered the army in 1810. By then he had abandoned Catholicism and never returned to the fold. He eventually married Frances Ridgway in Dublin in 1821, whose mother was the daughter of the Church of Ireland antiquarian Edward Ledwich. James William then went on to have a glittering career in the army as chief surgeon at Kilmainham. One of his sisters also converted. The other, Catherine, however, remained true to the Catholic faith and eventually went on to found the Sisters of Mercy (with Quaker money).[73]

The exact balance between Irish Protestants and Catholics in the army intake will never be known accurately. Recruits were not required to declare their religious allegiance on entering the service. It is likely, though, it was in the

---

[71] Army doctors' database, DID 18. Details on Dease. Richard Dease may have been a Protestant, for his father William, a founding member of the Royal College of Surgeons, appears to have married out and Richard himself attended TCD. Richard's own son, William, however, is described as a Catholic in the TCD matriculation register: see Cameron, *Royal College*, pp. 313–14; Widdess, *Royal College*, p. 21; Burtchaell, *Alumni*, under Richard and William Dease.

[72] Army doctors' database, DID 335.

[73] Army doctors' database DID 322. Although Ledwich was a cleric, he appears to have taken a Reims degree in 1761: see BM Reims MS 2654, fol. 25. He probably spent some time on the continent after gaining his BA at TCD in 1760: see *ODNB*, *sub* Edward Ledwich.

region of two to one. Twenty-nine of the army sample of 95 definitely born in Ireland appear in the early nineteenth-century matriculation register of the Dublin faculty of medicine, where signatories (most unusually) had to declare their religious affiliation: 19 claimed to be Protestants (they were not divided up confessionally) and 10 Catholics.[74] If this was the case, then the Irish Protestant community was greatly over-represented in the army medical corps. A group that comprised perhaps eight per cent of the population of the British Isles provided 20 per cent of army medical practitioner during the French war.

Limited information, as we saw, is available about the future lives of eighteenth-century medical graduates. It can only be assumed that most returned to Ireland. Much more is known, on the other hand, of the fate of the army recruits. Some on leaving the service went home, where those, such as Dease, who were released relatively young set themselves up in civilian practice. Another more successful civilian doctor was Shekleton who was also placed on half-pay in 1816. He too had a relative already in practice in Dublin – his younger brother John – so was similarly encouraged to put up his plate in the city, where he specialised (perhaps oddly for a former army surgeon) in obstetrics. From 1817 virtually until his death in 1867 he was attached to the Rotunda Lying-in Hospital in Rutland Square and is credited with being the first Irish doctor to use chloroform in deliveries. The success of his practice can be judged by the fact that he ended his days at a fashionable address: 59 Leeson Street.[75] Other army surgeons after spending long years in the service, became wealthy or inherited fortunes from relations and came back to Ireland to retire. Typical was William Byrtt of Belfast, who came from a prosperous family of boot makers in the city. Born in 1786 and apprenticed to a Belfast surgeon called Robert McLuny, he entered the army aged 20. After 23 years of service he returned to Belfast to live as a gentleman at 40 Upper Queen Street. According to his obituary in the *Belfast Newsletter* of 14 October 1845, he devoted his retirement 'to the public good – the cause of the poor, the aged, the young, the fatherless and the widow was cherished by him.'[76]

However, the army surgeons who ended their days in Ireland were a minority. Less than 30 per cent still in service in 1815/16 appear to have done so.[77] Of the remainder, about a third died abroad. Most were still in the service, like Hennen, who eventually succumbed to a virulent fever epidemic in Gibraltar in 1828,

---

[74] TCD, MS 758.

[75] Army doctors' database, DID 57. His slow social advancement can be traced year by year in the *Dublin Directory* (1817–1867). His brother was appointed curator at the Royal College of Surgeons in 1820, where he was in charge of anatomical demonstrations; John died from septicaemia four years later,

[76] Army doctors' database, DID 139; *Belfast Directory* (1843–4), 279; *Belfast Newsletter*, 14 October 1845.

[77] Ackroyd et al., *Advancing with the Army*, pp. 229–32.

while running the medical station there.⁷⁸ But a few were permanent emigrants who settled on the continent of Europe or in the colonies. One long-serving surgeon perversely retired to Paris where he died in 1848. This was Andrew Browne, probably a surgeon's son from Ballinrobe, county Mayo, who entered the army in 1795 and left in 1830 with the high rank of Deputy Inspector General of Hospitals. Although childless he used his considerable fortune of £20,000 to launch a prominent Ulster dynasty: the Montague Brownes of Janeville, St John's Point, Ardglass, county Down. Browne almost certainly obtained a captaincy in the army for his much younger brother, Peter, then left more than half of his wealth to Peter's soldier son, another Andrew.⁷⁹

The largest proportion, nearly half, settled in England, often making successful careers for themselves, usually in spa towns where they pandered to the medical needs of retired army officers. One such was William Gibney (*c.* 1794–1872).⁸⁰ Born at Dormiston castle in county Meath into a decaying Protestant landowning family, Gibney boasted good connections. Like John Gabriel Rice Redmond, he was a distant relative of Wellington, but more importantly his uncle, John Gibney, who had gained a degree at Edinburgh in 1790, was a respected Brighton physician and intimate of the Prince Regent. The elder Gibney looked after his nephew's education – William was one of the few surgeons to have a medical degree, from Edinburgh – on entering the service. When William joined up (on his uncle's insistence) in 1813, he also found him a pukka regiment. The war was over within a few years, however, and William in 1818, still in his early twenties, was placed on half-pay and had to build a civilian career.⁸¹ He made a good start by marrying in 1820 a West Indian planter's daughter born in Warwickshire called Frances Dwarris, but his fortune was made when he settled in a rapidly expanding Cheltenham.⁸² For the next 40 years he was a pillar of the community, running the dispensary and the female orphan asylum but he did not teach his children to value their Irishness. His soldier son, Robert (1826–1906), the author of a racy account of the Indian mutiny, was so embarrassed by the family name,

---

⁷⁸ See *Principles of Military Surgery*, pp. xv–xvi.

⁷⁹ Army doctors' database, DID 11. The family is descended from a junior branch of the Montagues of Cowdray, a Sussex family. An ancestor had gone to Ireland in the sixteenth century. When the viscountancy of Cowdray died out, the family added Montague to their name; they no longer own Janeville. The present head of the family, Anthony Arthur Duncan Montague Browne (b. 1923), the army surgeon's great great nephew, now living in Kent, was Churchill's last private secretary. The Reims doctor, Patrick Browne, mentioned above, was probably from the same family.

⁸⁰ Army doctors' database, DID 24.

⁸¹ He left a detailed account of his education and time in the army: see William Gibney, *Recollections of an old army doctor* (London, 1896). Gibney never did an apprenticeship, evidence of his relatively elevated social status and good connections.

⁸² His brother-in-law Sir Fortunatus William Lilley Dwarris FRS (1786–1860) was a respected London judge: see *ODNB*, *sub* Fortunatus William Lilley Dwarris.

he later changed it to Dwarris[83] However, of those who established themselves in England, not all enjoyed the same measure of good fortune. Tully Daly of county Galway, born about 1780, who was apprenticed locally, then studied in Dublin and London before joining up, also came out of the army in 1818 and married an English woman. For ten years he tried to build a practice in Chelsea but his success must have been limited. In 1829 he and his family emigrated to Australia but he was drowned *en route* with his eldest son.[84]

It is possible that the entrants to the navy were more ready to settle back in Ireland on quitting the service, but in their case too there were many who never returned.[85] Indeed, it was the navy not the army who produced the most famous medical exile in this period in Sir William Beatty FRS (1773–1842), the surgeon on the *Victory* in 1805.[86] Beatty was born in 1773 in county Londonderry to a prominent local family. His father, uncle, grandfather and two great uncles were excisemen, while his great-grandfather, who was still alive (just), was Captain Beatty, one of the defenders of Derry against James II. He is one of the few army and navy surgeons of this era who has left no trace of his education but he was almost certainly apprenticed to his maternal uncle, George Smyth (d. 1821), who himself had joined the navy in 1778 and appears to have been living in county Londonderry on half-pay when Beatty was a teenager. Beatty entered the service in October 1791 and had an eventful but not particularly singular career until he had the good fortune to be the man who cared for the dying Nelson. The Admiral, it seems, had a penchant for Ulster surgeons. Beatty's predecessor on the *Victory* was George (later Sir George) Magrath, whom Nelson declared to be the finest medical man he had ever known, while the physician to the Mediterrean fleet in the two years before was Dr Leonard Gillespie (1758–1842)

---

[83] [Robert Dwarris], *My escape from the mutineers in Oudh* (1858).

[84] Army doctors' database, DID 145. Possibly related to the Dalys of Daly castle.

[85] Eighty-five of the 430 in the navy cohort spent some time on half-pay in Ireland. Of these 41 lived in the present six counties, the large majority in counties Antrim, Londonderry and Tyrone. Eight were based in Belfast, six in the city of Derry. Two, John Monteith (d. 1837) and William A. Dickson (d. 1860), lived in both cities. As the navy cohort comprises half the surgeons on the books in the 1830s, presumably there were about 80 naval doctors who had served in the French wars living in Northern Ireland on the accession of Victoria.

[86] Beatty became an FRS in 1818; like many other members of the Royal Society at this date, he never addressed the Society and published no scientific papers. He was knighted by the sailor-king, William IV, in 1831: Brockliss, Cardwell and Moss, *Nelson's surgeon*, pp. 174–5 and 180.

from Armagh.[87] Beatty traded on his luck.[88] For the rest of the war, he served as the chief medical officer at the naval hospital at Plymouth, and then after a short break gained the plum job of physician at Greenwich. Throughout the 1820s and 1830s he was a leading light in London society: he was a director of the Clerical, Medical Assurance Company; he was on the board of the London and Greenwich Railway; and he was on the organising committee that erected Nelson's column. There is no evidence he ever went back to Ireland after joining the navy. In fact, he seems to have buried his background completely. When he died in London, none of the obituaries mentioned his place of birth, and even today the official list of the *Victory*'s 1805 crew has him down as Scottish.[89]

**Conclusion**

This chapter has dealt with two very different groups of Irish medical practitioners in the long eighteenth century. The first part offered a somewhat speculative account of the 1,300 graduate physicians produced by the kingdom in the period 1680 to 1780. The large majority of these gained at least part of their medical training abroad and took their degree at Reims. Most were arguably Catholics, and most returned home to set up their plate in small town Ireland. Their number, it must be emphasised, was not large – at most the country was being asked to absorb a dozen or so new graduate physicians per year. The second part of the chapter examined much more securely the history of the more than 1,700 Irish surgeons who joined the army and navy medical corps during the long French war from 1793 to 1815, perhaps as many as 70 a year. They were not graduates; their medical education was confined to the British Isles; most were Protestants; and most left Ireland for good. What unites the two, it can be tentatively suggested, is the use of medicine as a vehicle of social mobility. Until the late eighteenth century, medicine was the only respectable lay profession open to Irish Catholics:

---

[87] Naval doctors' database, DID 39 (Magrath); Nelson to Lady Hamilton and Nelson to Baird, 27 and 30 May 1804: Sir Nicholas Harris Nicolas, *The dispatches and letters of Lord Nelson* (7 vols, London, 1844–1846), vol. 6, 30 and 41; R.S.J. Clarke, 'Ulster Connections with Nelson and Trafalgar', *Ulster Medical Journal*, 75/1 (2006): 80–84 (80–82) (Gillespie).

[88] Beatty became a national figure on the publication in January 1806 of his *Authentic narrative of the death of Lord Nelson* (London, 1807), which remains the accepted, though highly suspicious, account of the Admiral's last hours: see Brockliss, Cardwell and Moss, *Nelson's surgeon*, chapter 4.

[89] Both the old and new DNBs say nothing of his provenance. Neither Magrath nor Gillespie went back to Ulster either. Magrath went on half-pay in 1825 and eventually set up in Plymouth; he became and FRS with Beatty's support in 1819 and was knighted in the same year as his Ulster friend in 1831. Gillespie retired on half-pay in 1809, then somewhat oddly went to live in Paris in 1815. Although he died in London, he was buried in Père Lachaise.

a medical degree placed its owner at the top of the medical ladder and gave him a social cachet and a marketable asset. Entering the army and navy medical service during the Revolutionary and Napoleonic wars served a similar function for the aspirant Protestant middle-classes of the island, especially in relatively depressed Ulster, from which so many people had emigrated to North America in preceding decades (including two of Sir William Beatty's family).[90] It was a chance to earn a decent salary and mix with the British landowning class, and it gave the surgeon the credentials, even the glamour, to be warmly received, if he eventually decided to set himself up far away from family and friends. In modern parlance both groups were pursuing exit strategies.

It must be stressed that there was nothing peculiarly Irish about this. The study of the English and Scottish surgeons who joined the army at the turn of the eighteenth century reveals that they too exploited a novel and, as it turned out, quite long-lasting opportunity to make money and improve their social status. If the English were under-represented among the recruits, it was just that in economically prosperous England there was more than one way to mount the social ladder.[91] In Ireland's case on the other hand it is interesting to speculate on the national effect of such behaviour. Presumably in the eighteenth century the ease with which middle-class Catholics could become respectable graduate physicians (with little formal study and at limited expense) helped to retain social cohesion in a fractured confessional society. Conversely, the permanent relocation of so many army and navy surgeons in the first decades of the Union can hardly have assisted the development of a feeling of Britishness in early nineteenth-century Ireland. The officer corps of the army and navy must have been the one section of the population of the British Isles that had a positive and emotional primary British identity at the close of the French wars. Messes and wardrooms were a mix of nationalities bound together in a common endeavour. The Presbyterian Scot James McGrigor, for instance, began his career as a medical officer in the newly formed Connaught Rangers, where apparently all the officers except the commanding officer, Major Keppel, came from county Galway and were related in some way to General de Burgh (later earl of Clanricarde) who had raised the regiment.[92] Military surgeons in particular, once back in Civvy Street or permanently based in the British Isles, were well placed to play a significant role in promoting Britishness, in that their daily

---

[90] Brockliss, Cardwell and Moss, *Nelson's surgeon*, p. 37 (family tree).

[91] Significantly, an important proportion of English recruits to the army medical corps came from nonconformist and hence relatively disadvantaged families. The army doctors' database contains information about the religious background of 33 of the 85 surgeons definitely born in England: eight of these were Protestant nonconformists and one a Catholic: Ackroyd et al. *Advancing with the army*, p. 92. Confessional background, it should be said, is a particularly difficult piece of biographical data to uncover.

[92] Sir James McGrigor, *The scalpel and the sword: the autobiography of the father of army medicine*, ed. Mary McGrigor (Dalkeith: Scottish Cultural Press, 2000), p. 33.

practice brought them continually into intimate and sympathetic contact with people from all ranks of society (even the very poor in hospitals). Many factors made it difficult, perhaps impossible, to unite the islands of Ireland and Britain in the first half of the nineteenth century, but the readiness of the Gibneys and Beattys to turn their back on their homeland and lose rather than celebrate their Irishness, cannot have made the task any easier. [93]

---

[93] It is sometime assumed that the Union was doomed from the beginning, but it is now clear that the government in London from 1830–60 made a real effort to create a single country: see K. Theodore Hoppen, 'Nationalist mobilization and governmental attitudes: geography, politics and nineteenth-century Ireland', in Laurence Brockliss and David Eastwood (eds), *A Union of multiple identities. The British Isles c.1750–c.1850* (Manchester: Manchester University Press, 1997), pp. 169–73. The failure then of a leading section of the 'British' British to second the government's endeavours takes on real significance.

Chapter 5

# Domestic Medication and Medical Care in Late Early Modern Ireland

James Kelly

**Introduction**

The inauguration of the modern tradition of diagnostic and institutional medicine in Ireland can be securely dated to the late early modern era. The establishment in the eighteenth century of a modest network of hospitals and dispensaries was one notable achievement, but the fact that the main medical professions – the physician, surgeon, apothecary and dentist – were still only assuming their recognisable modern form at the end of the century, attests to its embryonic character.[1] The paucity of medical personnel was of greater consequence given that most illness was treated in the home, for though the way was paved in the eighteenth century for the dramatic rise in the number of medical practitioners that occurred in the early nineteenth century, large parts of the country and large elements of the population had little access to, or seldom sought professional medical assistance.[2] The observation of James Reynolds, a physician, resident in county Tyrone, in 1793 that there were 'but two physicians to take care of a tract of country thirty miles in extent' provides a telling perspective on the situation in mid-Ulster at the end of the eighteenth century. The position was comparable in west Cork into the 1820s, as, according to Rev Horace Townshend Fleming of Ballydevlin, 'the

---

[1] See James Kelly, 'The emergence of scientific and institutional medical practice in Ireland, 1650–1800' in Greta Jones and Elizabeth Malcolm (eds), *Medicine, disease and the state in Ireland, 1650–1940* (Cork: Cork University Press, 1999), pp. 21–39; L.M. Geary, *Medicine and charity in Ireland, 1718–1851* (Dublin: UCD Press, 2004).

[2] The number of medical practitioners available at any time in the eighteenth century remains a grey area. The small number of fellows, candidates and licentiates admitted by the College of Physicians between 1693 and 1793 (63, 51 and 74 respectively) did not even meet the needs of Dublin, which had 61 practitioners in 1774. What is apparent is that the number of university trained practitioners grew rapidly in the early nineteenth century until, by the 1840s, there was an estimated 1,381 (the 1841 census) to 1,989 physicians (*Croly's Directory of 1846*); J.D.H. Widdess, *The Royal College of Physicians of Ireland, 1654–1963* (Edinburgh: E. and S. Livingstone, 1963), pp. 71, 102; Laurence M. Geary, 'Medical practice among the pre-Famine Irish poor' (unpublished paper delivered at History of Medicine seminar, University of Limerick, May 1998); see Brockliss chapter 4 in this collection.

medical element was non existent' there in his youth. Fleming recollected that his mother had to bring a doctor from Skibbereen, which was 'some 20 miles away', when medical assistance was required.[3] Yet the fact that help was then within reach, albeit not always easily, was a distinct improvement on circumstances a century earlier, when it was sometimes not possible even to obtain the ingredients required to make basic medicines. Writing from Phillipstown, Queen's county in 1724, Robert, first Viscount Molesworth observed anxiously that he was 'in a place where no herb or drug that I might occasion for (either a clyster or oat drink) can be had nearer than Tullamore', which was some thirty miles distant.[4] Clearly, circumstances improved in the course of the eighteenth century as apothecaries, surgeons and, in smaller number, physicians established practices in towns across the country, but their availability remained inherently uneven.[5] The implications of this were inescapable; adults were obliged to assume responsibility for their own health care, and for that of their children and adult dependents.

In this respect, Ireland resembled eighteenth-century England, of where it has been observed that 'the sick were not patients in the modern sense of the term' because they, or close family members, assumed direct and personal responsibility for medical care. In other words, individuals with no formal medical training not only engaged in the diagnosis of illness and the prescription and administration of medication, but also (frequently) made up or simply purchased the remedies that were administered and, of course, tended to those who were ill.[6] If this is attributable, in the first instance, to the shortage of appropriate medical assistance, it was made possible by the fact that medical remedies were shared between and transferred across generations by the exponential rise in the availability of proprietary medicine, and by the improved access to medical information in print. In addition, as confidence in the efficacy of the long dominant Galenist system diminished in advance of the emergence of a replacement, reliance on domestic and self-medication appreciated.[7] This assumed different forms. It can be seen in the

---

[3] James Kelly (ed.), *Proceedings of the Irish House of Lords, 1771–1800* (Dublin: Irish Manuscripts Commission, 2008), vol 2, p. 430; Rosemary ffolliott, *The Pooles of Mayfield* (Dublin: Hodges Figgis, 1958), p. 252.

[4] Viscount Molesworth to Lady Molesworth, 3 May 1724 in HMC, *Reports on manuscripts in various collections* (London: Her Majesty's Stationary Office, 1913), vol 8, p. 369.

[5] See James Kelly, 'Bleeding, vomiting and purging: ill health and the medical profession in late early modern Ireland' in Maria Luddy and Catherine Cox (eds), *Culture of care in Irish medical history, 1750–1950* (Basingstoke: Palgrave, forthcoming).

[6] Roy Porter (ed.), *Patients and practitioners: lay perceptions of medicine in pre-industrial society* (Cambridge: CUP, 1985), introduction; L.W.B. Brockliss, 'The development of the spa in seventeenth-century France' in Roy Porter (ed.), *The medical history of water and spas* (London: Medical History supplement 10, 1990), pp. 23–47 (43).

[7] Brockliss, 'The development of the spa', pp. 40–42.

proliferation of medical receipts books, in the recourse to hydrotherapy identifiable from the 1680s,[8] in the greater consumption from the 1720s of commercial proprietary medicines, and in the publication of increasingly compendious works that assisted with the provision in a domestic setting of medical care.[9]

It is not possible in the context of this initial exploration of domestic medication in Ireland to provide more than an introduction to the phenomenon, but the fact that it was resorted to widely illustrates that in Ireland, as in Great Britain, there was 'no single privileged medicine' because 'many types of healing co-existed'.[10] Domestic medication drew, in the first instance, on the shadowy realm of traditional medicine, which raises the difficult question of the impact of the native medical tradition. It is tempting to assume that the situation in Ireland resembled that in Scotland, where the population at large relied on remedies derived from ancient and medieval herbals and traditional medical practices. These were communicated across and within generations by word of mouth, through ballads and songs, and in writing, in family manuscripts and, increasingly, in print.[11] However, the traditional medical schools, which drew on established Galenist precepts, did not survive beyond the mid-seventeenth century, and because so few have been studied it is difficult to assess their medical legacy.[12] It is reasonable to assume that they had some impact on the medical care dispensed among the Irish speaking population, though the strength of popular belief in the curative powers of holy wells suggests that this population adhered to an essentially faith-based medical tradition.[13] By contrast, the island's Anglophone population drew primarily on an Anglican tradition of self and domestic medication that slowly percolated, in tandem with the embrace of English commercial practices and the English language.

---

[8] See James Kelly, 'Drinking the waters: balneotherapeutic medicine in Ireland, 1660–1850' in *Studia Hibernica*, 35 (2008–9): 99–145.

[9] See James Kelly, 'Health for sale: mountebanks, doctors, printers and the supply of medication in eighteenth-century Ireland', *RIA proc.*, 108C (2008): 75–113; below pp. 123–7.

[10] Roy Porter, 'The people's health in Georgian England', in Tim Harris (ed.), *Popular culture in England* (New York: St Martin's Press, 1995), p. 126; see also Churchill chapter 7 in this collection.

[11] V.G. Hadfield, 'Domestic medicine in eighteenth-century Scotland' (unpublished Ph.D. thesis, University of Edinburgh, 1980); see also Dillon chapter 2 in this collection.

[12] For a short overview see Aoibheann Nic Dhonnchadha, 'Early modern Irish medical writings' in *Newsletter of the School of Celtic Studies*, 4 (1990): 35–9; and for an account of one of these schools see Aoibheann Nic Dhonnchadha, 'The medical school of Aghmacart, Queen's county', *Ossory, Laois and Leinster*, 2 (2006): 11–43.

[13] Among other work, see Patrick Logan, *The holy wells of Ireland* (Gerrards Cross: Colin Smythe, 1980); Caoimhín Ó Danachair, 'The holy wells of county Dublin', *Reportorium Novum*, 2 (1955): 68–87; Eugene Broderick, 'Devotions at holy wells: an aspect of popular religion in the diocese of Waterford and Lismore before the Famine', *Decies*, 54 (1998): 53–74 (55–6).

Moreover, domestic medication within Ireland's English-speaking population was not a static or unchanging phenomenon. Pursued within essentially narrow parameters during the late seventeenth and early eighteenth centuries when medical options were limited, it was increasingly influenced in the eighteenth century by the commercial medical marketplace, which gave the consumer access from the 1720s to an expanding menu of commercial nostrums. This commercial medical culture was dependent on the newspaper for promotion, but print also influenced the practice of self-medication directly, since it was the medium through which many medical remedies were conveyed to the public. Much of this information may have originated with medical practitioners, consistent with the fact that the boundaries between the main branches of medicine were more permeable than the guardians of disciplinary exclusivity deemed appropriate. Moreover, there were many in the profession eager to make knowledge available to assist with medication in the domestic environment.[14] As a result, by the end of the eighteenth century the public had access to an unprecedented amount of information – traditional, popular and reputably scientific – to which they could appeal not only to manage illness when it occurred, but also to prevent illness ever happening.

## The rationale for domestic medication

While the candour with which correspondents discussed intimate details of their personal health in the seventeenth and eighteenth centuries is indicative that the more relaxed conception of personal privacy then prevailing in England also obtained in Ireland, it is still more illustrative of the vulnerability of people when faced with illness, and of their reliance on friends and family to assist them to negotiate the problems caused by ill-health.[15] As this suggests, individuals assumed personal responsibility for the diagnosis and treatment of illness, and did not hesitate either to seek advice or to offer assistance to others. This was a feature of the whole period, but it was at its strongest during the late seventeenth and early eighteenth centuries when professional medical assistance was at a premium. Thus Sir George Rawdon, of Moira, county Down made clear his gratitude in 1670 to Viscount Conway of Carnaervon for a 'prescription' sent him in anticipation that it might be helpful in overcoming an unspecified 'distemper', though he (Rawdon)

---

[14] See the observations of Bishop Edward Synge on the activities of the surgeons and apothecaries he encountered at Elphin and surrounding towns: M.L. Legg (ed.), *The Synge Letters: Bishop Edward Synge to his daughter, Alicia, Roscommon to Dublin 1746–1752* (Dublin: Lilliput Press for the Irish Manuscripts Commission, 1996), *passim*.

[15] See, for example, the openness with which in January 1691 the Rev John Hawkins (writing from Dromoland, county Clare) discussed his bowel problems: Sir John Ainsworth (ed.), *The Inchiquin Manuscripts* (Dublin: Irish Manuscripts Commission, 1961), p. 33; more generally see, Roger Chartier (ed.), *A history of private life: passions of the Renaissance* (Cambridge, Mass.: Belknap Press, 1989), pp. 354–5.

had already recovered by the time it arrived.[16] Robert, Viscount Molesworth, was also forthcoming; he counselled his wife in 1713 when remedies were required for gout and consumption that the best option in the case of the former was to drink 'pretty frequently a large glass of strong wine', and in the case of the latter that there was 'no place in the world so proper … as Montpellier' because of the excellence of the 'air and diet'.[17] Because few outside the medical profession were as well informed on matters medical as Molesworth, the more usual response was to convey a list of medicines, the recipe for a particular remedy or a suggested cure, though this was not without hazard. Jonathan Swift, the steward of the King's Inns and father of the more famous author of the same name, took mercury on recommendation in 1667 in the hope that it would cure a case of 'the itch' (scabies) he acquired 'in some foul bed' while on circuit, but it had precisely the contrary impact; he responded aversely and died.[18]

Because of the limitations of the available remedies, and of the diagnoses on which they were based, it is unsurprising that individuals who possessed the gift of healing were assured steady custom. The most influential 'healer' in the late seventeenth century was Valentine Greatrakes, the impact of whose activities in counties Waterford and Cork in the early 1660s was reinforced by the publication in Dublin in 1668 of 'a brief account' of the 'strange' and 'marvailous cures' he effected in London 'by the stroaking of the hands'.[19] Saliently, belief in the efficacy of non-medical healing transcended social station and religion. It has been claimed that Georgian England 'possessed fewer holy healers' than France or Italy, and that this can be attributed to religious conviction, but if so, it had little impact in Ireland where healers were resorted to throughout the eighteenth century. Thus in 1701, Belleis King, a relation of the Church of Ireland archbishop, William King, attended a woman at Dungannon, who had 'cured many', in search of relief for a troubling 'distemper in his neck'.[20] Significantly, this healing woman emphasised

---

[16] Cited in J.F. Fleetwood, *History of Irish medicine* (2nd edn, Dublin: Skellig Press, 1983), pp. 63–4.

[17] Viscount to Lady Molesworth, 28 April [1713], 30 May 1713 in HMC, *Various collections,* vol 8, p. 262.

[18] Hoare to Bonnell, 4 June 1722 (NLI, Smythe of Barbavilla papers, MS 41580/29); Knightley Chetwood to John Ussher, 16 April 1726 in Lady Mahon (ed.), 'The Chetwood letters, 1726', *Journal of the Kildare Archaeological Society,* 9 (1918–21): 273–6 (275); Arch Elias, (ed.) *The memoirs of Laetitia Pilkington* (2 vols, Athens, Georgia: University of Georgia Press, 1997), pp. 31, 401.

[19] Valentine Greatrakes, *A brief account of Mr Valentine Greatrak's and divers of the strange cures by him lately performed by himself in a letter… to … Robert Boyle (Dublin, 1668);* Henry Stubbe, *The miraculous conformist: or an account of several marvailous cures performed by the stroaking of the hands of Mr V. Greatarick …* (Oxford, 1666); *ODNB, sub* Valentine Greatrakes.

[20] Roy Porter, *Bodies politic: disease, death and doctors in Britain 1650–1900* (London: Reaktion Books, 2001), p. 197; Eleaner Brown to William King, 22 July 1701 (TCD, King papers, MSS 1995–2008 fol. 817).

her *bona fides* by declining 'to charge anything' until her patients were cured. The fact that others were more grasping indicates that this was an area replete with fraud – fiscal as well as medical. Be that as it may, the continuing attraction of the miracle cure is attested to by the variety of those who claimed to possess the healing powers of 'a one and twentieth son born in wedlock', as well as by the publication of cures for ailments such as 'barrenness in one sex and impotency in the other', 'scrophulous disorders', asthma, epilepsy, tinnitus, and other conditions, which defeated 'the whole art of surgery and all other human means'.[21]

Given this reality, and the frequency with which individuals were deemed to possess 'noe hopes of recovery' because of ostensibly modest conditions, illness prevention was a matter to which the health conscious devoted considerable time and effort.[22] It was commonly assumed, moreover, that there was a connection between a raffish lifestyle and serious illness. Thus William Fitzwilliam of Dublin observed in November 1757 of the Irish peer Edward, Lord Digby, who was then mortally ill, that he had 'simply and imprudently thrown away his life' by not living in a manner appropriate to his 'tender constitution'. Digby certainly did not assist his case in the estimation of contemporaries by declining medical advice that he should 'shut himself up at home and take a little physick', but though this was deemed a serious transgression, it was still less culpable than egregious excess, be this in consumption or conduct.[23] Thus Tom Burgess, a 'hearty honest farmer' from county Cork was deemed to have contributed to his own premature demise when, in 1747, after a night's 'hard drinking', he precipitated the physical collapse that hastened his death by consuming a 'draught' of 'milk and water'.[24] Sudden death was less likely, it was believed, if one possessed a strong constitution, but this did not excuse excess, as Richard Mathew of Dublin acknowledged in 1747 when he made a faster than usual recovery from surgery. 'We', he observed of his family at large, 'owe much to our genitors for this strength of nature ... but a great deale depends on our frugal management of whatever is imparted to us'.[25] These were not sentiments with which many disagreed, and it accounts for the continuous counsel Bishop Edward Synge of Elphin offered his teenage daughter

---

[21] *Dublin Gazette*, 2 October 1731; *Harding's Impartial Newsletter*, 16 May 1722; *Faulkner's Dublin Journal*, 10 March 1730, 5 October 1731; *Dublin Weekly Journal*, 22 August 1730; *Pue's Occurrences*, 28 April 1752, 6 May 1758, 19 June 1759; *Universal Advertiser*, 13 October 1753, 7 October 1755, 9 March 1756; *Dublin Chronicle*, 29 March 1770.

[22] William Pearde to Francis Price, 20 May 1746 (NLW, Puleston papers, MS 3579 fol. 104).

[23] Fitzwilliam to Lord Fitzwilliam, 22 November 1757 (NAI, Pembroke Estate papers, 97/46/1/1/27/103); Kelly, 'Bleeding, vomiting and purging'.

[24] Edmund Spencer to Francis Price, 16 October 1747 (NLW, Puleston papers, MS 3580 fol. 61).

[25] Mathew to Lord Fitzwilliam, 30 July 1747 (NAI, Pembroke Estate papers, 97/46/1/2/5/45).

Alicia on the necessity of regular exercise. Horse riding was his preference, but even this had to be pursued in a particular manner for optimal results; it was, for example, unwise to ride in the afternoon or in the heat of the day.[26]

Part of the allure of riding was that it provided individuals with an opportunity 'to take the air'. 'Pure air and exercise are indispensable for the preservation of ... life', Dr James Reynolds informed the House of Lords in 1793, and when faced with the prospect of imprisonment, he protested that his incarceration in 'the foul air of Newgate would be to send me to speedy execution'.[27] Reynolds' constitution was more robust than he suggested, but it is noteworthy that peers did not ignore his plea; they responded by instructing that he should spend his detention in the modern, airy, accommodation available at Kilmainham jail.[28]

As well as 'air and exercise', diet was also critical to well-being, particularly for those who had negotiated illness. There were as many suggestions on this point as there were recovered patients, consistent with the fact, Archbishop King observed perceptively, that 'experience makes everyone a physician'. Of the various options appealed to, asses milk, goat's whey, broth, and a general regimen of plain food were deemed particularly efficacious.[29] Fruit, by contrast, had few advocates because of the dangers associated with its consumption. Unripe fruit was believed to be a major cause of 'gripes', but it was also regarded warily because it was 'productive of many disorders to young persons, by vitiating the blood, breeding worms, injuring the appetite etc.'. It was particularly unhealthy if taken while embarked on a regime of water drinking, because fruit and imported mineral waters, which were consumed in substantial volume, were deemed a volatile combination.[30] Moreover, this belief proved as enduring as the conviction that 'those who lived abstemiously', which could mean 'staying at home and feeding ... sparingly' at times (like Christmas) when feasting was the norm, and who took plenty of exercise were more likely not only to enjoy good health, but also to inhibit the return of troubling conditions.[31]

Such preventative strategies were well intended though they were built on problematical medical foundations. This is true also of the belief, which had

---

[26] Legg (ed.), *The Synge letters*, pp. 82, 168, 170, 171.

[27] Pearde to Price, 27 June 1746 (NLW, Puleston papers, MS 3579 fol. 106); Kelly (ed.), *Proceedings of the Irish House of Lords, 1771–1800,* vol 2, pp. 430–31.

[28] 'Diary of Anne Cooke', *Journal of the Kildare Archaeological Society*, 8 (1915–7): 104–32 (119).

[29] King to Delasay, 2 June 1715 (TCD, King papers, MS 2536 fol, 307); Fitzwilliam to Lord Fitzwilliam, 7 February, 7 March 1758 (NAI, Pembroke Estate papers, 97/46/1/2/7/106, 107); Legg (ed.), *The Synge letters*, pp. 15, 458; James Kelly, 'Drinking the waters', 108–9.

[30] Legg (ed.), *The Synge letters*, pp.139; Kelly, 'Drinking the waters', 133; *Hibernian Journal*, 10 August 1789.

[31] Bishop Stearne of Dromore to King, 29 January 1715, Ward to King, 25 March 1728 (TCD, King papers, MSS 1995–2008, fols 1574, 2178).

professional as well as popular sanction, that alcohol possessed useful health-giving properties.[32] Indeed, it was widely accepted that individual wines, like mineral and spa waters, possessed properties that were particularly useful in arresting particular conditions. Thus hock was useful in combating jaundice, and, when 'drank in whey', in combating fever. By contrast, Moselle, Sack and Canary wines were perceived to possess properties that were more generally beneficial. It is notable that Bishop Synge recommended that his stock of each was maintained to assist with the recovery of friends and retainers when they fell ill.[33] The suggestion that those who were susceptible to gout should eat and drink their full underlines the strength of the belief in the medicinal virtues of wine. This perception is supported by Bishop Synge's complacent observation in 1749 that a combination of 'my usual quantity of wine at dinner' and 'three or four hours riding every day' ensured 'sufficient vigour and motion to my blood', though he conceded that when he left off drinking wine at night it was 'of great service to me'.[34] In reality, it is unlikely either regimen warded off illness, but it is noteworthy that Synge was guided in his behaviour by this objective. Others pursued still more problematic choices, as exemplified by the decision of John Giffard, the diehard municipal politician, to take up smoking in 1812 to combat 'the very worst diseases of the lungs'.[35] Disturbed by a 'salt and sorry rheum in my throat, which ... kept me constantly coughing, almost to convulsion', he concluded that if he could 'divert this humour and throw it off by saliva the cough would cease', and with this end in mind he commenced smoking. He was so pleased by the results he invoked the cry '*Vive le Tabac*' in an account of his improved condition.[36]

**Caring in the domestic environment**

As evidenced by the manifold strategies – wise, foolish and useless – that were employed to avert the onset of illness, or to respond to it when it occurred, late early modern Ireland was, to echo Roy Porter's arresting phrase, as much a sickness society as contemporary England. The most obvious justification for this

---

[32] For example, Daniel O'Connell was advised by his doctor in 1794 to consume a bottle of port a day to combat a 'slow nervous fever': M.R. O'Connell (ed.), *The correspondence of Daniel O'Connell* (8 vols Dublin: Irish University Press for the Irish Manuscripts Commission, 1972–80), vol 2, pp. 18–19.

[33] H.F. Berry, 'Notes from the diary of a Dublin lady in the reign of George II', *Journal of the Royal Society of Antiquaries of Ireland*, 28 (1898): 142; Legg (ed.), *The Synge letters*, pp. 205, 212, 246.

[34] King to Mountjoy, 14 February 1715 (TCD, King papers, MS 2536, fol. 188); Legg (ed.), *The Synge letters*, pp. 166, 168.

[35] *Saunders' Newsletter*, 14 December 1767.

[36] John to A.H. Giffard, 17 February 1812 in A.H. Giffard, *Who was my grandfather: a biographical sketch* (London: privately published, 1865), p. 73.

designation is the extended duration of most illnesses, and the generous allocation of time allowed those who were indisposed to recuperate. For example, Richard Godwin was granted six weeks' leave of absence from the revenue service in 1730 so he could have a fistula attended to; in the estimation of his surgeon, this was the time required to prepare Godwin for surgery and to enable him to cure.[37]

In most households, the burden of attending to those who were indisposed was assumed by women, though men, as evidenced by Edward Newenham who sat up with his wife for six nights when she was ill in 1778, did assist on occasion.[38] Be that as it may, it was not unusual for wives, mothers and daughters to watch over ill relatives through the night as well as the day, though this was often draining, physically as well as emotionally. There are plenty of examples, but a useful illustration of the commitment demanded is provided by the medical history of Edmund Spencer of Renny in county Cork. Spencer spent most of the winter of 1744–5 in bed 'consumed with nocturnal sweats and irregular hecticks', from which he did not declare himself recovered until March. During the winter of 1755–6, he was prostrated by a 'violent' attack of cholic that at one moment caused his physicians to fear for his life, and he spent a further 44 days 'laid up on his back' in 1758 with an ailment that manifested itself as cholic but which defied the best efforts of his physicians even to identify. In Spencer's case, his primary carer was his daughter Rosamond.[39] Her selflessness was widely replicated even though, as Bishop Synge observed of 'the dutifull affectionate care' lavished on the terminally ill archbishop of Tuam (Josiah Hort, d.1751) by his daughters, the toll it took on the health of carers gave cause for concern.[40] This was true also of wives, as evidenced by the case of John Freke, whose wife Elizabeth 'watched with him eight nights together' in 1704 when the fever that confined him to bed for 'above three months' was at its worst.[41] Given the demand involved in maintaining a 24-hour watch over an ill family member, it was inevitable that the duty was also entrusted to servants and attentive companions, and that they fulfilled the role usually performed by family when the latter was not available. The debt Alicia Synge owed her French governess and companion is manifest in her admission

---

[37] Minutes of revenue commissioners, 9 April 1730 (TNA, CUST1/21, fol. 418).

[38] James Kelly, *Sir Edward Newenham, MP: defender of the Protestant constitution* (Dublin: FCP, 2004), p. 144.

[39] Edmund Spencer to Francis Price, 18 January, 4 March 1745, Spencer to Alice Price, 22 December 1756, 21 February 1757, Rosamond Spencer to Alice Price, 18 September 1758 (NLW, Puleston papers, MS 3580, fols 28, 29, 106, 107, 120).

[40] Legg (ed.), *Synge letters*, p. 386.

[41] R.A. Anselment (ed.), *The remembrances of Elizabeth Freke, 1671–1714*, Camden, Fifth Series, vol. 18, (Cambridge: CUP, 2001), p. 79; R.A. Anselment, 'The want of health: an early eighteenth-century self-portrait of sickness', *Literature and Medicine*, 15 (1996): 225–43 (232–4).

that she could 'never repay the same friend and nurse' for all she had done on her behalf.[42]

The expectation that women would accept the primary responsibility of nursing those who were ill is exemplified by the Quaker community, where health care was normally defined as a female responsibility. In this, Mary Leadbeater's attitude was not untypical. She tended her husband William devotedly in 1797 when he was struck down by a fever, and was so determined to minister to his every need, that even when she was counselled by her 'doctors' not to sleep in the same room because she was heavily pregnant, she 'sate up most of the night in the adjoining one' listening.[43] Since her husband recovered, Leadbeater could reasonably conclude that the sacrifice she made was justified. Susanna Day's experience provides a different perspective. Obliged over the period of 18 months in 1801–2 to devote herself to the care of her terminally ill husband, she wrestled with the conflicting demands of caring and her desire for a normal life: 'My TD's weak state calls for my constant care and prevents my moving from home to see any of my friends but those who reside in town – and very short visits must suffice – but I hope my mind is in a comfortable degree reconciled to my present allotment.' Susanna coped stoically at first, but as her husband's condition worsened, she found the demand overwhelming: 'for sixteen months I have washed and dressed and led him and fed him when necessary ... I cannot now do for him without assistance', she observed plaintively.[44]

Though Susanna Day was only relieved of her onerous burden by her husband's demise, the positive consequence of such experiences for Quaker communities was that women who were adept at diagnosing and treating illness performed a function elsewhere provided by male professionals, and they were widely resorted to as a result. Because they did this on top of their other duties (domestic as well as religious), it is apparent that the prospect of 'patients as if without end' was not always agreeable, though most responded with remarkable good cheer.[45] This positive attitude was encouraged by the belief that caring was a natural womanly function, and many young women were, as Mary Wollstonecraft advised, 'taught the elements of anatomy and medicine so they could care for themselves and their families' for this reason.[46] The provision of nursing care by wives and daughters was an obvious manifestation of the importance of the family unit in dispensing medical care, but since the effective nursing of those who were stuck down by any of the many life-threatening ailments that were endemic involved the administration of remedies, knowledge was also crucial.

---

[42] Legg (ed.), *Synge letters*, p. 485.

[43] Riana McLaughlin, 'The sober duties of life: the domestic and religious life of six Quaker women, 1780–1820' (NUI, Galway, MA thesis, 1993), 95.

[44] McLaughlin, 'The sober duties of life', pp. 98–9. TD was the shorthand Susanna Day employed when referring to her husband.

[45] McLaughlin, 'The sober duties of life', p. 69.

[46] Janet Todd, *Rebel daughters: a story of 1798* (London: Viking, 2003), p. 142.

## Accessing medical information

The primary repository of medical information in the domestic environment was the medical 'receipt' book – a compendium of medical nostrums – that assisted families to respond to ailments and illnesses as they arose. Because of the obvious fallibility of the remedies contained within a typical receipt book, it is tempting to conclude that 'the hotch-potch of so-called "receipts" recorded in such collections' was emblematical of the desperation of contemporaries to do something to counter illnesses they did not understand and diseases they were largely powerless to cure.[47] However, receipt books can better be seen as the epitome of 'the entrenched and enduring pluralism of pre-modern medical care', and as a practical manifestation of the fact that, since domestic medication was an intrinsic feature of household management, the organisation of medical care within the household, like the organisation of diet, was a primarily a female responsibility.[48]

As a practice, the collection of medical 'receipts' was introduced into Ireland as part of the process that witnessed the emergence of an Anglophone settler community in the seventeenth century. This explains the presence in the muniments of the Parsons of Birr of a vellum bound volume of medical and kitchen recipes, assembled between 1645 and 1652. Consistent with its date of composition, it includes herbal remedies for wounds as well as cures for kidney stones. The remedies favoured by the next generation of the same family, as instanced by the 'booke of choice receipes' prepared by Dorothy Parsons in 1666, possess a more obvious 'medical' character, and embrace remedies for a wider range of ailments (rheumatism, deafness and cancer) and contagions (plague, small pox and consumption).[49] Saliently, this pattern is still more in evidence in the receipt book assembled by Mrs Jane Bury c. 1700, which includes 'a medicine for a cold', and ointments for head and other aches, boils, broken bones and 'old wounds'. There are also recipes of English origination for plaisters.[50]

A majority of the remedies included in receipt books from the late seventeenth and early eighteenth centuries were herbal.[51] This is consistent with the enduring strength of herbal medicine in England and Scotland, but this medical culture also drew heavily on animal parts for cures that were recommended for life-threatening conditions. Consumption is a case in point. The remedy included in Jane Bury's recipe book was for distilling a liquid from a variety of ingredients that included

---

[47] Porter, 'The people's health', p. 124.
[48] Porter, 'The people's health', p. 124.
[49] Receipe/receipt books, 1645–52, 1666 (Birr Castle, Rosse papers, MSS A/4, A/17).
[50] Mrs Jane Bury's recipe book, 1700 (NLI, Townley Hall papers, MS 9563).
[51] Mrs Jane Bury's recipe book, 1700; R. Lohan and T. Quinlan, 'Some receipts and hints from an eighteenth-century household', in *Irish Archives*, Spring 1995, p. 16; Twigge receipe book (NAI, MS 6231).

a calf's lung, a peck of garden snails, eggs, nutmeg and milk.[52] A comparable remedy for snailwater, (which was deemed particularly helpful in combating consumption), in the recipe book of Diana and Jane Twigge, probably of county Limerick, involved earth worms as well as snails, and a large selection of herbs. It is noteworthy that this echoed a nostrum included by Elizabeth Freke on a list of remedies that she assembled during her lifetime.[53] Compared with these, the receipts for snailwater inherited by Mary Granville (Mrs Delany), passed down through three generations of that family, were straightforward. One recipe involved creating a solution by mixing snails with sage and brown sugar; another could be composed by binding potato, red cow's milk, aniseed and snail shells.[54] If these ingredients could be acquired, these were not difficult medicines to make, which may partly explain why remedies requiring ingredients of animal derivation remain popular curatives for consumption. In a receipt included in a collection dating from the mid-eighteenth century, it was advised that brown candy sugar be dissolved in urine from the 'the bladder of a young steer' to create a palatable drink that was to be taken by consumptives three times a day.[55]

Though receipts using animal products are not hard to locate, they are less commonplace in Irish receipt books than in equivalent documents of English and Scottish origins. Indicatively, a series of ointments and oils from Scotland dating from 1670 that involved roasting frogs and black snails in the abdomen of a fat dog have no equivalent in the Irish record.[56] This is largely true also of many of the older and more magical of the extensive listing of remedies prepared by Elizabeth Freke. Her eclectic assemblage, drawn from mainly English sources, includes directions on the making and taking of laudanum among a colourful listing of receipts that endorsed the consumption of powdered house mice in beer to relieve whooping cough; the use of fox grease to ease ear ache; the ashes of the skull of a 'coal black cat' for failing eyesight; the ground powder of an unburied human skull for palsy; and various other exotics such as the powdered liver of a hedgehog for dropsy, powdered woodlice for declining sight, and burned bees in ash for hair loss, that are not duplicated in documents of purely Irish origin.[57] This is not to suggest that Irish consumers resisted the inclusion of exotic animal parts in their medications. However, as a more recently settled society, its Anglophone

---

[52] As note 51.

[53] Porter, 'The people's health', p. 124; Elizabeth Freke 'A table of physical receits for my own use …,' printed in Mrs Elizabeth Freke, her diary, 1671–1714', *Journal of the Cork Archaeological and Historical Society*, 2nd series 19 (1913): 134–47(144).

[54] Cookery and medicinal recipe book of Anne Granville (Folger Library, Washington, MS V.A.430).

[55] Medicinal and cookery recipe book (NLI, Lenihan papers, MS 13603).

[56] See the extracts from the Landess diary in John Stevenson, *Two centuries of life in county Down* (Belfast: McCaw, Stevenson and Orr, 1917), pp. 457–8.

[57] Freke 'A table of physical receits for my own use …', 144–7; for additional examples, see Fleetwood, *History*, pp. 61–2, 63.

component was at greater liberty to adopt and to discard particular medicines. This (ostensibly precocious) rejection of exotic animal ingredients is in keeping with a diminishing belief in the efficacy of these products and with the greater reliance on proprietary and patent medicine that is identifiable from the 1720s.[58] It is appropriate therefore that the contents of medical receipt books dating from the mid and late eighteenth century suggest a continuing diminution in the appeal of remedies that involved the powdering of earthworms or the usage of the vital organs of rodents. Animal ingredients continued to feature in cures for consumption, and there is an interesting example of a lotion for deafness involving the usage of fat rendered from baked eels in the 'receipt book' maintained at Townley Hall, county Meath between 1734 and 1782. Nevertheless, the preferred approach was more orthodox, and involved a combination of herbal remedies and humoral basics such as bleeding.[59]

Indicatively, remedies were drawn increasingly from medicinal circles. When Elizabeth Freke assembled her capacious 'table of phisycall receits' early in the eighteenth century, she attributed a larger proportion to ladies of her acquaintance than to herbalists and medical men such as Nicholas Culpeper, John Pechey and John Gerard.[60] Subsequent compilers reversed this, and it is notable from the mid-eighteenth-century receipt book of Townley Hall and Lady Florence Balfour's book, which dates from the end of the century, that the proportion of cited remedies originating with named physicians continued to grow. Thus, among others, the former includes the 'late Dr Smyth of Dawson's Street' remedy for rheumatism, and the latter Dr Hay's remedy for scurvy.[61] This did not eclipse the practice of ladies exchanging remedies, but it is notable that the print media grew in importance as a source of information. This is symbolised by the presence in the Townley Hall receipt book of news-cuttings as well as by the inclusion on a smaller list generated by the same household of a cure for rabies that was published in the *Dublin Gazette* in 1737.[62] Indeed, remedies were culled from far and wide. The latter Townley Hall receipt book also includes a 'famous American receipt for rheumatism', while a comparable compilation held at Killeen Castle, the seat of the earls of Fingall, included the Duke of Portland's recipe for rheumatism and Mr Rawlins' fistula wash.[63]

It may be that no more than a fraction of the remedies included in an average medical receipt books were ever resorted to. Yet, the fact that most landed families

---

[58] Kelly, 'Health for sale', *passim*.

[59] NLI, Townley Hall papers, MS 9560.

[60] Freke 'A table of physical receits for my own use ...', 144–7; Anselment, 'The want of health', 225–6.

[61] NLI, Townley Hall papers, MSS 9560, 9561.

[62] NLI, Townley Hall papers, MSS 9560, 11884; *Dublin Gazette*, 30 January, 18 October 1737.

[63] NLI, Townley Hall papers, MS 11884; NLI, Fingall papers, MS 8041/1.

possessed volumes of this sort,⁶⁴ that some were equipped with indices, and others manifest all the signs of frequent use suggests that men as well as women in these circles reached automatically for their receipt book for guidance when family members showed symptoms of indisposition. It is notable, in this context, that an impressive number of the remedies contained in Lady Florence Balfour's compilation were devised for children, and that many of the receipts contained therein could have been made from readily available kitchen condiments, and resorted to without apprehension. Others experimented with more elaborate and ambitious medications. The presence in the papers of William Parsons of Birr of a receipt dating from 1689 'for a purging infusion of gum Arabic and worms ointment' is illustrative of this tendency. It is still more manifest in the medical bills of Charles Daly, esq., which reveal that he expended £38 1s. 5d. in 1766 on a range of pills, ointments and ingredients that could be used directly or fashioned into various lotions, potions and medications, such as featured in various receipt books.⁶⁵

A further, and more reliable, indication that receipts were collected for use is provided by the readiness with which they were exchanged. In 1726, Knightly Chetwood of Dublin 'gave the receipt for my ointment' for burns to assist the child of a family friend who 'was burned by her running against a warming pan'.⁶⁶ Edmund Spencer of Renny, county Cork did likewise; he conveyed the receipt of the 'one remedy' he possessed for sore eyes to Alice Price at Wrexham in 1759 with the advice that she should not take alarm if it 'smart[ed] a little' as he knew from experience that 'two nights bathing with a little of it after I am in bed eases all inflammation'.⁶⁷ Similarly, Bishop Edward Synge instructed his daughter to search 'among your Mama's receits' for a remedy for scrofula that he wished to convey to an apothecary at Elphin for use by a 'poor boy'.⁶⁸ In common with many such remedies, this cure proved less than entirely efficacious, but such experiences did little to diminish belief in the merits of maintaining medical receipt books, or of the practice of self-medication that sustained them.

---

⁶⁴ For other examples, see NLI, de Vesci papers, MS 39250/1; PRONI, Medical recipes of Elizabeth Conolly, 1805, D2400; NAI, Receipe Book, 1775, MS 999/90. For comparable English examples in the Suffolk Record Office, see HA 67, 457, 458, 461, 468/1, HA30/50/22/27.3.

⁶⁵ Receipt made out to William Parsons, 23 December 1689 (Birr Castle, Rosse papers, A/1/6); Medical account of Charles Daly, 6 September 1766 (NLI, MS 8720).

⁶⁶ Chetwood to Ussher, 16 April 1726 in 'The Chetwood letters', 275.

⁶⁷ Spenser to Price, 31 December 1759 (NLW, Puleston papers, MS 3580 fol. 115).

⁶⁸ Legg (ed.), *Synge letters*, pp. 50, 229.

## Print and domestic medication

In order that the tradition of domestic medication should remain vigorous, it was critical that it was constantly replenished and invigorated with new remedies and solutions, and as the role of the press in conveying information on all subjects appreciated from the 1720s, an expanding volume of medical information was presented to the public through this medium. The importance of the newspaper as a source of medicinal information is symbolised by a manuscript addition to the National Library of Ireland copy of *Pue's Occurrences* for 1746 of a 'receipt for a flux'.[69] It is not apparent how this came about, but since Thomas Prior, one of the founding members of the Dublin Society, looked to the press to convey medical remedies to the public, it constitutes a symbolic affirmation of the importance of the newspaper in the dissemination of medical knowledge that was of use to the domestic practitioner.[70]

The potential of print as a source of medical information was first manifested in the 1720s at the same time that there was a veritable explosion in the marketing of commercial medicine. One of the first such interventions – a broadside with a list 'of choice receipts in physick and surgery for the cure of diseases insident [sic] to man's body' attributed to John Audouin, a surgeon, who was executed in 1728 for murdering his maid servant – was a blatant attempt to cash in on Audouin's notoriety by an opportunistic publisher.[71] Others sought to capitalise on the demand, and, from the early 1730s, the public was plied with a rich diet of folk and self-help remedies. The press led the way. In the main, the remedies conveyed to the public through this medium avoided the exotic ingredients readily found in domestic receipt books. Instead, they favoured largely herbal concoctions for ailments as diverse as the stone and gravel, colds and coughs, consumption, cholera, ague, fluxes, rheumatism and rabies, which were accompanied by detailed instructions as to how medications could be made and administered.[72] These remedies were no less problematic than the salves, balms, drugs and potions

---

[69] *Pue's Occurrences*, 1746, NLI.

[70] A.A. Luce, *The life of George Berkeley, Bishop of Cloyne* (London: Nelson, 1949), p. 198.

[71] *Doctor Audouin's last legacies to the world containing choice receipts in physick and surgery for the cure of diseases insident to man's body* (Dublin, 1728); for the Audouin case see James Kelly, *Gallows speeches from eighteenth-century Ireland* (Dublin: FCP, 2002), pp. 224–6; James Kelly, '"A most inhuman and barbarous piece of villainy": an exploration of the crime of rape in eighteenth-century Ireland', *Eighteenth-Century Ireland*, 9 (1994): 7–43.

[72] *Faulkner's Dublin Journal*, 3 August 1731, 15 December 1746; *Dublin Gazette*, 3 February 1730, 10 January 1733, 30 January, 18 October 1737, 26 June, 10 July 1739, 14 November 1741; *Dublin Newsletter*, 20 January 1740; *Dublin Evening Post*, 3 February 1733; 13 July 1734, 9 August, 6 September 1735; *Dublin Courant*, 29 December 1744; *Munster Journal*, 15 November 1750.

medical retailers offered for sale, but the frequency with which certain nostrums were recycled suggests that they were popular with the newspaper buying public.[73] As a result, the press quickly became a useful source of information in respect of such conditions as stone and gravel, calculi, rabies, ague, consumption, scurvy and headaches, though more serious afflictions such as cancer were not ignored. In the main, the quality of the advice depended on the source from which it emanated, but the publication, first in the *Gentleman's Magazine* in 1763 and subsequently in the *Freeman's Journal* in 1785, of the suggestion that boiled quicksilver might be administered to children to 'cure worms and cutaneous disorders' is indicative not only of the potential dangers but also of the enduring appeal of some hazardous remedies.[74] This was true of only a minority of conditions. The relentless pursuit of a cure for hydrophobia (rabies), by contrast, encouraged the publication of an exceptional number of ephemeral remedies, culled from a great variety of domestic and foreign sources.[75] Inevitably, their usefulness varied, though it is not apparent how contemporaries were expected to differentiate between the absurdity of taking spider's web in pill form followed by an hour's vigorous exercise as a cure for ague and the wisdom of a regimen of bed rest and fluid consumption for colds and flu.[76]

In reality, the practitioner of domestic medicine could avoid making such decisions by appealing to one of the proliferating number of medical guides. In this respect, Ireland was considerably in arrears of Great Britain, which had in Nicholas Culpeper's many publications alone, a rich seam of usable texts. Culpeper was not unknown in Ireland; in the 1670s, the rector of Dunaghy, county Antrim, Andrew Rowan, possessed a copy of *A directory for midwives*.[77] However, there was no Irish edition of any of Culpeper's works until 1740, or of such 'landmarks

---

[73] As illustrated by the following examples: stone and gravel (*Faulkner's Dublin Journal*, 3 August 1731; *Dublin Gazette*, 31 July 1731, 10 July 1739); colds and coughs (*Dublin Gazette*, 30 January 1733; *Dublin Evening Post*, 3 February 1733); rabies (*Dublin Evening Post*, 16 July 1734, 6 September 1735; *Dublin Gazette*, January 1735, 30 January, 18 October 1737); Mrs Stephens' recipe for the stone (*Dublin Gazette*, 26 June 1739, 14 November 1741).

[74] *Hibernian Journal*, 11 November 1789, 2 June 1790; *Freeman's Journal*, 7 October 1777, 28 April, 3 September 1785, 7, 12 December 1786, 28 June 1788, 4 September 1792; *Gentleman's Magazine*, January 1763, p. 45.

[75] *Munster Journal*, 22 February, 6 December 1750; *Hibernian Journal*, 13 December 1771, 30 July 1790; *Freeman's Journal*, 2 May 1775, 28 August 1787, 10 May 1791.

[76] *Hibernian Journal*, 6 September 1780; *Freeman's Journal*, 29 November 1788.

[77] D.A. Chart, 'An account book of the Rev. Andrew Rowan, rector of Dunaghy, county Antrim, c. 1672–1680', *Ulster Journal of Archaeology*, 3rd series, 5 (1942): 67–76 (75). Interestingly, an edition of Culpepper's *Midwife* was published in Belfast in 1766 (see J.R.R. Adams, 'Some aspects of the influence of printed material on everyday life in eighteenth-century Ulster' in Alan Gailey (ed.), *The use of tradition: essays presented to G. B. Thompson* (Cultra: Ulster Folk and Transport Museum, 1988), p. 119) and the first Irish edition of his influential *The English physician enlarged* in Dublin in 1787.

of popular medicine' as Luigi Cornaro's *Sure and certain methods of attaining a long and healthful life*, Eliza Smith's vastly popular *The Compleat Housewife, or accomplish'd gentlewoman's companion*, which included 'two hundred receipts of medicines', or of most of George Cheyne's works.[78] Indicatively, it was not until the 1730s, synchronous with the adoption by the press of an interest in the publication of remedies, that popular medical guides were published in Dublin. One of the first was Thomas Dover's *The ancient physician's legacy to his country, being what he has collected himself in forty-nine years practice*, which was a best seller in the early 1730s when it went to six editions in London and two in Dublin.[79] Yet, despite this obvious success, works on an equivalent scale were seldom published in Ireland during the following three decades. There was, for example, only one Irish edition of John Wesley's classic *Primative Physic* (1752), which presented some 'four hundred of the most useful and valuable receipts'. Instead, Irish publishers concentrated on producing pamphlets that engaged with a restricted list of conditions, or offered 'specifick remedies', for challenging ailments such as 'convulsive distemper.[80] The publication in 1764 by John Wade, a Dublin chemist, of 'a collection of useful family remedies', of John Theobald's 'complete collections of efficacious and approved remedies', and of Theophilus Lobb's 'useful family physician', suggests that demand for accessible medical information was then on the increase, but Irish publishers were reluctant to forsake the tried and trusted pamphlet medium.[81] Indeed, the re-publication in this format in 1770 of the London edition of Robert Johnson's 'directions for the sick'; in 1771 of John Ball's *The female physician*; in 1772 of *Nature the best physician*; and in 1776 of *The modern family physician*, which was essentially a compilation of cures prepared by a number of legendary doctors, indicate that it was an enduringly

---

[78] Ginnie Smith, 'Proscribing the rules of health' in Porter (ed.), *Patients and practitioners*, pp. 256–7; Luigi Cornero (1475–1566), *Sure and certain methods of attaining a long and healthful life, with means of correcting a bad constitution* (London, 1702; 3rd edn, Dublin 1740); Eliza Smith, *The compleat housewife: or accomplish'd gentlewoman's companion ... to which is added a collection of above two hundred receipts of medicines* (London, 1727).

[79] Thomas Dover, *The ancient physician's legacy to his country, being what he has collected himself in forty-nine years practice* (4th edn, Dublin, 1733).

[80] John Wesley, *Primative Physic, or an easy and natural method of curing most diseases* (Dublin, 1752); *An easy and infallible cure of several diseases, especially colick, the gout, gravel ... worms, whereby any person may acquire a perfect knowledge of his distemper, and also of the effectual means of curing himself* (Dublin [,1747]) advertised in *Dublin Courant*, 14 February and *Pue's Occurrences*, 24 February 1747.

[81] John Wade, *The family physician: being a collection of useful family remedies* (Dublin, 1764); John Theobald, *Every man his own physician. Being a complete collection of efficacious and approved remedies, for every disease incident to the human body* (Dublin, 1764); Theophilus Lobb, *The Good Samaritan: or useful family physician, containing observations on the most frequent diseases of men and women* (Dublin, 1764, 1774).

popular medium for the circulation of medical information.[82] The pamphlet was not sufficient to meet the public's need for general and accessible information, however, and, beginning in the mid-1760s, publishers began to produce larger, compendious works that enhanced the capacity of the individual and of the family to self-medicate.

The first such work, Samuel Auguste Tissot's seminal *Advice to people in general with respect to their health*, originally published in French at Lausanne in 1761, was published in two volumes in Dublin in 1766, the same year that it saw print in Edinburgh.[83] Tissot was a skilled clinician, and it was the manner in which he combined clinical description with therapy, and the emphasis he attached to prophylaxis that made his book special.[84] There is a lack of specific information as to how it was received in Ireland, but the fact that further Irish editions were published in 1769 and 1774 suggests that it excited considerable interest. It certainly served to encourage publishers to be more adventurous, and the early 1770s witnessed the publication by James Potts, the main medical publisher of the day, of an enhanced and expanded list of texts by various authors including John Trusler (1735–1820).[85] None of these emulated Tissot, but the latter was to lose his premier place in the domestic setting with the publication in 1773 of an Irish version of the second edition of William Buchan's remarkable *Domestic medicine: or a treatise on the prevention and cure of diseases by regimen and simple medicine* by a consortium of Dublin printers.[86]

Buchan's *Domestic medicine* was both more accessible and immediately relevant than Tissot's *Advice*. Written with the specific purpose of removing 'the veil of mystery, which still hangs over medicine', and which Buchan averred, in the preface to the third edition, 'renders it not only a conjectural, but even a suspicious art', it consciously eschewed Latin and technical terminology (as

---

[82] Robert Wallace Johnson, *Some friendly cautions to the heads of families, containing ample directions for the sick, and women in child-bed* (Dublin, [1770]); John Ball, *The female physician: or every woman her own doctor* (Dublin, [1771]); *Nature the best physician, or everyman his own doctor, containing rules for the preservation of health and long life* (Dublin, 1772); *The modern family physician, or the art of healing made easy, being a plain description of diseases ... extracted from ... Sydenham, Mead ... and other eminent physical writers* (Dublin, 1776).

[83] Samuel Auguste Tissot, *Advice to people in general with respect to their health* (Dublin, 1766); *Dublin Chronicle*, 30 January 1770.

[84] Antoinette Emch-Dériaz, *Tissot: physician of the Enlightenment* (New York and Bern: Peter Lang, 1992); Séverine Pilloud and Michel Louis-Courvoisier, 'The intimate experience of the body in the eighteenth century: between interiority and exteriority', *Medical History*, 47 (2003): 451–3.

[85] *The New Dispensatory* (3rd edn, Dublin, 1770); Thomas Marryat, The new practice of physic (2nd edn Dublin, 1770); John Trusler, *An easy way to prolong life, by a little attention to what we eat and drink* (Dublin, 1773).

[86] William Buchan, *Domestic medicine: or a treatise on the prevention and cure of diseases by regimen and simple medicine* (2nd edn, Dublin, 1773).

'not only ridiculous [but also] dangerous') in favour of 'the common language of the country'. This ran the risk of antagonising the medical establishment, which was not Buchan's intention. His stated aim was to 'lay ... medicine more open to mankind', and it was with this in mind that he set about preparing 'a comprehensive domestic manual' in which (in contrast to Tissot who 'confine[d] himself to ... acute diseases') he dealt with the full range of what might be termed quotidian conditions and attached greater emphasis to 'the patient's own endeavours' and on 'the prophylaxis, or preventative part of medicine'. He justified this approach on the grounds that since it was 'always in the power of the patient or of those about him, to do as much towards his recovery as can be effected by the physician', it was critical that the public possessed the requisite information. Like many of his contemporaries, Buchan attached enormous importance to regimen, but he also believed that carers and patients could be entrusted to administer most 'medicines ... with great freedom and safety', which he described in a more comprehensive manner and at greater length than any of his contemporaries.[87]

Because Buchan's *Domestic medicine* was more broadly focussed than Tissot, less technical than Lobb, more up to date than Cornaro, Culpeper or Cheyne, and more comprehensive than Wesley, it achieved immense popularity. Its appeal in Ireland is attested by the publication in Dublin of editions of the second, third, sixth, seventh, ninth (two), twelfth and fifteenth editions of the text between 1773 and 1797.[88] This was unprecedented for a work of this kind, and it provided families with access to a large amount of comparatively easily negotiated information. Its domestic appeal was highlighted by the fact that the text commenced with a substantial chapter on children, but the work was equally pioneering for the emphasis Buchan attached to prevention, and by the inclusion of chapters on cleanliness and infection. Yet, *Domestic medicine* is first and foremost about medical care and the text included an extensive appendix with 'a list of [such] drugs and medicines as may be necessary for private practice', and a guide to how all the major 'medicinal preparations' were readied.[89] Taken together with the bulging receipt books that were commonplace, it meant that there were few Anglophone households that did not have access to sufficient information to equip them to provide domestic care that, if administered with wisdom and prudence, could be as efficacious as that forthcoming from trained medical practitioners.

---

[87] William Buchan, *Domestic medicine, or a treatise on the prevention and cure of diseases by regimen and simple medicines* (3rd edn, Dublin, 1774), preface for the quotations cited in this paragraph; C.J. Lawrence, 'William Buchan: medicine laid open', *Medical History*, 19 (1975): 20–35.

[88] Buchan, *Domestic medicine, or a treatise on the prevention and cure of diseases by regimen and simple medicines* (2nd edn, 1773; 3rd edn, 1774; 6th edn, 1777; 7th edn, 1781; 9th edn, 1784; 12th edn, 1792; 9th edn, 1796; 15th edn, 1797). William Slater was the only printer involved in the publication of all editions, and of the first Irish printing of Tissot's *Advice*.

[89] Buchan, *Domestic medicine* (3rd edn), appendix.

## The practice of self-medication

In keeping with his membership of the Royal College of Physicians at Edinburgh, William Buchan anticipated that *Domestic Medicine* would assist 'to destroy quackery'.[90] This assumed that the medicine-consuming public was at one with him in perceiving a clear distinction between orthodox and unorthodox medicine, which was not the case. What is certain is that, given the increased availability of medicines of all kinds, guides such as Buchan's *Domestic Medicine* were invaluable in assisting those who engaged actively in self-medication. The extent to which this happened is difficult to assess, but references in correspondence to the effectiveness of 'balsam of capivi' and 'oyl of turpentine' in easing the passage of a kidney stone, to the frequency with which individuals 'took physsick', and the readiness with which opium was consumed indicates that there was a considerable amount of casual self medication.[91] This may well have been more prevalent among those for whom the expense of a professional consultation was not a minor consideration. Nicholas Peacock, the county Limerick agent farmer, is a case in point. Peacock routinely 'took physick' to ward off the threat of a cold or to relieve the feeling of 'being unwell'.[92] Mary Lucas of Drumcavan, county Clare, who took a vomit in May 1741 to combat the impact of illness is another such example. Richard Griffith, who led a precarious lifestyle as a landowner and retainer, may fit the same bill, though he was one of many who were drawn by the temptations of opium, the dangers of which had become a subject of comment by the 1780s.[93]

Because of their awareness of the hazards, medical practitioners cautioned repeatedly of the dangers of self-medication. However, patients were wilful, and unwilling always to be guided by medical advice, which was unnervingly fallible in any case. Moreover, as medical retailers developed their sales networks to the extent that it was possible to have select proprietary medicines 'sent, sealed up, to any part of Ireland ... with full and plain directions', and as the belief in the possibility of medicinal cure intensified, the willingness of the public to treat itself seems to have grown proportionately.[94] Others used private networks to the same end. Edmund Spencer of Renny requested Francis Price in Wales in 1747 to send him 'a little of the Jesuits' Drops' in anticipation that he would be enabled to repeat the 'great cures' he had previously achieved with this product. The Countess of Kildare was so convinced of the merits of Ward's drops, which were widely taken

---

[90] Buchan, *Domestic medicine* (3rd edn), preface.

[91] Bishop Nicolson to Archbishop Wake, 1 September 1719 (Gilbert Library, Wake papers, MS 27 fols 236–7).

[92] M.L. Legg (ed.), *Diary of Nicholas Peacock, 1740–51* (Dublin: FCP, 2005), pp. 89, 107.

[93] Brian O Dalaigh (ed.), 'The Lucas diary, 1740–41', *Analecta Hibernica*, 40 (2007): 122; Griffith to Flood, 30 June 1774 (Birr Castle, Rosse papers, C/1/8); *Freeman's Journal*, 3 May 1788.

[94] *Pue's Occurrences*, 6 May, 22 August 1758.

for stomach complaints, that she reminded her husband in 1759 to get her a bottle in London. Bishop Edward Synge placed an equal confidence in Jesuits' Bark, but all took second place in the market place to James's Powder.[95]

James's Fever Powder was probably the most popular proprietary medicine of the eighteenth century. Nobody in Ireland seems to have held it in quite the high esteem that caused George Washington famously to describe it as 'one of the most excellent medicines in the world'. Yet it was still enormously popular, and following its introduction in the 1740s, sales appreciated rapidly, and it was readily available in all the major medical retail outlets and in most (if not all) of the main urban centres in the kingdom by the 1790s.[96] Its popularity was based first and foremost on belief in its efficacy, and that it could be auto-prescribed. This was certainly the implication of the observation by the clerk to the British Privy Council, William Sharpe, who related to the Lord Lieutenant of Ireland in 1762 that a mutual acquaintance had conquered a fever 'by Dr James's Fever Powder, which he took contrary to the opinion of his physicians'.[97] The experience of Edmond Sexten Pery sustained such impressions; his recovery in 1763 from 'spotted fever' with the assistance of James's Powder was deemed all the more remarkable because his physicians had given up hope.[98] The impact of these and similar anecdotes were reinforced by aggressive advertising, which ensured that James's Powder was already firmly established as the most popular fever medicine and general pick-me-up by the early 1770s, when it was a familiar presence in private medical chests. Elizabeth Upton of county Down is a case in point; her accounts indicate that she purchased a dozen packets of James's Powder, and four boxes of James's pills for her personal use in 1772–3.[99] Others were more cautious, and with good reason. James's Powder was not an innocent placebo; it was an 'antimonial powder', comprised of one part oxide of antimony and two parts phosphate of calcium. It was a diaphoretic, which meant that it induced perspiration,

---

[95] Spencer to Price, 16 June 1747 (NLW, Puleston papers, MS 3580 fol. 59); Dorothy Porter and Roy Porter, *Patient's Progress: doctors and doctoring in eighteenth century England* (Stanford: Stanford University Press, 1989), p. 48; Legg (ed.), *Synge letters*, p. 204.

[96] Kelly, 'Health for sale'; Roy Porter, *Health for sale: quackery in England, 1660–1800* (Manchester: Manchester University Press, 1989), p. 45; *Freeman's Journal*, 17 December 1774, 18 June 1776, 18 October 1777; *Hibernian Journal*, 29 April 1776; *Waterford Herald*, 22 May 1792.

[97] Sharpe to Halifax, 25 March 1762 (NAI, Index to interdepartmental letters and papers, 1760–1789, vol. 1, p. 45).

[98] Waite to Wilmot, 17, 19 February 1763 (PRONI, Wilmot papers, T3019/4507, 4511).

[99] Accounts of Mrs Upton, 1772–1773 printed in Stevenson, *Two centuries of life in county Down*, p. 469; Ben Domville to Sir W. Lee, 17 December 1772 (NAI, MS 3418); Lady Louis Connolly to Lady Charleville, 29 December 1807, 28 January 1808 (NUL, Marlay papers, My33, 34).

and while this could have a positive effect if one was feverish, it could also prove deleterious. Cases such as that of Dorothea Stackpoole of Edenvale, county Clare, who died of fever though she took eight James's Powders, and that of the army officer, Thomas Ash Lee, who 'lost his life by it' encouraged caution.[100] Indeed, Bishop Synge responded to news of the death of Major Lee by counselling against its use.[101] However, such concerns proved short-lived, as the imperatives of illness encouraged men and women to spend freely on the purchase of drugs and other medical paraphernalia. It was, for example, possible in Dublin in the 1770s to buy a stocked medical chest 'of the utmost utility to families' complete with a copy of *The Family Physician* to suit one budget.[102] Such facilities were beyond the resources of most, but the preparedness of Lady Louisa Conolly to spend £42 on health-related items ensured not only that the medical market remained vibrant, but also that James's Powder and other heavily advertised nostrums continued to sell well.[103] Indeed, even trained physicians integrated their usage into their proscribing practices. William Drennan, who practiced medicine at Newry during the 1780s, certainly did so. He favoured tartar emetic in instances of fever for the simple reason that it could be 'more safely applied', but recognising that other, more experienced, doctors did not share his reservations ('they [James's Powder] are ordered in the slightest feverish cases, and even to children'), he came to adopt a more relaxed attitude.[104] He remained convinced that it did not possess the 'quieting' properties that many ill persons required, but his willingness to prescribe the Powder in small quantities in combination with opium, hemlock and camphor to assist his sister overcome a debilitating fever was indicative.[105]

Because of the risks attached to the consumption of medication, many opted to drink mineral water in the belief that this was a safer way to health. The preferred option was to visit a spa, and depending on its perceived therapeutic worth either to drink or bath in the water. Because the most highly esteemed mineral waters were abroad, members of the Irish elite who could afford it, featured prominently among the visitors to Bath and Bristol Hotwells in England, and Spa in the Austrian Netherlands in the eighteenth century. However, Ireland developed its own spa network and, beginning in the late seventeenth century, locations such

---

[100] T.J. Westropp, 'Burial of Dorothea Stacpoole in Bath Abbey', *Journal of the Royal Society of Antiquaries of Ireland*, 32 (1902): 64–5; Legg (ed.), *Synge letters*, p. 426.

[101] Legg (ed.), *Synge letters*, pp. 400–401, 426–7.

[102] *Hibernian Journal*, 22 May 1772; *Freeman's Journal*, 29 July 1773.

[103] Kelly, 'Health for sale'; Todd, *Rebel daughters*, pp. 76–7; *Freeman's Journal*, 29 April 1815.

[104] McTier to Drennan, 14 June 1783, Drennan to McTier, [1784], McTier to Drennan, 1785, Drennan to McTier, 1785, McTier to Drennan, 1785 in Jean Agnew (ed.), *The Drennan–McTier letters* (3 vols, Dublin: Irish Manuscripts Commission, 1998–99), vol. 1, pp. 108–11, 168, 224, 223, 225.

[105] McTier to Drennan, 1789, Drennan to McTier, [1789], Drennan to McTier, 1789 in Agnew (ed.), *The Drennan–McTier letters*, vol 1, pp. 335–9.

as Chapelizod, Templeogue and Lucan in county Dublin, Ballyspellan in county Kilkenny, Mallow in county Cork and Swanlinbar in county Cavan, along with many other less firmly established destinations, played host to a steady flow of visitors who came to drink the waters for therapeutic reasons.[106] For those who could not visit a spa, for reasons of convenience or cost, drinking bottled mineral water was an option, and it was possible to purchase bottles of an expanding variety of spa waters in Dublin from the 1740s. It is a measure, indeed, of belief in the merits of water drinking that the craze for tar water promoted by Bishop George Berkeley proved remarkably resilient. Everyone was not equally convinced of its virtues. William Buchan observed tartly of tar water that it 'falls greatly short of the character which has been given of it', but he accepted that it possessed 'some medicinal virtues'. His decision to include it in the extensive list of medicines he appended to the text of *Domestic medicine* was consistent with the commitment Berkeley and he shared to self-medication.[107]

**Accessing medical advice**

Although the late early modern public had good reason to regard the medical profession sceptically, the recognition that they possessed useful information served to ensure that the public did not hesitate to appeal for professional medical assistance when this was available. However, they were equally disposed (when they could afford it) to seek a second, or a third or fourth medical opinion. This was not always possible, of course, even for those with deep pockets, with the result that the health conscious were obliged to have resort to a variety of different strategies to compensate. One response, identified by Lord Molesworth in 1724 and put into practice by Bishop Synge of Elphin in the 1740s, was to limit one's movements to those parts of the country where good medical assistance was available. This was not a practicable solution of course, and because the slow percolation of apothecaries, surgeons and physicians during the eighteenth century did not facilitate all who sought access to appropriate medical assistance, people were obliged to develop other strategies to assist with the diagnosing of illness and the prescription of drugs.

One tactic that was widely employed to overcome the implications of the shortage of medical expertise was the epistolary consultation. It is not possible to estimate how commonplace this was, but evidence for the practice in England and continental Europe and from family papers of Irish origin indicates that both the ill and their carers had little hesitation in appealing by letter to knowledgeable

---

[106] A fuller exploration of the themes introduced in this paragraph can be found in Kelly, 'Drinking the waters'.

[107] Buchan, *Domestic medicine*, appendix.

physicians for information and direction.[108] Anne Hamilton of Tullymore, county Down is one such example. She knew Hans Sloane, who was born at Killyleagh in the same county in 1660. Between 1708 and 1721 she openly sought his 'directions in what you think may be proper' when her own health or that of members of her family members was poor, or when she was simply dissatisfied with the advice of her regular doctor. She was not, as this suggests, a passive receptor of information; she had her own ideas on what was appropriate, as evidenced by the fact that she informed Sloane on one occasion that she was resolved 'to blister this night' to ease a 'disorder in my head'.[109]

Though Sloane's replies to Mrs Hamilton are not available, there is sufficient evidence to suggest that many medical practitioners were willing to provide detailed instructions on paper. The Dublin physician, Thomas Kingsbury, advised Francis Price, in response to a query in 1736 as to how he should deal with the fact that he was 'spitting blood', to 'draw a little blood' and to 'take supping meats of a tenacious kind'. A year later when Price's son was ill, Kingsbury conveyed 'a list of purgatives' to induce vomiting as well as his usual directions as to diet, and he offered comparable advice some months later in respect of a similar ailment, when he instructed Price how to administer 'a vomit of twelve grains of ipecacuanha powdered' to a child still at nurse. These were comparatively straightforward problems. The treatment of a 'falling of the womb' was more complex, but this did not discourage Kingsbury, who conveyed a complex medication to Francis Price to make up with advice on how it should be administered.[110]

By no means all queries were answered with the clarity displayed by Thomas Kingsbury, but it is clear that both patients and their relatives expected an informed and reasoned response when they consulted a physician. Bishop Synge made this explicit when he observed of his daughter's physician in 1752 that he 'told me facts without giving any opinion either of the nature or causes of your complaints'.[111] It is apparent also that among the social elite at least the power in the doctor–patient relationship lay squarely with the latter. This may be attributable ultimately to their relative social stations and economic power, but it was a manifestation also of the fact that members of the elite were more than ordinarily informed medically, and not at all disinclined to display or to use that knowledge.

It was desirable, of course, in a world where so much medication was auto-administered, where the ill were attended to domestically, and where skilled medical operatives were not always available, that someone within the family unit was medically aware. The problem, as Bishop Synge conceded when he admitted

---

[108] Porter and Porter, *Patient's progress*, pp. 76–8; Pilloud and Louis-Courvoisier, 'The intimate experience', 452–3; Brockliss, 'The development of the spa', pp. 40–42; see also Churchill chapter 7 in this collection.

[109] Stevenson, *Two centuries of life in Down*, pp. 464–9.

[110] Kingsbury to Price, 30 May 1736, 3 December 1737, 1 April 1740, n.d., (NLW, Puleston papers, MS 3584 fols 23, 45, 76, 106).

[111] Legg (ed.), *Synge letters*, pp. 13, 77, 456, 459, 472.

his incapacity to offer 'proper answers to ... very proper questions', was that most family experts were possessed of quite limited knowledge. This did not deter Synge who was disposed to recommend 'purges' and other decoctions for those within his circle that experienced stomach or abdominal ailments, and (still more worryingly) horse ointment for piles. However, Synge was at least conscious of his limitations. Thus, when his efforts to assist a young boy at Elphin, by administering 'spirit of opodeldock' for a serious 'pain in the thigh', proved unsuccessful, he did not hesitate to admit that the 'disorder is beyond us', or delay in seeking a place for this patient, and others with equally resistant conditions, in a Dublin hospital.[112]

Advice, to be sure, was available in abundance. Indeed, it was the norm when news of illness spread for friends and family to stand forward with medical counsel as well as morale support.[113] The experience of Hercules Langford Rowley who expressed his thanks in August 1759 to Lord Fitzwilliam 'for the trouble and pains you have taken to procure the medicine for my son from Lord Montague, to whom I think myself highly indebted for so great an obligation', is not untypical.[114] Others offered advice that would have satisfied even a doctor, as Sir Richard Musgrave demonstrated when he informed Bishop Thomas Percy in 1799 on how to deal with a persistent cough:

> I would recommend to you to bathe your feet at least three times a week in hot water going to bed, and if you don't wear flannel next to your skin apply some to your breast and shoulders. Should your cough continue to keep you awake at night take 15 or 20 drops of laudanum going to bed in whey.[115]

There was an inherent danger that advice from well-intentioned but misguided friends might serve to exacerbate rather than to ease a troubling condition, but there was little alternative when, as Archbishop Cleaver of Ferns observed despairingly of the experience of his daughter in 1798, 'various prescriptions' issued by medical professionals failed to work.[116]

A minor ailment could be complicated by a culture of domestic medication that permitted patients, and their families, a major say in how illness was treated. This was more likely when a family member or close companion was seriously ill,

---

[112] Legg (ed.), *Synge letters*, pp. 108, 114, 141, 257, 261, 316, 395, 458–9; Spirit of Opodeloc was a solution of soap in alcohol with camphor and oils of origanum and rosemary.

[113] See, for example, Stella Tillyard, *Citizen Lord: Lord Edward Fitzgerald* (London: Chatto and Windus, 1998), p. 10.

[114] Rowley to Fitzwilliam, 18 August 1759 (NAI, Pembroke Estate papers, 97/46/1/2/6/26). Anthony Browne, sixth Viscount Montagu (1686–1767) was one of the small number of English Catholic peers.

[115] Musgrave to Pery, 20 February 1799 (NLI, Musgrave–Percy papers, MS 4157 fol. 9).

[116] Cleaver to Egremont, 24 July [1798] (Petworth House, Egremont papers).

as evidenced by the reaction of Lady Louisa Conolly to the 'dreadful' experience of the death in acute pain of her sister, Cecelia. It was, Lady Louisa observed, a most 'distressing scene' because of the powerlessness of those in attendance to ease her sister's suffering: 'we could not sometimes hit upon any position of her poor emaciated frame, or the pillows to give her an easy posture, and her poor countenance looked so distressed that it went to one's heart'.[117] Experiences such as this were intensified by the avowal by candid members of the medical professions that there were many conditions 'it was not in the power of medicine to remove'.[118] As a result, by the beginning of the nineteenth century, there was a striking increase in belief in the curative efficacy of nature. This took its most tangible form in the increased enthusiasm for sea-bathing, but it also sustained a strong belief in the therapeutic value of residing in a 'drier and warmer' climate.[119] Since neither of these options was available to more than a minority, and both were of little value in dealing with serious illness, there was no reduction in resort to proprietary or other medicines. Moreover, the strength of the tradition of domestic medicine ensured not only that people were as willing as ever to try the newest remedy, but also that they took more than was appropriate in a desperate, and sometimes counterproductive, attempt to secure relief.[120] It is hardly surprising therefore that Louisa Conolly was prompted to observe 'how delightful the next world will be, free of all these vexations ... and all sorrow and sickness is at an end'.[121]

## Conclusion

Though the experiences of pain and distress chronicled by Lady Louisa Conolly bear ample witness to the limitations of medical care at the beginning of the nineteenth century, conditions had improved over the previous 150 years. In this, as in so much else in medical history, Ireland resembles England, of which it has been said that by the early nineteenth century 'a broad, better education public had emerged, far more familiar with medical book-knowledge than had been

---

[117] Lady Louisa Conolly to Lady Charleville, 22 August 1808 (NUL, Marlay papers, My36); see also Cleaver to Egremont, 29 March 1799 (Petworth House, Egremont papers).

[118] Lady Louisa Conolly to Lady Charleville, 2 August 1810 (NUL, Marlay papers, My45).

[119] Kelly, 'Drinking the waters', 138–9; Lady Louisa Conolly to Lady Charleville, 13 August 1800 (NUL, Marlay papers, My46).

[120] Bishop Barnard to Isabella Barnard, 12, 14 June 1800 in A.D. Powell (ed.), *Barnard letters 1778–1823* (London: Duckworth, 1928), pp. 123–4, 125; Lady Leitrim to Lord Leitrim, 26 July 1824 (NLI, Killadoon papers, MS 36033/3).

[121] Lady Louisa Conolly to Lady Charleville, 20 Feb. 1816, 30 August 1817 (NUL, Marlay papers, My59, 60).

the case a century earlier'.[122] It is true that the improvement in personal health was more modest, but the Anglophone population of the early nineteenth century was certainly more aware of the possibilities of diagnostic medicine and of the nature of disease. Yet, it was knowledge hard learned as the system of diagnostic medicine inaugurated in the seventeenth century was so rude and underdeveloped that the population was long obliged to look for medical assistance wherever it could be procured. One of the most important consequences of this was the development of an elaborate tradition of domestic and self-medication. This was premised on the realisation that it was incumbent on each household, and on its adult members in particular, to assume direct responsibility for the well-being of all its members both while in a state of health as well as when ill. In order to assist with this, households needed information, and they sought to collect and preserve this in receipt books that were passed, like family heirlooms, across generations. The information they contained was of doubtful value in many instances, but the changing content of these books over time bears witness to the displacement of the once dominant magico-medical cures by more ostensibly practical medications, which was in keeping with the greater amount of medical information that was made available. Much of this information, like the proprietary medicines that were consumed, may have originated with unorthodox and irregular medical practitioners (quacks). Nonetheless, it played its role in convincing a population that had to come to terms with the reality of illness and disease that for all their ubiquity these were not conditions that had simply to be endured. There was, to be sure, much endurance required in the face of illness in late early modern Ireland, but it could have been still worse. The recognition that intervention could make a difference served to equip people with an enhanced understanding of the body. It also prepared them to accept professional medication, when the reliance on the home and on the tradition of domestic medication that was such a crucial aspect of the medical culture of the early modern era, gave way in the nineteenth century to the hospital, the dispensary and the doctor's surgery as the primary sources of dependable medical care.

---

[122] Porter, 'The people's health', pp. 141–2.

Chapter 6
# Institutional Medicine and State Intervention in Eighteenth-Century Ireland

Andrew Sneddon

So modern 'pothecaries, taught the art
By doctor's bills to play the doctor's part,
Bold in the practice of mistaken rules,
Prescribe, apply, and call their masters fools.

Alexander Pope, *An essay on criticism* (1711)

## Introduction

In recent years the history of medicine in the early modern period in Ireland has begun to move beyond the 'official' institutional histories that dominated the medical historical landscape during the nineteenth and twentieth centuries.[1] Nevertheless, much work still remains to be done on medical institutions and on the constituent elements of the Irish medical profession[2] if we are to maintain with confidence that the eighteenth century saw medicine become institutionally based and increasingly state funded, and that this provided the foundations upon which

---

[1] The medical institutions include the Royal Colleges of Physicians and Surgeons, voluntary hospitals, county infirmaries, houses of industry, medical supply dispensaries for the poor, and various medical schools, societies and guilds, notably the Apothecaries' Guild and Barber-Surgeons' Guild. Dates are given old style, with the exception that the year is taken to have started on 1 January rather than 25 March, a common practice before 1752.

[2] Recent relevant literature includes: James Kelly, 'The emergence of scientific and institutional medical practice in Ireland, 1650–1800' in Greta Jones and Elizabeth Malcolm (eds), *Medicine, disease and the state in Ireland* (Cork: Cork University Press, 1999), pp. 21–39; L. M. Geary, *Medicine and charity in Ireland, 1718–1851* (Dublin: UCD Press, 2004); James Kelly, 'Health for Sale: mountebanks, doctors, printers and the supply of medication in eighteenth-century Ireland', *RIA proc.*, 108C (2008): 75–113; Patrick Fagan, *Catholics in a Protestant country: the papist constituency in eighteenth–century Dublin* (Dublin: FCP, 1998), chapter 3; Toby Barnard, *A new anatomy of Ireland: the Irish Protestants, 1649–1770* (London: Yale University Press, 2003), chapter 7; Eamon O'Flaherty, 'Medical men and learned societies in Ireland, 1680–1785' in H.B. Clarke and Judith Devlin (eds), *European encounters: essays in memory of Albert Lovett* (Dublin: UCD Press, 2003), pp. 253–69.

modern medical structures were built.³ Little research, for example, has been undertaken into the nature and timing of the funding of Irish medical institutions by the state in the form of parliamentary grants and appropriations. Furthermore, no systematic analysis has been dedicated to examining how often, in what ways, and with what degree of success the Irish parliament attempted to regulate, reform and develop these institutions. This omission is all the more striking as this was a period when the Irish parliament grew in both influence and importance, and was increasingly disposed to stimulate economic regeneration and development through the use of legislation and the allocation of public monies.⁴

This study seeks to redress this gap in the historiography by examining institutional medical legislation.⁵ A total of 65 measures of this description (see Appendix) were initiated by the Irish parliament in the eighteenth century. They can be disaggregated into five main categories, pertaining to voluntary hospitals, county infirmaries and houses of industry; medical education; the formation of the Royal College of Surgeons (RCSI); the sale and production of drugs and medicines; and the regulation of the 'practice of physic' by preventing the unlicensed (druggists, apothecaries and surgeons, among others) from prescribing to patients or administering internal medicines.⁶ This article focuses on the latter two categories,⁷ in order to establish the extent to which the Irish parliament concerned itself with the regulation of both practitioners and the provision of drugs. In the process, it will provide new perspectives on the preoccupations, aims and legislative objectives of the main eighteenth-century medical institutions and practitioners, and extend our understanding of the process whereby interest groups

---

³ See, Kelly, 'Emergence', pp. 21–39.

⁴ D.W. Hayton, 'Introduction: the long apprenticeship', and Eoin Magennis, 'Coal, corn and canals: parliament and the dispersal of public moneys, 1695–1772' in David W. Hayton (ed.), *The Irish parliament in the eighteenth century* (Edinburgh: Edinburgh University Press, 2001), pp. 12, 71–86; James Kelly, 'Harvests and hardship: famine and scarcity in Ireland in the late 1720s', *Studia Hibernica*, 26 (1991–2): 65–106 (79, 95–100); Andrew Sneddon, 'Bishop Francis Hutchinson: a case study in the culture of eighteenth-century improvement,' *Irish Historical Studies*, 35 (2006–2007): 289–310 (304–5); Andrew Sneddon, 'Legislating for economic development: Irish fisheries as a case study in the limitations of improvement' (forthcoming).

⁵ Institutional medical legislation is defined as any bill or heads of a bill relating to medical institutions. This definition precludes legislation dedicated to the containment of disease, such as the 1721 heads of a bill, 'To oblige ships coming from infected places more effectually to perform their quarantine, and for the better preventing of the plague being brought from foreign parts into this kingdom' (8 George I c.3).

⁶ This legislation has been identified through the Irish Legislation Database (ILD), a Leverhulme Foundation-funded database project based at Queen's University Belfast directed by D.W. Hayton and James Kelly, which details every piece of legislation initiated in the Irish parliament between 1692 and 1800. This is available for consultation on the Queen's University website (www.qub.ac.uk/ild/) [Accessed 14 August 2009].

⁷ See Appendix, heads of bills, numbers 1, 2, 4, 6, 7, 9, 11, 15, 19, 22, 23, 46, 47, 55.

lobbied Ireland's executive and legislature, a subject still to be explored in detail by political historians, especially for the early to mid-eighteenth century.[8]

## Medical regulation in Ireland in the late seventeenth century

Consistent with the pattern established during the reign of Elizabeth I, the regulation of Irish medicine at the end of the seventeenth century was firmly vested in the hands of the main bodies of practitioners. Thus, the Guild of Barber-Surgeons, now governed by a charter issued in 1687 by James II, oversaw the interests and concerns of surgeons, though their unhappiness that they were bound in an institutional connection with the less skilled craft of barbering ensured that it was far from being an efficient or respected body. It was not ineffective at representing and protecting the interest of surgeons against encroachment, but it made little attempt either to police those who practiced or to uphold high standards of care, and seems to have devoted its energies primarily to non-medical issues.[9]

By comparison, the College of Physicians, which received its charter in 1666, was both more vigorous and possessed of fuller power to regulate the medical marketplace. It was granted a new charter in 1692 during the reign of William III and his wife Mary. As provided for by this document, the newly constituted College comprised a president and 14 fellows, from among whom four censors were chosen. Fellows held office for life unless removed for misconduct, and replacements were chosen by election. All fellows were Protestant, and were expected to be well-disposed to the monarch. Significantly, the College's charter stated that only physicians licensed by it were allowed to practise in Dublin or within a seven-mile radius. The unlicensed could be fined £10 for every month they practised, whereas graduates in physic from the universities of Cambridge, Oxford, or Dublin would be licensed, upon paying a fixed fee, by the College without further examination. As this indicates, the College of Physicians possessed extensive powers to examine and licence those who sought to practice physic, but it was more than just a licensing body for physicians. Its powers extended over the other branches of medicine, surgery excepted. Thus, physicians working outside of the capital (unless graduates from the above universities) were to be examined by the president and censors and provided with a written testimonial, which allowed them license to practice if found suitably qualified. Midwives likewise were required to be examined and licensed, and those who failed to do so could be penalised for plying their trade without authorisation, while druggists,

---

[8] For a discussion of the Irish Quaker lobby during the reign of William and Mary, see John Bergin, 'The Quaker lobby and its influence on Irish legislation, 1692–1705', *Eighteenth-Century Ireland*, 19 (2004): 9–36.

[9] See Lyons chapter 1 in this collection; H.F. Berry, 'The ancient corporation of barber-surgeons, or gild of St Mary Magdalene, Dublin', *Journal of the Royal Society of Antiquaries of Ireland*, 33 (1903), 230–34.

apothecaries and pharmacists operating in the capital were liable to be examined on their expertise and professionalism. Indeed, the College of Physicians was empowered to search apothecaries' shops and houses, and authorised to destroy all medicines and drugs deemed unsound or unsafe. In addition, Dublin's apothecaries were precluded, subject to a penalty of £20, from employing an apprentice who had not been examined by the College for his expertise in Latin: a clause included to ensure apprentices could read the prescriptions given to them by physicians.[10]

Though the physicians believed these regulations justified, they were also acutely conscious that they were not easily enforced, and eager to affirm their medical ascendancy and the authority of their charter, they sought repeatedly during the 1690s and early decades of the eighteenth century to secure legislation giving it statutory force, in order to ensure that those without the appropriate university qualifications and/or licenses did not encroach on the prestigious, often very profitable, professional territory of the physician. Such legislation would have served also to give them greater influence over the trade in drugs. However, one should not conceive of their campaign as simply self-motivated. Altruistic, philanthropic and charitable instincts, combined with the enlightened, fashionable desire to 'improve' Ireland and the Irish, also informed their actions. It was these ideals after all that motivated activists involved with the voluntary hospital movement of the eighteenth century. Furthermore, as well as the College of Physicians, Dublin's well-to-do physicians were prominent in the Dublin Philosophical Society, the [Royal] Dublin Society, and other improving societies of the day.[11]

## The College of Physicians of Ireland seek to have their charter confirmed in law, 1695–1703

At their second ever meeting, on 20 January 1693, the College of Physicians resolved that every fellow was to 'concurr proportionally to carry on the passing of our patent [charter] into ane act of Parl[iamen]t and be att charges accordingly'.[12] A week later the College selected two of their number, the President, Patrick Dun, and the censor John Madden, to ask the solicitor general, Sir Richard Levinge, and one of the judges of the Court of Common Pleas, Richard Cox, to draft a bill that would give their charter statutory authority.[13] After perusing the draft bill

---

[10] *Records of the King and Queen's College of Physicians in Ireland ...* (Dublin, 1866).

[11] Barnard, A *new anatomy*, pp. 130–35, 141–2; Geary, *Medicine and charity*, p. 15. See also Barnard chapter 8 in this collection.

[12] RCPI, College Journals, 1692–1717, vol. 1, p. 2 (20 January 1693).

[13] RCPI, College Journals, vol. 1, p. 2 (27 January 1693). Levinge, it seems, was ever willing, especially when rewarded materially for doing so, to provide interest groups, such as those representing Ireland's Quakers and Roman Catholics, with political intelligence

and accompanying petition (which were conveyed via the lord lieutenant, Henry Sydney, 1st Earl Romney), the Irish Privy Council, which included Levinge and Cox among its members, unsurprisingly gave it their assent.[14] However, since the 1692 parliament did not resume following its controversial prorogation in December, when the lord lieutenant refused to accede to MPs assertion that they possessed the 'sole right' to initiate financial legislation, the bill stood no chance of reaching the statute book at this time, and the Irish Privy Council effectively killed it by not forwarding it for consideration at the English Council Board.

Though the failure of this first attempt to secure legislative confirmation of their chartered rights was a setback, the members of the College of Physicians were determined to reanimate the matter at the earliest opportunity. In May 1695, nearly three months before the Irish parliament reconvened, the College established a 'committee to consider and order the affairs relating to the bill for confirming our charter by act of parlament [sic]'.[15] It evidently concluded that there was no likelihood of their 1693 bill ever emerging out of the Irish Privy Council. Perceiving that they were more likely to obtain the legislation they desired by appealing to parliament, the Physicians' bill committee resolved in September 1695 to petition parliament to initiate an appropriate measure. It was further decided that Richard Cox should be employed to draft a petition embracing their request for presentation to the House of Commons.[16] In deciding to proceed in this manner the physicians rested their hopes on a sympathetic parliament, and since, as James Kelly has pointed out, 'the 1695 session established that the Irish parliament would be afforded an active role in the making of law for the Kingdom of Ireland by acknowledging its entitlement to initiate legislation in the form of heads of bills', this was a logical way to proceed.[17] Unfortunately, for the College of Physicians, it too encountered an insuperable obstacle.

On completion, Cox's petition was 'fairly transcribed' and revised by the original bills committee. It was then delivered to the Tory MP for Carlingford, Sir John Hanmer, to present to the House of Commons.[18] Meanwhile, the College of Physicians bade its fellows to canvass as many MPs as possible to ensure that the Commons both acceded to the demands of the petition and supported

---

and to represent their position before Parliament and the Irish Privy Council: see *Journal of the House of Commons of the kingdom of Ireland, 1613–1800* (4th edn, 21 vols, Dublin, 1796–1802) (henceforth *Commons Journals, Ireland*) vol. 3, pp. 77–8, 80–81; *British Weekly Mercury*, 2 February 1716; Bergin, 'Quaker lobby', 20, 24, 26–7.

[14] J.D.H. Widdess, *A history of the Royal College of Physicians of Ireland 1654–1963* (Edinburgh: E and S. Livingstone, 1963), p. 36.

[15] RCPI, College Journals, vol. 1, p. 40 (21 May 1695).

[16] RCPI, College Journals, vol. 1, p. 48 (23 September 1695).

[17] James Kelly, *Poynings' Law and the making of law in Ireland, 1660–1800* (Dublin: FCP, 2007), p. 115.

[18] RCPI, College Journals, vol. 1, p. 49 (6 October 1695).

the consequent heads of a bill.[19] In addition, to discourage petitions being lodged against their passage through parliament, a circular letter was 'sent to the chief surgeons and apothecaries to be by them subscribed, allowing of the usefulness of our charter to the publique'.[20]

The College of Physicians' petition was brought before the House of Commons on 20 November 1695, and the House immediately gave William Ponsonby, MP for county Kilkenny, leave to bring in the heads of a bill entitled, 'For the confirmation of the charter granted to the College of Physicians'.[21] This petition, and the legislation that arose from it, made explicit its intentions to regulate the apothecaries' trade, as well as to suppress the unregistered from practising as physicians.[22] However, despite the College's efforts, the surgeons and apothecaries of the Barber-Surgeons' Guild determined to oppose the measure, and they presented a petition seeking permission to present their concerns on 23 November 1695.[23] The Guild's petition persuaded the Commons' select committee, to whom the heads of a bill to confirm the College of Physicians charter had been referred, to allow a delegation from the Guild to appear before them to present their case. This was sufficient to convince MPs not to proceed with the measure and it was dropped soon afterwards by the House.[24]

The petition of the Barber-Surgeons' Guild shows clearly that it was the 'practising physic' clauses of the proposed legislation, and their effective banning of anyone but trained physicians from prescribing to patients and administering internal medicines, that most concerned surgeons. The petitioners argued that the legal enforcement of a prohibition on apothecaries and surgeons 'practicing physic' would affect the health, and thus the performance, of his majesty's navy and army, as most ships did not possess both a surgeon and a physician. The barber-surgeons had decided shrewdly when they chose to oppose the measure on these

---

[19] RCPI, College Journals, vol. 1, p. 49. This tactic was also used by Irish Quakers: see Bergin, 'Quaker lobby', 20.

[20] RCPI, College Journals, vol. 1, p. 51 (26 October 1695).

[21] *Commons Journals, Ireland*, vol. 2, p. 117; Edith Mary Johnston-Liik, *History of the Irish parliament 1692–1800: Commons, constituencies and statutes* (6 vols, Belfast: Ulster Historical Foundation, 2002), vol. 6, p. 98.

[22] *Commons Journals, Ireland*, vol. 2, p. 117.

[23] *Commons Journals, Ireland*, vol. 2, p. 121. During the first half of the eighteenth century surgeons became increasingly disillusioned with their association with barber-surgeons, and after the 1750s few joined the Barber-Surgeons' Guild. This dissociation was largely the result of the rising status of many surgeons, a consequence of their association with the burgeoning voluntary hospital and county infirmary systems. After three unsuccessful attempts during the mid-1770s to secure legislation to set up their own representative body, Irish surgeons received a royal charter to form the College of Surgeons in 1784. They were now able to regulate their own membership and develop a system of surgical education: schools of anatomy and surgery were founded, a licensing system put in place, professors appointed, and students enrolled.

[24] *Commons Journals, Ireland*, vol. 2, p. 125.

grounds, given the geo-political reality of the near total war then raging between the three kingdoms of Ireland, Scotland and England, and Catholic France. In addition, the petition suggested that an act giving the physicians' charter the force of law would affect the health of the poorest in society as it would oblige those who were ill to seek the services of all three branches of the medical profession (which they could not afford to do), rather than just the all-encompassing aid of a surgeon or apothecary. Finally, it was contended that because the act prevented unlicensed non-physicians from preparing or administering medical compositions, the ability of surgeons to perform their trade must be severely affected, as nearly every ailment required both internal and external medicines, many of which they alone had the skill to prepare.[25]

Despite this further discouraging setback, the College of Physicians tried on three further occasions during the next eight years to have their charter given the force of law, only to witness each initiative fail in its early stages. In July 1697, the College paid Counsellor William Usher five guineas to study 'all such acts as are relateing to the practise of physique in England',[26] as well as the charter of the College of Physicians of Ireland, 'and thence to draw [up] a short publique bill as he shall think fitt'.[27] This done, the Solicitor General, Richard Levinge, was invited on 9 September 1697 to peruse the draft heads and to present it to the House of Commons at the earliest opportunity, in return for which he was given a gold watch. Payment of this type may have been felt by the College of Physicians to be a more discreet way of rewarding the services of a privy councillor and law officer than a monetary fee.[28] In any event, it secured Levinge's goodwill, and a fortnight later, on 24 September, he was given leave by MPs to bring in the heads of a bill 'to regulate the practice of physic'.[29] These heads were referred to a select committee, which promptly rejected them for reasons unknown. It is probable that their actions were prompted by pressure, or anticipated pressure, from the Barber-Surgeons' Guild.[30]

A year later, on 27 October 1698, Sir John Meade, lawyer, legal official and MP for county Tipperary, was given leave by the House of Commons to bring in a heads of a bill entitled, 'To regulate the practice of physic in this kingdom'; while five years later, on 29 September 1703, Benjamin Burton, a committed social

---

[25] *Commons Journals, Ireland*, vol. 2, pp. 121–2.

[26] RCPI, College Journals, vol. 1, p. 66 (21 July 1697). The College of Physicians of London's charter of 1518, which prevented anyone from practising physic in London, or within a seven-mile radius, who had not been licensed by the College, was given statutory force in 1523 (14 & 15 Henry VIII c.5). While an act of 1540 (32 Henry VIII c. 42) gave the College the power to enter grocer or apothecaries' shops, examine their wares and destroy unsound medicines or drugs.

[27] RCPI, College Journals, vol. 1, p. 66 (21 July 1697).

[28] RCPI, College Journals, vol. 1, p. 67 (9 September 1697).

[29] *Commons Journals, Ireland*, vol. 2, p. 208.

[30] *Commons Journals, Ireland*, vol. 2, p. 208.

and economic improver and MP for Dublin city, brought in heads entitled, 'For regulating the practice of physic and chirurgery, and of apothecaries, in the city of Dublin'. Both heads were given leave, presented and referred to a select committee for consideration, but once again they proceeded no further. It is probable that they too were rejected by the House in anticipation of the type of opposition that had defeated the proposition in 1695.[31]

## The 1725 heads of a bill to confirm the charter of the College of Physicians

Following the rejection of the 1703 measure, the College of Physicians went silent on the subject of giving its charter the authority of law for almost fourteen years. The fact that successive presidents and fellows devoted much of their energies to medical education may partly explain this hiatus: in 1715 it established the first King's professorship in medicine, a post funded by the will of Sir Patrick Dun. Furthermore, it could not have escaped the attention of the Irish College of Physicians that the campaign pursued over two centuries by the London College of Physicians to extend and revive its legal right to prevent those who were unlicensed from practising physic had recently come to an abrupt halt.

In 1704, the House of Lords in Westminster ruled, in their judgement on the infamous 'William Rose Case', that apothecaries might prescribe to patients in the same way as physicians as long as they did not charge for their advice but only the drugs they supplied.[32] Alarmed by this, and determined to protect the privileged position of physicians, the College of Physicians of London pursued a similarly protracted, if marginally more successful, parliamentary battle for the legal right to regulate the production and sale of drugs and medicines than its Irish equivalent. In 1723, an act was passed, in the face of opposition from the Company of Apothecaries of London, which gave the London College of Physicians the power to examine the premises of apothecaries, 'druggists' and 'chymists' and destroy anything deemed unsound or unsafe.[33] Although this act was temporary, valid initially for a period of four years, it was renewed for a further three years in 1727, once more in the teeth of opposition, on the same grounds, from the

---

[31] *Commons Journals, Ireland*, vol. 2, p. 257, vol. 3, pp. 322, 327; Johnston-Liik, *History of Irish parliament*, vol. 3, pp. 316–18, vol. 5, pp. 235–36.

[32] Juanita G.L. Burnby, *A study of the English apothecary from 1660 to 1760* (London: Medical History, supplement no. 3, 1983), pp. 8–9.

[33] *An act for the better viewing, searching and examining drugs, medicines, waters, oyls, compositions ... in all places where the same shall be exposed to sale ... within the City of London and suburbs thereof or within seven miles circuit of the said city* (10 George I c.20).

Company of Apothecaries. However, when it expired in 1730 it was not renewed because of the continuing vehement opposition of the apothecaries.[34]

Meanwhile, having concluded, based on their own experiences and what they gleaned of events in England, that there was no prospect of their securing legislative recognition of their intrinsically monopolistic claims, the College of Physicians sought in 1716 to combat abuses and to protect their own privileged position by using the powers provided them by their charter. They were particularly anxious to prevent 'apothecaries from practicing physic',[35] on the grounds that if this problem continued to be ignored Dublin's physicians would greatly 'suffer in their business'.[36] To this end, it was decided that a circular letter should be sent to Dublin's apothecaries[37] threatening to remove the lucrative custom of the city's leading physicians from those who continued to 'practise physick':

> Whereas several apothecarys of this city have presumed to practice physick, and that in many cases to the great detriment of the sick, and to the apparent neglect of their own proper business, which is to prepare, keep and dispense good and wholesome medicines, and not to prescribe physick to patients, we, the president and censors of the College of Physicians do, by order of the said College signifie to you that the members thereof, whether fellows, candidates or licentiates will not for the future direct any note or prescription to the shop of any apothecary, who shall be convict before them of practicing physick without the advice, consent or direction of some physician approved by the College.[38]

This admonition failed to achieve the hoped for result, and in June 1725 the College of Physicians, possibly buoyed by the success of the London College of Physicians in securing a drugs act at Westminster in 1723, decided to attempt once again to secure a charter act.[39] On 1 November 1725, the College paid Henry Singleton, MP for Drogheda, £6 sterling to draw up a draft heads for an act to confirm their charter.[40] A fortnight later the College ordered that the 'treasurer do give the president, Richard Helsham, ten moiders for the feeing of five lawyers in order to have their opinion on our bill'.[41] A special committee was also appointed

---

[34] Sir George Clark, *A history of the Royal College of Physicians of London* (3 vols, Oxford: OUP, 1964–6), vol. 2, pp. 459–60, 465; 476–9, 493–5; W.S.C. Copeman, *The worshipful Society of Apothecaries of London: a history, 1617–1967* (London: Pergamon, 1967), pp. 43–8; Burnby, *English apothecary from 1660 to 1760*, pp. 5–13.

[35] RCPI, College Journals, vol. 1, p. 211 (29 October 1716).

[36] RCPI, College Journals, vol. 1, p. 212 (14 January 1717).

[37] RCPI, College Journals, vol. 1, pp. 213–14 (29 April 1717), p. 215 (24 June 1717).

[38] RCPI, College Journals, vol. 1, p. 216 (2 July 1717).

[39] RCPI, College Journals, vol. 2, 1717–1743, pp. 52–3 (4 June 1725).

[40] RCPI, College Journals, vol. 2, pp. 58–9 (1 November 1725).

[41] RCPI, College Journals, vol. 2, pp. 60–61 (15 November 1725).

to liaise with leading Dublin surgeons and apothecaries to dissuade them from petitioning against the charter heads of a bill once it appeared in parliament.[42]

The College of Physicians' petition requesting parliament to give their charter legal recognition was heard in the House of Commons on 1 December 1725, and immediately Singleton was given leave to bring in a heads of bill 'for preventing the abuses in the practice of physic, and for searching and examining all drugs, medicines, waters, oils, and compositions used or to be used for medicines ... exposed to sale or kept for that purpose within the City of Dublin.'[43] These heads resembled previous initiatives in all but title, and the reaction was comparable. Once more the College of Physicians' canvassing proved futile, as the heads came under sustained challenge from the representatives of Dublin's surgeons, druggists and apothecaries, who presented three petitions against the measure. Resorting to what was now established opposition rhetoric, they complained that if the proposed heads were passed they would detrimentally affect the profitability of their business and their ability to treat the sick. This was sufficient reason for MPs to hesitate, and the measure was rejected after a division of the House.[44] The campaign had cost the fellows of the College of Physicians a total of 'thirty pounds eleven shillings and two pence' in fees.[45]

Between 1692 and 1725, the College of Physicians pursued a time-consuming and expensive, two-pronged, legislative campaign to regulate the production and sale of drugs and medicine and the 'practice of physic'. Their object was to secure legislation that would both cement their privileged position at the top of the Irish medical profession as well as improve public health. During this campaign, the College of Physicians proved skilled at lobbying, gathering political intelligence, producing meticulously drafted heads of bills, and indentifying and canvassing sources of opposition to them. This was in keeping with the fact that its fellows were often wealthy and possessed of a wide array of political and social contacts in the upper reaches of Protestant society.

Unfortunately for the College of Physicians, the surgeons, apothecaries and druggists they were eager to regulate were still more adept at raising opposition to their initiatives. These interests argued that, if made law, the provisions provided for in the 1692 charter would prevent them from prescribing and producing compounds, drugs or medicines as they saw fit, and that this would not only rob them of a large part of their livelihood but also diminish their ability to attend to those who could not afford the services of a physician. It was this influential argument, first and foremost, that doomed every legislative venture launched by the College of Physicians between 1695 and 1725. In pre-1782 parliaments, petitioning was an extremely effective form of lobbying (and one that was used

---

[42] RCPI, College Journals, vol. 2, pp. 60–61 (26 November 1725).
[43] *Commons Journals, Ireland*, vol. 3, p. 429.
[44] *Commons Journals, Ireland*, vol. 3, p. 433.
[45] RCPI, College Journals, vol. 2, pp. 62–3 (17 January 1726); appendix, bill number 7.

frequently, especially before 1732). Both Irish MPs and peers, as well as British and Irish privy councillors, regularly rejected or respited legislation that parties, representing a variety of religious, corporate or individual interests, asserted either disadvantaged them or society at large.[46]

The financial cost and loss of face that resulted from the failure of successive legislative campaigns, along with the fact they were becoming increasingly involved in matters of medical education,[47] convinced the College of Physicians at some point in the mid-1720s to cease their efforts to have their charter confirmed in law. They were probably encouraged to do so by the fact that their counterpart in London also abandoned its attempt to secure a 'practice of physic' act. It was thus ironic that when the College of Physicians finally obtained the legal right to regulate the way medicines were made and sold in Ireland but they did so as a result of the efforts of a fully apprenticed apothecary, Charles Lucas.

## Charles Lucas and the regulation of the Apothecaries profession

Lucas, a keen amateur natural historian and topographer, conducted his trade from premises in Charles Street, Dublin.[48] By the early 1730s, his experiences had convinced him that the apothecary's trade was 'neglected and un-cultivated' and 'over-run with errors, abuses and frauds', all of which were 'little liable to discovery or punishment'.[49] These 'secret corruptions',[50] he maintained, served not only to 'destroy the reputation of the most careful and judicious physicians and chirurgeons' who dispensed their unsound or adulterated medicines,[51] but also 'endangered and often destroyed' lives, and robbed 'thousands of their fortunes'.[52] By drawing the public's attention to these corruptions, as only an insider could, and by convincing parliament to put in place legal measures for their detection and punishment, Lucas hoped both to promote 'the health and temporal happiness of a considerable part of mankind', and, by reviving the fortunes of his trade, to enable

---

[46] Kelly, *Poynings' Law*, pp. 56–7, 71, 212–16, 233–4.

[47] See Appendix, heads of a bill number 10.

[48] Charles Lucas to Sir Hans Sloane, 11 November 1736 (BL, Sloane MS 4025, fol. 155).

[49] Charles Lucas, *Pharmacomastix: or, the office, use, and abuse of apothecaries explained; ... humbly addressed to a member of parliament, with intent to shew the necessity of amending and continuing a temporary statute, for preventing frauds and abuses committed in the making and vending unsound, adulterate, and bad drugs and medicines, now near expiring. By the author of the scheme on which the said statute was founded* (Dublin, 1741), p. 7; *ODNB, sub* Charles Lucas; Sean J. Murphy, 'The Lucas affair: a study of municipal and electoral politics in Dublin' (M.A. thesis, UCD, 1981), 49.

[50] Lucas, *Pharmacomastix*, p. 4.

[51] Lucas, *Pharmacomastix*, p. 7.

[52] Lucas, *Pharmacomastix*, p. 8.

it to 'shine in its pristine lustre and beauty, restored to its original use, worth and dignity'.[53] In short, it was enlightened ideals of improvement, philanthropy and human betterment, as well as more prosaic professional concerns that sustained Lucas's reform campaign at this point.

Consistent with the respect traditionally shown to physicians, Lucas was convinced that the statutory regulation of the sale and production of drugs and medicines, as well as the licensing and training of the apothecary, should be overseen by their representative body, the College of Physicians. He even tried, albeit unsuccessfully, to implement a watered-down version of the second, more controversial, part of the physicians' charter on a number of occasions in the 1740s, 1760s and 1770s. Although Lucas's legislative plans for his trade aroused no opposition, or indeed much concrete support, from the College of Physicians they provoked sustained, vehement parliamentary opposition from Dublin's apothecaries, surgeons and druggists, as well as from members of the Apothecaries' Guild, which was constituted as a new and distinct guild in 1747. As far as the apothecaries were concerned, Lucas's legislative proposals placed *de facto* control of their trade in the hands of Dublin's leading physicians.

The establishment of the Apothecaries' Guild by charter formally acknowledged the apothecaries' right to an independent identity separate from the Guild of Barber-Surgeons. Although the College of Physicians retained a controlling voice in drug matters, a privilege afforded by the drugs act of 1735 (see below), the making of by-laws, along with the day-to-day running of their institution, was left in the hands of the Apothecaries' Guild. For most of the eighteenth century, only a minority of practicing apothecaries were members of the Guild: the illiterate and untrained stayed away, as did those who were Catholic. This latter fact is particularly significant as the trade of apothecary was the most Catholic of all the branches of medicine in Ireland for most of the eighteenth century.[54]

Ireland's apothecaries did not achieve a real degree of power over their own trade until the formation of the Apothecaries' Hall by an act of parliament of 1791.[55] The Hall opened its doors in Mary Street, Dublin, in 1792. The 1791 act gave it the power to regulate the education level, training and appointment of apothecaries' apprentices. It was also now able to determine who was proficient enough in their art to run an apothecary's shop. Furthermore, the Apothecaries Hall functioned as a store for high quality drugs and medicines for the sale to apothecaries. It also held a monopoly over the importation of drugs and medicines into Ireland, and controlled the sale of poisonous substances.

---

[53] Lucas, *Pharmacomastix*, pp. 3–4, 68.

[54] Fleetwood, *History of medicine*, p. 83; Fagan, *Catholics in a Protestant country*, pp. 92, 94, 99.

[55] See heads of a bill number 47; for the failed attempt to pass this heads, see number 46, and for an unsuccessful attempt to amend it, see number 55.

## The 1735 Drugs Act

Lucas commenced his campaign to reform the apothecaries' trade in the mid-1730s by penning a pamphlet, no longer extant, entitled, *A short scheme for preventing frauds and abuses in pharmacy, humbly offered to the consideration of the legislature* (Dublin, 1735).[56] The pamphlet was the basis for the act '*for preventing [the] frauds and abuses committed in making and vending unsound, adulterated, and bad drugs and medicines*', which became law in 1735.[57] First presented to the House of Lords on 29 November 1735 by William Stewart, Viscount Mountjoy, it gave four fellows of the College of Physicians, assisted by 'any two [Dublin] apothecaries of good repute', the authority to inspect apothecaries' shops, destroy or confiscate any unsound medicines, and fine those who obstructed such searches. It also prevented any person from practising the 'occupation of apothecary, chymist or druggist' in Dublin, or within a seven-mile radius thereof, unless they had served a five-year apprenticeship and had registered with the College. Finally, it laid down regulations both for admission into the Barber-Surgeons' Guild and for the correct preparation and dispensing of drugs and medicines.[58]

The question that must be posed is, why did Lucas's heads of a drugs bill succeed when previous bills had failed? The answer lies in its content. Simply put, the 1735 measure was not as controversial as its predecessors because it did not include a 'practising physic' clause. What remained was an initiative that, in essence, aimed to remove adulterated drugs and medicine from circulation – an end that no right-thinking medical practitioner could, at least publicly, deny as worthwhile. The plausibility of Lucas's act explains the minimal, and ultimately ineffectual, nature of the parliamentary opposition to it. Unable to secure the support of both the Barber-Surgeons' Guild[59] and the College of Physicians,[60] a small group of Dublin's leading apothecaries petitioned parliament in early December to protest that any attempt to regulate their profession would endanger their livelihood.[61] Lucas responded directly to their objections when he defended his heads in person before a committee of the whole House of Lords to which the

---

[56] Murphy, 'The Lucas affair', 50.

[57] Murphy, 'The Lucas affair', 50; 9 George II c.10.

[58] *The statutes at large, passed in the parliaments held in Ireland, from the third year of Edward the Second, A.D. 1310, to the First Year of George the Third, A.D. inclusive, with marginal notes, and compleat Index to the whole* (8 vols, Dublin, 1765), vol. 6, pp. 203–206; *ODNB*, sub Charles Lucas; Fleetwood, *History of medicine*, pp. 82–3; Barnard, *A new anatomy*, pp. 139–40.

[59] Minute book of the Dublin Company of Barber-Surgeons, 1703–1757 (TCD, MS 1447/8/1); Minute book of the Dublin Company of Barber-Surgeons, 1724–1792 (TCD, MS 1447/8/2).

[60] RCPI, College Journals, vol. 2, pp. 133–4 (1 December 1735).

[61] *Journals of the House of Lords of the kingdom of Ireland* (8 vols, Dublin, 1779–1800), vol. 3, p. 320.

measure was referred, and the measure negotiated this hurdle on the way to the statute book.[62]

## The 1741 drugs bill

On 19 December 1741, Lord Mountjoy presented the House of Lords with the heads of a bill to revive, expand and strengthen the 1735 act.[63] The measure, which was the handiwork of Charles Lucas, was primarily concerned with improving the effectiveness of the College of Physicians' inspections of apothecaries' shops. It stipulated that the College's inspection teams should be expanded to include two surgeons (who had to be members of the Barber-Surgeons' Guild) and a civil officer. It further suggested that teams be rotated regularly by allowing each member to serve a maximum of one year in every four, the practical application of which was to be aided by increasing the number of fellows of the College of Physicians. And, in order to ensure that rural as well as urban apothecaries were inspected, local inspectors were to be appointed in lieu of official teams from the metropolis. Furthermore, all inspection teams were now to examine apothecaries' equipment and apparatus as well as their drugs.[64]

In the 1741 heads, Lucas, for the first time, included 'practising physic' clauses. These differed from the provisions in the College of Physicians' charter in that they allowed untrained, non-physicians to prescribe medicines to the sick in life and death situations, where the services of a physician or a surgeon could not be obtained. Furthermore Lucas defined a trained physician as someone with a medical degree, not necessarily a licentiate of the College of Physicians.[65] These clauses made Lucas's heads of a bill controversial and led to its rejection by the Lords.[66]

Lucas aspired to prevent drug sellers from 'practising physic' because he believed that they endangered life, lacking as they did proper medical training, education and judgement.[67] In his view, the trained physicians practicing in Ireland constituted a profession whose practitioners were 'inferior to none in Europe, in erudition, judgement and probity'.[68] His respect for the office of physician may have been shaped by his own wish to enter that profession – an aim he fulfilled in the early 1750s when he obtained medical degrees from the universities of Reims and Leiden. Shortly afterwards, he tried unsuccessfully to break into the closed

---

[62] *Lords Journals, Ireland*, vol. 3, p. 328.
[63] *Lords Journals, Ireland*, vol. 3, p. 512; see Appendix, heads of a bill number 11. The 1741 heads was based on Lucas's *Pharmacomastix*, pp. 1–3.
[64] Lucas, *Pharmacomastix*, pp. 68–77.
[65] Lucas, *Pharmacomastix*, p. 73.
[66] See ILD, QUB (see note 6 above).
[67] Lucas, *Pharmacomastix*, pp. 7, 21–2, 42–3.
[68] Lucas, *Pharmacomastix*, p. 7.

shop that was the 'practice of physic' in Bath, England. In June 1759, he became a licentiate of the Royal College of Physicians of London, and set up a successful practice there between 1759 and 1761.[69] One of his more successful cases involved James Caulfeild, the first earl of Charlemont, who claimed in 1760 that he was cured of rheumatism, 'after an excruciating course of pains and physicians', by Lucas's 'tender care and effectual abilities'.[70]

The 1741 heads may not have made it to the statute book, but Lucas's 1735 act, initially valid for three years, was successively renewed until 1756.[71] During this time, the College of Physicians had recourse to the powers they were afforded by the act.[72] However, Lucas was occupied during most of this time with other matters, and medical regulation slipped down the legislative agenda.[73] This hiatus highlights a key characteristic of Lucas's medical reform campaign: it was sporadic, interspersed with various political intrigues and battles fought at both a local and national level. This is evident from Lucas's published work: of the 217 publications attributed to him only nine can be categorised as relating to medical matters; the rest were political ephemera written for specific political purposes and in response to immediate events and crises.[74]

**Drugs legislation, 1761–71**

When Lucas returned to a less politically volatile Dublin in 1760, after a period of self-imposed exile in Europe and England in order to escape the political fall-out from his controversial by-election campaign of 1748–49, he was returned, almost

---

[69] [William Baylies], *Letters of Doctor Lucas and Doctor Oliver; occasioned by a physical confederacy discovered at Bath* (Bath, 1757); *ODNB*, sub James Caulfeild, first earl of Charlemount; *ODNB*, sub Charles Lucas; Murphy, 'The Lucas affair', 216–17, 235; David Harley, 'Honour and property: the structure of professional disputes in eighteenth-century England' in Andrew Cunnigham and Roger French (eds), *The medical enlightenment of the eighteenth century* (Cambridge: CUP, 1990), pp. 149–50.

[70] HMC, *The manuscripts and correspondence of James, first earl of Charlemont* (2 vols, London: Her Majesty's Stationary Office, 1891–1894), vol. 1, pp. 8–9; *ODNB*, sub James Caulfeild, first earl of Charlemount; see also, HMC, *Report on manuscripts in various collections* (8 vols, London: His Majesty's Stationary Office, 1913), vol. 8, p. 187.

[71] Widdess, *History of Royal College of Physicians*, p. 64.

[72] RCPI, College Journals, vol. 3, p. 41 (6 June 1748), pp. 102–03 (7 April 1755).

[73] For Lucas's political career see, Sean Murphy, 'Charles Lucas and the Dublin election of 1748–1749', *Parliamentary History*, 9 (1983): 93–105; Sean Murphy, 'The Corporation of Dublin', *Dublin Historical Record*, 37/1 (1983): 26–30; *ODNB*, sub Charles Lucas; James Kelly, *Sir Henry Newenham MP, 1734–1814: defender of the Protestant constitution* (Dublin: FCP, 2004), pp. 28, 39.

[74] This quantitative and qualitative analysis of Lucas's writing is based on the *English short title catalogue, 1473–1800* (3rd edn, London: Thomson Gale, 2003).

immediately, to the Irish parliament as an MP for Dublin city.[75] Eager to progress medical reform, on 26 January 1762, he presented the House of Commons with the heads of a bill 'for preventing frauds and abuses in the vending, preparing and administering drugs and medicines'.[76] Apart from the omission of clauses to prevent drug sellers from practising physic, there were two main differences between the 1762 heads and its 1741 counterpart.[77] Firstly, it required physicians to note down, in a signed prescription, the exact details of the formula of internal or external medicines they wished a druggist or apothecary to compound.[78] Secondly, it empowered the College of Physicians to 'frame and publish a code or pharmacopoeia, containing a catalogue of such drugs or simple medicine, as they shall judge necessary for the prescriptions and uses of physicians and chiurgeons, together with forms and rules for preparing and compounding the same chemically and galenically', a guide that drug sellers were to follow under penalty of a £10 fine.[79]

On 5 February 1762, the Apothecaries' Guild held a special meeting to discuss Lucas's proposal.[80] A week later the Guild presented a petition against the measure to the House of Commons in which it was stated that although members did 'in principle, oppose the sale of unsound, adulterated or bad drugs', they believed Lucas's heads of a bill to 'be injurious to the petitioners', and 'prejudicial to commerce, the linen and dy[e]ing manufactures, the revenue of the crown, and oppressive to the liberty of the subject'.[81] However, they did not recommend the outright rejection of the bill; they requested that it was amended to meet their concerns, and that they were involved in the process.[82]

Opposing Lucas's heads in the Commons proved to be an expensive business for the Guild (it cost over £85), and it required the Guild to draw on its savings and to levy its members half a guinea each to assemble the required funds.[83] It was also in vain, as the heads successfully negotiated the Commons, following which they were forwarded to the Irish Privy Council.[84] The Guild responded by establishing a subscription list to defray the cost of presenting a petition to the Privy Council, but this too proved ineffectual, and the bill was conveyed, without amendment, to

---

[75] *ODNB*, *sub* Charles Lucas.

[76] *Commons Journals, Ireland*, vol. 7, p. 110; Fleetwood, *History of medicine*, pp. 66–9; O'Flaherty, 'Medical men and learned societies', p. 258.

[77] Lucas, *Pharmacomastix*, pp. 70–6; *The statutes at large, passed in ... Ireland ...* , vol. 7, pp. 848–58.

[78] *The statutes at large, passed in ... Ireland ...* , vol. 7, p. 856.

[79] *The statutes at large, passed in ... Ireland ...* , vol. 7, p. 852.

[80] GA. Minute Books of the Apothecaries' Guild, 1747–1833, 5 February 1762, p. 100 (NLI microfilm, p. 929).

[81] *Commons Journals, Ireland*, vol. 7, p. 117.

[82] *Commons Journals, Ireland*, vol. 7, p. 117.

[83] GA, Minute Books, 27 February 1762, p. 101 (NLI microfilm, p. 929).

[84] *Commons Journals, Ireland*, vol. 7, p. 148.

the British Privy Council.[85] Although the British Council changed the wording of the heads slightly, this did not alter its intent or overall purpose, and the bill was returned to Ireland for presentation to the Irish parliament.[86] As parliament was not permitted, according to the arrangement provided for under Poynings' Law, to amend the returned bill, the Guild, on 20 April 1762, petitioned the House of Lords to reject the measure in its entirety, but they were unsuccessful.[87] Lucas's bill was given the royal assent on 30 April 1762 and became law on 1 May (1 George III c.14).[88]

The Guild's objections were not entertained by parliament because the apothecaries were unable to garner support beyond the ranks of their trade. This can be attributed, at least in part, to the fact that Lucas's heads of a bill, minus a 'regulating physic' clause, was little more than an enhanced version of the temporary 1735 drugs act, which had been allowed lapse only in 1756, and which the influential College of Physicians had resort to on a regular basis. Furthermore, Lucas was now an MP and was able, for the first time, to meet the objections raised against his heads by the apothecaries in parliament, as soon as they arose.[89]

Like the 1735 act, Lucas's 1761 drugs act was 'to continue in force for the term of three years, and from thence to the end of the next [session of parliament]'.[90] Since it had elapsed by the time MPs assembled in parliament for the 1767–8 session,[91] Lucas applied for, and was given leave by the House of Commons on 28 November 1767 to bring in a bill 'for reviving and amending an act entitled an act for preventing frauds and abuses in the preparing and vending of drugs and medicines.'[92] By the time the heads was read for the second time and forwarded on 6 February to a committee of the whole house (of which Lucas was a member), its title had been enlarged to '*an act for reviving and amending an act entitled an act for preventing frauds and abuses in the preparing and vending of drugs and medicines, and for the better regulating the professions and practice of physic, pharmacy and chirurgery in this kingdom*'.[93]

The enlargement of the heads of the bill to embrace the physicians' venerable aspiration of preventing apothecaries and surgeons from 'practising physic'

---

[85] GA, Minute Books, 2 March 1762, p. 102 (NLI microfilm, p. 929).

[86] Privy Council Registers, 31 March 1762, (TNA, PC 2/109, p. 151).

[87] *Lords Journals, Ireland*, vol. 4, p. 252.

[88] See ILD, QUB.

[89] *Acts and statutes made in a parliament begun at Dublin, the twenty-second day of October, ann. dom. 1761, in the first year of the reign of our most gracious sovereign Lord George the Third before his excellency Dunk, Earl of Halifax, lord lieutenant general, and general governor of Ireland* (Dublin, 1762).

[90] *The statutes at large, passed in ... Ireland ...* , vol. 7, pp. 848, 858.

[91] GA, Minute Books, 17 January 1768, p. 127 (NLI, microfilm p. 929); *Acts and statutes ... 1761*.

[92] *Commons Journals, Ireland*, vol. 8, p. 206.

[93] *Commons Journals, Ireland*, vol. 8, pp. 223, 234–5.

was unexpected, but it can be accounted for by reference to Lucas's changed circumstances. Now a trained physician, though not a member of the College of Physicians, Lucas shared the desire of physicians everywhere to prevent surgeons and apothecaries from appropriating business from him and his fellow practitioners by presuming to 'practise physic'. Thus, the Edinburgh University educated, physician, poet and political reformer, William Drennan, who was then working as an obstetrician in Newry, county Down, complained in 1788 that:

> my profits here will never be great, but I think one or two junior physicians would rather increase them by preventing the apothecaries, etc., from filling up so great a part of the practice and leaving us the bad cases – whenever these grow serious then the physician is called – much too much for form sake.[94]

Although it negotiated the Commons unopposed, Lucas's 1767 heads failed to emerge out of the British Privy Council.[95] Despite being made freeman of the Apothecaries' Guild in March 1768, in what can be seen as an attempt by the corporation to persuade Lucas to abandon his legislative campaign,[96] Lucas made two more attempts to have his 'charter heads' enacted, first in 1769 and then again in 1771. However, both measures failed to proceed beyond committee stage.[97] The reasons why these bills failed to negotiate the Irish parliament remains to be established, but since each contained a 'practising physic' clause, and, as we have already seen, every previous attempt to prevent surgeons, druggist and apothecaries from prescribing to patients or administering internal medicines prompted resistance, it is reasonable to assume that this was the cause. In any event, the 1771 heads was one of Lucas's last political acts, as he died the following November.[98]

Lucas may have failed to amend the 1761 statute to include clauses preventing the untrained from practicing as physicians, but the original act was continued in various temporary statute acts from 1771 until 1788, and was made perpetual under the Apothecaries' Hall act of 1791. During this time, censors and fellows of the College of Physicians, assisted by apothecaries appointed by the Apothecaries' Guild, continued to inspect apothecaries' shops and condemn and punish the abuses and inadequacies they often found there. In the late 1780s and early 1790s the College of Physicians even considered petitioning parliament to increase their

---

[94] Dr William Drennan to Mrs Martha McTier, January 1788, D.A. Chart (ed.), *The Drennan letters, being a selection from the correspondence which passed between William Drennan, M.D. and his brother-in-law and sister, Samuel and Martha McTier, during the years 1776–1819* (Belfast: Public Record Office of Northern Ireland, 1931), p. 45; *ODNB, sub* William Drennan.

[95] ILD; see Appendix, heads number 19.

[96] GA, Minute Books, 31 March 1768, p. 129 (NLI, microfilm p.929).

[97] ILD; see Appendix, heads numbers 22 and 23.

[98] *ODNB, sub* Charles Lucas.

powers to punish such offenders. The College only formally discontinued these inspections in 1863.[99]

In one sense then, Lucas's legislative campaign can be seen as a more successful continuation of that of the College of Physicians the early part of the century. Motivated by ideals of charity, improvement and human betterment, as well as a concern to professionalise and raise the social status of his first trade, Lucas was able to procure two acts, which allowed the College of Physicians a large measure of control over the activities of Dublin's apothecaries. The College continued to exercise these powers far beyond the establishment of the Apothecaries Hall. Moreover, Lucas even expanded his regulation of drugs campaign, albeit unsuccessfully, in the 1740s, 1760s and early 1770s, in an attempt to ensure that only university educated physicians prescribed drugs to patients.

## Conclusion

What has emerged from this case study of drug regulation and 'practice of physic' legislation is that the former enjoyed a 100 per cent success rate, and the latter a 100 per cent failure rate. This was not because members of the Irish Houses of Commons or Lords favoured heads relating to drugs and regarded the 'practice of physic' bills as pernicious, rather it was that parliament consistently rejected legislation which encountered formal, parliamentary opposition. And it so happened that drug legislation bills created far less disquiet among Ireland's medical practitioners, and their representative bodies, than those relating to the 'practice of physic'.

The parliamentary opposition that drug regulation legislation engendered, especially as the century wore on, came from disgruntled apothecaries and the Apothecaries' Guild. They argued that drug regulation bills gave the College of Physicians of Ireland financially ruinous, unwarranted and intrusive powers of inquisition into what the apothecaries sold and made, as well as over their professional training. That Charles Lucas's drugs acts of 1735 and 1761 did indeed impact on the way their trade was conducted, in the capital at least, is beyond a doubt as these laws gave the College of Physicians a pretext to police the shops and premises of the capital's apothecaries, chemists and druggists for a large part of the eighteenth century. How frequent and systematic these inspections were is a

---

[99] GA, Minute Book, 20 July 1788, p. 104 (NCI, Microfilm, p. 929); RCPI, College Journals, vol. 4, 1785–1802, p. 41 (27 October 1788), p. 96 (2 February 1791), pp. 114–5 (June 1792), p. 116 (9 July 1792), p. 120 (5 November 1792), pp. 121–2 (26 November 1792); *The statutes at large, passed in ... Ireland ...* , vol. 10, pp. 28, 257, 611, 819, vol. 12, p. 306; T.P.C. Kirkpatrick, *Henry Quin, M.D. president and fellow of the King and Queen's College of Physicians of Ireland and Professor of the Practice of Physic, 1718–1791* (Dublin: University Press, 1919), p. 28.

question that cannot be answered here and one that deserves to examined in detail as part of a larger and much needed examination of Irish apothecaries in general.

The opposition of the apothecaries to drug regulation legislation was both muted and ineffectual, as they were unable to draw other medical practitioners to their cause. Untroubled by the apothecaries' professional concerns, physicians and surgeons were disposed to look positively on such attempts as were made to take damaging and dangerous drugs out of circulation – an aspiration that even apothecaries found hard to object to as the century wore on.

Those measures dedicated to the regulation of the 'practice of physic', on the other hand, could not lay claim to an equivalent imperative. Plausibly enough, they were perceived by surgeons, druggists and apothecaries alike as an attempt by elite physicians to control the medical market for their own gain and to the detriment of the health of that part of Ireland's population who could neither obtain nor afford the services of a physician. The differences that were plainly visible over the College of Physicians' efforts to have their charter enshrined in law between 1693 and 1725 thus fit almost exactly with the model of medical disputes in eighteenth-century England developed by David Hartley; he contends that medical disputes in that period often involved issues that 'posed a threat to the status and power of elite groups accustomed to maintaining an appearance of non-competitive activity'.[100] Although the College of Physicians' campaign was a failure it demonstrates that it realised very early that the new heads of bills arrangement provided them with an opportunity to introduce legislation into parliament. It also highlights that they were as reliant as their opponents on lobbying.

The medical reform campaigns pursued by Lucas and others has also thrown light on the much larger issue of the nature and extent of state intervention in the Irish medical world in the eighteenth-century. It is clear that parliament's involvement in medicine in that period was reactive, and that the Irish executive and legislature, largely indifferent to such matters, left their agitation to committed individuals and interest groups. Despite this, it is clear also that Ireland's emerging medical institutions and practitioners took parliamentary legislation very seriously as they recognised that it was able both to impact positively and negatively on the way their trade or profession was conducted.

---

[100] Harley, 'Honour and property', p. 160.

# Appendix

Table 6.1  Heads of bills and bills initiated in the Irish parliament and relating to institutional medicine, 1695–1800

| Bill number | Title | Statute number |
|---|---|---|
| 1 | For the confirmation of the charter granted to the College of Physicians (1695) | Failed |
| 2 | To regulate the practice of physic (1697) | Failed |
| 3 | To erect hospitals and workhouses in this kingdom (1697) | Failed |
| 4 | To regulate the practice of physic in this kingdom (1698) | Failed |
| 5 | For erecting hospitals and workhouses within the city of Dublin, for the better employing and maintaining thereof (1703) | Failed |
| 6 | For regulating the practice of physic and chirurgery, and of apothecaries, in the city of Dublin (1703) | Failed |
| 7 | For preventing the abuses in the practice of physic, and for searching and examining all drugs, medicines, waters, oils, and compositions used or to be used for medicines in all parts where the same shall be exposed to sale or kept for that purpose within the city of Dublin or suburbs thereof, or within five miles circuit of the said city (1725) | Failed |
| 8 | For finishing and regulating the hospital founded by Richard Stevens, esquire, Doctor of Physic (1729) | 3 George II c.23 |
| 9 | For preventing frauds and abuses committed in making and vending unsound, adulterated, and bad drugs and medicines (1735) | 9 George II c.10 |
| 10 | For vacating the office of the King's Professor of Physic in Dublin upon the death or surrender of the present King's professor, and for erecting three professorships of physic in the said city instead thereof (1741) | 15 George II c.3 (private) |
| 11 | For amending and making more effectual an act, entitled, an act for preventing frauds and abuses committed in the making and vending unsound, adulterated and bad drugs and medicines (1741) | Failed |
| 12 | For enabling the governors and guardians of the hospital founded by Dr Richard Steevens, to grant a piece of ground in fee-farm to the governors of St. Patrick's hospital, Dublin, for the site of that hospital (1747) | 21 George II c.1 (private) |
| 13 | For regulating the hospital founded by Mary Mercer, spinster (1749) | 23 George II c.18 |

| Bill number | Title | Statute number |
|---|---|---|
| 14 | For establishing an infirmary in the city of Cork, and to vest the house called the infirmary house, and the back yard thereunto belonging, which is built at the east end of the church yard of St Mary Shandon, otherwise St Ann's in the liberties of the city of Cork, in certain trustees forever, and to give such trustees, such powers as may be necessary to promote and execute the purposes of an infirmary in the city of Cork, and for uniting several small parishes in the suburbs of the said city (1751) | 25 George II c.23 |
| 15 | For preventing frauds and abuses in the vending, preparing and administering drugs and medicines (1761) | 1 George III c.14 |
| 16 | To enable tenants for life to make perpetual leases of grounds whereon to erect public hospitals (1761) | 1 George III c.8 |
| 17 | For erecting public county infirmaries in this kingdom (1765) | Failed |
| 18 | For erecting and establishing public infirmaries or hospitals in this kingdom (1765) | 5 George III c.20 |
| 19 | For reviving and amending an act entitled an act for preventing frauds and abuses in the preparing and vending of drugs and medicines, and for the better regulating the professions and practice of physic, pharmacy and chirurgery in this kingdom (1767) | Failed |
| 20 | To amend an act made the last session of parliament for erecting and establishing public infirmaries or hospitals in this kingdom (1767) | 7 George III c.8 |
| 21 | For directing the application of the sum of £7,000 granted to the Dublin Society for the encouragement of such trades and manufactures as should be directed by parliament (1767) | 7 George III c.15 |
| 22 | For reviving and amending an act entitled an act for preventing frauds and abuses in the preparing and vending of drugs and medicines, and for the better regulating the profession and practice of physic, pharmacy and chirurgery in this kingdom (1769) | Failed |
| 23 | For preventing frauds and abuses in the preparing, vending and administering of drugs and medicines, and for the better regulating the practice and professions of physic, pharmacy and chirurgery in Ireland (1771A) | Failed |
| 24 | For establishing an infirmary in the south suburbs of the city of Cork, and to vest an house and front lot of ground in the south suburbs of the said city, or any other house or grounds that may be taken, in certain trustees forever, and to give such trustees such power as may be necessary to promote and execute the purposes of an infirmary in the south suburbs of the city of Cork (1771B) | 11 & 12 George III c.23 |

| Bill number | Title | Statute number |
|---|---|---|
| 25 | For badging such poor as shall be found unable to support themselves by labour, and otherwise providing for them, and for restraining such as shall be found able to support themselves by labour or industry from begging (1771B) | 11 & 12 George III c.30 |
| 26 | For explaining and amending an act passed in the 5th year of his present majesty's reign entitled an act for erecting and establishing public infirmaries or hospitals in this kingdom (1773) | 13 & 14 George III c.43 |
| 27 | For the better regulating the profession and practice of chirurgery in this kingdom (1773) | Failed |
| 28 | For the relief of the out-pensioners of the hospital of King Charles II, for ancient and maimed officers and soldiers of the army of Ireland (1775) | 15 & 16 George III c.23 |
| 29 | For amending an act made the last session of parliament entitled an act for badging such poor as shall be found unable to support themselves by labour, and otherwise providing for them, and for restraining such as shall be found able to support themselves by labour or industry from begging (1773) | 13 & 14 George III c.46 |
| 30 | To improve and regulate the art and practice of chirurgery (1775) | Failed |
| 31 | For amending and rendering more effectual an act passed last session of parliament entitled an act for reviving and continuing several temporary statutes, and to prevent the destructive practice of trawling for fish in the bay of Dublin, and for explaining and amending another act made in the 13th and 14th years of the reign of his present majesty entitled an act for explaining an act passed in the 5th year of his present majesty's reign entitled an act for erecting and establishing infirmaries or hospitals in this kingdom (1775) | 15 & 16 George III c.31 |
| 32 | To enable testamentary guardians of minors to make leases for the purpose of building county infirmaries or hospitals on the estates of such minors, subject to restrictions hereinafter mentioned (1777) | 17 & 18 George III c.15 |
| 33 | For incorporating the surgeons of Dublin (1777) | Failed |
| 34 | To amend an act passed in the 5th year of the reign of his present majesty entitled an act for erecting public infirmaries or hospitals in this kingdom (1777) | Failed |
| 35 | For making and amending public roads in the county of Dublin, and regulating, applotting and levying of money in the county of the city of Dublin (1779) | 19 & 20 George III c.44 |
| 36 | For extending the provisions of an act passed in this kingdom in the 6th year of the reign of his present majesty entitled an act for erecting and establishing public infirmaries or hospitals in this kingdom (1781) | 21 & 22 George III c.13 |
| 37 | For establishing a complete school of physic (1783) | Failed |

| Bill number | Title | Statute number |
|---|---|---|
| 38 | For the due accounting for all money granted for public works, charities and hospitals, and for the ordering a regular account in future of all monies entrusted to the corporation for carrying on the inland navigation, the trustees of the linen manufacture, the Dublin Society, the paymaster of the corn premiums, the corporation for paving the streets of Dublin, and for other purposes therein mentioned (1783) | 23 & 24 George III c.26 |
| 39 | For establishing a complete school of physic in this kingdom (1785) | 25 George III c.42 |
| 40 | For the completing and effectually lighting and watching Rutland Square, and for the better support and maintenance of the hospital for the relief of poor lying-in-women in Great Britain Street, Dublin, and for other purposes therein mentioned (1785) | 25 George III c.43 |
| 41 | For the more effectual lighting and watching Rutland Square, and for the better support and maintenance of the lying-in hospital, and for other purposes therein mentioned (1785) | Failed |
| 42 | For further extending the provisions of an act passed in this kingdom in the 5th year of the reign of his present majesty entitled an act for erecting and establishing public infirmaries or hospitals in this kingdom (1785) | 25 George III c.40 |
| 43 | To carry into further effect an act passed in the last session of parliament in this kingdom entitled an act for the due accounting for all money granted for public works, charities and hospitals, and for the ordering a regular account in future of all monies entrusted to the corporation for carrying on the inland navigation, the trustees of the linen manufacture, the Dublin Society, the paymaster of the corn premiums, the corporation for paving the streets of Dublin, and for other purposes therein mentioned (1785) | 25 George III c.63 |
| 44 | For extending the provisions of an act passed in this kingdom in the 5th year of the reign of his present majesty entitled an act for erecting and establishing public infirmaries or hospitals in this kingdom (1785) | 25 George III c.39 |
| 45 | To explain and amend an act entitled an act for establishing a complete school of physic in this kingdom, so far as the same relates to clinical lectures (1788) | Failed |
| 46 | For more effectually preserving the health of his majesty's subjects throughout the kingdom of Ireland, and for erecting an apothecaries hall, and regulating the business of an apothecary within the city of Dublin, and the suburbs and liberties thereof (1790A) | Failed |
| 47 | For the more effectually preserving the health of his majesty's subjects, for erecting an apothecaries hall in the city of Dublin, and regulating the profession of an apothecary throughout the kingdom of Ireland (1791) | 31 George III c.34 |

| Bill number | Title | Statute number |
|---|---|---|
| 48 | To explain and amend an act, entitled, an act for establishing a complete school of physic in this kingdom (1791) | 31 George III c.35 |
| 49 | For regulating the care of deserted children throughout the kingdom of Ireland, for the regulation of county infirmaries, and for providing hospitals or other places for the reception of persons for whom no effectual provision has hitherto been made (1791) | Failed |
| 50 | For reviving and continuing several temporary statutes (1791) | 31 George III c.44 |
| 51 | For directing the application of certain sums of money granted for providing and maintaining a botany garden, and for the appointment of trustees for that purposes (1793) | Failed |
| 52 | For the relief of his majesty's Roman Catholic subjects of Ireland (1793) | 33 George III c.21 |
| 53 | To amend an act passed in this kingdom in the 5th year of the reign of his present majesty, entitled, an act for erecting and establishing public infirmaries or hospitals in this kingdom (1795) | Failed |
| 54 | To explain an act, entitled, an act for establishing a complete school of physic in this kingdom (1795) | 35 George III c.22 |
| 55 | To explain, amend and make more effectual an act, entitled, an act for more effectually preserving the health of his majesty's subjects, for erecting an apothecaries hall in the city of Dublin and regulating the profession of an apothecary throughout the kingdom of Ireland (1796A) | Failed |
| 56 | For the further regulation of public infirmaries or hospitals (1796A) | 36 George III c.9 |
| 57 | To amend an act passed in the 5th year of the reign of his present majesty, entitled, an act for erecting and establishing public infirmaries or hospitals in this kingdom (1796A) | Failed |
| 58 | For the better governing and managing the house of industry, for the relief of the poor in Dublin (1796B) | 37 George III c.34 |
| 59 | To continue for a limited time the government and management of the house of industry, for the relief of the poor in Dublin, under the present acting governors thereof (1798) | 38 George III c.34 |
| 60 | For the better management of the workhouse and foundling hospital in Dublin, and to continue for a limited time the government and management of the house of industry for the relief of the poor in Dublin, under the present acting governors thereof (1798) | Failed |

| Bill number | Title | Statute number |
|---|---|---|
| 61 | To continue an act passed in the 38th year of his present majesty's reign, entitled, an act to continue for a limited time the government and management of the house of industry for the relief of the poor in Dublin, under the present acting governors thereof, and also, one other act passed in the same year, entitled, an act for the better management of the workhouse and foundling hospital in Dublin (1799) | 39 George III c.38 |
| 62 | For extending to the county of Waterford the different laws passed in this kingdom for erecting, establishing and regulating of public infirmaries or hospitals (1799) | 39 George III c.17 |
| 63 | For the better governing and managing the infirmary of the county of Clare (1800) | 40 George III c.32 |
| 64 | For the better regulation and management of the house of industry established for the relief of the poor in Dublin (1800) | 40 George III c.40 |
| 65 | For repealing an act passed in the 25th year of his present majesty, entitled, an act for establishing a complete school of physic in this kingdom and also for repealing an act passed in the 35th year of his present majesty, entitled, an act to explain and amend an act establishing a complete school of physic in this kingdom (1800) | 40 George III c.84 |

Source: *Irish Legislation Database* (www.qub.ac.uk/ild/)

Chapter 7

# Gendered Medical Advice within Anglo-Irish Correspondence: A Case Study of the Cary-Jurin Letters*

Wendy D. Churchill

**Introduction**

During the early modern period, correspondence was an important medium connecting patients, generally of the middling and upper social orders, and practitioners, as well as practitioners to other practitioners across the British Isles, continental Europe and the Americas. Social historians of medicine have utilised examples of such correspondence from the seventeenth and eighteenth centuries to illuminate socio-economic, gendered, and professional aspects of medicine in England, Scotland, and continental Europe.[1] Since the late 1980s, scholars have incorporated correspondence alongside other primary sources in their examinations of early modern British medicine, or have specifically focused on consultation correspondence.[2] Recent work on women and gender demonstrates the riches that written medical exchanges offer.[3] Such correspondence also presents ample

---

\* This study has profited enormously from the feedback of Dr J.D. Alsop. I am also grateful to Dr D. Charters for helpful suggestions.

[1] Examples include A.F. Oakley, 'Letters to a seventeenth-century Yorkshire physician', *History of Medicine*, 2/4 (1970): 24–8; Guenter Risse, '"Doctor William Cullen, physician, Edinburgh": a consultation practice in the eighteenth century', *Bulletin of the History of Medicine*, 48/3 (1974): 338–51; Laurence Brockliss, 'Consultation by letter in early eighteenth-century Paris: the medical practice of Étienne-François Geoffroy' in A. La Berge and M. Feingold (eds), *French medical culture in the nineteenth century*, The Wellcome Institute Series in the History of Medicine, Clio Medica 25 (Amsterdam: Rodopi Press, 1994), pp. 79–117.

[2] For instance: Dorothy Porter and Roy Porter, *Patient's progress: doctors and doctoring in eighteenth-century England* (Cambridge: Polity Press, 1989); Steven Shapin, 'Trusting George Cheyne: scientific expertise, common sense, and moral authority in early eighteenth-century dietetic medicine', *Bulletin for the History of Medicine*, 77/2 (2003): 263–97. See also notes 3 and 4 below.

[3] See Lisa W. Smith, 'Reassessing the role of the family: women's medical care in eighteenth-century England', *Social History of Medicine*, 16/3 (2003): 327–42; Wendy D. Churchill, 'The medical practice of the sexed body: women, men, and disease in Britain,

– and, to date, largely unexplored – opportunities to study the nature of patient – practitioner relationships in early modern Ireland, while simultaneously situating such relationships within the medical, professional, and social networks that linked Ireland and England during this period.

This study examines the correspondence of the Church of Ireland bishop, Mordecai Cary, with the prominent London-based physician Dr James Jurin (bap. 1684, d. 1750) during the 1730s.[4] Writing from Ireland, Cary conveyed details of his wife's breast ailment to his friend and former tutor in the expectation that he would secure advice on her treatment. In addition to its gendered dimensions, this correspondence demonstrates that members of the English elite resident in Ireland were part of a wider, interconnected, cosmopolitan web of medical knowledge and expertise, and how they availed of this when they were unable to secure the desired medical assistance locally.

**Mordecai Cary and James Jurin**

By the time of their correspondence in the 1730s, Cary and Jurin had known each other for 25 years, both having attended Christ's Hospital, London, and Trinity College, Cambridge. After Jurin received his BA and was elected fellow of Trinity, he served as Cary's tutor for 1708–09. During this time, the two men travelled to Leyden where they attended the lectures of the Dutch physician Herman Boerhaave.[5] Following their return to England, Cary and Jurin completed

---

circa 1600–1740', *Social History of Medicine*, 18/1 (2005): 3–22; Lisa Smith, 'The relative duties of a man: domestic medicine in England and France, ca. 1685–1740', *Journal of Family History*, 31/3 (2006): 237–56.

[4] The Cary–Jurin letters have been by examined by Andrea Rusnock and Wayne Wild: see Andrea A. Rusnock (ed.), *The correspondence of James Jurin (1684–1750): physician and secretary to the Royal Society*, The Wellcome Institute Series in the History of Medicine, Clio Medica 39 (Amsterdam: Rodopi Press, 1996), pp. 42, 396–7, 398, 399, 402–405; Wayne Wild, 'Doctor–patient correspondence in eighteenth-century Britain: a change in rhetoric and relationship', *Studies in Eighteenth-Century Culture*, 29 (2000): 47–64 (47–50); Wayne Wild, *Medicine-by-post: the changing voice of illness in eighteenth-century British consultation letters and literature*, The Wellcome Series in the History of Medicine, Clio Medica 79 (Amsterdam: Rodopi Press, 2006), pp. 81–93. Nevertheless, these letters have not been used to explore how members of the ruling elite in Ireland appealed to England for medical help. This paper utilises the Cary–Jurin correspondence to explore this subject and issues of gender, social rank and professional status, and religion.

[5] John Venn and J.A. Venn, *Alumni Cantabrigienses: a biographical list of all known students, graduates and holders of office at the University of Cambridge, from the earliest times to 1900* (10 vols, 2 pts, Cambridge: CUP, 1922), vol. 1, pt 1, p. 292; J.B. Leslie, 'Killala: biographical succession list', 1938, p. 12 (RCBL, MS 61/2/9); Rusnock (ed.), *The correspondence of James Jurin*, pp. 9–12; *ODNB*, sub James Jurin; Wild, *Medicine-by-post*, pp. 62, 81–2.

their education and training and rose to prominent positions in their respective professions of religion and medicine. Cary received his BA and MA from Cambridge and was made fellow of Trinity College before he was ordained as a deacon in London in 1714. After holding posts as a headmaster, a perpetual curate, and a rector, he received his DD in 1731.[6] Meanwhile, Jurin graduated from Cambridge, MD, in 1716 and was elected as a fellow of the Royal Society of London in 1717. Two years later, he became a candidate and a fellow of the Royal College of Physicians. While serving as secretary of the Royal Society from 1721 to 1727, Jurin cultivated an extensive network of correspondents on topics of natural philosophy that encompassed science, medicine, mathematics, and meteorology. His voluminous correspondence vividly illustrates the importance, utility and vitality of communication networks amongst elite men who shared similar educational and socio-economic backgrounds. Andrea Rusnock has demonstrated that the vast majority of Jurin's correspondents were professionals, especially those in medicine, from across England. Nevertheless, a substantial proportion of the letters were from continental Europe and North America, and smaller numbers from Ireland, Scotland and Wales. The writers and recipients of this correspondence were virtually exclusively male. Jurin appears to have written directly to only one woman, and this was subsequent to his time as secretary to the Society.[7]

In the first eight of his 12 surviving letters to Jurin, Cary described in detail the health of his wife Katherine and requested Jurin's medical opinion about her condition.[8] All eight letters were penned between June 1733 and February 1735; seven were from the Irish diocese of Clonfert, county Galway, and one from Dublin. At the commencement of the letters, the Cary family had been in Ireland for only two years, during which time Cary served briefly as chaplain to the Lord Lieutenant of Ireland, the Duke of Dorset, prior to his elevation to the episcopal bench as Bishop of Clonfert in 1732. In 1735, he was promoted to the united diocese of Killala and Achonry.[9] Throughout this period, Jurin (who had

---

[6] Venn and Venn, *Alumni Cantabrigienses*, p. 292; RCBL, MS 61/2/9, p. 12.

[7] Rusnock (ed.), *The correspondence of James Jurin*, pp. 9–12; *ODNB*, sub James Jurin; Wild, *Medicine-by-post*, pp. 62, 81–2; Andrea Rusnock, 'Correspondence networks and the Royal Society, 1700–1750', *British Journal for the History of Science*, 32/2 (1999): 155–69 (156–9).

[8] Letters from Mordecai Cary to James Jurin, M.D., 1733–42 (WL, MS 6140/1–12). Four of Cary's eight letters to Jurin are included in Rusnock (ed.), *The correspondence of James Jurin*. Katherine is not mentioned by name in any of the letters; instead, Cary referred to her as 'my wife' throughout, and once as 'Your patient' (WL, MS 6140/4 (28 July 1733)). She was, however, identified by her first name in his will: see 'Will of Mordecai Cary, Bishop of Killala and Achonry, 1735–51', *The Journal of the Irish Memorials Association*, 12/2 (1926): 369–71.

[9] Venn and Venn, *Alumni Cantabrigienses*, p. 292; F.J. Byrne, F.X. Martin, and T.W. Moody (eds), *A new history of Ireland, IX: maps, genealogies, lists* (Oxford: OUP, 1984),

previously served as physician to Guy's Hospital) was situated in London, where he practiced medicine and maintained his active correspondence and publication record on a wide variety of scientific and medical topics.[10]

## Medical consultation by correspondence: the Cary–Jurin case

An analysis of the Cary–Jurin correspondence presents several challenges. First, only Cary's side of this exchange has survived (aside from a few brief notations and prescriptions penned by Jurin on Cary's letters).[11] Second, there is no known surviving first-hand account by Katherine of her illness and treatment. Her voice has to be reconstructed through the words of her husband. Cary presented his wife's case in great detail, relaying Katherine's descriptions of her symptoms in addition to his own observations, and the advice of various medical practitioners in Ireland. Despite these limitations, the letters illuminate the gendered, social, professional and religious dimensions of the medical consultation experience of the ruling elite in eighteenth-century Ireland. It is clear that, in addition to drawing on the medical marketplace in Ireland, these patients accessed medical advice from practitioners based in England through networks of correspondence constructed within shared social, educational and professional backgrounds.

As a physician, James Jurin treated both male and female patients. Similar to other medical practitioners of his day, he also consulted with, and prescribed for, patients via written correspondence. As the Cary letters suggest, however, this communication tended to be with other males even when the subject of the consultation was a woman. For instance, Jurin also treated the wives of prominent physicians such as Hans Sloane (1660–1753) and John Huxham (1692–1768). As with the Katherine Cary case, Jurin diagnosed and prescribed for these women primarily by corresponding with their husbands.[12] These men, who shared a professional identity, participated in such exchanges not only as doctors but also as patriarchs and concerned husbands.

Such male-to-male discourse about the health of female patients is commonplace in consultation letters of seventeenth- and eighteenth-century England. Although a small number of women personally entered into such correspondence, the medical concerns of female patients were more often the subject of an interaction between

---

pp. 434, 437.

[10] *ODNB*, sub James Jurin; Rusnock (ed.), *The correspondence of James Jurin*, pp. 3–61.

[11] There exist two extant letters written by Jurin to Cary in 1742, but they do not contain any reference to Katherine's health. Copy letter from James Jurin to Mordecai Cary, 10 June 1742 (WL, MS 6146/26); Copy letter from James Jurin to Mordecai Cary, n.d. [post-30 October 1742] (WL, MS 6146/27).

[12] See Rusnock (ed.), *The correspondence of James Jurin*, pp. 15–17, 30–35, 42, 191–2, 196, 196–7, 198–9, 435–6; Wild, *Medicine-by-post*, pp. 95–6, 98, 100 n. 70.

two males: the medical practitioner and the head of the household. In a majority of cases, the male relative was either the father or husband, but it could also be a brother, brother-in-law or uncle.[13] Lisa Smith has recently demonstrated that patients, regardless of their sex, were more likely to write to medical practitioners for others (family, friends or household members) than for themselves, highlighting the fact that medical networks were not solely gendered toward the masculine.[14] In addition, she has revealed that the roles of males within early modern family medical care were more diverse and important than has generally been acknowledged. Smith asserts that such roles were consistent with societal expectations of the function of patriarchy within the family and household.[15] Thus, it was in their roles as care providers, if not necessarily as care givers, although some were, for their wives, daughters and other female relatives that men such as Mordecai Cary solicited medical advice from male medical practitioners through correspondence.

The involvement of husbands in the medical diagnosis and treatment of their wives during this period was useful, or even necessary, for a variety of reasons.[16] In law, a married woman was regarded as *feme covert*, which meant that in theory she could not enter a contract on her own behalf. This encompassed medical contracts.[17] A partial explanation for the rapidly growing popularity of medical consultation by correspondence[18] appears to have been that it represented a contractual agreement that was more subtle, 'polite', and flexible than earlier forms of written 'contracts for cure' in which payment was contingent on the efficacy of the treatment.[19] Thus, medical consultation by correspondence reflected the evolution of the contractual agreement within early modern medicine.[20] Husbands acted as the principal

---

[13] Smith, 'Reassessing the role of the family', 333; Wendy D. Churchill, 'Female complaints: the medical diagnosis and treatment of British women, 1590–1740' (unpublished Ph.D thesis, McMaster University, 2005), 24–5, 60–61, 72.

[14] Smith, 'The relative duties of a man', 241–3.

[15] Smith, 'The relative duties of a man', 249.

[16] For further discussion see Catherine Crawford, 'Patients' rights and the law of contract in eighteenth-century England', *Social History of Medicine*, 13/3 (2000): 381–410 (402–405, 408); Smith, 'Reassessing the role of the family', 330–31, 333–4, 338–9, 341; Smith, 'The relative duties of a man', 238, 242–5, 249.

[17] Sara Mendelson and Patricia Crawford, *Women in early modern England, 1550–1720* (Oxford: Clarendon Press, 1998), pp. 37–8; Crawford, 'Patients' rights and the law of contract', 398–404; Lisa Wynne Smith, 'Women's health care in England and France (1650–1775)' (unpublished Ph.D. thesis, University of Essex, 2001), 204–205; Smith, 'Reassessing the role of the family', 330–1; Churchill, 'Female complaints', 61.

[18] Brockliss, 'Consultation by letter in early eighteenth-century Paris', p. 80; Wild, *Medicine-by-post*, p. 17.

[19] Helen M. Dingwall, '"General practice" in seventeenth-century Edinburgh: evidence from the Burgh Court', *Social History of Medicine*, 6/1 (1993): 125–42; Crawford, 'Patients' rights and the law of contract', 390.

[20] Churchill, 'Female complaints', 60–61, 252–4.

representatives regarding the health of their wives because it was legally necessary, as well as socially expected and practically useful. Networks between men based on their shared gendered experiences in education, training and occupation, and their positions as heads of households meant that male family members could be effective in procuring medical advice from other males.[21]

Cary's concern about Katherine's breast ailment, and, apparently, what this meant for her overall health, is evident in the tone and language of his letters. After providing details regarding the nature and progression of Katherine's symptoms in his first letter, written from Clonfert on 1 June 1733, Cary implored Jurin for his medical advice: 'Now Dear Doctor, I have told You the case, I must beg Your advice by the next Post ...'.[22] On 9 June, Cary wrote again, with a sense of urgency conveyed through his prefatory comment: 'Now I must beg pardon for this second trouble'.[23] In his 12 June letter, Cary's concern that Katherine's ailment might be cancer is clearly evident: 'Pray, Dr., is there reason to fear a Cancer? and if it prove a Cancer, ... what must we do?'.[24] Faced with a long-standing chronic breast condition that presented a variety of symptoms and resisted accurate diagnosis and effective treatment, the Carys were clearly worried. Early modern patients and practitioners alike believed that conditions such as abscesses and ulcers could advance into cancerous tumours.[25] Through her husband's letters, Katherine described her symptoms and made clear her concerns. For instance, Cary informed Jurin that 'whenever she stoops she finds a tugging as she calls it at the breast bone under the suspected part of the breast and she is afraid, whenever she shall leave off the poultice, that the breast, tho now soft and little, will grow hard and big again'.[26] Anxiety over Katherine's condition is reflected not only in Cary's words, but also in the amount of space and attention devoted to the subject; it was discussed in eight out of 12 of his extant letters, comprising the *sole* topic of discourse in three and representing the chief purpose for the other five.

The breast disorder afflicting Katherine, who was in her mid-forties at the time,[27] involved pain, swelling and discomfort of the left breast, which was sometimes accompanied by pain in the right breast and her armpits and hips.[28]

---

[21] See Crawford, 'Patients' rights and the law of contract', 402–405, 408; Smith, 'Women's health care', 181–3, 185, 212–13, 227–9, 231; Smith, 'Reassessing the role of the family', 331, 333–4.

[22] WL, MS 6140/1 (1 June 1733). The majority of the palaeographical abbreviations in the manuscripts have been silently expanded. The symbol < > signifies where Cary inserted a letter, word, or phrase above his original text, while the presence of a — indicates text that has been scored through.

[23] WL, MS 6140/2 (9 June 1733).

[24] WL, MS 6140/3 (12 June 1733).

[25] Churchill, 'Female complaints', 125–6, 129–30.

[26] WL, MS 6140/2.

[27] WL, MS 6140/7 (20 November 1734).

[28] WL, MS 6140/1.

Cary's letters reveal a detailed, careful approach in describing her condition. Prior to sending his letters, he made numerous corrections and additions to the sections relating to Katherine's ailment, indicating his desire to represent her medical case as faithfully and completely as possible.[29] Furthermore, Cary's words were selected to distinguish between his own observations, his wife's descriptions, and those instances in which they agreed upon her symptoms. For example, Cary wrote on 1 June 1733 that:

> her left breast ... has been ... in great pain with little intermissions or rather removals of the pain, as sometimes into her hands sometimes into one hip <sometimes into her right breast and right armpit:> but her most constant complaint is of the bone under the left breast and of her back bone betwixt the scapulae and thereabouts. The breast has been much swelled, then abated, and now it is a little bigger than the other whereas when she is well, the less than the other. We find no lump, nor sign of inflammation ... Her wandring pains into her arms and hips, and shoulders and other parts we are apt to think Rheumatick. That gnawing pain in the breast it self, which as she complains draws down her neck, and hinders the free use of her left arm and goes to the bone under the breast and to the back-bone and sometimes to the left breast and to t her armpits and sides[.] I suppose [it] proceeds from some contraction or affection of the nerves of the left breast. She has complained of the pain's running about in and under her breast like some living creature; but that complaint is much abated: or as she expresses it, the mouse that us'd to grow run up and down is much lessen'd ... Her pain excepted, she is not sick ... The pain of her breast she sometimes compares to <that of> forks or darts stabbing the part.[30]

Cary performed multiple roles as husband, observer, and recorder of his wife's condition. By relaying Katherine's account of her symptoms, Cary was speaking on her behalf. This did not mean, however, that Katherine was obliged to take a passive role in the care of her own health. Cary's letters contain detailed descriptions and questions, seemingly originating from Katherine herself, alongside information generated from Cary's visual and manual examinations. In his 12 June letter, Cary informed Jurin:

> The place aggriev'd of my wifes breast is <close to the bone in the> the [sic] very highest part of it <in a> perpendicular dividing the breast into two <equal> parts right and left. There is not <an acute> pain in it, nor swelling or hardness [that] I can perceive (for I felt it very freely this morning) but my [wife] says there is a little hardnes[s] and a constant tugging as she calls it. The great vein of her left arm which comes to the back of the hand and distributes veins to the fingers, is often very remarkably full and quite astrut, and then her arm is in pain

---

[29] Wild, 'Doctor–patient correspondence', 50; Wild, *Medicine-by-post*, pp. 82, 89.
[30] WL, MS 6140/1.

till she holds up her hand above her head, and then the vein sinks and the pain abates.[31]

By assembling such data, Cary presented himself to Jurin as a surrogate medical practitioner, albeit one with intimate access to the patient by virtue of his roles as husband and learned professional male who had studied medicine (albeit to a limited extent). However, although Cary presented Jurin with detailed information regarding Katherine's symptoms, he did not venture a diagnosis. He left that to Jurin.

It is clear from Cary's letters that Katherine's left breast had been 'lanced' sixteen years earlier, when she was resident in England. At the time of this procedure, c. 1717, the Carys had been married only a year and Katherine was 28 years old.[32] Although Cary did not offer a detailed description of this earlier condition, it must have involved a cyst or abscess to justify surgery. William Cheselden (1688–1752), the prominent London surgeon and anatomist, performed the procedure.[33] Despite this, according to Cary, Katherine continued to experience pain in her breast, 'at times, these 16 years; as often as she has got cold, or almost before every rain'.[34]

By the spring of 1733, the Carys judged Katherine's breast condition serious enough to warrant further medical intervention. Cary's letters to Jurin commenced on 1 June, approximately one month after the reappearance of symptoms. As well as self-treatment, this prompted Katherine to have recourse to the services of a diversity of local medical expertise in Ireland that included several local women, an apothecary and a physician.[35] She also underwent bloodletting, likely performed by surgeons or barber-surgeons.[36] However, when these local avenues of care failed to elicit any improvement in her symptoms, it was Jurin – not Cheselden – to whom the Carys appealed for medical advice. Saliently, Cary's letters contain no reference to Katherine seeking or receiving treatment from Cheselden after 1717. As will be argued below, the search for efficacious treatment was the dominant consideration for the Carys, just as it was for patients elsewhere in the British Isles.[37] It is also possible that Katherine wished to avoid or to delay further surgical

---

[31] WL, MS 6140/3.

[32] These details have been established from WL, MS 6140/1, 7, 8 (8 February 1734/5); RCBL, MS 61/2/9, p. 12.

[33] WL, MS 6140/1; Rusnock (ed.), *The correspondence of James Jurin*, pp. 396–7, 397 (n. 2); *ODNB*, sub William Cheselden; Wild, *Medicine-by-post*, p. 83.

[34] WL, MS 6140/1.

[35] It is unclear whether Cary's reference to 'the advice of a physician' in WL, MS 6140/1 refers to the same physician whose account of Katherine's breast disorder was provided by Cary to Jurin and who is mentioned in MS 6140/5 (1 August 1733) and MS 6140/6 (15 January 1733/4).

[36] WL, MS 6140/1–2, 8.

[37] Churchill, 'Female complaints', especially 71–4, 79.

procedures; there was no guarantee that they would provide relief or affect a cure[38] and such procedures were often accompanied by pain and the risk of disfigurement, infection and/or death.[39]

In his initial letter on 1 June 1733, Cary advanced an explanation for the reappearance of Katherine's symptoms: 'Above a month ago my wife took cold by going into new rooms when the walls were damp, after a walk that had heated her. Hereupon her left breast ... has been ever since in great pain with little intermissions ...'.[40] Rather than attribute the reappearance of Katherine's symptoms to the Irish geography or climate, Cary ascribed them to changes in her immediate environment.[41] Early modern aetiology held that such fluctuations could precipitate an imbalance of bodily humours that brought on illness, with the female body being especially vulnerable due to its cold, moist nature.[42] Katherine's treatment closely followed a seasonal course of physick as part of her medical regimen;[43] this would have aimed to balance the bodily humours with the seasonal qualities and astrological and climatic changes that were associated with the specific time of year.[44] Regardless of where they resided, British female patients were diagnosed and treated according to the same set of criteria pertaining to Galenic humoral medicine in the late seventeenth and eighteenth centuries.[45]

Between the consultation with Cheselden and the appeal to Jurin for medical advice, the Carys explored a number of medical options in an attempt to alleviate Katherine's symptoms. Following their arrival in Ireland, they had recourse to self-treatment, lay healers, and irregular and regular practitioners.[46] Their reliance on medical practitioners of different ages, sexes, social ranks and professional status supports the scholarly argument that early modern patients and their families viewed medical expertise in a broad and flexible manner and were guided primarily by the desire to secure effective treatment. This conclusion is consistent

---

[38] Lucinda McCray Beier, *Sufferers and healers: the experience of illness in seventeenth-century England* (London: Routledge and Kegan Paul, 1987), pp. 5, 209, 257.

[39] Andrew Wear, *Knowledge and practice in English medicine, 1550–1680* (Cambridge: CUP, 2000), pp. 238–40; Andrew Wear, 'The discourses of practitioners in sixteenth- and seventeenth-century Europe' in Robert Baker and Larry McCullough (eds), *The Cambridge world history of medical ethics* (Cambridge: CUP, 2009, pp. 379–90); Churchill, 'Female complaints', 78–80.

[40] WL, MS 6140/1.

[41] WL, MS 6140/1, 4, 6–7.

[42] Churchill, 'Female complaints', 125–6.

[43] WL, MS 6140/4, 6–8.

[44] Wear, *Knowledge and practice*, pp. 37–8.

[45] Churchill, 'Female complaints', chapter 3; Wendy D. Churchill, 'Bodily differences? Gender, race and class in Hans Sloane's Jamaican medical practice, 1687–88', *Journal of the History of Medicine and Allied Sciences*, 60/4 (2005): 391–444, (391, 416–26, 431, 437–9, 441–2).

[46] See also Kelly chapter 5 in this collection.

with the evidence found in practitioner casebooks, consultation correspondence and medical treatises throughout Britain of patients who sought treatment for female-specific ailments, including breast and menstrual disorders.[47]

In her self-treatment, Katherine simultaneously played the role of patient and medical expert. Her own treatments included applying a poultice of 'an herb bruised and fryed in Lard' to her afflicted breast, drinking 'a Chalybeate Water [that is, water infused with iron] ... about a quart in a morning before breakfast ...',[48] and consuming millipedes (woodlice), which was frequently prescribed for menstrual and other obstructions in female patients.[49] As Roy Porter and others have shown, self-treatment was one of the primary therapies resorted to by those who were ill in the early modern period.[50]

Katherine also sought medical advice in Ireland from several women of various ages and different socio-economic backgrounds. Cary's letters of 12 June and 28 July 1733 reveal that Katherine employed the services of an 'old woman' with a reputation for 'cur[ing] many sore breasts' and who applied 'an Oyl made of white Lily roots and butter',[51] and that she followed the advice of 'some Neighbouring Ladies' who recommended applying a plaster to the sore breast.[52] This constituted the totality of local female assistance. In addition, Katherine sought the advice of an unnamed male physician[53] and filed prescriptions with a male apothecary.[54]

There is no evidence in Cary's letters to suggest that Katherine preferred to be treated by other women or was hesitant to receive medical care at the hands of male practitioners. The intention was simply to obtain efficacious treatment from a competent practitioner. Given the pluralism of the early modern medical marketplace, the point at which the patient, or her family or 'friends', deemed either the practitioner or the treatment to be untrustworthy or ineffective was as likely as not to precipitate the termination of the medical consultation,[55] which seems to have been the outcome in this particular instance. When discussing the

---

[47] Churchill, 'Female complaints', chapter 2.

[48] WL, MS 6140/2; Rusnock (ed.), *The correspondence of James Jurin*, p. 398 n. 2.

[49] WL, MS 6140/3; Rusnock (ed.), *The correspondence of James Jurin*, p. 399 n. 1; Churchill, 'Bodily differences?', 418–19.

[50] Porter and Porter, *Patient's progress*, chapter 3; Roy Porter, 'The patient in England, c. 1660–c. 1800', in Andrew Wear (ed.), *Medicine in society: historical essays* (Cambridge: CUP, 1992; repr. edn, 1996), pp. 96–114.

[51] WL, MS 6140/3.

[52] WL, MS 6140/4. This was probably the same group Cary referred to as 'the good women' in MS 6140/2.

[53] WL, MS 6140/5.

[54] WL, MS 6140/4.

[55] Ronald C. Sawyer, 'Friends or foes? Doctors and their patients in early modern England' in Yosio Kawakita, Shizu Sakai and Yasuo Otsuka (eds), *History of the doctor–patient relationship: proceedings of the 14th international symposium on the comparative history of medicine – east and west: September 3–September 9, 1989, Susono-shi, Shizuoka*

approach of the 'old woman', Cary remarked critically that 'she makes very light of my wifes ailing, and pretends to cure it without fail'.[56] The fact that he made no further reference to her in his letters suggests that the patient–practitioner bond had been broken or, perhaps, never firmly established.[57]

Relatively little can be gleaned directly about what Cary or his wife thought about the state of medicine in Ireland. However, in seeking diagnostic and treatment advice from Jurin, it is clear that they were not content to rely on the available local options. Cary's appeal to Jurin for assistance was spurred, at least partially, by the inability of various local medical practitioners to procure an improvement in Katherine's symptoms. And although the letters are not forthcoming with the name or professional status of Katherine's local physician, Cary's position as an Anglican bishop would have provided him with access to the most eminent medical practitioners in Ireland. The disposition of patients to choose from among the full range of available medical options was not particular to members of the ruling Anglophone elite in eighteenth-century Ireland. This was the inclination also of patients of both sexes, but especially those of high socio-economic standing, throughout early modern England.[58] With the exception of Cary's comments about the old woman, the absence of explicit or implied criticism in his letters about the training, qualifications or expertise of local medical practitioners suggests these may not have been matters of particular concern. Cary's letters to his friend certainly would have included such information if this had been the case and if he had regarded it as pertinent to his wife's diagnosis and treatment. It is clear that the Carys did not view medical expertise as being restricted to only university educated, formally trained or licensed male medical practitioners.

## Mordecai Cary, religion and medicine

Cary's letters do not specify whether the local medical practitioners involved in Katherine's case were native-born Irish, nor do they provide information about their religious convictions. And while it is impossible definitively to establish Bishop Cary's opinion of the state of medical practice in Ireland, it is possible to

---

(Tokyo, Japan: Ishiyaku EuroAmerica, 1995), pp. 42, 49–50; Smith, 'Women's health care', 175–6; Churchill, 'Female complaints', 71–4, 77–9.

[56] WL, MS 6140/3.

[57] For further discussion on issues of advice and trust see Shapin, 'Trusting George Cheyne', 284–92; Porter and Porter, *Patient's progress*, pp. 58–66, 87–8; Harold J. Cook, 'Good advice and little medicine: the professional authority of early modern English physicians', *Journal of British Studies*, 33/1 (1994): 1–31 (especially 11). For the importance and function of trust between female patients and male practitioners see Smith, 'Women's health care', 132–70; Churchill, 'Female complaints', 81–5.

[58] Churchill, 'Female complaints', 12–15, 24–6; Sawyer, 'Friends or foes?', pp. 44–9.

surmise something concerning his general attitude towards the Irish. Could health issues – and, specifically, the quest for effective diagnosis and treatment – trump religious differences for a Church of Ireland bishop such as Cary?

Given Cary's position in the Church of Ireland, it is hardly surprising that he targeted Catholicism for criticism in his two published sermons.[59] In a sermon delivered on 18 March 1743 to the Incorporated Society in Dublin for Promoting English Protestant Schools in Ireland,[60] Cary strongly commended the Irish charter schools, conceiving of them as practical manifestations of Christian charity that were performing the invaluable service of working to 'convert the *Popish* Natives of this Kingdom to our own Persuasion'.[61] This sentiment was shared across the ruling Protestant elite in Ireland (and, particularly, the Anglican clergy) in the first half of the eighteenth century, and it reflected their conviction that the Catholic and Gaelic-speaking Irish majority needed to be brought 'out of the Darkness and Slavery of Superstition, into the Light and Liberty of the Gospel'.[62] Such views could well have meant that it was unlikely that a Protestant clergyman recently arrived from England would have sought medical advice from Catholics.

The detailed nature and familiar tone of his letters suggest that *if* Cary had deemed it pertinent to allude to the religion of the medical practitioners whom he and his wife consulted in Ireland then he would have addressed this in his letters to Jurin; he certainly provided other relevant descriptors of the practitioners.[63] The overwhelming majority of Ireland's population was Catholic throughout the early decades of the eighteenth century.[64] Moreover, medicine represented the only profession from which Catholics were not inhibited from practicing by the anti-

---

[59] Mordecai Cary, *A sermon preach'd in Christ-Church, Dublin, on Wednesday the 5th of November, 1735, being the anniversary of the Gun-Powder-Plot, before his grace, Lionel Duke of Dorset, lord lieutenant general, and general governor of Ireland, and the lords spiritual and temporal in parliament assembled ...* (Dublin, 1735); Mordecai Cary, *A sermon preached at Christ-Church, Dublin, on the 18th day of March, 1743, before the Incorporated Society, for Promoting English Protestant Schools in Ireland ... with a continuation of the Society's Proceedings to the 25th of March, 1744* (Dublin, 1744).

[60] For the Society and its aims during this period, see Kenneth Milne, *The Irish Charter Schools, 1730–1830* (Dublin: FCP, 1997), especially pp. 11–33.

[61] Cary, *A sermon preached at Christ-Church, Dublin, on the 18th day of March, 1743*, p. 17.

[62] Cary, *A sermon*, p. 17; Toby Barnard, 'Integration or separation? Hospitality and display in Protestant Ireland, 1660–1800' in Laurence Brockliss and David Eastwood (eds), *A Union of multiple identities: the British Isles, c. 1750–c. 1850* (Manchester: Manchester University Press, 1997), pp. 127, 129.

[63] See WL, MS 6140/1–5.

[64] S.J. Connolly, *Religion, law, and power: the making of Protestant Ireland, 1660–1760* (Oxford: OUP, 1992), pp. 146 (Figure 5.1), 147; Patrick Fagan, *Catholics in a Protestant country: the Papist constituency in eighteenth-century Dublin* (Dublin: FCP, 1998), pp. 31, 44–5, 51 (appendix 5).

popery laws.[65] Many Protestant inhabitants, in all likelihood, would have found it necessary to consult Catholic medical practitioners, particularly when resident outside Dublin. It is probable, therefore, that the local practitioners to whom the Carys had recourse were Catholic. The fact that Cary espoused anti-Catholic views in relation to religion, politics and education was not incompatible with utilising the medical services of local Catholics. As T.C. Barnard has cautioned, interpreting anti-popery sentiments as evidence of conflict at all levels of relations between Protestants and Catholics overstates the extent to which eighteenth-century Ireland was 'polarised along the lines of religious difference ...'.[66] Rather, as Barnard contends, 'demographic realities meant that most Dublin Protestants were served in shops and in their own houses by Irish Catholics. Such routine contacts widened the gap between the horror of popery in the abstract, or as political and theological system, and the practical coexistence'.[67] For the Carys, then, the demographics of Clonfert, coupled with anxieties about Katherine's health and the desire to obtain efficacious treatment, took precedence over any aspirations they may have entertained of observing religious divisions in their choice of practitioners.

Social historians of medicine have shown that professional medicine was often not the first recourse of early modern patients, even wealthy ones.[68] Moreover, as Cary's letters demonstrate, the use of lay and professional medical practitioners sometimes overlapped in the search for effective treatment; thus, medical consultations by patients did not routinely follow a straightforward, linear progression from lay to 'professional' medicine. Rather, patients in Ireland, like their counterparts in England, moved easily between various forms of medical expertise.[69] The largely unregulated nature of the early modern medical marketplace not only resulted in variety and competition amongst practitioners, but also afforded patients agency and choice within the consultation process.[70] This notwithstanding, the degree to which – and the manner in which – patients

---

[65] Fagan, *Catholics in a Protestant country*, p. 77.

[66] T.C. Barnard, '"Grand Metropolis" or "The Anus of the World"?: the cultural life of eighteenth-century Dublin' in Peter Clark and Raymond Gillespie (eds), *Two Capitals: London and Dublin 1500–1840*, Proceedings of the British Academy, vol. 107 (Oxford: Published for the British Academy by OUP, 2001), p. 188.

[67] Barnard, '"Grand Metropolis"', p. 188.

[68] Robert Jütte, 'A seventeenth-century German barber-surgeon and his patients', *Medical History*, 33/2 (1989): 184–98 (191, 193–4); Sawyer, 'Friends or foes?', pp. 44–9; Churchill, 'Female complaints', 71–2, 126–8, 137–8, 247.

[69] For England, see Porter and Porter, *Patient's progress*; Wear, *Knowledge and practice*, especially pp. 40–45.

[70] N.D. Jewson, 'Medical knowledge and the patronage system in 18th century England', *Sociology*, 8/3 (1974): 369–85; Porter and Porter, *Patient's progress*, pp. 17, 26–8, 208–209; Mary E. Fissell, *Patients, power, and the poor in eighteenth-century Bristol*, Cambridge History of Medicine (Cambridge: CUP, 1991), pp. 51, 68–70, 72–3; Smith, 'Women's health care', 2–3.

exercised this agency in England was influenced by gendered and socio-economic factors.[71] This statement also holds true for Ireland, especially for those who, like the Carys, possessed money, status and education. Nevertheless, due to differences in demography and religion, the medical options available to them in Ireland, particularly when outside Dublin, were fewer and more confined when compared with what was available in England.[72] For those of the English elite who lived outside Dublin, the difficulties involved in obtaining medical care may have been compounded by those religious and linguistic circumstances that placed them into minority positions in these regions.

**Trust, friendship, and patronage networks**

It was in this context that Cary wrote to Jurin for medical advice on behalf of his wife. Although he did not possess specialisms in either breast disorders or cancer, Jurin, like many early modern physicians, probably counted a high proportion of female patients amongst his clientele.[73] As such, Jurin would have treated women for a variety of conditions, including those of a female-specific nature such as menstrual suppressions and breast ailments.[74] In addition to the friendship that bound the two men, it is evident that Cary appealed to Jurin, rather than Cheselden, for medical advice because he was regarded as the more qualified practitioner. It was physicians, not surgeons, who dispensed 'advice' at a distance and who instructed others to carry out their directions.[75] The Carys also may have expected that the friendship between Cary and Jurin would facilitate the patient-practitioner relationship and the consultation process, not least because both had to be transacted by letter.

The friendship that existed between Cary and Jurin also helps to explain why the letters exchanged between the two men contain no reference to monetary payment. Their correspondence was grounded on a relationship that was equal and

---

[71] Crawford, 'Patients' rights and the law of contract', 396–401, 404, 409; Smith, 'Women's health care', chapter 6 and pp. 17–20, 263, 270–71; Smith, 'Reassessing the role of the family', *passim.*; Churchill, 'Female complaints', chapter 1 and pp. 239–40, 246.

[72] On the Dublin-centred nature of medical expertise see James Kelly, 'The emergence of scientific and institutional medical practice in Ireland, 1650–1800' in Greta Jones and Elizabeth Malcolm (eds), *Medicine, disease and the state in Ireland, 1650–1940* (Cork: Cork University Press, 1999), p. 32; Fagan, *Catholics in a Protestant country*, p. 97; Tony Farmar, *Patients, potions, and physicians: a social history of medicine in Ireland, 1654–2004* (Dublin: A. & A. Farmar in association with the Royal College of Physicians, 2004), p. 34.

[73] For sex ratios amongst physicians' casebooks, see Churchill, 'Female complaints', chapter 1.

[74] Churchill, 'Female complaints', chapter 2.

[75] Cook, 'Good advice and little medicine', *passim.*

reciprocal. It was not through any overt evocation of his elevated social rank as a bishop that Cary appealed to Jurin for his advice. Instead, he drew more directly on the intellectual foundations of their social relationship as well attested by the presence in his letters of commentary on classical literature, Greek and Latin, and politics, as well as news about common friends and acquaintances. Jurin might well have enhanced his medical reputation if he managed successfully to diagnose and to treat Katherine Cary. However, since his reputation was already firmly established by the 1730s, it is doubtful if this was as compelling a consideration as his desire to maintain his standing and friendship with Cary. It was through such friendships and correspondence that educated men in the eighteenth century cultivated and sustained mutually beneficial intellectual pursuits.

The letters indicate that Katherine no longer availed of the medical expertise of local practitioners after 28 July 1733. By then, Cary had provided Jurin with the requisite information concerning his wife's case and Jurin's medical advice had begun to produce a measure of observable improvement in Katherine's symptoms.[76] Convinced that they could trust themselves fully to Jurin's care, Cary informed his friend in his sixth letter, written from Dublin on 15 January 1734, that Katherine was unwilling to consult any other physician:

> Some times she has been so free from pain that she has flatterd her self with hopes that all was over: but still the pain returns, especially in any thing of sharp weather, in the upper part of her left breast, her scapula and armpit. Besides this, she complains of a pricking pain like that of a foot or hand asleep as we call it, but sharper, all over her back and breast. … I could not perswade her to come to Town [that is, to Dublin from Clonfert]: there's no Physician she can trust in, but Dr Jurin. You will be so good as to order when she is to begin her course [of physick] again …[77]

Such a declaration of trust in Jurin's abilities reinforced the patient–practitioner relationship of Katherine Cary and James Jurin. By explicitly – and one assumes consciously – expressing her confidence in Jurin, Katherine appears to have been invoking one of the most basic tenets of the consultation process in the expectation that it would elicit a reciprocal response from Jurin, and that this (as well as his sense of professional duty) would yield prompt and useful medical advice regarding her ailment.

Considering that the Carys were not long resident in Ireland when Katherine's symptoms reappeared, it is hardly surprising that once local practitioners failed to provide the required relief they turned their gaze towards the London medical marketplace. What is more telling is that they did not do so immediately upon the reoccurrence of Katherine's breast pain. The fact that they utilised a variety of local medical options in Ireland before seeking Jurin's advice is suggestive

---

[76] WL, MS 6140/4–5.
[77] WL, MS 6140/6.

on several levels. In the first place, as previously noted, it is illustrative of the tendency of patients to seek efficacious treatment wherever it could be found within the prevailing competitive, pluralistic medical marketplace, which afforded patients and their families a great deal of choice and agency. Secondly, there was an important and obvious logistical variable. The distance and difficulties involved in travelling between Ireland and London meant that a face-to-face medical consultation with an English practitioner was hardly feasible. Instead, it was necessary to obtain medical advice from England through correspondence, a medium that practitioners and patients alike recognised could be problematic.[78]

Both practitioners and patients had plenty of reason to doubt the reliability and efficiency of the postal service or individual messengers, in addition to the reasonable concerns they must have entertained concerning possible misdiagnoses or improper treatments resulting from a lack of reliable information or the misinterpretation of that information.[79] As Wayne Wild has remarked, 'both patients and their doctors had an obligation to be very precise if medicine-by-post was to work effectively'.[80] Despite its inherent problems, however, medical consultation by correspondence was widely resorted to during the late seventeenth and eighteenth centuries. Although it has been argued that its popularity speaks to the rudimentary nature and unimportance of visual and physical examinations within early modern medical practice,[81] recent research on female patients in early modern Britain questions this interpretation by highlighting the ways that visual examinations and hands-on diagnostic procedures could extend beyond cursory viewing and pulse-taking.[82] Such a critique does not, however, negate the primacy of the patient's narrative within the consultative relationship. While medical correspondence was recognised as a useful means through which consultations could be obtained across distance and geography,[83] some eighteenth-century practitioners explicitly identified the absence of an in-person medical consultation as a significant deficiency of this method.[84] This may help to explain why Jurin asked Cary to supply him with

---

[78] John Powell, M.D., to surgeon Charles Bernard, 14 July 1701 (BL, Sloane MS 1786, fol. 149r); Wild, *Medicine-by-post*, p. 80.

[79] WL, MS 6140/8; BL, Sloane MS 1786, fol. 149r; Oakley, 'Letters to a seventeenth-century Yorkshire physician', 25; Risse, '"Doctor William Cullen, physician, Edinburgh"', 343. See also Rusnock, 'Correspondence networks', 159; Wild, *Medicine-by-post*, pp. 182–3.

[80] Wild, *Medicine-by-post*, p. 80.

[81] See, for instance: Porter and Porter, *Patient's progress*, pp. 76–8; Roy Porter, 'The rise of the physical examination' in W.F. Bynum and Roy Porter (eds), *Medicine and the five senses* (Cambridge: CUP, 1993), p. 183; Brockliss, 'Consultation by letter in early eighteenth-century Paris', p. 79; Wild, *Medicine-by-post*, p. 17.

[82] Churchill, 'Female complaints', 66–70, 75–7, 86.

[83] Wild, *Medicine-by-post*, pp. 17–18.

[84] For example: BL, Sloane MS 1786, fol. 149r.

an account of Katherine's condition as described by her physician in Ireland. Cary pointed out in response that this information would add very little to that which he had already provided, but because he was 'unwilling to omit any thing which ... [Jurin] thought of any use ...' he enclosed the account from the local physician in his letter of 1 August 1733:

> The D[octo]rs State of my wifes Case.
> Mrs Cary has the same pains all over <her> body especially under the Omoplatae that she feels in her breasts. She complains of a Twitching of the Nerves and fibrous Contractions. There seems to be a great Sizyness of her blood from a pulsation or something moving in all parts of her body such as I apprehend from a certain degree of lentor circulating through the Capillary Arteries and from the painfull swelling on the back of her hand which seemed Rheumatick. This swelling is now much abated.
> The pains often remit but have no certain periodical return.[85]

Although Cary presented this statement as if it was taken verbatim from a document prepared by his wife's physician in Ireland, it is noteworthy that he followed it with supplementary information based upon his own observations. Cary added: 'I would take notice to You as I said in my last [letter] that the upper part of the left Breast, at or near the Sternum, is the chief seat of pain; and I would add that she is easier in the breast when she is up than when in bed ...'.[86] One can readily understand why Jurin sought a statement from a medical professional whom he likely believed had consulted with Katherine in person (although it is unclear if any such consultation took place), as it would serve to validate or to disprove Cary's account of his wife's symptoms. Trust, after all, was a two-way process in the consultative relationship, and the practitioner also needed to be certain that the patient (or the patient's family or friends) provided case details that were complete and accurate.[87] In addition, he needed to know that the patient followed his medical advice precisely and to the letter.[88] Both requirements were especially important when diagnosing by correspondence because the physician was unable in such cases to monitor the progression of symptoms and the effects of treatment through conversation, observation or (visual or physical) examination.

Another important dimension of the medical consultation by correspondence exchanged between Ireland and England was its contribution to the maintenance

---

[85] WL, MS 6140/5. See also discussion in Wild, *Medicine-by-post*, pp. 81, 89–91.

[86] WL, MS 6140/5.

[87] Wild, *Medicine-by-post*, pp. 9, 67–8, 81, 122–3; Churchill, 'Female complaints', 60–65, 97–8, 162–3.

[88] George Cheyne to Hans Sloane, 1 April 1723 (BL, Sloane MS 4034, fol. 348r); Shapin, 'Trusting George Cheyne', 282–5; Wild, *Medicine-by-post*, pp. 9, 25, 47, 122–3, 142.

of patronage networks. By connecting medical practice in the colonies to that in the British Empire's metropolis, patronage networks that were sustained through correspondence helped to overcome the challenges presented by geographical location and physical distance.[89] Craig Bailey has argued that the dichotomous position of Ireland within the eighteenth-century empire was typified by 'professional Irish migrants ... [who] acted as colonisers alongside their English, Scottish and Welsh colleagues, [while] they nevertheless retained strong connections with their homeland'.[90] Such networks facilitated the exchange of 'skills, knowledge and resources ...'.[91] To date, little attention has been devoted to identifying the ways in which members of different English professions functioned within circles of professional patronage and expertise in imperial contexts and geographies, including Ireland.[92] Yet, when the evidence for the medical professionals in Ireland gleaned from the Cary–Jurin case study is positioned alongside that for Irish migrants in London provided in Bailey's study it appears that the ethnic, professional/occupational and social connections within (and, perhaps, between) the two groups were comparable both in form and function. The Cary–Jurin correspondence reveals that social and medical networks performed a similar function for the English living in Ireland during this period. In this manner, then, medical correspondence functioned as a form of social patronage that reinforced networks, which were based on shared gendered, professional, and/or social identities and interests.

## Conclusion

In concluding this case study, it is appropriate to return to Katherine Cary. Despite the anxieties expressed by Cary in his letters to Jurin, it is unlikely that Katherine's breast was cancerous. Instead, it appears to have been a chronic condition that plagued her for at least 18 years until February 1735, after which there is no mention of this ailment – or, indeed, any reference to Katherine's health – in Cary's surviving letters to Jurin.[93] Moreover, her ailment was evidently not terminal in nature. She was still alive at Cary's death in 1751, by which time she would have been aged 63.[94] Scholars of early modern medicine

---

[89] Craig Bailey, 'Metropole and colony: Irish networks and patronage in the eighteenth-century empire', *Immigrants & Minorities*, 23/2–3 (2005): 161–81, *passim*, (especially 161–2).
[90] Bailey, 'Metropole and colony', 162.
[91] Bailey, 'Metropole and colony', 169.
[92] For the phrase 'imperial geographies', see Bailey, 'Metropole and colony', 176.
[93] WL, MS 6140/9–12.
[94] 'Will of Mordecai Cary', 369–71. See also discussion in Churchill, 'Female complaints', 129–30 (n. 149).

have rightly cautioned against retrospective diagnoses[95] and thus one will not be attempted here.

In his seventh letter, written on 20 November 1734, Cary reported that Katherine's symptoms had improved significantly, although they had not disappeared entirely: 'She finds her breast better than she expected ever to find it: tho in sharp weather or upon taking the least cold, she feels the return of her old pains'.[96] Cary then requested Jurin's advice for a 'new complaint, that is of an intolerable Itching in back, belly and thighs; in which parts upon the least scratching or even rubbing (though she forbears as much as possibly she can) there riseth and remaineth a red scurfy spot, as broad as ~~my finger~~ <her thumb>'. Cary ascribed these symptoms to physiological changes associated with middle age,[97] adding that 'next February she will be 46 years old; [and] ... before her last Course of Physick she found the menses not so regular as they should be ... Since said 10th October she has seen nothing of 'em, tho by her breath I percieve 'em to be in her body'.[98] It is apparent from Cary's subsequent letter, dated 8 February 1735, that Jurin's prescription had procured an improvement in those new symptoms:

> She is quite clear of the itching scrufy spots which she says were chiefly on her thighs where from the breadth of a silver penny they us'd to spread into that of a Crown piece. All her complaint Now is, that she grows very fat. She had the menses 9 Dec.[,] 5 Jan. and 5 Feb. after which she always finds her self very easy.[99]

In this same letter, Katherine conveyed that she was 'pretty well' in regard to her breast condition and queried if her 'Spring Course' of physick would be necessary. Cary informed Jurin that 'she almost thinks she needs not; but she will follow Your direction'.[100]

As is clear from this, the Carys' concern for, and request for medical advice pertaining to, Katherine's health was not restricted to her breast disorder. They also sought Jurin's guidance on other female-specific health issues. The attention to female health in the Cary–Jurin correspondence is consistent with recent scholarship that has revealed the centrality of female patients within medical

---

[95] Ronald C. Sawyer, 'Patients, healers, and disease in the southeast Midlands, 1597–1634' (unpublished Ph.D. thesis, University of Wisconsin-Madison, 1986), 461–5; Brian Nance, *Turquet de Mayerne as baroque physician: the art of medical portraiture*, The Wellcome Series in the History of Medicine, Clio Medica 65 (Amsterdam: Rodopi Press, 2001), p. ix.
[96] WL, MS 6140/7.
[97] Wild, *Medicine-by-post*, p. 93.
[98] WL, MS 6140/7.
[99] WL, MS 6140/8.
[100] WL, MS 6140/8.

practice – especially that of physicians – throughout the British Isles during the early modern period.[101] It also points to the importance and agency (that is, at least for this particular elite woman) of the matriarch within the medical consultation process, even when this correspondence was penned and maintained by the patriarch.

---

[101] For instance, see Churchill, 'Female complaints', *passim*.

Chapter 8

# The Wider Cultures of Eighteenth-Century Irish Doctors

Toby Barnard

**Introduction**

This essay seeks to describe and explain the disproportionate influence exerted over the wider culture of eighteenth-century Ireland by medical practitioners. Their prominence within successive groups dedicated to enquiry and experiment is notable. From William Petty, the state physician, in the circle of Samuel Hartlib's followers in Dublin during the 1650s, through the Dublin Philosophical Society (of which Petty was president) to the Dublin Society, the complementary Physico-Historical Society of the 1740s, and its successor, the Medico-Philosophical Society, doctors are conspicuous.[1] In addition, Paul Pollard noted that medical men – after the clergy and lawyers – constituted the calling known to have assembled most substantial libraries in the eighteenth century.[2] At least one of these collections, that of Dr Edward Worth, survives intact and is currently being analysed thoroughly. Medical doctors, having travelled, sometimes to educate themselves, but also to please patrons and to find patients, might share their impressions. Bernard O'Connor published an account of Poland; Hans Sloane toured the Caribbean and made collections there; Patrick Browne from Mayo wrote a *Civil and Natural History of Jamaica*.[3] Others participated in politics,

---

[1] T.C. Barnard, 'The Hartlib circle and the origins of the Dublin Philosophical Society', *Irish Historical Studies*, 19 (1974): 56–71; T.C. Barnard, 'The Hartlib circle and the cult and culture of improvement' in Mark Greengrass, Michael Leslie and Timothy Raylor (eds), *Samuel Hartlib and universal reformation* (Cambridge: CUP, 1994), pp. 381–97; Michael Herity, 'The Physico-Historical Society and its precursor, "Hibernia", 1738–1752', *Studia Celtica Japonica*, 8 (1996): 65–85; K.T. Hoppen, *The common scientist in the seventeenth century: a study of the Dublin Philosophical Society, 1683–1708* (London: Routledge and Keegan Paul, 1970); Eoin Magennis, '"A land of milk and honey": the Physico-Historical Society, improvement and the surveys of mid-eighteenth-century Ireland', *RIA proc.*, 102C (2002): 199–217; Eamon O'Flaherty, 'Medical men and learned societies in Ireland, 1680–1785' in Judith Devlin and H.B. Clarke (eds), *European encounters: essays in memory of Albert Lovett* (Dublin: UCD Press, 2003), pp. 253–69.

[2] M. Pollard, *Dublin's trade in books, 1550–1800* (Oxford: OUP, 1989), p. 215.

[3] Patrick Browne, *The civil and natural history of Jamaica* (London, 1789).

usually of a radical hue. Petty can be counted among them, but most conspicuous are Charles Lucas and William Drennan. Several explanations can be offered tentatively for this breadth of interests.

First, medicine was the one profession in late seventeenth- and eighteenth-century Ireland not subject to confessional tests as a condition of entry. In consequence, well-connected and talented Catholics as well as Protestants established themselves in profitable practice. Notionally, at least, any of talent might qualify. In reality, training was protracted and costly, especially for the would-be physician or surgeon. *Bourses*, such as those that subsidised the studies of youths intending for the Catholic priesthood, were occasionally available.[4] Economical options, like the cheap medical degrees awarded by the University of Reims, were another strategy.[5] Even so, given the restricted opportunities for Catholics to prosper between the 1690s and 1780s, the financial hurdles obstructed their recruitment into the higher reaches of medicine. Nevertheless, by 1760, it is estimated that a dozen of 49 known Dublin physicians were Catholic.[6] In Limerick at the same time one of its best-known surgeons was the Catholic Sylvester O'Halloran. Equally Presbyterians, such as Duncan Cumyng and Victor Ferguson, and other Protestant dissenters (like the Quaker John Rutty) flourished as medical practitioners, particularly in Dublin and the north-east.[7]

A second factor in accounting for the participation of medics in the wider cultural scene is the nature of their training. In the absence of a medical school in Dublin before the early nineteenth century, those aiming for the upper reaches – practising as a physician – had to travel. Would-be surgeons, too, were often apprenticed outside Ireland. For some trainees, it meant journeys no further than Edinburgh or London.[8] Nevertheless, even these travels enlarged horizons. More chose to study in continental Europe, where France and the United Provinces

---

[4] Liam Chambers, 'Irish *fondations* and *boursiers* in early-modern Paris, 1682–1793', *Irish Economic and Social History*, 35 (2008): 1–22. I am very grateful to Dr Liam Chambers for letting me read this in advance of its publication.

[5] See also Brockliss chapter 4.

[6] Toby Barnard, *A new anatomy of Ireland: the Irish Protestants, 1649–1770* (New Haven and London: Yale University Press, 2003), pp. 128–42; Patrick Fagan, *Catholics in a Protestant country* (Dublin: FCP, 1998), pp. 77–84; James Kelly, 'The emergence of scientific and institutional medical practice in Ireland, 1650–1800' in Elizabeth Malcolm and Greta Jones (eds), *Medicine, disease and the state in Ireland, 1650–1940* (Cork: Cork University Press, 1999), pp. 21–39.

[7] Barnard, *A new anatomy*, p. 129.

[8] R.G.W. Anderson and A.D.C. Simpson (eds), *The early years of the Edinburgh medical school* (Edinburgh: Royal Scottish Museum, 1976); C. Lawrence, 'Ornate physicians and learned artisans: Edinburgh medical men, 1726–1776' in W.F. Bynum and Roy Porter (eds), *William Hunter and the eighteenth-century medical world* (Cambridge: CUP, 1985), pp. 153–76; Lisa Rosner, *Medical education in the age of improvement in Edinburgh: students and apprentices, 1760–1826* (Edinburgh: Edinburgh University Press, 1991).

seem to have been the most popular destinations.⁹ Thereby, medical men were exposed to influences more varied even than those experienced by entrants to the profession that otherwise most closely resembled theirs: the legal profession. Lawyers had also to train outside the island. However, those intending for the Irish bar went only to London. Catholics were formally debarred from practising in the Irish courts. The ban could be circumvented, mainly through the stratagem of acting as chamber counsel. Such advisory work enriched the fortunate few, but conferred a different and unequal status from that of the Protestants who pleaded in the courts. It also differed from the professional freedom enjoyed by Catholic physicians.[10]

A third explanation of the conspicuous role occupied by some doctors, more difficult to evaluate, is the precocious development of hospitals in Georgian Dublin. Inevitably, physicians and surgeons served on the boards of governors as well as being retained by the institutions. Running the hospitals brought the medical directors into constant contact with the other, non-medical governors, recruited usually from the professional, intellectual and public-spirited elite of Protestant Dublin.[11] This cooperation in practical and charitable endeavour added to the contacts that abounded already in the intimate society of fashionable and prosperous Dublin. Charitable activity increased the occasions when medical men joined in the civic and associational life focussed on neighbourhood, parish vestries, clubs, freemasons' lodges and voluntary groups like the Incorporated Society, the Dublin Society and Physico-Historical Society.[12]

A fourth factor is even harder to assess with precision. Medical training involving dissection and observation encouraged investigatory and analytical techniques that might be applied elsewhere. Furthermore, close involvement with the often-parlous conditions of those admitted into the hospitals, and the

---

[9] Peter Froggatt, 'Irish students of medicine at Leiden' in B.P. Kennedy (ed.), *The anatomy lesson: art and medicine: an exhibition ... to celebrate the tercentary of the royal charter of 1692 of the Royal College of Physicians of Ireland* (Dublin: National Gallery of Ireland, 1992), pp. 134–43; E.A. Underwood, 'The first and final phases of the Irish medical students at the University of Leyden' in Eoin O'Brien (ed.), *Essays in honour of J.D.H. Widdess* (Dublin: Cityview Press, 1978), pp. 6–15; E.A. Underwood, *Boerhaave's men at Leyden* (Edinburgh: Edinburgh University Press, 1972). For Boerhaave's materialist and non-speculative approach: H.J. Cook, *Matters of exchange: commerce, medicine and science in the Dutch golden age* (New Haven and London: Yale University Press, 2007), pp. 383–96, 405–6.

[10] I am grateful to Dr John Bergin and Dr Liam Chambers for previews and discussions of their work on Irish Catholic chamber counsel.

[11] Minute book, governors of Mercer's Hospital, 1736–1772 (Mercer's Hospital, Dublin); Eoin O'Brien, *The Charitable Infirmary, Jervis Street, 1718–1987* (Monkstown: Anniversary Press, 1987), pp. 1–10.

[12] Toby Barnard, *Making the grand figure: lives and possessions in Ireland, 1641–1770* (New Haven and London: Yale University Press, 2004), pp. 361–8; Barnard, *A new anatomy*, pp. 33, 129–30, 137–8.

high levels of disease and mortality, stimulated speculation about the causes and possible solutions. Also, those studying in Edinburgh (and probably elsewhere) were drawn into clubs that discussed both technical and more general issues.[13] For some, the entire natural world became an object worthy of study. Not just human bodies were to be anatomised. Others were tempted to consider the social, political and cultural forces that related to, and perhaps explained, the problems of poverty and famine. The thoughtful recognised how vulnerable to epidemics and high mortality were large sections of the Irish population. Throughout the later seventeenth and eighteenth centuries, methods of amelioration and improvement were proposed and sometimes applied.

**The Medico-Philosophical Society**

The commitment to improvement – and the programme that it produced – can be discerned in the manifesto of the Medico-Philosophical Society, which was established in Dublin in 1756. The Society emerged out of a number of informal meetings. Henceforward, the discussions were to be formalised. The focus was on 'medical, natural and philosophical inquiries', which were deemed 'improving and entertaining'. Yet, definitions of suitable topics remained loose: natural history, natural philosophy, medicine, new improvements and entertaining subjects fell within the remit. So, too, did such novelties 'of arts, trades and manufactures as might conduce to the universal good of the public in general'. More specifically, the Society wished to hear of innovations that reduced poverty, provided jobs, combated disease and tackled a topical concern: the excessive consumption of alcohol.[14]

In its wide interests, the Medico-Philosophical Society followed predecessors like the informal Hartlib group of the 1650s and the Dublin Philosophical Society in the 1680s and 1690s. It overlapped with the larger and well-established Dublin Society. Consciously, it aspired to perform some of the functions attributed to philosophical societies across contemporary Europe. Its leading member was quickly in touch with a comparable organisation in London: the Royal Society of Arts.[15] Where the Medico-Philosophical Society differed from its forbears

---

[13] See, for example, John Hayman from Youghal, county Cork, drawn into such a group in Edinburgh: Charles Elliot ledgers (NLS, MS 43098, pp. 182, 264, 299, 302, 444; MS 43100, p. 504); will of John Hayman, 10 April 1777 (NLI, D 13351–13422/46); Barnard, *A new anatomy*, p. 258.

[14] RCPI, Minute books of the Medico-Philosophical Society, 1756–84, s.d. 3 February 1757, 16 June 1757. There is a copy in the Royal Irish Academy (RIA, MS 24 K 31); 'Repository ... entered and collected for the Medico-Philosophical Society' (RIA, MS 24 E 5). The Medico-Philosophical Society may resemble Amsterdam's private college of medicine of the previous century (see Cook, *Matters of exchange*, p. 286).

[15] Charles Smith to [ ], 10 June 1758 (RSA, London, Guard Book 3/14).

and contemporary societies elsewhere was in limiting membership to medical practitioners. This may have reflected a deliberate wish to avoid the difficulties that had beset earlier Dublin groups. Well-meaning members of the gentry expressed initial enthusiasm for attending fashionable meetings, but soon lost interest as fashion fixed on other activities. The indifference or fickleness that killed earlier experimental and speculative groups was felt to be a defining characteristic of the landed in Ireland. Its members were accused of being 'taken up with every method of aggrandizing their families and supporting luxury'.[16] Rather than be at the mercy of such unreliable backers, the Medico-Philosophical Society was made the preserve of the serious and civic-minded.

The author of the manifesto and animator of the Medico-Philosophical Society was Charles Smith, an apothecary from Dungarvan. Smith is one example useful in illustrating the range of interests shown by some medical men. For Smith, the smaller society was a means to continue the tasks that previously had been forwarded by the recently defunct Physico-Historical Society, in which he had also been prominent. If the new organisation was to survive – and it did so until 1784 – it needed to find a distinctive place alongside potential competitors such as the Dublin Society and the antiquarian societies that would eventually culminate in the Royal Irish Academy. The Medico-Philosophical Society did not altogether eschew antiquarianism. Old coins and archaeological finds were examined, natural phenomena, such as earthquakes and waterspouts, were discussed, and a collection of fossils was created.[17] More characteristic of the utilitarian concerns of the group were attempts to stop malpractices among the herb sellers around Dublin, to prepare a comprehensive and accurate pharmacopoeia, and to compare the bills of mortality for Dublin with those from London, Copenhagen, Vienna and Paris.[18]

The concern to prevent impositions on patients with spurious plants and drugs showed a practical and public spirit. It also expressed a type of patriotism: the import of expensive decoctions could be avoided if the home grown was correctly identified. Back in 1724, Dr William Stephens, a founding member of the Dublin Society, was put in charge of the recently established physick garden of Dublin University. He hoped that 'a set of experiments, accurately made upon the properties of vegetables, and especially the 'officianalls', would assist the medical profession.[19] It is noteworthy too that another apothecary (Charles Lucas)

---

[16] RCPI, Minute books of the Medico-Philosophical Society, 1756–84, s.d. 16 June 1757.

[17] RCPI, Minute books of the Medico-Philosophical Society, 1756–84, s.d. 1 and 8 July 1756, 6 January 1757, 1 September 1757, 3 September 1767.

[18] RCPI, Minute books of the Medico-Philosophical Society, 1756–84, s.d. 8 and 15 April 1756, 15 January 1761.

[19] Fergus Mulligan, *The founders of the Royal Dublin Society* (Dublin: Royal Dublin Society, 2005), pp. 32–5; A.A. Rusnock (ed.), *The correspondence of James Jurin (1684–1750): physician and secretary to the Royal Society*, The Wellcome Institute Series in the

sought to reform the supply of drugs before moving to the reform of corrupt political institutions.[20] In a similar spirit, John Rutty, also a member of the Medico-Philosophical Society, urged resort to Irish spas rather than the expensive habit of flocking to fashionable watering places in Britain and continental Europe. This patriotic move, too, had been an ambition of Lucas.[21] In his turn, Rutty prepared a pharmacopoeia in the hope of stopping frauds and ruinous imports.

Smith's own practicality was further revealed in a paper of detailed 'experiments and observation to show the utility of botanical knowledge in relation to agriculture and the feeding of cattle'.[22] In a more humdrum way, Smith utilised contacts in the medical trade as sources of information. An army surgeon, for example, stationed in Connacht first corresponded with the Medico-Philosophical Society, then was elected a member, and provided Smith with detailed descriptions of remote places. This satisfied more than mere curiosity, since the accounts were intended as the prelude to the better use of natural resources.[23]

David MacBride, who served as secretary to the Society, engaged in both microscopical and chemical experiments. The former he deemed an 'exceedingly entertaining branch of enquiry'.[24] MacBride, originally from the north of Ireland and educated at Glasgow, established a popular practice in Dublin. He was in

---

History of Medicine, Clio Medica, 39 (Amsterdam: Rodopi, 1996), p. 249; W. Stephens, *Botanical elements for the use of the botany school in the University of Dublin* (Dublin, 1727). On Jurin see also Churchill chapter 7 in this collection.

[20] Charles Lucas, *Pharmacomastix* (Dublin, 1741); see Sneddon chapter 6 in this collection.

[21] Charles Lucas, *An essay on waters* (London, 1756); Charles Lucas, *A cursory examination of the methodical synopsis of mineral waters* (Dublin, 1763); John Rutty, *An essay towards a natural, experimental and medicinal history of the mineral waters of Ireland* (Dublin, 1757); John Rutty, *A methodical synopsis of mineral waters* (London, 1757); John Rutty, *The analyser analysed* (London, 1758); John Rutty, *The argument of sulphur or no sulphur in waters discussed* (Dublin, 1762); Rutty on mineral waters (RIA, MS 24 E 5, no 15). Rutty, who took issue with Lucas's analysis, commented on the latter's disquisition, 'amidst a good deal of idle parade our author has certainly improved the unhappy opportunity of his exile' (RCPI, Minute books of the Medico-Philosophical Society, 1756–84, s.d. 5 April 1759).

[22] RCPI, Minute books of the Medico-Philosophical Society, 1756–84, s.d. 5 October 1758.

[23] RCPI, Minute books of the Medico-Philosophical Society, 1756–84, s.d. 22 July 1756; T. Wetherall, description of Gort, county Galway, 1752 in *The whole works of Sir James Ware*, ed. Walter Harris (Dublin, 1739), vol. 1, p. 636 (this is Charles Smith's copy presented by Walter Harris in Cambridge University Library, Hib. 3.739.1); T. Wetherall, account of stained marble (RIA, MS 24 E 5, no 31); T. Wetherall, letters of 2 November 1763 and 2 January 1764, T. Wetherall to J. Rutty, November 1767 (RIA, MS 24 E 5, nos 75, 76, 81); T. Wetherall, account of stained marble (RIA, MS 24 E 6, no 155).

[24] David MacBride to J. Ellis, 9 May 1770 (LS, Ellis correspondence, vol 2, item 11).

demand as an *accoucheur*. He corresponded widely, not just with the like-minded in Britain, but also with the Swedish naturalist, Daniel Solander. A particular concern, eventually achieved, was to find methods to prevent scurvy.[25] Also, in the course of his own researches he hit on a technique applicable to tanning. MacBride persuaded a Dublin tanner to try the process. It succeeded in cheapening considerably the preparation of hides. This promised enormous public benefits. However, MacBride was realist enough to know that unless it was adopted universally, traditional tanners would combine to ruin the innovator.[26]

The sociable speculation and experiment embodied in the Medico-Philosophical Society involved only a small proportion of the medical profession. It is the first specifically medical group in Ireland, which consciously interested itself in the wider world, and for which documentation survives. How far it fits into patterns that have been sketched elsewhere in Europe for an emergent public sphere emboldening the hitherto obscure, a self-conscious republic of letters, or Irish participation in an enlightenment, must await more detailed consideration.[27] Nevertheless, there are hints of its larger implications. Smith, Rutty and the other activists publicised the work of the Society through print, just as the Dublin Society and the Physico-Historical Society did.[28] Drawing on their contacts outside the Society, the members could hardly be regarded as hermetic and inward-looking. Through correspondence with non-members, it gathered and then disseminated useful information. Nor does the membership of the Medico-Philosophical Society exhaust the list of those medical personnel who concerned themselves with more than their patients.[29]

---

[25] David MacBride to J. Ellis, 9 May 1770, 19 January 1771 (LS, Ellis correspondence, vol 2, items 11 and 12); David MacBride, *Experimental essays on medical and physical subjects* (2nd edn, Dublin, 1767), pp. 185–242.

[26] David MacBride, *Some account of a new method of tanning* (Dublin, 1769); RDS, Proceedings of the Dublin Society, s.d. 31 March 1768, 14 April 1768, 16 June 1768, 15 December 1768, 19 January 1769.

[27] L.W.B. Brockliss, *Calvet's web: enlightenment and the republic of letters in eighteenth-century France* (Oxford: OUP, 2002), pp. 1–19; Thomas Broman, 'The Habermasian public sphere and science in the enlightenment', *History of Science*, 36 (1998): 123–49; Jim Livesey, 'The Dublin Society in eighteenth-century Irish political thought', *Historical Journal*, 47 (2004): 615–40; D.S. Lux and H.J. Cook, 'Closed circles and open networks: communication at a distance during the scientific revolution', *History of Science*, 36 (1998): 179–211; Andrea Rusnock, 'Correspondence networks and the Royal Society, 1700–1750', *British Journal for the History of Science*, 32 (1999):155–70.

[28] For example, the notice to be inserted into *Universal Advertiser*, 8 January 1757: RCPI, Minute books of the Medico-Philosophical Society, 1756–1784, s.d. 6 January 1757.

[29] In 1767, by which time Smith was dead, the recorded members are Span, Cleghorn, Bride, Archer, MacBride, Rutty, Jones, Croker, Purcell, Hamilton and Doyle.

## Charles Smith, the Medico-Philosophical Society and intellectual life in eighteenth-century Ireland

Charles Smith, the director of the group in 1756, expressed a desire to avoid partisanship. In reality, he proved highly partisan. His outlook had already been revealed in his work for the Physico-Historical Society, which resulted in the publication of three county histories (Cork, Waterford and Kerry) and the writing of at least two more (Limerick and Tipperary).[30] The intention in compiling such natural and civil histories, modelled on English accounts, was to assist with the identification and exploitation of resources. In turn, this aim was linked – unashamedly – with praise of English and Protestant settlers for promoting agriculture and industry. The philosophy reached back to the propaganda on behalf of English and Scottish settlement produced in the seventeenth century, including some issued under the auspices of the Hartlib circle during the 1650s.[31] The cause of improvement so dear to Smith would, it was believed, transform Ireland into a second England. The published and unpublished histories reflected this philosophy: a philosophy that underpinned the work of both the Hartlib group and, subsequently, of the Dublin Philosophical Society.

Smith's enslavement to this contentious, and intrinsically Protestant, vision of Ireland threatened the equanimity of the Medico-Philosophical Society, when he was drawn into what was an essentially sectarian dispute. In 1757, Smith was asked to comment on a pamphlet that had recently been published on the ancient and present state of Ireland. The tract was by the leading Catholic apologist, Charles O'Conor. Smith accused O'Conor of making a contrived connection between the recent famine that had afflicted part of the country in 1756 and the legal disabilities under which Catholics still lived. In addition, Smith mocked O'Conor's 'pert and affected style', questioned his historical account of Catholic loyalty, and conventionally and lamely attacked O'Conor for 'Jesuitical subterfuges'.[32]

As Smith's response attests, the apparent disinterestedness of the Medico-Philosophical Society's endeavours notwithstanding, this group, like so many others in eighteenth-century Ireland, possessed a vivid sectarian colouring. It was seldom so evident as in Smith's diatribe, but nevertheless it was implicit.

---

[30] C. Smith to [ ], 10 June 1758 (RSA, London, Guard Book 3/14); Toby Barnard, 'Improving Ireland's Past' in Toby Barnard, *Improving Ireland? Projectors, prophets and profiteers, 1641–1786* (Dublin: FCP, 2008), p. 116; W. Fraher, 'Charles Smith, 1715–1762: pioneer of Irish topography', *Decies*, 53 (1997): 33–44.

[31] G. Boate, *Irelands naturall history* (London, 1652); Toby Barnard, 'The cult and cultures of improvement' in Barnard, *Improving Ireland?...*, pp. 13–40.

[32] RCPI, Minute books of the Medico-Philosophical Society, 1756–84, s.d. 7 April 1757. For Catholic responses, see M. Reilly to C. O'Conor, 6 June 1752, 16 October 1755 (RIA, O'Conor papers, MS B i 1); R. Ousley to Sir L. O'Brien, 7 April 1769 (NLI, Inchiquin papers, 2806).

Catholics were not invited to join the Medico-Philosophical Society, although there were eminent practitioners within that confession. At least one corresponded with the Society.[33] Nor, at this time, did the Dublin Society elect Catholics to membership. In consequence, Smith, for all his insistence that partisanship should be avoided, could happily (almost unthinkingly) indulge in atavistic anti-Catholic sentiments.

Yet, as has been emphasised, Catholics were prominent within the medical profession, and shared with their Protestant counterparts a curiosity that extended far beyond their patients. Two must suffice to make the point. John Curry practised in Dublin. He wrote and published on fevers but his interests extended further.[34] A close collaborator with Charles O'Conor, Curry determined to refute the type of propagandist Protestant history that Smith venerated and imitated. So, alongside his medical work and learned treatises, Curry laboured on Irish histories. He was motivated less by intellectual curiosity than by an urge to challenge the prevalent Protestant arguments about past Irish Catholic behaviour.[35] Protestant accounts, particularly from the seventeenth century, were cited to justify and maintain the legal disabilities on the Catholics. Curry hoped to construct an alternative interpretation more sympathetic to the Catholic cause. In common with other Catholic professionals, Curry used some of his earnings to assemble a historical library. He was lent more volumes by O'Conor.[36] In time, Curry's known interest

---

[33] RCPI, Minute books of the Medico-Philosophical Society, 1756–84, s.d. 5 May 1757; RIA, MS 24 E 5, no 60.

[34] John Murray to Mrs Hoey, 29 January 1776, Murray to John Hoey, 8 April 1776 (NLS, John Murray papers, MS 41901); John Curry, *An essay on ordinary fevers* (Dublin, 1743); John Curry, *A brief account of the scorbutic fever* (Dublin, 1749); John Curry, *Some thoughts on the nature of fevers* (London, 1774); R.E. Ward, J.F. Wrynn and C.C. Ward (eds), *Letters of Charles O'Conor of Belanagare* (Washington, DC: Catholic University of American Press, 1988), pp. 115, 147, 320.

[35] John Curry, *An essay towards a new history of the Gun-Powder Treason* (London, 1765); John Curry, *An historical and critical review of the civil wars in Ireland* (2 vols, London, 1786).

[36] C. O'Conor to J. Curry, 17 August 1757, 29 February 1760, 4 April 1760; J. Curry to C. O'Conor, 10 March 1760, 25 October 1766, 1 and 4 November 1766, 17 September 1768, 16 April 1771, 19 November 1771, 2 May 1772, 12 October 1772, 10 January 1773, 2 and 24 August 1773, 4 April 1777, 24 October 1777, (RIA, O'Conor papers, MS B i I); Ward, Wrynn and Ward (eds), *Letters of Charles O'Conor*, pp. 23, 25, 27, 61,66, 70, 234, 278, 294, 320, 322, 327–30, 355–6, 370. One of the most notable libraries assembled by a Catholic physician was that of Dr John Fergus: John Fergus to C. O'Conor, senior, [10 October 1731] (RIA, O'Conor papers, MS B i I/92–3); Minutes of the select committee of Dublin Society for Antiquities, 1772–1774 (RIA, MS 24 E 7, pp. 114–17); *A catalogue of the libraries of John Fergus, M.D. and son, both deceased* (Dublin, 1766); D. Ó Catháin, 'John Fergus, MD, eighteenth-century doctor, book collector and Irish scholar', *Journal of the Royal Society of Antiquaries of Ireland*, 118 (1988): 142–3.

in history led others to send him materials from the seventeenth century.[37] Considerable effort went into the writing and eventual publication of this history, but Curry failed to displace the highly-coloured versions circulated by Protestant partisans.[38]

Similar motives emboldened another Catholic doctor to tackle the Irish past. Sylvester O'Halloran built up a lucrative and smart practice as a surgeon in and around Limerick in the mid-eighteenth century. He had probably been educated in France. Two of his brothers became priests in France, one rising to a French bishopric. Another brother was a successful silversmith and jeweller in Limerick and Cork. O'Halloran, like other ambitious medical practitioners, sought to advance himself in an overcrowded profession by writing and publishing.[39] After 1750, tracts on glaucoma, gangrene, amputation and injuries to the head (of particular relevance in Ireland) issued from his busy pen.[40] He also corresponded with the Medico-Philosophical Society.[41]

O'Halloran was not content simply to write on topics arising from his practice. Like Curry, he was stung by the frequent denigration of the Irish in historical accounts emanating from Britain. He wished to vindicate the Catholics and indigenous Irish against charges of barbarism, incivility and backwardness. Only through accurate and detailed history could 'the nature and spirit of the present constitution or extent of Poynings' Law' be understood, he privately

---

[37] J. Laffan to J. Curry, 1 February 1776 (RIA, O'Conor papers, MS B i I).

[38] J. Curry to C. O'Conor, 27 July 1774, 17 September 1774, 13 November 1775, 26 September 1777 (RIA, O'Conor papers, MS B i I).

[39] S. O'Halloran to J. Brown, 31 March 1788 (Palatine Heritage Centre, Rathkeale, Southwell–Brown papers, box 1, bundle 5); J.R. Bowen and Conor O'Brien (eds), *A celebration of Limerick's silver* (Cork: The Collins Press, 2007), pp. 196–7; Claire E. Lyons, 'A rediscovered letter of Sylvester O'Halloran to Dr De Salis, 1 February 1777', *Journal of the Galway Archaeological and Historical Society*, 59 (2007): 46–58; J.B. Lyons, (ed.), 'The letters of Sylvester O'Halloran [part 1]', *North Munster Antiquarian Journal*, 8 (1958–1961): 168–81; J.B. Lyons, (ed.), 'The letters of Sylvester O'Halloran [part 2]', *North Munster Antiquarian Journal*, 9 (1962–1965): 25–50; J.B. Lyons, 'Sylvester O'Halloran, 1728–1807', *Eighteenth-Century Ireland*, 4 (1989): 65–74; George Roberts, *Juvenile poems on various subjects* (Limerick, 1763), p. 165.

[40] Sylvester O'Halloran, *A new treatise on the glaucoma, or cataract* (Dublin, 1750); Sylvester O'Halloran, *A critical analysis of the new operation for a cataract* (Dublin, 1775); Sylvester O'Halloran, *A concise and impartial account of the advantages arising to the public from the general use of a new method of amputation* (Dublin, 1763); Sylvester O'Halloran, *A complete treatise on gangrene and sphacelus* (Dublin, 1765); Sylvester O'Halloran, *A new treatise on the different disorders arising from external injuries of the head* (Dublin, 1793).

[41] RCPI, Minute books of the Medico-Philosophical Society, 1756–84, s.d. 5 May 1757; paper from S. O'Halloran, 8 June 1762, Repository of the Medico-Philosophical Society (RIA, MS 24 E 5/60).

observed.[42] To this end, he mobilised well-heeled patients, fellow medical practitioners, neighbours and acquaintances first in and around Limerick, but then in a much wider orbit, which took in those of Irish background in Spain.[43] Even so, he bemoaned the lack of 'patrons or protectors' of historical 'science' in Ireland.[44] O'Halloran was both obsessive and wealthy enough to attend in person to the production of his historical disquisitions in London during the 1770s. The results, in terms of sales and influence, disappointed him. Even his co-religionists Curry and O'Conor, committed to the same cause, regretted his interventions as maladroit. Indeed, Curry described O'Halloran's writing as too 'scattery' to have the intended effect of moderating hostility to the Irish Catholics.[45]

In a variety of ways Smith, Curry and O'Halloran suggest how those active in the medical world participated in others. Public policy and a hope of influencing, even changing it, drove them. Apparently unpolitical – even indulgent – were the pursuits of a final example, Henry Quin, who came from a family of physicians. His father prospered as an apothecary in Dublin, serving as one of two wardens of the apothecary's guild in 1747[46], and two sons enjoyed success as physicians.[47] Henry Quin trained in France and Padua, then debated whether or not to establish his practice in England, but returned under parental pressure to Dublin. There he rapidly built up a smart *clientèle* and a high reputation.[48] Yet, the long sojourn on

---

[42] Sylvester O'Halloran to Sir J. Caldwell, 13 December 1777 (JRUL, Bagshawe muniments, B 3/10, letter 520); Sylvester O'Halloran, *Insula Sacra* (Limerick, 1770); Sylvester O'Halloran, *Ierne defended* (Dublin, 1774); Sylvester O'Halloran, *An introduction to the study of the history and antiquities of Ireland* (Dublin, 1772); Sylvester O'Halloran, *A general history of Ireland*, (2 vols, London, 1778).

[43] Subscription lists in Sylvester O'Halloran, *A complete treatise on gangrene and sphacelus* (Limerick, 1765); O'Halloran, *A general history of Ireland, passim*.

[44] S. O'Halloran to Sir J. Caldwell, 13 December 1777 (JRUL, Bagshawe muniments, B 3/10, letter 520).

[45] J. Murray to T. Ewing, 22 June 1772, 13 January 1773, 17 February 1773 (NLS, Murray papers, MS 41898); Murray to Sylvester O'Halloran, 5 February 1776, 18 May 1776, 3 August 1776, 19 September 1777, 4 November 1777, Murray to John Hoey, 19 September 1777 (NLS, Murray papers, MS 41901).

[46] J.T. Gilbert, *A history of the city of Dublin* (3 vols, Dublin, 1854–1859), vol. 1, p. 178.

[47] Minute Book, Apothecaries' Guild, s.d. 25 April 1747 (Apothecaries Hall, Dublin); *Faulkner's Dublin Journal*, 21–24 October 1758; Charles William Quin, *Dissertatio medica in angularis, de hydrocephalo interno* (Edinburgh, 1779); also Jean Agnew (ed.), *The Drennan–McTier letters*, (3 vols, Dublin: Irish Manuscripts Commission, 1998–1999), vol. 1, pp. 40–41 and vol. 3, pp. 446, 573. For comparable medical dynasticism in the United Provinces, see Cook, *Matters of exchange*, pp. 150–51.

[48] J. Quin to T. Quin, 19 December 1749 (NAI, MS 999/392/5/17); David MacBride to J. Ellis, 9 May 1770 (LS, Ellis correspondence, vol 2, item 11); draft will of Henry Quin, 1771 (NAI, MS 999/392/5/4); J. Murray, journal, s.d. 13, 18, 21 and 23 May 1775 (NLS, Murray papers, MS 43018); Lady Caldwell to Sir J. Caldwell, 10 February 1778

the continent and trips into Italy had stirred artistic interests.[49] Back in Ireland, Quin developed them further. Specifically he invited the Scot James Tassie to join him in experimenting in his Dublin laboratory in an attempt to fabricate the glass and semi-precious stones in which replicas of classical cameos, intaglios and gems could be made.[50] With Quin, Tassie discovered the formulae to do this, and soon exchanged life in Dublin for London. However, he did not sever his links with Quin; nor did the prominent Dublin physician cease experiments or patronising artists and artificers.

One visitor who dined with Quin in his splendid Dublin town house on St Stephen's Green commented, 'an enthusiast in Tassie's pastes and in all new inventions ... without you can converse to him upon these he had as lief you were silent.'[51] Yet, Quin, several times president of the Royal College of Physicians, never joined the obvious body dedicated to the improvement of both useful and decorative manufactures in Ireland: the Dublin Society. The unexpected side to Quin, fostered in part by his lengthy immersion in European life, reminds how successful doctors added to the complexity and vigour of eighteenth-century Ireland. Quin's activities, although presently not nearly so well known, parallel those of near-contemporaries in the medical profession such as Sir Hans Sloane and Richard Mead in London or William Hunter from Scotland. Sloane came from the north of Ireland; Mead had numerous links with both patients and aesthetes from Ireland. Hunter was prominent in the medical community in which many

---

(JRUL, Bagshawe muniments, B 3/29/61); Lady Llanover (ed.), *The autobiography and correspondence of Mary Granville, Mrs Delany*, 1st series (3 vols, London, 1861), vol. 2, pp. 549–50 and vol. 3, pp. 254, 558. Cf. Anne Crookshank and Desmond Fitzgerald, Knight of Glin, *Irish portraits, 1660–1860* (Dublin: Paul Mellon Foundation for British Art, 1969), pp. 94–6; The Georgian Society, *Records of Domestic Architecture and Decoration in Dublin* (5 vols, Dublin, 1909–1913), vol. 2, p. 97; T.P.C. Kirkpatrick, *Henry Quin, MD* (Dublin: University Press, 1919).

[49] Henry Quin to T. Quin, 11 September 1745, T. Quin to H. Quin, 30 January 1747[8] (NAI, MS 999/392/5/13, 14); H. Quin to J. Ellis, 24 March 1749[50], 19 April 1754 (LS, Ellis correspondence, vol 2, items 48 and 49); John Ingamells, *A dictionary of British and Irish travellers in Italy, 1701–1800* (New Haven and London: Yale University Press, 1997), pp. 791–2.

[50] H. Quin to J. Ellis, 29 January 1762 (LS, Ellis correspondence, vol 2, item 51); R.E. Raspe, *Account of the present state and arrangement of Mr James Tassie's collection of pastes and impressions* (London, 1786), p. 22; *A catalogue of impressions in sulphur, of antique and modern gems from which pastes are made and sold by James Tassie* (London, 1775), p. 16; J.M. Gray, *James and William Tassie: a biographical and critical sketch* (Edinburgh, 1894), pp. 5–6; James Holloway, *James Tassie, 1735–1799* ([Edinburgh]: National Gallery of Scotland, 1990).

[51] Letters of James Tassie to H. Quin, 17 April 1779–3 June 1778 (NAI, 999/392/5/46–64); Journal of John Murray, 18, 21 and 23 May 1775 (NLS, Murray papers, MS 43018).

aspirants from Ireland studied.⁵² In time, maybe, a figure from the eighteenth-century Irish medical world will be found whose varied interests, even if not so well documented, rival those of Ésprit Calvet in Avignon.⁵³

---

⁵² Barnard, *A new anatomy*, pp. 132, 136; P. Black (ed.), *'My highest pleasures': William Hunter's art collection* (Glasgow: the Hunterian Museum, 2007); Bynum and Porter (eds), *William Hunter and the eighteenth-century medical world*; A. MacGregor (ed.), *Sir Hans Sloane: collector, scientist, antiquary* (London: British Museum, 1994); M. Webster, 'Taste of an Augustan collector: the collection of Dr Richard Mead', *Country Life*, 29 January 1970: 249–51 and *Country Life*, 24 September (1970): 765–7.

⁵³ Brockliss, *Calvet's web: enlightenment and the republic of letters*.

Chapter 9

# Advancing the Medical Career Abroad: The Case of Daniel O'Sullivan (1760–c.1797)[*]

Fiona Clark

**Introduction**

Daniel O'Sullivan, physician-surgeon to the Second Battalion of the Infantry Division of Puebla de los Ángeles, disembarked in the port of Veracruz, Mexico in August 1789. His arrival marked the culmination of ten years of study, training and petitioning that path had led him from Ireland across Europe, to the kingdom of Spain in 1786.[1] Convinced of the quality of his medical training, his place within the republic of letters, and driven by a desire to succeed, O'Sullivan successfully established himself within months of his arrival in Mexico among the networks of the local elite, creating what on first impression appeared to be a promising medical and scientific career. By 1798, however, military correspondence indicates that he was dead, leaving as the only remnant of those early ambitions a series of largely unsuccessful petitions and a collection of four reports into a series of trials for an anti-venereal treatment held in the Hospital de San Andrés, Mexico City, between 1790 and 1791.[2] For O'Sullivan, the medical debacle that took place in San Andrés marked a downward turn in what had been, until that point, a steady

---

[*] This study has been made possible thanks to postdoctoral funding of the Irish Research Council for the Humanities and Social Sciences, the Society for Irish Latin American Studies, and the support of the History Department, St Patrick's College, Dublin City University.

[1] AHFM–UNAM, Leg. 2, exp. 6, fols 4r–5r; AGN, Historia, 3, fol. 33.

[2] These four reports comprise: *Oficio del Señor Subinspector acompañado por representaciones de los coroneles de los cuerpos veteranos que ocupasen esta capital sobre el mal método de administrar el mercurio a la tropa en el Hospital de San Andrés, y providencias para que los enfermos de gálico tomen las unciones en el de San Juan de Dios* (1791–4, AGN, Inquisición, 1337, exp. 11); *Representaciones hechas al Exmo Señor Virrey de México sobre los malos efectos del supuesto específico del Beato* (1791–3, RANM, fol. 16, leg, 14c, doc. 69); *Relación histórico-crítica de un supuesto nuevo methodo antivenereo vulgarmente llamado del Beato introducido en el Hospital de San Andrés de México en el Año de 1790, y establecido con exclusión del Mercurio en el de 91* (1792, RANM, fol. 40, leg. 14c., doc. 67); *Carta circular del doctor Don Daniel O'Sullivan a 25 médicos con sus respuestas y un apéndice sobre el específico antivenéreo del Beato* (1792, RANM, Leg. 14c, doc. 68).

path of professional advancement. All but written out of the official eighteenth-century accounts of the San Andrés anti-venereal trials, he seldom features in any modern studies of that period. Yet his reports indicate that, for a short time at least, O'Sullivan played a more active and respected role within colonial scientific circles than has hitherto been made evident. As a result, an exploration into the reasons for his failure provides a particularly interesting case study of the world outside of Europe in which some Irish physicians attempted to establish careers.

O'Sullivan's inability to progress professionally in colonial Mexico caused him to direct his gaze, via his Irish networks, to possible avenues of support within Spain as a means towards correcting perceived abuses within the Mexican medical system.[3] Contrary to his expectations, the lack of response to his reports in Spain and his increased marginalisation in Mexico may largely have resulted from his inability to manipulate the local frameworks of authority appropriately or to understand the nature of their relationship to the Iberian power structures.

In order to establish the context in which these reports originated this chapter shall consider four related areas: O'Sullivan's early training and formation in Europe and his use of the familiar 'discourse of emigration'; the colonial Mexican context within which he was working by the end of the 1780s; his attempts to negotiate the social, professional, and academic networks following his arrival in Mexico; and lastly, the particular backdrop of the anti-venereal trials at San Andrés to which his reports refer.

### Early training and formation

By the time Daniel O'Sullivan reached the shores of New Spain in 1789 he had, to all appearances, received a wide breadth of medical training and experience in France, England, Scotland, Ireland and Spain. A native of county Cork where he was born in 1760, his records indicate that, having received his preliminary education in his home, he completed his studies at the University of Toulouse in Philosophy and Mathematics (1777) where he was also awarded a 'General Prize'

---

[3] O'Sullivan corresponded with Timoteo O'Scanlan, a leading Irish physician in Spain through whom he maintained links with the Royal Academy of Medicine in Madrid. Two of O'Sullivan's letters appended to the 'Carta Cirular' (October 1792 and January 1793) refer to the fact that O'Scanlan had been charged with requesting a report from O'Sullivan into the anti-venereal trials, and that O'Sullivan had experienced several difficulties in carrying out the task. The reports were sent to Spain via another Irish merchant network, Patricio Joyes (Joyce) and Co., (RNAM, Leg. 14c, doc. 68). One of the witnesses called by the Protomedicato to validate O'Sullivan's petition for permission to practice medicine was Coronel Marcos Keating of the Royal Artillery (AHFM–UNAM, Leg. 2, exp. 6, fols 7r–7v).

before he progressed to study Theology (1780).⁴ Following his tonsure in 1780, he proceeded to matriculate in medicine at the same university, although he was later to count the entirety of the period from 1777 as dedicated to the study of that subject.⁵ In a manner typical to many medical students of the time, O'Sullivan's training encompassed a variety of medical institutions and hospitals both during and after his degree from Toulouse.⁶ By 1786, in response to the recommendations of Spanish medical students he met whilst travelling, we find him advancing his career in Spain where he was granted the post as military surgeon.⁷

As demonstrated by his dealings with the Spanish authorities and his petitions for various posts both in Spain and Mexico, O'Sullivan developed a strategy similar to that of those Irish emigrants described by Óscar Recio Morales as 'active, self-defining individuals'.⁸ This included the use of a specific discourse that highlighted the immemorial links between Ireland and Iberia, the common bond of Catholicism, the fight against Protestantism, and the reciprocity due as a result of Irish service to the Spanish king, which O'Sullivan most clearly attached to the historical weight of his surname. Moreover, given his status as a graduate of a French university, he was careful to state when petitioning the Spanish government during the late 1780s and early 1790s, when the French Revolution was in full swing, that he considered France to be a 'disgraced Empire'. He offered his services in whatever way possible in the fight against the 'abominable executioners of the king of France and to contribute ... to avenging the terrible assassination of that most Christian monarch, as one who had witnessed his paternal

---

⁴ AGS, SGU, Leg. 6974.2, fols 49 and 58; AHFM–UNAM, Protomedicato, leg. 2, exp. 6, fol. 116; see also L.W.B. Brockliss and Patrick Ferté, 'Prosopography of Irish Clerics in the Universities of Paris and Toulouse, 1573–1792', *Archivium Hibernicum*, 58, (2004): 71–166.

⁵ AGS, SGU, Leg. 6974.2, fol. 58.

⁶ O'Sullivan's accounts (see note 4) indicate that, as well as his studies in Toulouse and Montpellier, he gained experience in hospitals in Paris, London, and Edinburgh (two years), Glasgow, and Dublin (on visits). In his study of the French higher education system Laurence Brockliss states that from 1707 the French Crown made attempts to standardise the regulations governing medical students across the country, bringing the majority of universities into line with Montpellier where the statutes demanded three years of study. Later references to O'Sullivan's position as both surgeon and physician may be linked to the practice in some French universities of instructing medical students in surgery and pharmacy. Although the colleges of surgery were established in Montpellier in 1741 and Toulouse 1762, a separate degree in surgical medicine had already been instituted in Montpellier in 1732. L.W.B. Brockliss, *French higher education in the seventeenth and eighteenth centuries* (Oxford: Clarendon Press, 1987), 391, 393–4.

⁷ AHFM–UNAM, Leg. 2, exp. 6, fols 4r–5r; AGN, Historia, 3, fol. 33.

⁸ Óscar Recio Morales, 'Irish émigré strategies of survival, adaptation and integration in seventeenth and eighteenth-century Spain' in Thomas O'Connor and Mary Ann Lyons (eds) *Irish communities in early modern Europe* (Dublin: FCP, 2006), pp. 240–66.

love for his people and his august virtues'.⁹ Despite these assurances, O'Sullivan's links with Toulouse were a major reason for his rejection as candidate for the Chair of Mathematics and Astrology at the Royal Pontifical University in Mexico in 1795. According to the University authorities, a foreigner, imbued with the teaching of an institution so closely linked to the Revolution, could not be trusted to instruct Spanish students. To consider such a move, they argued, went against the laws of the land and the University regulations.[10] So rigid were they in this matter that even O'Sullivan's recently granted seal of royal approval for the post as Consulting Physician to the Royal Army was insufficient counterweight.[11] This rejection is indicative that the discourse that initially assisted O'Sullivan to make advances in Europe did not bring the same benefits when resorted to within the power structures of Puebla and Mexico City. In fact, O'Sullivan's correspondence from 1792 onwards reveals that he perceived himself to be a victim of systematic persecution by the local authorities as a result of his opposition to their methods. Whilst possibly true, this claim fails to take into account the fact that O'Sullivan may well have been a victim of his own success as regards the networks he formed in his early months in Mexico: networks that implanted him in the tensions that were a deep and enduring feature of the relationship of the *criollo* (Creole) elite and their European counterparts.[12]

## The Mexican context

O'Sullivan's arrival in Mexico came at the end of a century in which the Spanish Bourbon monarchy had undertaken a complete restructuring of colonial government in the Spanish Americas in an attempt to centralise and impose greater Peninsular authority, and to increase potential revenues. This policy had particular impact on Mexico during the visitation of José de Gálvez, the Minister of the Indies

---

⁹ AGS, SGU, Leg. 6974.2, fol. 49. All translations of the original text are the author's own.

[10] AGN, Universidad, vol. 27, Libro de Claustros, fols 209r–211v.

[11] The University authorities argued that this was merely proof of the one particular post, not of ability generally, and that none of O'Sullivan's claims had passed through the Council of Indies for official verification (AGN, Universidad, vol. 27, Libro de Claustros, fols 209r–211v).

[12] The term 'criollo' in New Spain should be understood to hold different connotations to the usage of Creole in the Caribbean. By the eighteenth century it was being substituted by the term 'americano', which was not limited in meaning to an individual born in America to Peninsular Spanish parents. Its meaning had instead already gained certain political, cultural and even economic connotations. As such, it not only denoted a specific ethnographic grouping, but also described a social class with a well defined social, cultural, educational outlook. For further discussion see Luis Reed Torres, *El periodismo en México: 500 años de historia* (México: Edamex, 1995), p. 64; and Juan José Arron, *Certidumbre de América* (Cuba: Letras Cubanas, 1988), p. 924.

(1765–71), and was epitomised by the expulsion of the Society of Jesus from the Americas in 1767. New departments and officials were assigned to curb the jurisdiction of those established previously under the Habsburgs; these positions were filled by men from the Iberian Peninsula and brought about a radical decrease in the number of *criollos* permitted into government office.[13] European Spaniards, in return, were perceived by many *criollos* to have little or no understanding of the Mexican situation and, therefore, to be incapable of the undertaking the responsibilities given to them. Their appointment to positions within social and scientific circles, and the influx of European ideas, was often regarded as a direct attack on the capacity of the *criollo*-educated elite.

Similar tensions were evident in medico-scientific circles. During the late eighteenth century, the Mexican scientific community played a central role to the various scientific expeditions and interchange of scholars organised and sponsored by the Spanish monarchy. However, two years before O'Sullivan arrived in Veracruz, the royal expedition to New Spain led by Aragonese physician, Martín de Sessé y Lacasta, began the process of establishing a Royal Botanical Garden in Mexico City and promoting the furtherance of the Linnean taxonomical system. Given the strong tradition of local science already existent, and the use of indigenous practices of classification, the Linnean system initially symbolised the enforced implementation of European methods over and against local knowledge of their own land and its natural resources.[14] Significantly, not only were the key positions in the Botanical Garden given to Iberian Spaniards, it was also decreed that the expenses of the Garden should be included within the budget of the Royal Pontifical University, and that only those students in medicine, pharmacy and surgery who had successfully completed a course in botany could proceed for final accreditation.[15] Such a move undermined the status of the established positions of authority in the university, held for the most part by members of the *criollo* population, and created a two-tier system by allowing the Iberian botanists privileges above and beyond those given to the *criollo* professors. The course in

---

[13] David Brading states that the social rift and jealousy between families of the original conquistadors and those of the *advenedizos* (more newly arriving from Spain) greatly intensified by the seventeenth century. He also argues that the lack of political repercussion arising from a 'denigration' of the Creole character may well have been in part due to the fact that most Creole intellectuals entered the priesthood where their varied roles allowed them ample opportunity 'to exercise their talents': see David Brading, *The origins of Mexican nationalism* (Cambridge: CUP, 1985), p. 911.

[14] See, for example, Iris H.W. Engstrand. *Spanish scientists in the new world: the eighteenth-century expeditions* (Seattle: University of Washington Press, 1981); Patricia Aceves Pastrana, *Química, botánica y farmacia en la Nueva España a finales del siglo XVIII* (México: Universidad Autónoma de México, 1993).

[15] For more detailed discussion of the struggle for authority and recognition between the Botanical Garden, the University and the Royal Protomedicato see Juan Carlos Arias Divito. *Las expediciones españolas durante el siglo XVIII: expedición botánica de Nueva España* (Madrid: Ediciones Cultura Hispánica, 1968).

Botany also impinged upon the authority of the Real Tribunal del Protomedicato (the Royal Medical Tribunal), a body comprising three eminent physicians, charged with the responsibility of certifying medical practitioners.[16]

O'Sullivan also encountered a society in the midst of substantial change in respect of how it addressed issues of public health and sanitation. As John Tate Lanning has stated in his study of the Protomedicato in Mexico, the eighteenth-century Spanish American idea of public health meant the 'proper licensing of doctors, phlebotomists, surgeons, and pharmacists; the inspection of hospitals and apothecary shops; the control of false or dangerous medical information; suppression of fakes and quackery; and rendering justice in medical cases'.[17] The Protomedicato performed many of these public health functions, yet at times of public health crises, for example epidemics, the political authorities comprised the main acting bodies.[18] Against this backdrop, two hospitals are of particular interest: the first, the Hospital de San Juan de Dios, established in 1541 for the treatment of venereal patients; the second, the Hospital General de San Andrés, where, from 1790 to 1791, O'Sullivan held a post as chief surgeon in the venereal department.[19] In the latter case, the establishment of a general hospital met two different needs.

---

[16] Originating in Spain in the fifteenth century, this tribunal was charged with regulating the practice of medicine. It comprised a board of three licensed physicians with two principle functions: the first, to certify medical practitioners and academic functions related to the organisation and teaching of medicine; the second, to regulate medical practice and administrative functions, and control over new knowledge in medicine. From the mid-1600s the role of President, or first Protomédico and Professor of *Prima de Medicina* (first chair in medicine) were rolled into one. In most cities the post of second Protomédico was tied to the chair of *Vísperas* (second chair) or the Dean of the Faculty, and the third Protomédico was named by the Viceroy. Individuals could appeal to the king when appealing tribunal decisions. Those living in the Americas from 1737, in recognition of the difficulties arising from distance, were allowed to address their appeals instead to the Viceroy or *audiencia* (form of appellate court): Pilar Gardeta Sabater, 'El nuevo modelo del Real Tribunal del Protomedicato en la América española: transformaciones sufridas ante las Leyes de Indias y el cuerpo legislativo posterior', *Dynamis*, 16 (1996): 237–59 (243).

[17] John Tate Lanning. *The Royal Protomedicato: the regulation of the medical profession in the Spanish empire,* ed. John Jay Tepaske (Durham, N.C.: Duke University Press, 1985), p. 351.

[18] Ana Cecilia Rodríguez de Romo, 'Inoculation in the 1799 smallpox epidemic in Mexico: myth or real solution', *Antilia: revista de historia de las ciencias de la naturaleza y de la tecnología,* 2/1(1997), http://www.ucm.es/info/antilia/revista/vol3–en/arten3–1.htm [Accessed 14 August 2009].

[19] San Andrés was originally established as a college for the Jesuit novitiate in 1626. In 1770, after the expulsion of the Jesuits from Spanish domains, the Junta Superior de Aplicaciones directed the college for use as a hospital for the treatment of men and women in all social classes, including soldiers and Indian peoples, but the latter only if the Hospital Real de Naturales could not accommodate them: see Josefina Muriel, *Hospitales de la Nueva España: fundaciones de los siglos XVII y XVIII* (2 vols México: UNAM, 1991) vol. 2, pp. 215–39.

First, the centralisation of patients under one roof instead of at a variety of specialist institutions, and second, the provision of an alternative to the poor care the soldiers received at the Hospital de San Juan de Dios.[20] Despite this rationale, the hospital was allowed to deteriorate to such an extent that it resulted in overcrowding and inhuman conditions for the soldiers.[21] In 1779, the then Archbishop of Mexico City, Alonso Núñez Haro y Peralta petitioned to be given responsibility for establishing a well-run hospital equipped to deal with 300 patients on the site.[22] He was granted complete control over the hospital in 1786, with the result that the hospital was not answerable to the government authorities with regard to either administrative or economic procedures.[23] This transfer of administrative authority facilitated the removal of venereal patients from San Juan de Dios to San Andrés rather than maintain a hospital specialising purely in the treatment of this illness.[24] San Andrés, following the manner of classifying illnesses as either internal or external, comprised departments of medicine, surgery, military surgery and

---

[20] Josefina Muriel states that the rough cost per bed in the 1770s came to 4 reales.

[21] One report to the archbishop, Núñez de Haro y Peralta, stated that the hospital building was disintegrating, horses had filled the wards, the place was full of leaks and grass grew on the windows: see Muriel, *Hospitales*, p. 218.

[22] Muriel states that he offered to fund this using extra finance from the Hospital Amor de Dios and his own funds, p. 218.

[23] Haro y Peralta personally provided the funding for all that the hospital required. Whilst the hospital administration was to provide the government with a yearly report on its financial accounts the Archbishop's plans led in 1796 to a special royal concession that stated that whilst Haro y Peralta was governor of the hospital there was no need for that institution to present accounts to the government. In 1788 it consisted of 39 rooms with capacity for 1000 beds, including some offices and an area for outpatient consultation: see Muriel, *Hospitales*, pp. 223, 229.

[24] In terms of administration, it was an institution governed by clerics with both the posts of Rector and the Vice-rector held by ecclesiastics. The *mayordomo* held responsibility for all the financial aspects of hospital life, with custody over all important paperwork relevant to both San Andrés and San Juan. Further to these specific roles, there were various committees that met at various times throughout the year to discuss the practical running of the institution and the methods and means of treatment. According to Xóchitl Martínez Barbosa, two main committees were responsible for hospital decision making. The *junta superior* (superior committee) comprised 10 members: the archbishop, president of subalterns, rector, mayordomo, vice-rector, senior chaplain, lawyer, first physician, senior surgeons and senior pharmacist. They met in January each year, at which point they dealt with all the issues pertaining to the patients' physical and spiritual health. The *junta económica y de gobierno* (committee on finance and government) was held on the 10th of every month, and on the 20th a medico-surgical reunion took place. Present were: the president, rector, mayordomo, vicerector, physicians, surgeons, senior pharmacist and senior practitioners. In this case the committee dealt with all matters pertaining to treatment and care of the patients, sanitation, pharmacy stocks, methods of treatment, and so on, and took stock of the illnesses that they observed most commonly in the hospital: see Xóchitl Martínez Barbosa, 'El Hospital de San Andrés' in (eds) Martha Eugenia Rodríguez Pérez

venereal treatment.[25] Whilst a series of committees were created to make decisions concerning the running of the hospital, the most significant positions of authority were held by ecclesiastics. It was a structure, heavily criticised by O'Sullivan in the context of the trials, that led to unnecessary ecclesiastical meddling in matters beyond their understanding. Given this background, we now turn to consider why the path that O'Sullivan attempted to forge in his new homeland did not lead to the success he had initially envisioned.

## O'Sullivan in Mexico: the path of advancement

Within two months of his arrival O'Sullivan applied to the Royal Protomedicato for a license to practise medicine freely in Mexico.[26] As an army surgeon this was not a necessity, but it was a course frequently followed by foreign practitioners who wished to keep all avenues open for the future, either for retirement purposes or in order to practise in a non-military hospital whilst in post, often as a means of boosting their income.[27] As Rodríguez Sala has indicated, there were many opportunities for ingenious and well-prepared army physicians and surgeons to advance within a variety of medical circles.[28] Although O'Sullivan initiated the process in August 1789, it was not until the following January that steps were taken by the Protomedicato to verify the documents and his identity.[29] The application

---

and Xóchitl Martínez Barbosa, *Medicina novohispana. Siglo XVIII* (México: UNAM, 2001) vol. 4, pp. 499–509.

[25] Men and women were treated separately throughout, and the Medical dept. for men included a room for prisoners. Other areas included a laundry, dispensary, kitchens, meeting rooms, living area for doctors and surgeons: see Lorenzo Barragán Mercado, *Historia del Hospital General de México* (México: Lerner Mexicana, 1968).

[26] AHFM–UNAM, Leg. 2, exp. 6, fol. 116.

[27] According to Rodríguez Sala, of the 56 military surgeons in their research cohort in the period between 1713 and 1820, only 3 served in both a military and a non-military hospital, 28 served solely within the military, and 25 served in the military and in another hospital linked to the military, either at the same time or shortly after leaving their post: María Luisa Rodríguez Sala, *Cirujanos del ejército en la Nueva España (1713–1820): ¿miembros de un estamento profesional o una comunidad científica?* (México: UNAM, 2005), p. 73.

[28] Rodríguez Sala, *Cirujanos del ejército*, p. 149.

[29] Included among these documents were: his baptismal records from the parishes of Killcoe and Aughadown in the Diocese of Ross, signed by the parish priest, Daniel Bourke, and countersigned by Bishop McKenna; a letter by Bourke regarding the documents written in Latin and a translation of the same into Spanish by Felipe de Samaniego, Knight in the Order of Santiago and Interpreter for the king's council in Madrid; the license granting O'Sullivan freedom to travel and work in New Spain and recognising his post as Surgeon in the Infantry of Puebla; and his medical degree certificate from the University of Toulouse (AHFM–UNAM, Leg. 2, exp. 6, fols 2r–5r).

process was lengthy and involved two stages. First, it was necessary to obtain confirmation of his identity from various individuals who knew him through the army or had known him at court in Madrid and could attest to the validity of his credentials; and second, it involved an examination of the theory and practise of medicine.[30] Once the Protomédicos were convinced they had sufficient proof validating O'Sullivan's qualifications and person, and that he was of good blood, he was sworn in and given authority to practise as a physician in Mexico City and any other town, village, or port belonging to Charles III, taking with him one or two assistants.[31]

Whilst this process was still underway, O'Sullivan became embroiled in a series of complaints relating to the treatment of soldiers in San Andrés. Correspondence between the army surgeons, that is, O'Sullivan and Cayetano Muns, the army chaplains, the Coronel, the Viceroy and the Archbishop, dating from the 7 January 1790, indicate that staff at San Andrés refused to admit soldiers whose illnesses were either unknown or incurable, and that those who were admitted left in a worse condition than when they entered. As a result the soldiers showed, in the words of O'Sullivan and Muns, 'a complete and invincible repugnance' to the idea of entering the hospital, often preferring to remain in prison.[32] As the two surgeons were quick to point out, this state of affairs came at great cost both to the soldiers' health and the service of the king, and was attributable, not to the lack of knowledge of the physicians, but to the lack of method and order in the hospital.

The disagreement centred on the question of whether or not San Andrés was obliged to receive the military, and the related matter of the hospital's complaint that the amount received as payment for the soldiers was not sufficient to cover the costs of treatment.[33] The resulting exchange over the treatment of soldiers continued until the early months of 1794, with a particularly intense period of correspondence between June and November 1791 prompted by the complaints by soldiers who were the unfortunate recipients of the new anti-venereal cure, the 'Beato method'. These reports form the first section of the information O'Sullivan sent to the Royal Academy of Medicine in Madrid in 1792 via Timoteo O'Scanlan.[34]

---

[30] AHFM–UNAM, Leg. 2, exp. 6, fol. 6r.

[31] The process of swearing in comprised: agreeing to uphold belief in the mystery of the pure and Immaculate Conception of the Virgin Mary; promising to use his position faithfully; and agreeing to obey and fulfil the laws and orders of the Tribunal to cure and assist the poor without recompense. Good blood referred to having no taint of Jewish or Muslim blood, and being a legitimate son of a good Catholic family. The license was finally granted and paid for by O'Sullivan on 23 January 1790, having taken just under four months to complete (AHFM–UNAM, Leg. 2, exp. 6, fols 9r–9v).

[32] AGN, Historia, 257, 9, fol. 1.

[33] AGN, Historia, 257, 9, fol. 1.

[34] For recent discussion on the importance of O'Scanlan within the Spanish context see Michael White, 'The role of Irish doctors in eighteenth-century Spanish medicine' in

Despite, or perhaps because of, this unsatisfactory situation, in May 1790 the Archbishop invited O'Sullivan to become Chief Surgeon of the venereal department at that same institution.[35] There is clear indication that this department was particularly problematic from the perspective of the hospital administrators as it incurred financial costs that far outweighed those of the departments of medicine and surgery.[36] In September 1789, the then chief surgeon of the venereal wards, Joachín Pío de Eguía y Muro, was obliged to resign because of over-spending in the hospital pharmacy. The Archbishop, shocked at the amounts in question, demanded that a more 'economical' individual be put in place by October to oversee the 'patrimonio de los pobres' (the assets of the poor).[37] This was to be the Valencian army surgeon, Francisco Javier Balmis. Eguía y Muro responded to his critics by denying any hint of malpractice on his part, stating that any over-expenditure was due to the far greater number of patients in this department compared to any other ward (double to treble the norm). This financial problem and the figure of Balmis were to come back and haunt O'Sullivan in the early months of 1791.

Remaining in 1790, however, it is clear that this year marked the peak of O'Sullivan's drive to establish his professional and intellectual standing within the educated elite of Mexico City. As we have seen, by mid-1790, he had gained approval to practise medicine throughout Mexico and he had obtained a hospital placement linked to his military posting in Puebla at the Archbishop's invitation. Moreover, he had also taken steps to enter the elite circles of Spanish science through contact with the director of the newly established Royal Botanical Gardens, Martín de Sessé, and the Chair of the department of Botany, Vicente Cervantes. In December 1789, only months after his arrival, O'Sullivan took part in the second public exercises held by the newly established course in botany, questioning José Mociño, one of the future great Mexican botanists, on his understanding of Linnean methodology and doctrine.[38] Following this, and possibly at the same time as he accepted the position in San Andrés, O'Sullivan began studying the

---

Declan M. Downey and Julio Crespo MacLennan (eds), *Spanish–Irish relations through the ages: new historical perspectives* (Dublin: FCP, 2008), pp. 149–74.

[35] O'Sullivan. *Relación histórico-crítica*, fol. 4. O'Sullivan records that he took up the position on 1 May 1790.

[36] AGN, Bienes Nacionales, 575, 35, fol. 15.

[37] AGN, Bienes Nacionales, 575, exp. 35, fol. 5.

[38] News of this event was published on 12 December 1789, in the official periodical in Mexico City, the *Gazeta de México*, vol. 3, no. 45, p. 439. The two examiners who appeared with O'Sullivan were Joseph Gracida and Gabriel Ocampo. The former, who was Professor of Anatomy and Surgery, was to join O'Sullivan the following year in undertaking a course in botany under instruction by Vicente Cervantes, and the latter would later become one of the competitors along with O'Sullivan for the Chair of Mathematics in 1795. Ocampo and Gracida also appear on the list of correspondents contacted by O'Sullivan regarding the efficacy of the Beato method as an anti-venereal specific: Gracida declared himself neutral, but Ocampo was firmly opposed (RANM, Leg. 14c, doc. 68, correspondence no. 13 and no. 25). O'Sullivan's name also appears in the list of Doctors and Graduates in Medicine

new botanical course under the tutelage of Cervantes, alongside José Gracida, Professor of Anatomy, in the Royal Pontifical University.[39] Arias Divito suggests that their attendance at the course over a period of two months came as result both of their desire to show their knowledge, and an attempt to increase the prestige of the course and to encourage students to attend classes regularly.[40] Although they were chosen for the public exercises scheduled to take place in December 1790, a dispute between the authorities in the Botanical Gardens and those in the University meant that neither man was allowed to display his knowledge publically.[41] Yet O'Sullivan continues to appear in reports relating to public exercises between 1792 and 1794.[42] Internal wrangling over the details of the continuation of public exercises was to have repercussions into the mid-1790s when Martín de Sessé was forced to appeal to the Viceroy to take action and intervene for the sake of the future of botany in the country.

O'Sullivan's attempt to identify and forge stronger links with the Botanical Gardens is indicative of his transference of the approach of the French universities, where a strong link existed between medicine and botany, to the Mexican context. It was, moreover, a direct link to Madrid because of the relationship of Sessé and Casimiro Gómez Ortega, Director of the Royal Botanical Garden in Madrid, who was one of the key supporters of the Sessé-led expedition to New Spain.[43] More importantly, Sessé had, since 1787, been petitioning Gómez Ortega to undertake an inspection of medical and pharmaceutical practices in Mexico in an attempt to reform the existing systems and institutions, and to correct abuses evident in the exercise of authority of the Protomédicos, especially that of José Ignacio García

---

and Surgery who attended lessons in botany and also participated in asking questions in the public defence events (AGN, Historia, 466, exp. 21, fols 23–5).

[39] AGN, Historia, 463, exp. 1, fol. 118. A variety of lessons in botany took place between the beginning of May or June and the end of October, on Mondays, Wednesdays, Fridays and Saturdays, from four to six in the evening, although it appears that Gracida and O'Sullivan attended extra classes. The public exercises at the end of the course were reserved for the most outstanding students as a space for them to show how much they had progressed under the tutelage of Cervantes and his staff, and receive prizes for their contribution. For further detail on the defence of the Linnean system maintained by José Mociño, in which O'Sullivan was involved: see Arias Divito, *Las expediciones*, pp. 107–108.

[40] Arias Divito, *Las expediciones*, p. 131.

[41] AGN, Historia, 463, fols 1r–9v. The dispute in question centred on a University constitution that stated that no doctor and faculty member could preside over another in an exam, in this way, Gracida could not be examined by Cervantes. Gracida did eventually sit his examination in 1795, but there is no further mention of O'Sullivan (AGN, Universidad, Libro de Claustros, vol. 27, fols 198–201).

[42] See Arias Divito, *Las expediciones*, p. 109.

[43] For further discussion of these expeditions see Engstrand, *Spanish scientists*.

Jove.⁴⁴ It can be no coincidence that the bitter criticism of García Jove published by O'Sullivan in his account of the anti-venereal trials at San Andrés, echoed the sentiments written by Sessé to Gómez Ortega in 1788, when, he made it clear that, at best, García Jove would sell his soul to Barabbas in order to advance his many scams.⁴⁵ The intransigence of the Mexican University authorities was, therefore, according to the Spaniards, a clear sign of the hostility with which they viewed the establishment of the Gardens and the course.

It is likewise unsurprising that O'Sullivan, trained in the precincts of Toulouse, Montpellier and Edinburgh, should, in April 1790, petition the Viceroy for permission to run a series of private lectures in his home on medicine and related sciences. This request was known to the University council by August 1790, by which point the documents report that it had passed through the hands of the Royal Protomedicato. On reflection, the University authorities concluded, with the University statutes in mind, that such a 'public academy' whilst laudable and useful in 'the republic', was not at present considered convenient in Mexico City. Despite some support for the implementation of the plan under certain regulations and guidelines, the application was finally denied.⁴⁶ According to the university's records, two factors worked against O'Sullivan in this instance: first, his status as a foreigner and a non-graduate of the University; and related to this, the argument that he lacked documentary proof of his 'latinidad', that is, recognised university qualifications as a physician.⁴⁷

These arguments against accepting the innovative move by the Irishman are indicative of the deeper divisions existing between sectors of the University and related institutions, such as the Royal Protomedicato and the Botanical Gardens. The nature of these overlapping relationships is still largely un-researched, and for this reason we are limited in the conclusions we can draw for their impact on cases such as O'Sullivan's. Several reasons do, however, present themselves as possible explanations for his rejection. On the one hand, given the fact that the Protomedicato had already authorised O'Sullivan based on the validity of his credentials and the proof of witnesses regarding his person, we may view this

---

⁴⁴ Arias Divito has written extensively on the correspondence between Sessé and Gómez Ortega and the power struggle between the Botanical Gardens and the Protomedicato. He states that Gómez Ortega recognised the justice of Sessé's complaints based on eye witness accounts that described the Protomédicos as: 'a mad man' (Juan José Matías de la Peña y Brizuela); 'a man as decrepit as the first was mad' (José Giral); and a man who 'could be useful ... if he used his talents, but he was such a bad vassal that he decried everything that came from Spain as if he were the firstborn son of Moctezuma and the Spanish crown had usurped his temple' (García Jove): see Arias Divito, *Las expediciones*, p. 124.

⁴⁵ Arias Divito, *Las expediciones*, p. 126, fn. 14.

⁴⁶ The proposal included O'Sullivan presenting himself for exam before the University on the subjects he wished to teach and allowing a continual monitoring of his classes (AGN, Universidad, Libro de Claustros, vol. 27, fols 72v–73v).

⁴⁷ AGN, Universidad, vol. 27, Libro de Claustros, fols 209r–211v.

decision as a manifestation of the internal dissension that existed between the University government and the authority of the Protomedicato. On the other hand, we must bear in mind that all three Protomédicos were professors of medicine at the University. While a license to practise as a physician in Mexico did not necessarily impinge upon their careers and financial prospects, the establishment of a private school aimed at university students would clearly affect the take up of their courses.[48] Furthermore, for some time faculty had been expressing discontent with their low income, especially in comparison to the posts linked to the newly established course in Botany.[49] O'Sullivan's involvement with the Botanical Gardens could not have gone unnoticed not least since his name was linked with their programmes in the *Gazeta de México*, the city's official periodical publication.[50] From this point on he became strongly associated with a 'foreign' element within Mexican society, and one that situated him on the side of the 'gachupines', the Iberian Spanish, without a clear local patron to support his cause. In addition, by August 1790, O'Sullivan had spent four months immersed in trials into a new antivenereal treatment at the Hospital de San Andrés. In this capacity he actively and openly opposed the methods and practices instigated by one of the most powerful men in Mexican medicine, the aforementioned Protomédico José García Jove.[51]

By the end of 1790, therefore, O'Sullivan had, either knowingly or inadvertently, aligned himself with individuals and camps within the local context by following a path consistent with his European training and experience. These circumstances were exacerbated by the role O'Sullivan played in the 'Beato method' trials in San Andrés to which we now turn.

---

[48] In 1790 all three faculty formed part of a group within the university who filed an official complaint regarding their low incomes compared to others in similar positions but in other departments, and asked for their salary to be improved: see Alberto María Carreño. *Efemérides de la Real y Pontificia Universidad de México según sus libros de claustros* (2 vols México: UNAM, 1963) vol. 2, p. 762.

[49] In April 1788 José Gracida, Professor of Anatomy, suggested that, in view of the liberal manner in which the king had awarded the Botanical faculty their income, it would be a propitious time in which to ask for a review of professors' pay, which apparently stood unchanged since the 1640s: see Carreño, *Efemérides*, p. 745. Although in 1787 the crown had consented to an increase in salary for certain faculty, the funds were never made available. As a result in 1790 the University requested permission to open a butcher's shop to raise the money: a request that was rejected: see Luz María Hernández Sáenz, *Learning to heal: the medical profession in colonial Mexico, 1767–1831* (New York: Peter Lang, 1997), p. 46.

[50] O'Sullivan's name appears several times in the *Gazeta de México* in relation to his activities in the Botanical Gardens (*Gazeta de México*, vol. 3, no. 45, p. 439 (1789); vol. 5, no. 26, pp. 242–4 (1793); vol. 6, no. 1, p. 4 (1794); vol. 6, no. 28, p. 226 (1794); no. 85, p. 703 (1794)).

[51] O'Sullivan, *Relación histórico-crítica*, fol. 122.

## The anti-venereal trials at the Hospital de San Andrés

Most accounts of the events in San Andrés, as described in modern historical narratives, derive from the minutes taken at the time of the trials, and later reports written by García Jove and Núñez de Haro y Peralta, alongside the additions and revisions to the cure later recorded by Francisco Javier Balmis.[52] The text most widely used by modern scholars is a later report by Balmis (1794) written as a response to criticism of similar trials he performed in Madrid in 1792.[53] In actual fact, Balmis was in Spain 1790–91, and his published text cannot be relied upon to provide anaccurate first-hand account of the process. This fact is frequently overlooked in later accounts in which Balmis is given credit for the origins of much of the cure.

The 'Beato method' originated with a 'curandero' or healer, Nicolás Viana, who arrived in Mexico City at the start of 1790, claiming that over the course of 30 years he had cured thousands of venereal patients, suffering from all manifestations of the disease, using a recipe based on two main ingredients: begonia and maguey/agave. This was administered to the patient over a period of nine to 10 days ensuring a complete and total cure by day 12.[54] The method, with the consent of Haro y Peralta, underwent three periods of testing, each comprising an increasingly larger cohort of patients. The first took place in San Juan de Dios over the course of a month; the last two in San Andrés comprised 18 patients for one month and 60 patients over more than two months respectively. Three meetings were held over the course of the trials to assess the progress of the cure. Although the first seems to have been restricted to hospital staff, such was the expectation of a favourable outcome that the later meetings included, at Haro y Peralta's behest, various of the city's notables and dignitaries, the Protomédicos, and friends and family related to the Archbishop.

According to the official reports, these trials took place in an orderly, well-monitored fashion under Viana's guidance. The method included noting a patient's history, symptoms, manifestation of venereal disease, medication administered, changes that took place and final outcome. Restrictions were set on staff interference in respect of the administration of treatment, and contact between the

---

[52] AGN, Bienes Nacionales, 593, exp. 3, fols 2r –62v.

[53] Francisco Javier Balmis. *Demostración de las eficaces virtudes nuevamente descubiertas en las raíces de dos plantas de Nueva España, especies de ágave y de begonia, para la curación del vicio venéreo y escrofuloso, y de otras graves enfermedades que resisten al uso del Mercurio, y demás remedios conocidos* (Madrid, 1794).

[54] The alcoholic extract of the agave was used as a sweating agent and the begonia was ground up as a purgative. Several other ingredients were also added, including a third formula comprising sarsaparilla and water, lemon and copal of Campeche, sassafras and sugar. Other more exotic elements initially included were snake flesh and a flower known as 'rosa de castilla', but the recipe was later simplified by Balmis (AGN, Bienes Nacionales, 593, exp. 3, fols 13r–14v, 37r–49r).

trial patients and others in the hospital was prohibited. As part of the assessment meetings the 'cured' patients were brought out praising God for their miraculous and swift healing. In each case a majority of the hospital staff declared the patients to be either perfectly well or much improved, although on occasion a small number were retained for further observation.[55] Whilst there are occasional references in the notes (including a mention of O'Sullivan) that suggest that opinion was less than wholly unanimous, the overwhelming consensus was that the 'Beato method' was a 'specific' cure, and that it should be administered in place of mercury without further delay. No doubt the fact that it was a more economical option both in terms of money and time held a strong appeal. That said, the inconclusive nature of the 1790 trial results led Haro y Peralta to call for a further period of observation in the hospital following a system that allowed the patients to choose between mercury and the vegetable-based cure.

By February 1791 a majority of patients were once again opting for the mercurial unctions, which caused the authorities to prohibit the further use of any form of mercury in order to promote their chosen method. At the same time O'Sullivan was removed from responsibility for the venereal department and placed on the medical wards, leaving the former in the hands of García Jove. Later that year Balmis returned from Spain to resume charge of the venereal patients, resulting in the return of García Jove to the medical wards, and the dismissal of O'Sullivan from the hospital on charges of financial mismanagement. In early 1792, further to some simplification of the recipe, Haro y Peralta, by then convinced of the efficacy of the cure, gained permission from the Viceroy for Balmis to take the recipe and samples of the plants to the hospitals in Madrid in order to demonstrate their virtues to the Spanish court.[56]

As they stand, the official reports provide a straightforward, concise depiction of the clinical trials and the decision making processes followed within San Andrés. Based on this fact, Alba Morales Cosme, in her recent work on the history of the hospital, has argued that the manner in which they dealt with the 'Beato specific' indicated that it was an institution open to examining new methods.[57] These events, she states, bear witness to the formation of a scientific community that, whilst not necessarily united in opinion, was unified by the will to consolidate a common institutional project. Yet these accounts, when read in tandem with O'Sullivan's reports, in actual fact reveal a world of infighting and conspiracy within the medical and ecclesiastical power structures as individuals struggled to protect or further their careers. The image of unity in support of a common institutional project is, therefore, attributable more to the fact that many voices were silenced than to a higher desire for the common good.

---

[55] AGN, Bienes Nacionales, 593, exp. 3, fols 2r–62v.

[56] AGN, Bienes Nacionales, 593, exp. 3, fols 65r–65v.

[57] Alba Dolores Morales Cosme, *El Hospital General de San Andrés: la modernización de la medicina novohispana (1770–1833)* (México: UAM, 2002), pp. 102–103.

## The historico-critical report

O'Sullivan's historico-critical report into the 'Beato method' cannot be described as a purely scientific or medical treatise, even by the standards of the period. It is, rather, a semi-scientific, semi-sensationalist critique of the structures and methods employed within institutional confines, written in language that would appeal to the most adventurous spirit. The central issue, as such, was not to question the chemical properties and compounds of the cure. Although O'Sullivan strongly promoted the greater efficacy of mercury as a 'specific' over and against the merely alleviative nature of the new recipe, his report focused primarily on the lack of correct medical procedures and the misuse of authority.

O'Sullivan undercuts Viana's claims to medical orthodoxy by placing him among the legions of quacks that had produced a long line of ineffectual cures for venereal disease. He informed the reader, Viana, was a little, ill-formed, 60-year old man of poor complexion, who had exchanged his profession as a tailor for that of a 'curandero'.[58] Not only had he stolen the cure from an inebriated country woman, he had also been threatened with a prison sentence by the Protomedicato only to find eventual success for his claims by disguising himself as a Franciscan (hence the title 'Beato') in a bid to gain the Archbishop's support. Viana was, O'Sullivan contended dismissively, a false prophet, a sheep in wolf's clothing, a conniver, a hypocrite, and an imposter who should suffer the worst punishments for gambling with human life for his own gain.[59]

Having established the questionable origins of the cure, O'Sullivan focused on three main areas: the failure of the ecclesiastics, carried away by the desire to serve humanity and gain renown for the hospital, to leave medical decision making in the hands of the physicians, only to be persuaded into a course of action by means that were both unscientific and lacking in the necessary degree of scepticism; the failure of hospital physicians and surgeons to follow correct method in the testing and implementation of the new treatment, which led them to engage in collusion, party-politics and deceit when their initial claims could not be substantiated; and the questionable exercise of authority and the public exhibition of patients throughout the process that discouraged disinterested examination and blocked all opportunity for dissention or opposition among the hospital staff. O'Sullivan, by contrast, is depicted as a silent, detached and disinterested observer whose methodological approach stood in clear opposition to that of the hospital staff and Protomédicos.

As the report progresses the reader's attention is drawn to a series of events, such as the loss and alteration of original medical reports by senior medical staff in a bid to conceal the failure of the vegetable-based cure, the secret introduction of mercury in the ongoing treatments, pantomimes of patients singing and dancing before rooms packed tight with observers, and ward rounds undertaken in the late

---

[58] O'Sullivan, *Relación histórico-crítica*, fols 5, 26–31.
[59] O'Sullivan, *Relación histórico-crítica*, fols 5–7.

hours of the night where no correct observation could be forthcoming. The use of narrative techniques, such as cliffhangers between sections, serve to build tension, climaxing in the murder of a patient whose declining health clearly pointed to the inefficacy of the cure, and the ensuing attempts to cover up the truth and O'Sullivan's dismissal as a result of his objections. Irony and humour abound, not least in the description of Viana's eventual fall from grace and his attempts to bolster the support of a fast disbelieving public through claims of death threats issued by the medical staff against him, necessitating the use of body guards at all times.[60] The brunt of the criticism, however, was reserved for Francisco Javier Balmis who, O'Sullivan stated, originally recognised the weaknesses of the 'Beato method' but chose to ignore these facts, even at the expense of human life, in order to pursue recognition and promotion, and curry favour with the ecclesiastical and medical authorities who could best further his advancement. In a manner similar to his criticism of Viana, O'Sullivan presented details that questioned Balmis's integrity both on professional and personal grounds, depicting him as a man of little education, who had recently returned to Spain under duress, in part as a result of his wife's continual petitioning but also as a means of escaping accusations levelled against him by the Protomedicato.[61]

There is no indication that the content of O'Sullivan's report was ever made known to the individuals who featured prominently within it, but the strength of feeling reflected in his words is indicative of the souring relationships within the local context. Following his dismissal from the hospital, an event he linked directly to the ongoing persecution he experienced because of his opposition to the 'Beato method', O'Sullivan had little or no opportunity within the local context to advance his arguments. The two parties most likely to serve in a medico-judicial manner in such situations – the Protomédicos and the hospital authorities – constituted central players in his drama. The limited circle of the educated medical elite in Mexico City and their dependence on the support of those in positions of authority for any form of advancement meant that the majority of his fellow physicians and surgeons were unwilling for obvious reasons to speak out openly against the authorities when O'Sullivan approached them to assess the Beato method at a later date.[62] Those who did provide him with negative assessments worked primarily within military circles, a fact that underlines the independence of these post holders. These circumstances caused O'Sullivan to turn to the two independent networks to which he had access: the army, which led him to the Viceroy; and his Irish mercantile and military connections, which linked him with Spain and the Royal Academy of Medicine in Madrid.[63]

---

[60] O'Sullivan, *Relación histórico-crítica*, fols 17–26, 31–60.

[61] O'Sullivan, *Relación histórico-crítica*, fols 59–67.

[62] This is evidenced by the language they use and the manner in which they respond to his request for personal assessment of the efficacy of the method in his *Carta circular* (1792).

[63] See footnote 3 above.

In terms of the first network, O'Sullivan contrived by submitting his reports to the independent appeals process of the army, to secure the removal of the soldiers from San Andrés and their transfer to a separate hospital for renewed mercurial treatments, and these are included as evidence within the portfolio he created for the Academy of Medicine.[64] It is notable that O'Sullivan gained an element of personal success within the latter network, for his reports earned him membership of the Royal Academy of Medicine in October 1793.[65] However, these were the limits of his advancement for despite the Academy of Medicine's approval of O'Sullivan's reports, and the fact that they were presented at the same time as the Spanish physician Piñera y Siles published his highly critical denouncement of Balmis and the Beato method, no attempt was made to limit the trials that Balmis pursued in the Madrid hospitals.[66] To all extents and purposes, O'Sullivan's reports seem to have reached the Academy's archives and remained there untouched and unused for the following two centuries.

Regardless of his best efforts to rouse the indignation of the republic of letters and to convince the scientific community to support scientific argument, O'Sullivan failed to elicit any support for his cause on a trans-Atlantic setting. He clearly believed that the weight of the European response would effect change within the local Mexican context, thus substantiating his position and lending him greater credence. It is unlikely, however, that the Madrid authorities had sufficient power over the Mexican medical authorities to instigate change, had they acted upon O'Sullivan's reports.[67] Instead, we find Balmis climbing the ladder of success and royal approval throughout the later 1790s, despite O'Sullivan's protestations that he was no more than a 'romancista' (non-university trained), whose person had never warmed the seat of any university to which he claimed allegiance.[68] Balmis, unlike O'Sullivan, successfully cultivated patrons in elevated positions both in Spain and Mexico, most notably the powerful figure of Manuel Godoy, Duque de la Alcudia. Whatever qualifications he lacked in his early years, this ingenious individual gradually gained them at a later stage even while progressing upward in

---

[64] Even in the new surroundings of the Hospital de San Juan de Dios the soldiers continued to experience maltreatment, supposedly because the baths used for the treatment of venereal disease were in disrepair and, when questioned, the Brothers excused this lack of facility on the basis that the army payments were insufficient to see to their proper functioning (AGN, Inquisición, 1337, fols 31–9).

[65] RANM, leg. 4, doc. 169.

[66] Bartolomé Piñera y Siles. *Narración histórica de las observaciones ó ensayos prácticos que se han hecho en los hospitales de San Juan de Dios, General y Pasión de esta corte, para examinar y comprobar la virtud anti-venérea de los dos simples americanos agave o pita, y begonia* (Madrid, 1792).

[67] This is further evidenced by the fact that the previously mentioned petitions of medical reform written by Sessé did not have the desired effect in Mexico: see Arias Divito, *Las expediciones*, pp. 119–43.

[68] RANM, fol. 40, leg. 14c., doc. 67, fols 61r–65r.

the social ranks.⁶⁹ Such was his success that history has recorded him as the figure responsible for spreading the use of inoculation throughout the Spanish empire.

But what of O'Sullivan? It would seem that he remained in Mexico, even after his regiment moved to Cuba, and between 1793 and 1794, he continued his involvement with the Botanical Gardens, taking part in public examinations and the collection of plants across the country.⁷⁰ The success of this connection with the Botanical Gardens is indicated by the fact that Martín de Sessé nominated O'Sullivan as his replacement as Director in his application to the then Viceroy, Branciforte, in June 1795, stating that O'Sullivan was, 'a physician of the highest reputation in the Capital [Mexico City], whose intelligence, personal disinterest and zeal for the public good I am sure will contribute to the better order and honour of the position'.⁷¹ Although, to date, no response by the Viceroy has come to light, O'Sullivan continued to petition for a variety of academic and medical positions in Mexico between 1794 and 1796, such as Consulting Physician to the Royal Army and the position of 'First physician' in New Spain.⁷² Branciforte finally conceded the former post but on a non-stipendiary basis.⁷³ A few months later O'Sullivan applied as candidate for the Chair of Mathematics and Astrology at the University, only to be rejected. O'Sullivan interpreted this as a further instance of persecution and, once more, resorted to the Viceroy to redress the situation. On this occasion, however, the Viceroy upheld the University authorities and instructed them to disregard O'Sullivan.⁷⁴ The only further evidence we have at this time of the Irish physician are references to his involvement as interpreter in the trials of Frenchmen accused of freemasonry and acting as translator for Pedro Valenzuela in the Real Sala del Crimen.⁷⁵ By 1798 the army had reported his death and was once more seeking a replacement.⁷⁶

---

⁶⁹ Balmis dedicated his *Demostración de las eficaces virtudes* (1794) to the Duke and was also in correspondence with him from Mexico, as well as seeking his support through Haro y Perlata, see for example the following correspondence (AGI, Estado, vol.1, 40, n. 6 and AGI, Estado, vol. 1, 41, n. 10).

⁷⁰ *Gazeta de México*, vol. 6, no. 85, p. 703 (23 December 1794).

⁷¹ 'D. O'Sulivan, Médico de primera reputación en esa Capital, cuya inteligencia, desinterés, y celo por el bien público estoy seguro que contribuirán al mejor orden, y honor de la Facultad' (AGN, Indiferente Virreinal, Exp. 002, Real Audiencia, Caja 3706).

⁷² His petitions are forwarded repeatedly between 1794 and 1795 (AGN, Correspondencia de Virreyes, vol. 178, fols 109r–110v; AGN, Reales Cédulas, vol. 160, fol. 132; AGS, SGU, Leg, 6774.2, fol. 3v).

⁷³ AGS, SGU, Leg. 6974.2, fol. 60r.

⁷⁴ AGN, Universidad, Libro de Claustros, vol. 27, fols 213v–214r.

⁷⁵ AGS, SGU, Leg. 6974.2, fols 57r/v.

⁷⁶ AGN, Correspondencia de Virreyes, 190, 1031, fol. 79.

## Conclusion

Although there are many unknowns surrounding the circumstances in which Daniel O'Sullivan operated, his life serves to highlight the complexities of the local situations in which physicians and surgeons functioned when they moved abroad. O'Sullivan maintained a Eurocentric approach throughout his interactions in Mexican medical circles, proceeding down a path that may well have functioned successfully in other circumstances, but in this case failed to comprehend the subtleties of local polemics and the sensitive structures of power and authority. His belief that scientific/medical truth would overcome all contested points within the republic of letters was essentially doomed when faced with the systems of patronage, while his reasoning that the Spanish institutions held authority over their Mexican counterparts also fell short of the reality of the world in which he operated. His foreign identity and his sense of independence did not assist his situation, and in the end consigned him to relative obscurity. Testament of this fact can be found in the name given to the plant over which so much of the anti-venereal polemic took place and which eventually would prove worthless in the treatment of syphilis: the Begonia Balmisiana.

# Index

Page references in **bold** denote the chapter(s) in which the subject is primarily addressed. The letter *t* following a page number denotes a table

Aberdeen 78
Achonry, diocese of 80t
accoucheur, *see* midwives
Aghmacart, county Laois 6–7, 42, 43, 47, 111n12
anatomy 62, 44, 63, 64, 69, 71, 81, 82, 118, 143n23, 207
Angers, France 77–8t, 85n27, 79
Anglophone population/community 5, 11, 50, 111, 119, 120–121, 127, 135, 173. *See also* Protestantism
animal 48, 49, 60, 63, 64, 119, 120, 121
Anjou, France 74
antiquarianism 13, 102, 187
anti-venereal trials, *see under* venereal disease
Antrim, county 30, 48, 84, 100, 105, 124
apothecaries 2, 3, 4, 5, 11, 12, 19, 20, 22, 33, 36, 73, 74, 75, 104, 109, 110, 131, 135, 138, 139–40, 142, 143, 144–6, 147–55, 156, 170, 172, 187, 201, 202, 203n24
Apothecaries' Guild 12, 137n1, 148, 152–3, 154, 155, 193
Apothecaries' Hall 12, 148, 154, 160–61t
apprentices and apprenticeship 20, 74, 76, 98, 99, 102, 103, 104n81, 105, 140, 147, 148, 149, 184
Archdekin, Richard 55–6, 57, 61n48
Ardagh, diocese of 80t
Ardfert and Aghadoe, diocese 69, 80
Aristotelianism 59, 60, 61, 72
Armagh, archdiocese of 27, 30, 80t, 100t, 106
Armstrong, William 102

army surgeons 9, 36, 86n29, 76, 87, 91, 96–108, 142, 159t, 188, 200, 204, 205, 206, 214–216
Arthur, Thomas 8, 14–15, 17–19, 23, 24–5, 28–32, 33, 35–7
asylums, lunatic 2; orphan 104
Audouin, John 123
Austrian Hapsburgs 45; Austrian Netherlands 130; Austrian Succession, war of 45, 86n29, 87;
Australia 105
autopsy 26
Avignon, France 195

Bailey, Craig 180
Balfour, Lady Florence 121, 122
Ball, John, *The female physician* (1771) 125
Ballyspellan spa 131
Balmis, Francisco Javier 206, 210, 211, 213, 214, 215; *Demostración de las eficaces virtudes* (1794) 215n69, 216
Bannerman, John 44
barber-surgeons 20, 22, 32, 75, 142, 170
Barber-Surgeons' Guild 12, 19, 21, 32, 75, 139, 142, 143, 148, 149, 150
Barrett, John 90n39
Barry, Nathaniel (c. 1724–85) 90–91, 92, 93n50, 97
Barry, Sir Edward (1696–1776) 14–15, 90
Bath 130, 151
bathing *see* hydrotherapy
Beaghan, Timothy 64, 65
Beato method 197–8, 205, 206n38, 209, 210–214. *See also* Viana, Nicolás

Beatty, Sir William (1773–1842) 105–106, 107, 108; *Authentic narrative of the death of Lord Nelson* (1807) 106n88
Bedell, William 27, 28
begonia 210, 214, 216. *See also* anti-venereal treatment; Beato method,
Beere, Thomas 27
Belfast 48, 101, 103, 105n85, 124n77
*Belfast Newsletter* 103
Bellini, Lorenzo 59
Berkeley, Bishop George 131
Bertrucius, Nicolaus (d. 1347) 43
Birr, county Offaly 119, 122
Blount, Charles 57, 62
Boate, Arnold 36
Boerhaave, Herman 4, 8, 164, 185, n9
bones 63, 62, 73, 99, 119, 168, 169
Bonny, Robert 29n45, 30, 31
Bordeaux, France 18
Borri, Giuseppe Francesco 69
botany: 32, 82, 161t, 188, 202; Royal Botanical Garden, Madrid 207; Royal Botanical Garden, Mexico City 201, 206, 207, 208, 209, 215
Boyle, Robert 56,
Boyne, Michael de 46
Branciforte, Viceroy 215
Brooke, Sir Basil 23
Browne, Andrew 104
Browne, Anthony, sixth Viscount Montague (1686–1767) 133n114
Browne, Edward 61n52, 62
Browne, John (1642–1702) 71n122
Browne, Patrick (1720–90) 87, 104n79, 183; *Civil and Natural History of Jamaica* (1789) 183
Browne, Sir Thomas 62
Browne, Thomas (grandson) 62
Brussels 40, 61
Buchan, William, *Domestic Medicine* (Dublin, 1773) 126–7, 128, 131
Bulkeley, Richard 57
Burton, Benjamin 143–4
Bury, Jane 119–20
Butler, James, 12th earl of Ormond 35
Butler, Colonel Walter 19, 45
Byrtt, William 103

Caen 84t
Callanan, John 87, 88
Calvet, Ésprit 195
Cambridge 8, 9, 25, 28, 36, 61, 63, 79n14, 81n16, 87, 93n49, 139, 164, 165
Canada 98t
Cantwell, Andrew 87n30
Cardwell, John 98
Caribbean 183, 200
Carlow 100t
Carnaervon 112
Carrickfergus, county Antrim 30
Cary, Katherine 13–14, 165, 166, 168–73, 175, 177, 179–81
Cary, Mordecai 13–14, **163–82**
Cashel, diocese of 80t
Cassin, Conly 22
Catholicism 4, 7, 8, 10, 13, 14, 18–19, 25, 35, 44, 45, 54, 55, 56, 69, 70, 71, 72, 87, 91–103, 106–107, 140n13, 148, 174–5, 184, 185, 190–193, 199, 205n31; Confederate Catholic 19, 35, 36n75, 36n77
Caulfeild, James, 1st earl of Charlemont 151
Cavan, county 100t, 131
census (1841) 109n2; (1851) 73, 76n12
Cervantes, Vicente 206, 207
Chambre Royale de Médicine 58–9
Champagne, Faculty of Medicine 88, 92, 93
Chapelizod spa 131
charitable activity 6, 140, 155, 174, 185; Charitable Infirmary 21, 90n40, 92n44
Charles I, 25–6
Charles II (Spain) 20, 159t
Charles III 205
Cheselden, William (1688–1752) 170, 171, 176
Chetwood, Knightley 113, 122
Cheyne, George 125, 127,
Christ's Hospital, London 164
Church of England 70, 71. *See also* Protestantism; Presbyterianism; Quakers
Church of Ireland 8, 13, 30, 53, 93, 102, 113, 164, 174. *See also* Protestantism; Presbyterianism; Quakers

Clanchy, James 87
Clare, county 39, 86, 112, 128, 130, 162t
Clavell, John 28–30, 33–5
Cleaver, Archbishop Euseby 133
Clement XII, Pope 69
Clerical, Medical Assurance Company 106
clergy 46, 53, 55, 60, 69, 73, 80–81t, 93, 174, 183; ecclesiastical 56, 203, 204, 212, 213
Clogher, diocese of 80t
Clonfert, diocese of 13, 81t, 165, 168, 175, 177
Clonmacnoise, diocese of 80t
Cloyne, diocese of 80t
Collegio Veneto Artista 82n18
Colles, Abraham 99
Company of Apothecaries 144, 145. *See also* apothecaries
Complaints; *see* illness
Connacht 39, 188
Connaught Rangers 107
Connor, diocese of 80t
Connor, Bernard (c. 1666–98) 9–10, **53–72**, 91, 93, 183; *Dissertationes medico-physicæ* (1695) 61n52, 62n57, 63; *Evangelium Medici* (1697) 9, 10, 54, 55, 58, 61n52, 62–3, 65–9, 71–2; *History of Poland* (1698) 55, 63, 69, 91
Conolly, Lady Louisa 130, 134
consumer 15, 75, 112, 120. *See also* Medical marketplace
Conway, Edward, third Viscount 112
Copenhagen 187
Cork 33, 80, 81, 83, 87, 88, 94–5, 100, 101, 109, 113, 114, 117, 122, 131, 158t, 186n13, 190, 192, 198; Cork Corporation 21
Cornaro, Luigi 127; *Sure and certain methods of attaining a long and healthful life* (1702) 125
Council of Trent 45
Cox, Richard 140, 141
credentials 19, 92, 95, 107, 205, 209
*criollo* ('creole') 200, 201
Cromwell, Henry 36
Cuba 215
Culpeper, Nicholas 121, 124, 127

Cunegunda, Princess Teresa 61
cures/curing 7, 10, 11, 30, 31–5, 40, 49, 50, 56, 64, 65, 113, 114, 117, 119, 121–8, 165, 151, 167, 171, 173, 205, 210, 211, 212, 213. *See also* herbal remedies; hydrotherapy; receipt books *under* medicine

Currer, William 36
Curry, John (1702/3–80) 91–2, 93, 191–2, 193
*Cursus medicus* (1655) 31

Dalitz, R.H. 55, 70
Daly, Charles 122
Daly, Tully 105
Daunt, George 88, 90, 93n50
Day, Susanna 118
De Danann, Tuatha 49
De Laney, James 86
Dease, Francis 86
Dease, Oliver 101–102, 103
Dease, Richard 99, 102
degree, medical, *see* medical graduates
deism 57n23, 70, 72n125
Delaune, Paul 19, 25, 27, 28
dentist 3, 109
Devenish, George 23
Derry, diocese of 80t
diagnosis 4, 11, 13, 30, 31, 32, 34, 51, 59, 74, 110, 112, 167, 168, 170, 173, 174
Digby, Lord Edward 114
disorders, *see* illness
dispensaries 2, 104, 109, 135, 137n1, 204n25
distance 20, 176, 178, 180, 189, 202
doctors, *see* physicians
Domhnail of Lisaniskey 17
Donegal, county 100t
Donore, county Kildare 43
Douai 84t
Dover, Thomas, *The ancient physician's legacy to his country* (1733) 125
Down, county 100t, 104, 112, 129, 132, 154
Down, diocese of 80t
Drennan, William 5, 96, 130, 154, 184

Drogheda, county Louth 30, 145
Dromore, diocese of 80t
druggists, *see* apothecaries
drugs 123, 127, 130, 131, 138, 140, 143n26, 146, 156, 187, 188; Act (1723) 144, 145; Act (1735) 12, 148, 149–50, 151, 153, 155; bill, (1741) 150–151; legislation (1761–71) 152–58. *See also* medication; potions and nostrums
Dublin 7, **17–37**, 75, 76, 77–8t, 79, 80, 81, 82, 83, 84t, 88, 89t, 90, 91, 92, 93n51, 94, 95n53 &n55, 97, 99, 100, 101, 102, 103, 105, 109n2, 113, 114, 122, 123, 125–7, 130, 131, 133, 139, 140, 144, 145, 146, 148, 149, 151, 155, 157–62t, 165, 174, 175, 176, 177, 184, 185, 186, 187, 191, 193, 194, 199n6; Dublin Castle 25, 26, 33, 43; *see also* St Patrick's Hospital; Trinity College
*Dublin Directory*, see *Wilson's Dublin Directory;*
*Dublin Gazette* 121
Dublin Lying-in Hospital, *see* Rotunda, the
Dublin Philosophical Society 12, 56–7, 140, 183, 186, 190
Dublin Society 140, 183, 186, 187, 189, 191
Dumbill, John 31
Dun, Sir Patrick 90–91, 140, 144
Dungannon, countyTyrone 46, 86, 113
Dungarvan, county Waterford 187
Dutch Republic, *see* Netherlands
Dwarris, Frances 104
Dwarris, Robert (*was* Gibney) 104–105
Dwarris, Sir Fortunatus William Lilley 104n82

*Ecole française* 31
economics of medicine 1, 5, 6, 14, 39, 40, 50, 58, 62, 87, 93, 130, 132, 156, 164, 165, 166, 173, 174, 176, 182, 185, 197, 200, 201, 206, 213
Edinburgh 9, 77–8t, 79, 81, 82, 84t, 88, 89t, 92, 93n49, 93n51, 95n53, 96, 99, 100n69, 104, 126, 128, 154, 184, 186, 199, 208

Eguía y Muro, Joachín Pío de 206
élite 1, 5, 6, 14, 39, 40, 44, 50, 58, 62, 87, 93, 130, 132, 156, 164–5, 173, 174, 176, 182, 165, 197, 200, 201, 206, 213
Elizabeth I 19, 20n11, 139; charter (1577) 19–21
Elphin, diocese of 81t, 112n14, 114, 122, 131, 133
Emly, diocese of 80t
England 7, 11, 15, 24, 30, 34, 56, 57, 58, 61, 62, 70, 72, 73, 74, 75, 76, 79, 81n16, 87, 94t, 95n52, 98t, 104, 105, 107, 110, 112, 119, 126, 130, 131, 134, 143, 145, 151, 152, 156, 163, 164, 165, 166, 170, 173, 174, 175–6, 178, 179, 190, 193, 198

Falkland, Henry Cary, first Viscount 19, 25–6, 28, 30
Fennell, Gerald 17, 18, 19, 35–7
Ferguson, Victor 184
Fermanagh, county 39, 46, 100t
Ferns, diocese of 80t, 133
Fildens, Jacobus 18
Fitzpatrick, Sir Jeremiah (1740–1810) 91, 93
Fitzwilliam, William 114
Fitzwilliam, Richard sixth Viscount 133
Fleetwood, Charles 36
Fleming, Patrick 45
Fleming, Rev Horace Townshend 109–110
folk medicine 7, 123, 124
Fothergill, John (1712–80) 95n52
France 86, 98t, 113, 199; medical training 10, 15, 17, 59, 79, 84, 85, 184, 192, 193, 198; war with 81, 82, 96, 143
fraud 114, 147, 149, 152, 153, 157–8t, 188
*Freeman's Journal* 124
freemasons 87, 185, 216
Freke, Elizabeth 120, 121
Freke, John 117
French Revolution 79, 82, 199, 200

Gaelic Irish medical practice 6–7, **39–52**
Gaddesden, John of 41, 51; *Rosa Anglica* (1314) 41, 51

galenism 4, 5, 6, 7, 10, 24, 31–32, 39, 59, 60, 64, 110, 111, 152, 171
Gálvez, José de 200
Galway 100t
García Jove, José Ignacio 207–8, 209, 210, 211
*Gazeta de México* 206n38, 209
gender 2, 13, **163–80**
*Gentleman and Citizen's Almanach, The* 88n38
*Gentleman's Magazine* 124
gentry 5, 25, 40, 43, 87, 102, 187. *See also* élite
Gerard, John 121
Gibney, John 104
Gibney, Robert (*later* Dwarris) (1826–1906) 104–105
Gibney, William (c. 1794–1872) 104, 108
Giffard, John 116
Gillespie, Leonard (1758–1842) 105–106
Gillespie, Raymond 53, 69
Glasgow 9, 75, 75n7, 77–8t, 79, 82, 83, 84, 88n38, 89t, 92, 93n51, 97, 188, 199n6
Glorious Revolution 64
Goddard, Jonathan 36
Godoy, Manuel 214
Godwin, Richard 117
Gómez Ortega, Casimiro 207–208
de Gordon, Bernard, *Lilium Medicinae* (1305) 41–2
Göttingen 82
Goubert, Jean-Pierre 74
Gould, Anna 23
Grace, Sheffield 90n40
Gracida, José 206n38, 207, 207n39 & n41, 209n49
graduate physicians 5, 8, 9, **17–37**, 46, 61n49, 74, 75, 76–96, 100, 103, 106–107, 139, 206-7n38. *See also* medical training and education
Granville, Mary (Mrs Delany) 120
Greatrakes, Valentine 56, 113
Greek language 44, 177
Griffith, Richard 128
Guild of Barber-Surgeons, *see* Barber-Surgeons' Guild
Guy's Hospital, London 166

Hally, John 84
Hamilton, Anne 132
Hanmer, Sir John 141
Haro y Peralta, Alonso Núñez 203, 210, 211
Harrach, Cardinal Arnošt 45
Hartley, David 156
Hartlib, Samuel, and his circle 183, 186, 190
Harvey, William 82n18; *De Motu Cordis et Sanguinis* (1628) 32
Hayley, William 58, 70–71
healers and healing 4, 7, 12, 24, 40, 47, 48–9, 56, 73, 74, 75n6, 111, 113–114, 171; lithotomists 32, 88
Helsham, Richard 145
Hennen, John 99, 103
Henry IV 19
herbal remedies 5, 33n65, 49, 50, 111, 119, 120, 121, 123
hereditary medical practice 6, 10–11, 19, 39–43, 44, 47, 50, 53; medical families 39–41, 42, 42, 43, 46, 47, 50
Hickey, Nicholas 20
Hippocrates 44; *De Lege Naturae* 24
*HMS Victory* 105, 106
Holland, *see* Netherlands
Hoppen, K. Theodore 12, 57
Hort, Josiah (d. 1751) 117
Hospital de San Andrés 197–8, 202, 203, 205, 206, 208, 209, 210, 211, 214
Hospital de San Juan de Dios 202, 203, 210, 214n64
Hospital Real de Naturales 202n19
hospitals and infirmaries 1, 2, 5, 6, 81, 90, 91, 99, 108, 109, 135, 157–162t, 185; voluntary 137n1, 138, 140, 142n23. *See also individual hospitals*
houses of industry 2, 137n1, 138, 161–2t
Hume, David 57
humours, bodily 4, 31, 34, 64, 116, 121, 171
Hunter, William 194
Huntington, Robert 57
Huxham, John (1692–1768) 166
hydrotherapy 104, 111, 116, 122, 130–131, 133, 188, 214n64

iatrochemical thought 10, 59, 64
Iberia, *see* Spain and Spanish culture
illness/illnesses 5, 24, 35, 40, 47, 49, 53, 114, 115, 124, 129, 132, 133, 154, 168, 169, 170, 172, 176–82; ague 59, 123, 124; ankylosing spondylitis 54, 63; asthma 114; barrenness 114; boils 119; breast ailment 164, 168-72, 176, 177, 179, 180–81; cancer 119, 124, 168, 176, 180; cholera 123; cholic 31, 117; colds 119, 123, 124, 128, 170, 171, 181; consumption 15, 75, 112, 120; coughs 49, 116, 120, 123, 124, 133; deafness 119, 121; distemper 112, 113, 125; dropsy 23, 120; ear ache 120; epilepsy 34, 35, 114; failing eyesight 120; fever 23, 51, 53, 116, 117, 118, 129, 130, 191; fistula 117, 121; gout 113, 116; headaches 124; impotency 114; kidney ailments 31, 34, 49, 119, 128; menstrual disorders 172, 176; palsy 120; piles 133; plague 21, 22, 32, 119, 138n5; rabies 121, 123, 124; rheumatism 119, 121, 123, 151; scrofula 64, 65,114, 122; scurvy 121, 124, 189; smallpox 119; stomach complaints 30, 31, 34, 60, 129, 133; stone and gravel 123, 124; tinnitus 114; vomiting 128, 132; whooping cough 120. *See also* medical marketplace; venereal disease.
Incorporated Society in Dublin for Promoting English Protestant Schools 174, 185
Ingolstadt 84
ipecacuanha 132
Innes Smith, R.W., 4, 9, 83n22
Irish Legislation Database (ILD) 138n6, 162
Irish parliament; *see* parliament
Israel, Jonathan, 57
Italy 61, 113, 194

James II 105, 139
James's Powder 129–30
Jebb, Frederick (d. 1781) 90, 90, 93n50

Jersey 98t
Jesuits 45, 55, 56, 60, 61
Jesuits' Bark (drops) 128, 129, 190, 202n19
Johnson, Robert 125
Jurin, James (1684–1750) 13–14, **163–82**

Keating, Coronel Marcos 198n3
Keill, John 69
Kelly, James, 10, 11, 141
Keogh, John 84
Kerry, county 39, 58, 69, 71, 100, 190
Kildare 43, 80t, 100t, 128
Kilfenora, diocese of 80t
Kilkenny 35, 36, 43, 100t, 131, 142
Killala, diocese of 81t, 165
Killaloe, diocese of 80t
Kilmacduagh, diocese of 81t
Kilmore, diocese of 28, 80t
King, Archbishop William 113, 115
King, Belleis 113
King's professorship in medicine (1715) 144, 157t
Kingsbury, Thomas 132
Knott, John 54, 55

Lambay Island 30
Laois, county 6, 42
Latin 29, 41, 42, 44, 93n49, 99n65, 126–7, 140, 177, 204n29
laudanum 120, 133
Leadbeater, Mary 118
Leadbeater, William 118
Lebrun, François 74
Ledwich, Edward 102
Lee, Thomas Ash 130
Le Fanu, W.R. 54, 55
Legge, William 61
Leiden 4, 8, 9, 18, 44, 77–8t, 79, 82, 83, 84, 85n27, 86, 87, 87, 88n38, 89t, 90, 92, 93n49, 93n51, 94, 95, 96, 150
Leighlin, diocese of 80t
Leinster 7, 39, 43
Lettsom, John Coakley (1744–1815) 95n52
Leuven/Louvain 56, 77–8t, 79, 83, 84t, 85n27, 86, 87, 91
Levinge, Sir Richard 140–141, 143

Limerick 18, 23, 25, 29, 32, 35, 80–81t, 87, 90n39, 95n55, 100t, 120, 128, 184, 190, 192, 193
Linnean taxonomical system 201, 206, 207n39
Lismore diocese 80t
Lithuania 63
Lobb, Theophilus 125, 127
Locke, John 58, 62
Loftus, Adam 25–6, 30, 33, 34
London 9, 10, 13, 15n30, 22, 24–8, 32, 36, 54n5, 61, 63, 64, 65, 66, 71, 75, 76n11, 81, 83, 84t, 87, 91, 93, 99, 100n69, 104n82, 105, 106, 108n93, 113, 125, 129, 143n26, 144, 145, 147, 151, 164, 165, 166, 170, 177, 178, 180, 184, 185, 186, 187, 193, 194, 199n6; London and Greenwich Railway 106
Londonderry, county 100t, 105
Longford, county 101t
Louth, county 101t, 45
Louvain, see Leuven 56, 84t
Lucas, Charles (1713–71) 12, 92, 146, 147–55, 156, 184, 187, 188
Lucas, Mary 128
Lyne, Marmaduke 36

Mac Giollapádraig family 42, 43
McAdam, Robert 48, 49
Macauley, James William 102
MacBride, David (1726–78) 97, 188–9, 193n48
MacDomhnaill, Aodh 48–50; *Fealsúnacht/ Philosophy* 47–50, 51 (extract)
MacGrath, Raymond 86n29
McGauley, James 102
McGrigor, James 97, 107
McLuny, Robert 103
Madden, John 140
Madrid 204n29, 205, 207, 210, 211, 214; Royal Botanical Garden 207; Royal Academy of Medicine 198n3, 206, 214
Magrath, George (*later* Sir) 105, 106n89
Malpighi, Marcello 59
Mathew, Richard 114
Mayo, county 87, 99, 101t, 104, 183

Mead, Richard 194
Meade, Sir John 143
Meath, county 101t
mechanical philosophy 10, 54, 55, 56, 60, 63n66, 64, 66, 68, 71, 72
medicine: domestic care and medication 10–11, 13, 15, **109–35**; medical advice and consultation 14, 23, 65, 112, 114, 124, 128, 131–4, 144, 145; by correspondence 13–14, 64, 128, 131–2, **163–82** (Cary–Jurin); medical families, *see* hereditary medical practice; Gaelic medicine **39–52**; medical networks and circles 15, 33, 50, 58, 61, 70, 121–2, 128, 164, 165, 166, 167, 168, 176–80, 182, 183, 190, 197, 198, 200, 201, 204, 206, 214; medical ingredients 25, 65, 110, 119, 120–23, 210; medical legislation 12, **137–62;** medical marketplace 28, 74n3, 75n9, 112, 139, 166, 172, 175, 177, 178 (*see also* consumer)
medical practitioners – physicians and doctors 2, 3, 4, 5, 7, 8, 9, 10, 12, 13, 54, 56, 59, 62, 69, 73, 105–106, 109, 110, 115, 117, 121, 125, 127, 129, 130, 131, 132, 139–40, 164, 166, 170, 172, 173, 176, 177, 179, 182, 183–5, 193, 194, 198, 202, 203n24, 205, 208, 209, 212, 213, 215, 216; graduates **17–37**, 74, 75, 76–96, 106–107; 'practice of physic' 26, 64, 65, 69, 75, 138, 143, 144, 146, 147, 150, 151, 152, 153–4, 155, 156, 157–8t (*see also* Royal College of Physicians); medical reform 7, 25, 148, 149, 151, 152, 156, 188, 208, 215
medical texts: books 11, 22, 40, 41, 44, 50, 123, 124–7; manuscripts 41–4, 47–52, 111; newspapers 123, 124; pamphlets and treatises 125–6, 172, 212; receipt books 11, 111, 119–122, 123, 125, 127, 135, 210–212
medical training and education 4, 7–9, 14, 24, 42, 44–7, 50, 59, **73–108**, 138, 142n23, 144, 147, 148, 150, 165,

168, 197, 198, 199n6, 213. *See also* graduates; *individual place names*
medication 2, 5, 6, 11, 13, 15, 31, 32; domestic **109–135**, 211. *See also* drugs; herbal remedies; potions and nostrums; self-medication; ipecacuanha; James Powders; Jesuit Bark; Spirit of Opodeloc; Ward's drops; Rawlins fistula wash; quacks and charlatans
Medico-Philosophical Society 13, 183, 186–95
Mercer's Hospital 90n40, 157t
Metcalfe, James 25
Mexico 10, **197–216**
midwifery 5, 32, 73, 82, 91, 124, 139, 189
miracles 9, 10, 53–8, 61n48, 62, 64, 65–72; *Miracles, no violations on the laws of nature* (1683) 57
Mociño, José 206, 207n39
Molesworth, Lord Robert 110, 113, 131
Moloney scholarship 96n56
Monaghan, county 101t
Montagu, Charles 61n52
Montague Browne family 104
Montague, Viscount, *see* Browne, Anthony
Monteith, John (d. 1837) 105
Montpellier 8, 41, 58, 62n53, 77–8t, 79, 82, 84t, 86n27, 87n30, 91, 113, 199n6, 208
Mountgarret, Edmund Butler, second Viscount 43
Mountjoy, William Stewart, third Viscount 149, 150
Muns, Cayetano 205
Munster 7, 36, 39
Musgrave, Sir Richard 133

natural philosophy 57, 59, 63, 165, 186
navy surgeons 9, 76, 96–106, 107
Nelson, Admiral Horatio 105–106
Netherlands 8, 61, 77–8t, 83, 85, 95n95, 184–5. *See also* Austrian Netherlands *under* Austrian Hapsburgs
New Spain, *see* Spanish America
Newenham, Sir Edward 117
Newry, county Down 5, 130, 154
North America 107, 165

nostrums, *see* potions and nostrums
nurses and nursing 3, 73, 117, 118; nursing homes 2

Ó Conchubhair, Donnchadh 42, 43, 44
Ó Conchubhair, Risteard (1561–1625) 5, 42–3, 44
Ó Cuív, Brian 43
Ó Glacán, Neil 22n20, *Cursus Medicus* (1655) 31
O'Cassidy, William 46
O'Connor, Bernard, *see* Connor, Bernard
O'Conor, Charles 190–191, 193
O'Devlin, Johannes Ludovicus Matthias 46
O'Halloran, Sylvester 184, 192–3
O'Meara, Dermot 7, 8, 17–19, 22–5, 26n35, 29, 33, 35; *Pathologia hereditaria Generalis* (1619) 19, 22, 23
O'Meara, Edmund 18, 22
O'Meara, William 17
O'Moltolly, William 21
O'Neill, Edmund (John) 46, 86n27
O'Scanlan, Timoteo 198n3, 205
O'Shiel, Owen 36
O'Sullivan, Daniel (1760–c.1797) 9, 10, 87n32, **197–216**
Ocampo, Gabriel 206, 207n38
opium 128, 130
Ossory diocese 42, 80t
Oxford 7, 8–9, 18, 36, 61, 63, 70, 71, 79n14, 81n16, 93n49, 97n59, 139

Padua 25, 82, 193
Paracelsian influences 10, 24, 64
Paris 8, 18, 24, 58, 59, 62n53, 63n62, 82, 83, 84, 85–6, 88, 90, 91, 92, 93n50, 95, 96, 100n69, 104, 106n89, 187, 199n6
parliament, Ireland: 11, 15, 138, 141, 152, 153, 154, 157–62t; House of Commons 141, 142, 143, 146, 152, 153, 154, 155; House of Lords 75, 115, 144, 149, 150, 153, 155
Parsons, Dorothy 119
Parsons, William 122
patent 11n27, 20, 26, 121, 140
patient agency 5, 175, 176, 178, 182
patriotism 187, 188

Peacock, Nicholas 128
Pechey, John 121
Percy, Thomas, Bishop of Dromore 133
Pery, Edmond Sexten 129
Petty, Sir William 36, 183, 184
pharmacists, *see* apothecaries
pharmacopoeia 49, 152, 187, 188
*Philosophical Transactions* 62n54, 63
phlebotomists 202
Physico-Historical Society 13, 183, 185, 187, 189, 190
Piñera y Siles, Bartolomé 214
Poland 9, 59, 60, 61, 63, 91, 183. *See also under* Connor, Bernard, *History of Poland*
Pollard, Paul 183
Ponsonby, William 142
Porter, Roy, 75, 116, 172
potions and nostrums 11, 33, 35, 47, 112, 119, 120, 122, 123–4, 130
Potts, James 126
Poynings' Law 153, 192
Prague 8, 44, 45–7, 77–8t, 79, 83, 84, 85n27
Presbyterianism 9, 184; Ulster Presbyterian Synod 48, 107
Price, Alice 122
Prior, Thomas 123
Privy Council (British) 129, 141, 153, 154
Privy Council (Irish) 26, 141, 147, 152
profession and professionalisation 1, 2, 3, 5–14, **17–37**, 39, 41, 43, 44, 46, 47, 50, 70, 71, 73, 76, 79, 82, 83, 95, 106, 109, 112, 113, 115, 118, 128, 131, 133, 134, 135, 137, 140, 143, 146, 148, 149, 150, 151, 154, 155, 156, 158–61t, 163, 164, 165, 166, 170, 171, 173, 175, 177, 179, 180, 184, 185, 187, 189, 191, 192, 194, 198, 202, 206, 212, 213
Protestantism 8, 10, 45, 69, 81, 82n18, 87, 92–5, 96, 101, 102–103, 104, 106, 107, 139, 146, 174, 175, 184, 185, 190, 191–2, 199; *see* Presbyterian, Church of England, Church of Ireland
Protomédicos 74, 198n3, 201n15, 202, 204, 205, 207, 208, 209, 212, 211, 213

Puebla de los Angeles 197, 200, 206
purgatives 46, 132, 210n54, 122, 133

quacks, charlatans, irregular, curanderos 4, 7, 12, 15, 21, 22, 23, 28, 33, 35, 47, 50, 64n74, 73, 76, 128, 135, 171, 202, 212. *See also* healers
Quakers 95, 102, 118, 139n8, 140n13, 142n19, 184
Quin, Henry 193–4

Radcliffe, John 61n52, 62
Raphoe, diocese of 80t
Rawdon, Sir George 112–113
Rawlins' fistula wash 121
receipt books, *see under* medical texts
Redi, Francisco 59
Redmond, John Gabriel Rice, 102, 104
regularization 24, 86, 171
Reims 4, 8, 9, 17, 18, 24, 25, 35, 44, 58, 77–96, 100, 104n79, 106, 150, 184
Reynolds, James 109, 115
Richards, John 69
Ridgway, Frances 102
Riverius 44
Robinson-Hammerstein, Helga 45
Rome 53, 69
Roscommon, county 101t
Rose, William 75, 144
Ross, diocese of 80t
Rotunda, the (Dublin Lying-in Hospital) 2, 90, 103, 160t
Rowley, Hercules Langford 133
Royal Academy of Medicine, Madrid 198n3, 205, 213
Royal Botanical Garden, Madrid *see under* botany
Royal Botanical Garden, Mexico City *see under* botany
Royal College of Physicians of Ireland 1n1, 3, 8, 11, 12, 15n30, 17, 19, 20, 25, , 28, 37, 88, 91, 92, 97, 109n2, 137n1, 139–56, 194; in London 22, 24, 25, 26, 36, 61, 63n66, 65, 66, 75, 139-56, 165; in Edinburgh 128.
Royal College of Surgeons, Dublin 3, 12, 88, 99, 102n71, 103n75, 137n1, 138, 142n23

Royal Dublin Society 123, 140, 158t, 160t, 183, 185, 186, 187, 189, 191, 194
Royal Irish Academy 187
Royal Pontifical University, Mexico 200, 201, 207, 208, 209, 215
Royal Protomedicato *see* Protomédicos
Royal Society of Arts 186
Royal Society, London 61, 62, 63, 64, 66, 90, 91, 105n86, 165
Rutty, John 95n52, 184, 188, 189

St Andrews 78
St George's Hospital, London 87
St John, Sir Oliver 19
St Patrick's Hospital, Dublin 157t
Samaniego, Felipe de 204n29
scepticism 5, 53, 72, 212
Scotland 9, 57, 79n14, 81, 82n18, 93, 94t, 98t, 99, 107, 111, 119, 120, 143, 163, 165, 190, 180, 198; Gaelic 39, 40, 44
self-medication 11, 110, 112, 122, 123, 126, 128–31, 135
Sessé y Lacasta, Martín de 201, 206, 207–208, 215
Sharpe, William 129
Shekelton, Robert 99, 103
Simcockes, Thomas 83
Singleton, Henry 145, 146
Slater, William 127n88
Sligo county 101t
Sloane, Sir Hans (1660–1753) 61n52, 62, 78, 91, 132, 166, 183, 194, 195
Smith, Charles 13, 187, 188, 189, 190–191, 193
Smith, Eliza, *The Compleat Housewife* (1727) 125
Smyth, George (d. 1821) 105
Sobieski, John 59, 61
social mobility 5, 96, 73-108
Solander, Daniel 189
Sorbonne 44
Spain and Spanish culture 10, 25, 61, 74, 193, 197, 198, 199, 200, 201, 202n16, 204n29, 206, 208n44, 209, 210, 211, 213, 214, 215, 216; Spanish America 198, 200, 201, 202, 204n29, 207–208, 215

spas *see* hydrotherapy
Spencer, Edmund 117, 122, 128
Spinoza, *Tractatus Politico-Theologicus* (1670) 57
Spirit of Opodeloc 133n112
Stearne, John 22, 28, 37
Stephens, William 187
Stevens, Richard 157t
Stone, Gerald C. 55, 70
Sulliard, Sankey 36
surgeon-apothecaries 76, 90, 96
surgeons 2, 3, 4, 5, 11, 12, 19, 20, 36, 56, 71, 73, 74, 75, 88, 90n39, 109, 110, 112n14, 117, 123, 131, 138, 139, 142, 143, 146, 148, 150, 153, 156, 159t, 170, 176, 184, 185, 192, 197, 199, 202, 203n24, 206, 212, 213, 216. *See also* army surgeons; barber-surgeons; navy surgeons; Royal College of Surgeons; surgeon-apothecaries; surgery
surgery 19, 32, 74, 81, 91, 114, 117, 123, 139, 170, 199n6, 201, 203, 206
Sydney, Henry, 1st Earl Romney 141
Synge, Alicia 114–115, 117
Synge, Edward, Bishop of Elphin 112n14, 114–15, 117–18, 122, 129, 130, 131, 132–3

Taafe, Colonel Patrick 45, 46
Talbot, Christopher 17, 19, 25
Talbot, Sir William 32
Taranta, Valescus de (fl. 1382–1418) 43
Tassie, James 194
Temple, Sir John 27
Tenison, Thomas, Archbishop of Canterbury 62, 66
Theobald, John 125
Thwaites, Ephraim 83, 88n38
tinnitus 114
Tipperary, county 29, 86, 143, 190
Tissot, Samuel Auguste 126, 127; *Advice to people in general with respect to their health* (1761) 126
Tobin, Maurice 64–5
Toland, John 72; *Christianity not Mysterious* (1695) 10, 57–8, 71

Toulouse 87n32, 198, 199, 200, 204n29, 208
Townley Hall 121
Trinity College Dublin 4, 8, 9, 27, 28, 78t, 87, 90, 91, 92, 93, 95n55, 102
Trinity College, Cambridge 164, 165
Trumbull, Sir William 70
Trusler, John (1735–1820) 126
Tuam, diocese of 80–81t, 117
Tuatha De Danann 49
Tullamore, county Offaly 110
Tullymore 132
Twigge, Diana and Jane 120
Tyrone, county 85n27, 101t, 105n85, 109
Tyrrell, James 62, 71

Ulster 32, 39, 43, 46, 49, 50, 80, 97, 100, 101, 104, 105, 106n89, 107, 109
Ulster Gaelic Society 48
United Provinces, *see* Netherlands
Upton, Elizabeth 129
urine 34, 49, 51, 120
Usher, William 143
Ussher, James, Archbishop of Armagh 27, 30, 32, 62

Valenzuela, Pedro 215
Van Helmont, Johann Baptista (1579–1644) 7, 40–41
venereal disease 10, 197–216; anti-venereal trials 197, 198, 204, 208, 209, 210–212, 214, 216. *See also* Beato method; Viana, Nicolás
Venice 59
Veracruz 197, 201
Verdon, John 25
Viana, Nicolás 210, 211, 212, 213. *See also* Beato method; anti-venereal trials *under* venereal disease

Vienna 45, 82, 84t, 89t, 187
Vota, Father 60

Wade, John 125
Wales 73, 81, 94t, 98t, 165, 180
Waller, Richard 62
Walsham, Alexandra 71n124
Ward's drops 128
Warsaw 59
Washington, George 129
Waterford, county 80t, 101t, 113, 162t, 190
Wellington, Duke of (Arthur Wellesley) 97, 102, 104
Wentworth, Thomas 34
Wesley, John, *Primitive Physic* (1752) 125, 127
West Indies 87, 98t
Westmeath, county 86, 91
Wexford, county 101t
Wicklow, county 101t
Wielopolski, Jan 59
William III 70n118, 139
William IV 105n86
Willis, Thomas 32
*Wilson's Dublin Directory* 88, 89, 90, 103n75
Wollstonecraft, Mary 118
women 11, 14, 21, 22, 34, 73, 117, 122, 130, 160t, 163, 166, 167, 170, 172, 173, 176, 202n19, 204n25. *See also* midwives; nurses
workhouses 2, 157–62t
Worsley, Benjamin 36
Worth, Edward 183

Xavier, Francis 56

Yarner, Abraham 36–7

For Product Safety Concerns and Information please contact our EU
representative  GPSR@taylorandfrancis.com
Taylor & Francis Verlag GmbH, Kaufingerstraße 24, 80331 München, Germany

www.ingramcontent.com/pod-product-compliance
Lightning Source LLC
Chambersburg PA
CBHW071352290426
44108CB00014B/1515